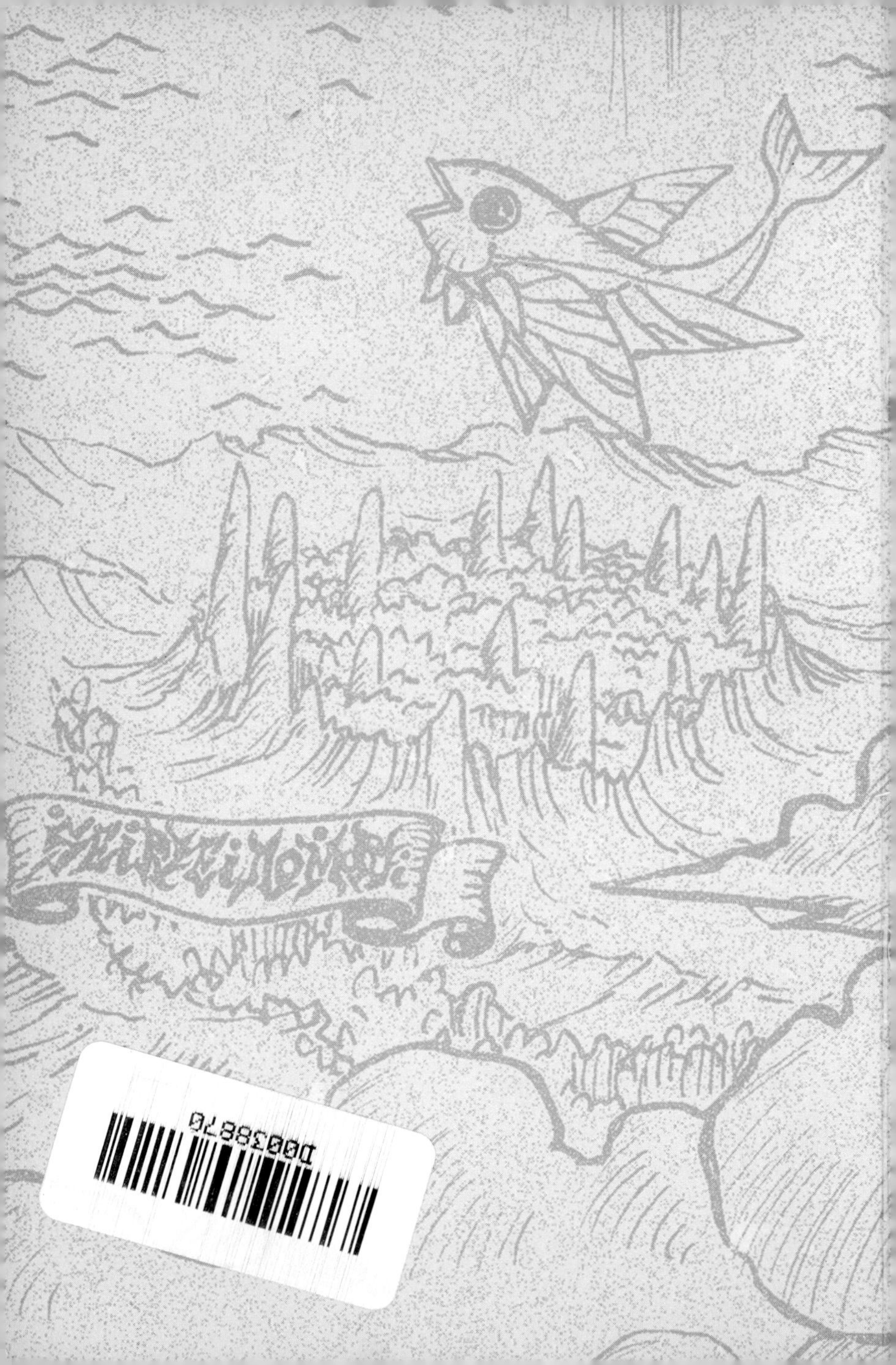

Other 100% Authentic Manga Available from TOKYOPOP®:

COWBOY BEBOP
All-new adventures of interstellar bounty hunting, based on the hit anime seen on Cartoon Network.

MARMALADE BOY
A tangled teen romance for the new millennium.

REAL BOUT HIGH SCHOOL
At Daimon High, teachers don't break up fights...they grade them.

MARS
Biker Rei and artist Kira are as different as night and day, but fate binds them in this angst-filled romance.

GTO
Biker gang member Onizuka is going back to school...as a teacher!

CHOBITS
In the future, boys will be boys and girls will be...robots? The newest hit series from CLAMP!

SKULL MAN
They took his family. They took his face. They took his soul. Now, he's going to take his revenge.

DRAGON KNIGHTS
Part dragon, part knight, ALL glam. The most inept knights on the block are out to kick some demon butt.

INITIAL D
Delivery boy Tak has a gift for driving, but can he compete in the high-stakes world of street racing?

PARADISE KISS
High fashion and deep passion collide in this hot new shojo series!

KODOCHA: Sana's Stage
There's a rumble in the jungle gym when child star Sana Kurata and bully Akito Hayama collide.

ANGELIC LAYER
In the future, the most popular game is Angelic Layer, where hand-raised robots battle for supremacy.

LOVE HINA
Can Keitaro handle living in a dorm with five cute girls...and still make it through school?

Also Available from TOKYOPOP®:

PRIEST
The quick and the undead in one macabre manga.

RAGNAROK
In the final battle between gods and men, only a small band of heroes stand in the way of total annihilation.

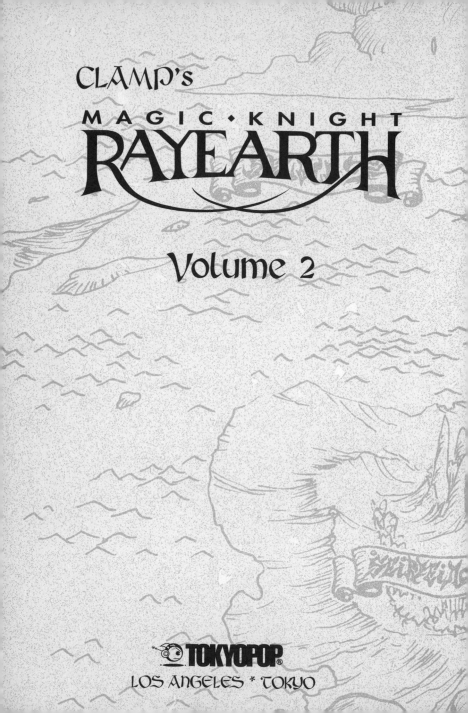

CLAMP's

MAGIC · KNIGHT
RAYEARTH

Volume 2

TOKYOPOP®

LOS ANGELES * TOKYO

Translator - Anita Sengupta
English Adaptation - Jamie S. Rich
Cover Design - Patrick Hook
Layout - Monalisa DeAsis
Copy Editor - Bryce Coleman

Editor - Jake Forbes
Production Manager - Mario Rodriguez
Art Director - Matthew Alford
VP Production- Ron Klamert
Publisher- Stuart Levy

Email: editor@TOKYOPOP.com
Come visit us online at www.TOKYOPOP.com

A TOKYOPOP Manga
TOKYOPOP ® is an imprint of Mixx Entertainment Inc.
5900 Wilshire Blvd. Ste 2000, Los Angeles, CA 90036

ISBN: 1-59182-083-9

First TOKYOPOP® printing: November 2002

10 9 8 7 6 5 4 3 2 1

Manufactured in the USA

The Story So Far...

Hikaru, Umi and Fuu were Tokyo schoolgirls with nothing else in common, until one fateful day, during a fieldtrip to Tokyo Tower, the three of them were summoned to the magical land of Cephiro. Upon their arrival, they were greeted by Guru Clef, the greatest magician in the land, who told them that they must save Princess Emeraude from the sinister Priest Zagato. In order to do this they must first release the Mashin, powerful elemental gods, so that they can become the Legendary Magic Knights. They must complete this quest before they can return home to Tokyo. Before sending them on their way, Clef gives them Evolving Armor and connects them with their magical abilities. Their parting is cut short when one of Zagato's minions, the witch Alcione, attacks Clef and the girls. Clef summons a spirit creature to bear the girls to safety while fending off the witch on his own.

The creature carries them to the Forest of Silence, where they find a seemingly empty workshop. After venturing inside, Hikaru, Umi and Fuu find themselves caught in a trap set by the workshop's owner, Presea. After explaining their situation, the girls are released and Presea introduces herself as a Pharle, an artisan who fashions weapons. She offers to make weapons for the girls, but in order to create weapons befitting the Magic Knights, she'll need the Legendary Mineral Escudo. The problem is, this material can only be found accross the Forest of Silence (where magic cannot be used) in the spring Eterna. After receiving loaner weapons from Presea, Hikaru, Umi and Fuu set off in search of the Escudo. They soon face their first monster all alone, and through their combined skills manage to defeat it. But a second monster right away proves more troublesome. Suddenly, a strange swordsman appears and defeats the monster. Could this be a new friend, or another of Zagato's minions?

5

Cast of Characters...

Hikaru Shidou: She may be short, but she's just as old as Umi and Fuu (14, to be exact). Her family runs a Kendo Dojo, so she's experienced with the sword. A constant optimist and loyal friend, Hikaru is eager to help the people of Cephiro. Her magical element is fire.

Umi Ryuzaki: Umi's the only child of wealthy parents, so she's used to getting what she wants. She starts off her journey a bit of a snob, but she has a good heart and has proven herself a true friend to Hikaru and Fuu. A fencer in her club, she's also adept with the sword. Her magical element is water.

Fuu Houji: Fuu is a bright student and an overachiever. She stays very calm under pressure and deals with their fantastic situations in a logical manner. She was a member of the archery team in school. Her magical element is wind.

Mokona: A mysterious "Holy Beast," no one knows what Mokona is exactly, but there's only one of it. The only thing it says is "Puu." It acts like it doesn't understand anything, but it might know more than it lets on.

Princess Emeraude: The "Pillar" of Cephiro, it is Emeraude's prayers that keep the land safe. Now that she's imprisoned, evil has begun encroaching. She summoned the three girls from another world to become the Magic Knights.

Zagato: A former Sol, a priest who protected Emeraude, he is now keeping her in the Water Dungeon for unknown purposes. He sends his strongest minions to destroy the Magic Knights.

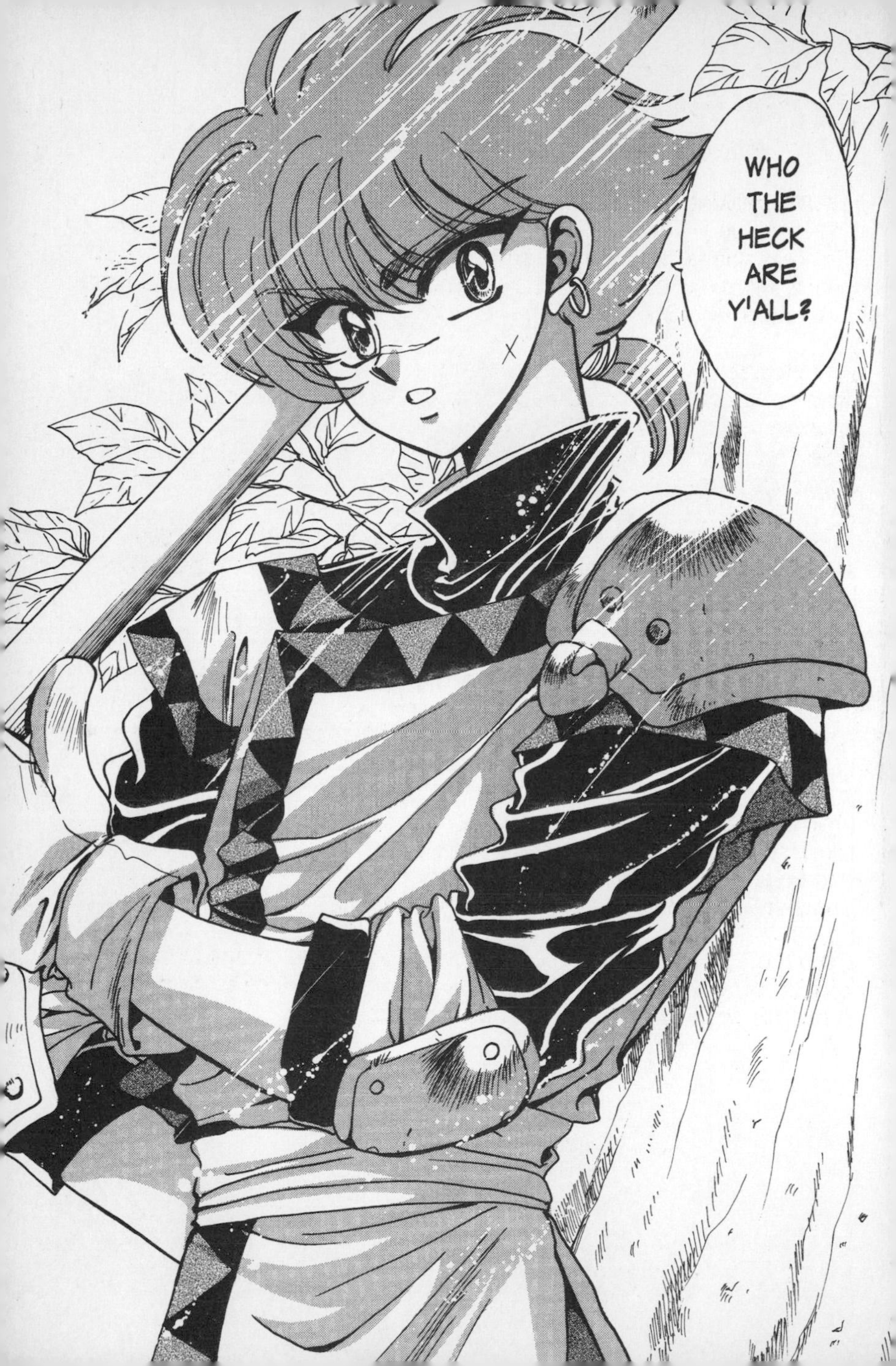
WHO THE HECK ARE Y'ALL?

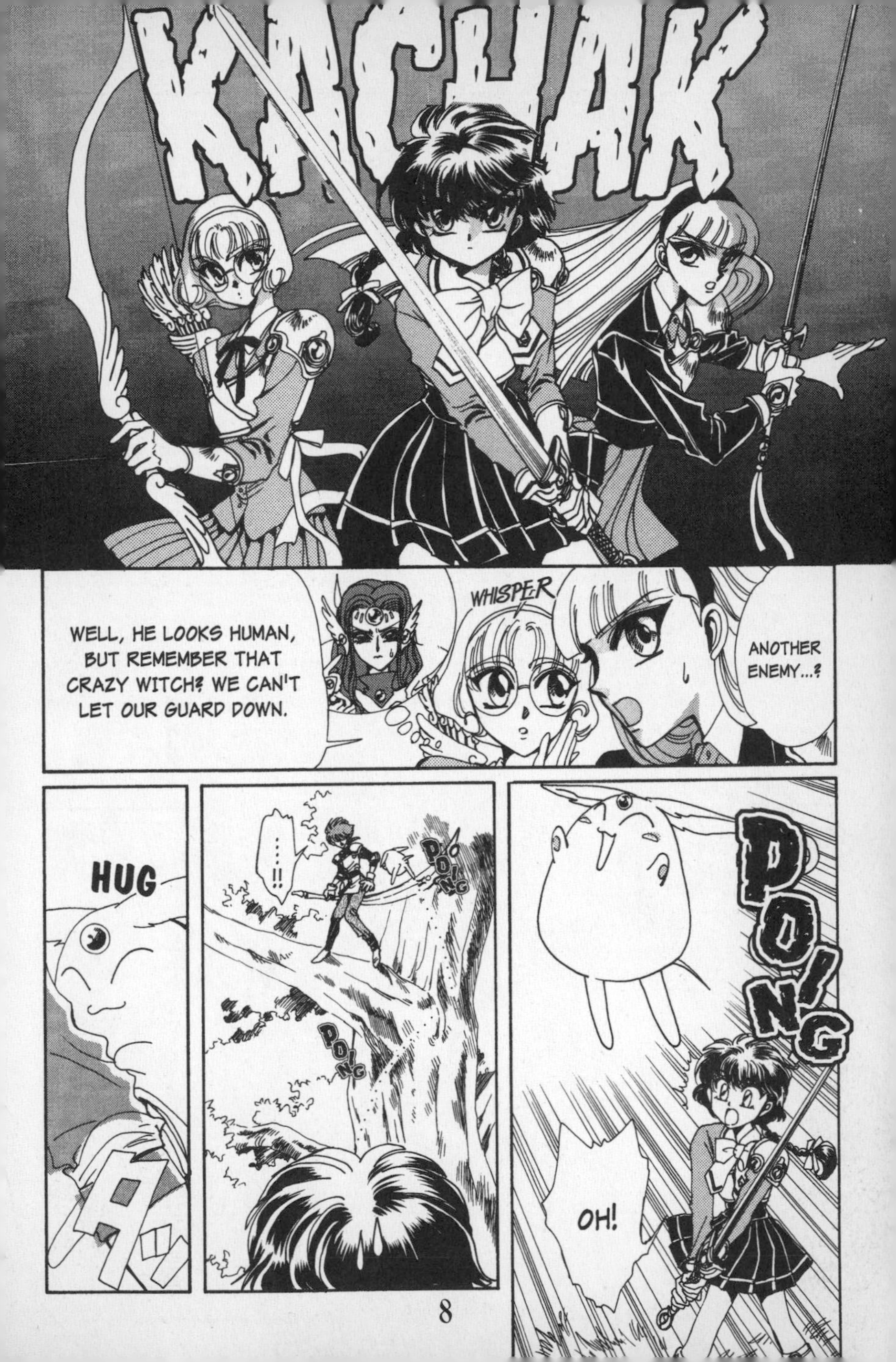
KACHAK
ANOTHER ENEMY...?
WHISPER
WELL, HE LOOKS HUMAN, BUT REMEMBER THAT CRAZY WITCH? WE CAN'T LET OUR GUARD DOWN.
POING
OH!
......!!
POING
POING
HUG

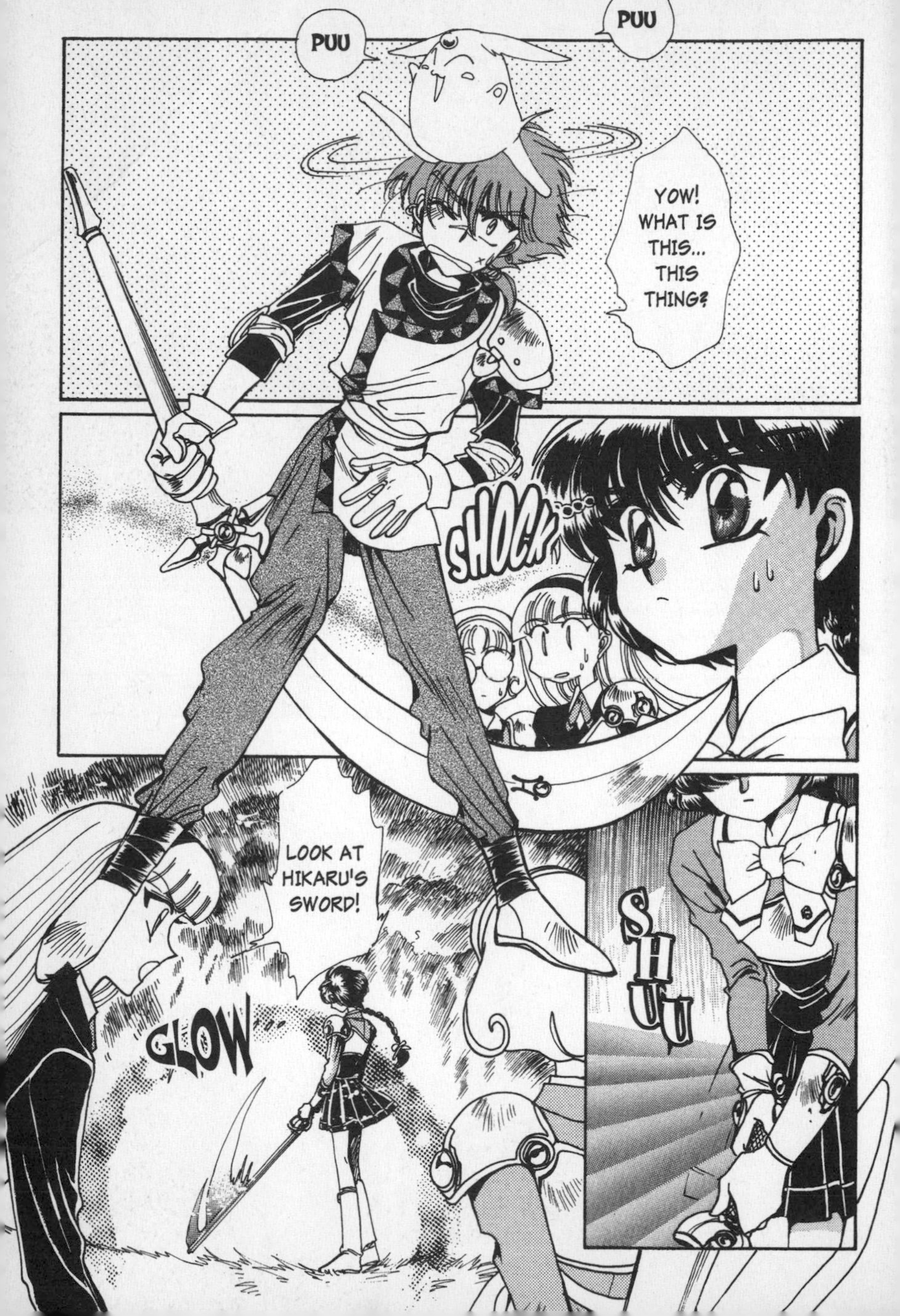
PUU
PUU
YOW! WHAT IS THIS... THIS THING?
SHOCK
SHUU
LOOK AT HIKARU'S SWORD!
GLOW

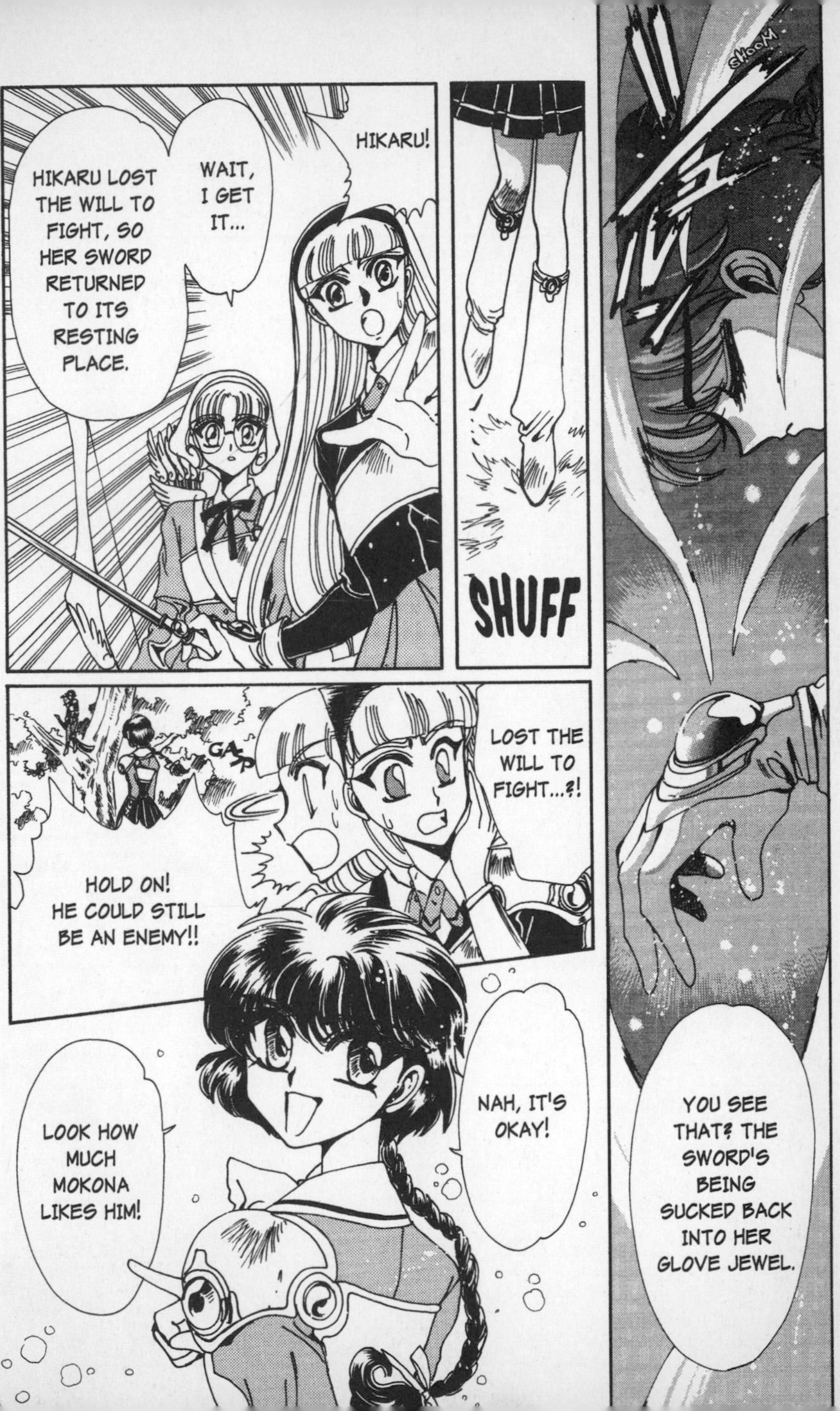
SHOOM
YOU SEE THAT? THE SWORD'S BEING SUCKED BACK INTO HER GLOVE JEWEL.
SHUFF
HIKARU!
WAIT, I GET IT...
HIKARU LOST THE WILL TO FIGHT, SO HER SWORD RETURNED TO ITS RESTING PLACE.
LOST THE WILL TO FIGHT...?!
GASP
HOLD ON! HE COULD STILL BE AN ENEMY!!
NAH, IT'S OKAY!
LOOK HOW MUCH MOKONA LIKES HIM!

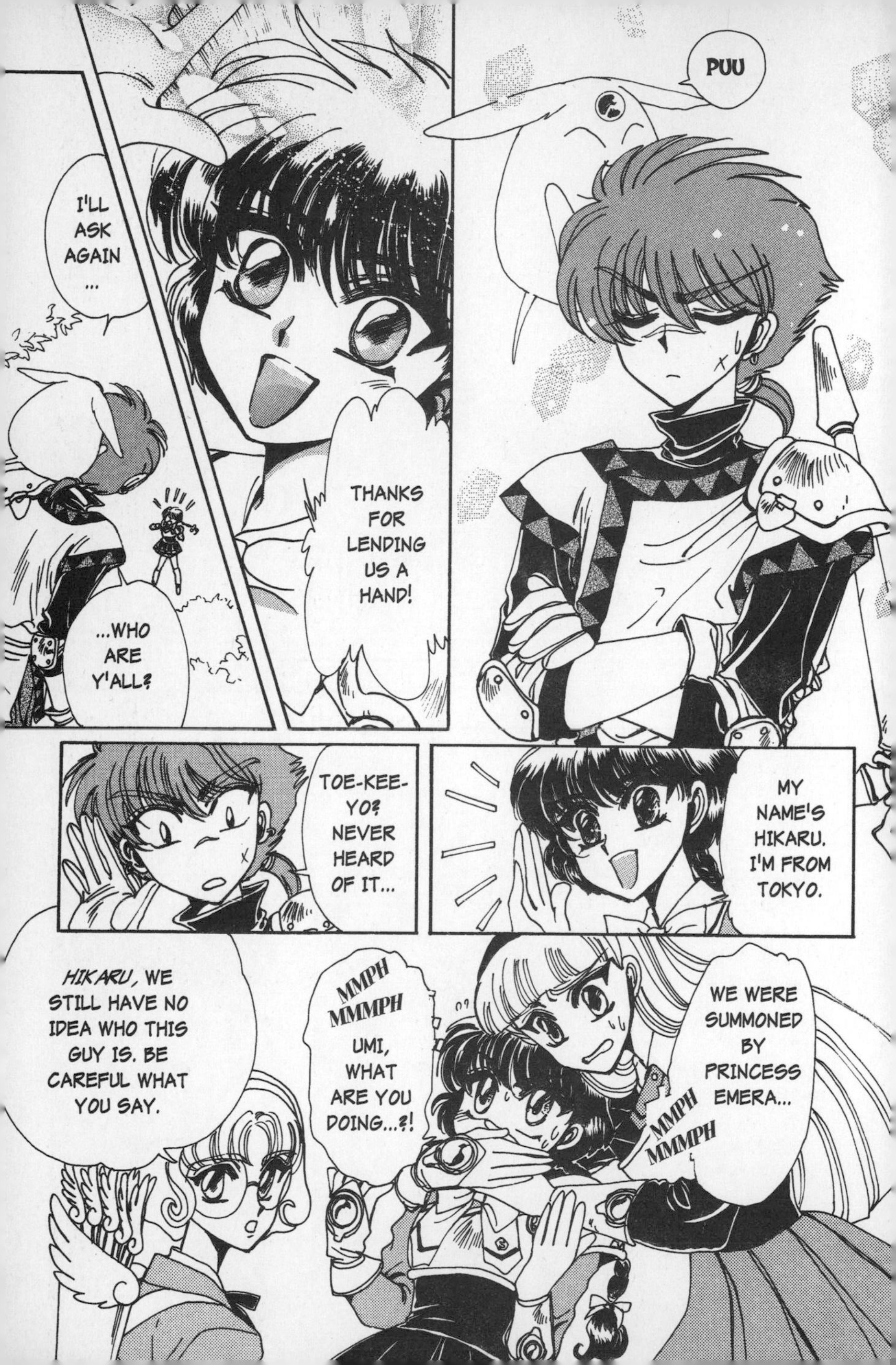
PUU
THANKS FOR LENDING US A HAND!
I'LL ASK AGAIN ...
...WHO ARE Y'ALL?
MY NAME'S HIKARU. I'M FROM TOKYO.
TOE-KEE-YO? NEVER HEARD OF IT...
WE WERE SUMMONED BY PRINCESS EMERA...
MMPH MMMPH
MMPH MMMPH
UMI, WHAT ARE YOU DOING...?!
HIKARU, WE STILL HAVE NO IDEA WHO THIS GUY IS. BE CAREFUL WHAT YOU SAY.

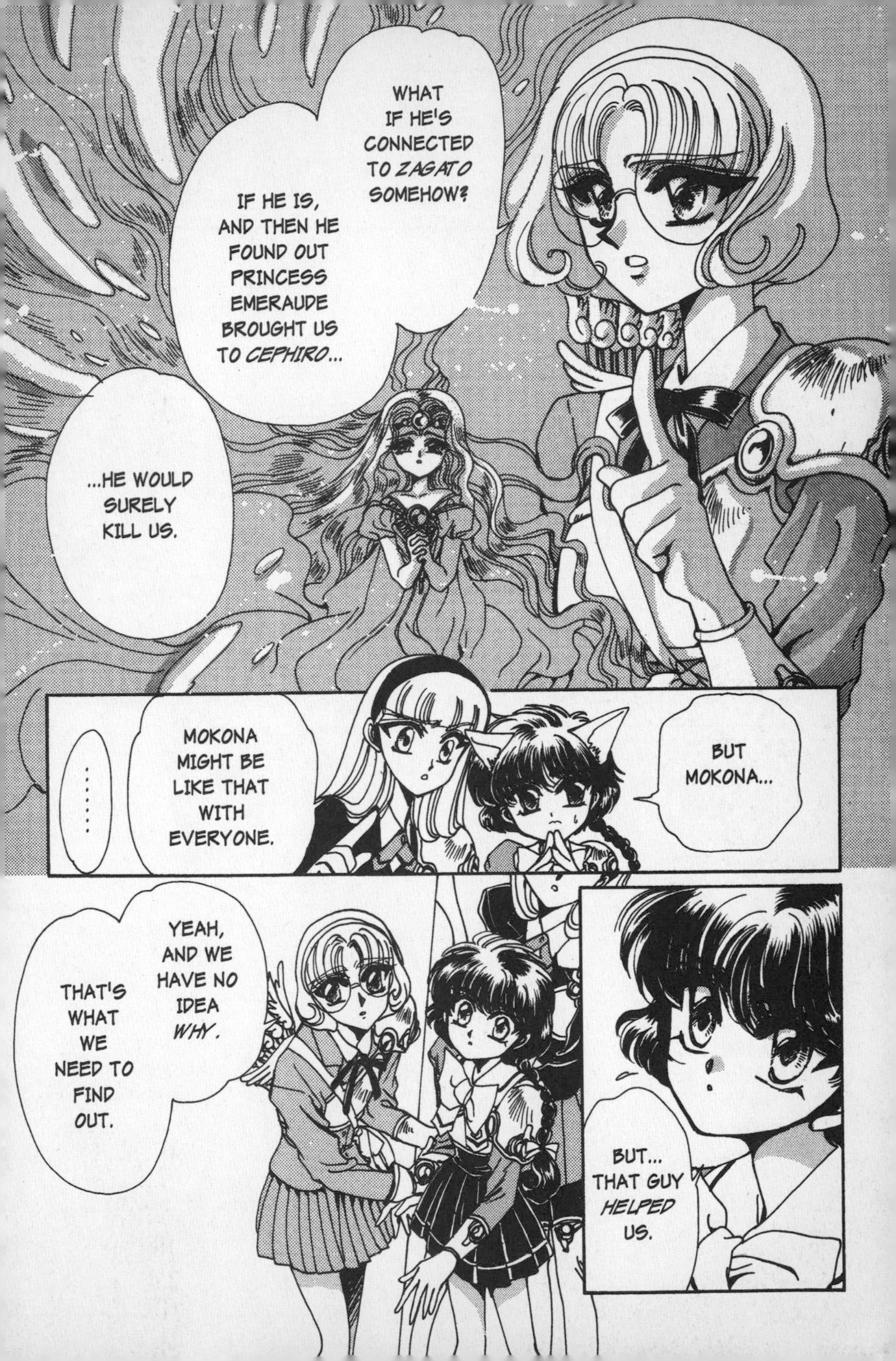
WHAT IF HE'S CONNECTED TO *ZAGATO* SOMEHOW?
IF HE IS, AND THEN HE FOUND OUT PRINCESS EMERAUDE BROUGHT US TO *CEPHIRO*...
...HE WOULD SURELY KILL US.
BUT MOKONA...
MOKONA MIGHT BE LIKE THAT WITH EVERYONE.
......
BUT... THAT GUY *HELPED* US.
YEAH, AND WE HAVE NO IDEA *WHY*.
THAT'S WHAT WE NEED TO FIND OUT.

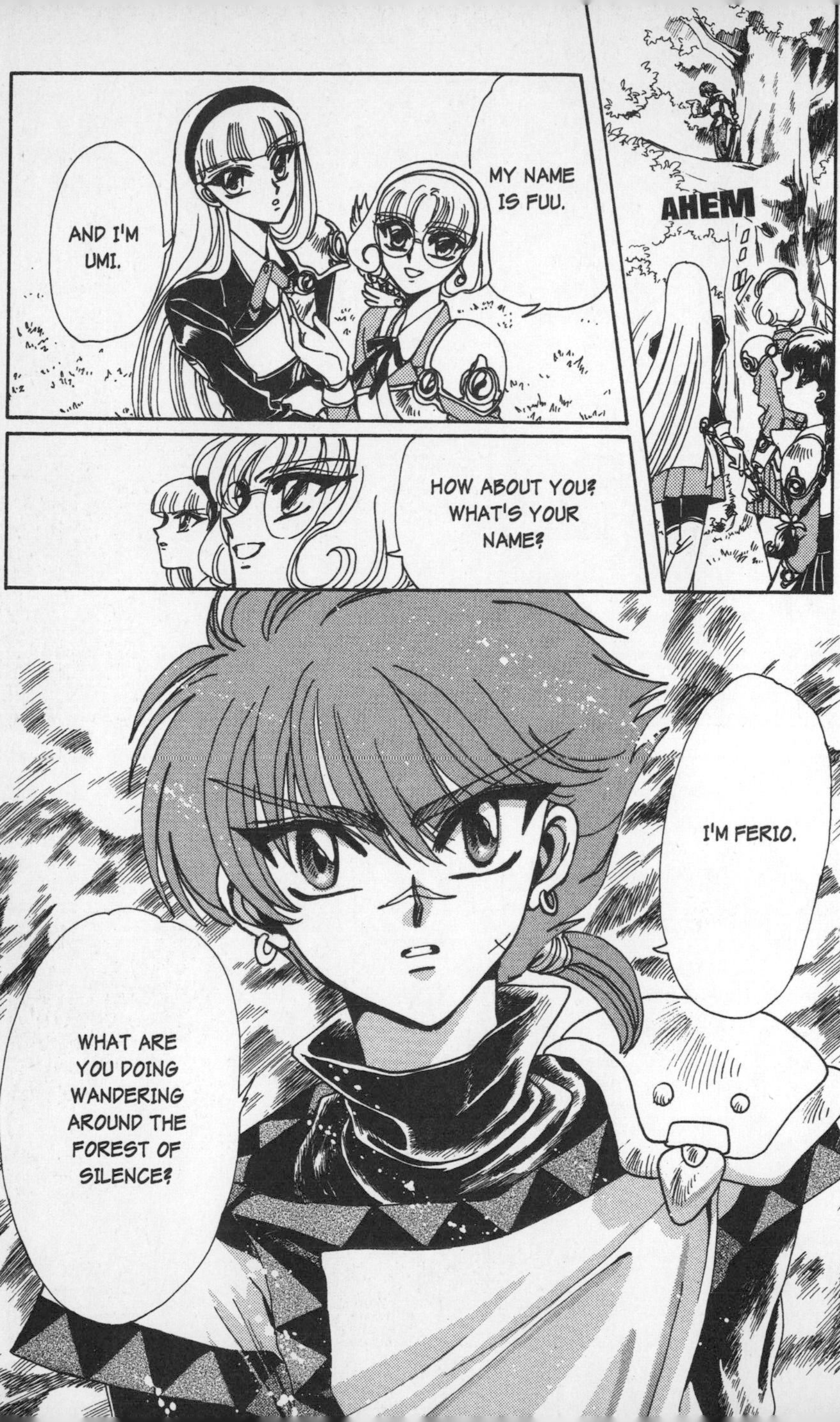
AHEM
MY NAME IS FUU.
AND I'M UMI.
HOW ABOUT YOU? WHAT'S YOUR NAME?
I'M FERIO.
WHAT ARE YOU DOING WANDERING AROUND THE FOREST OF SILENCE?

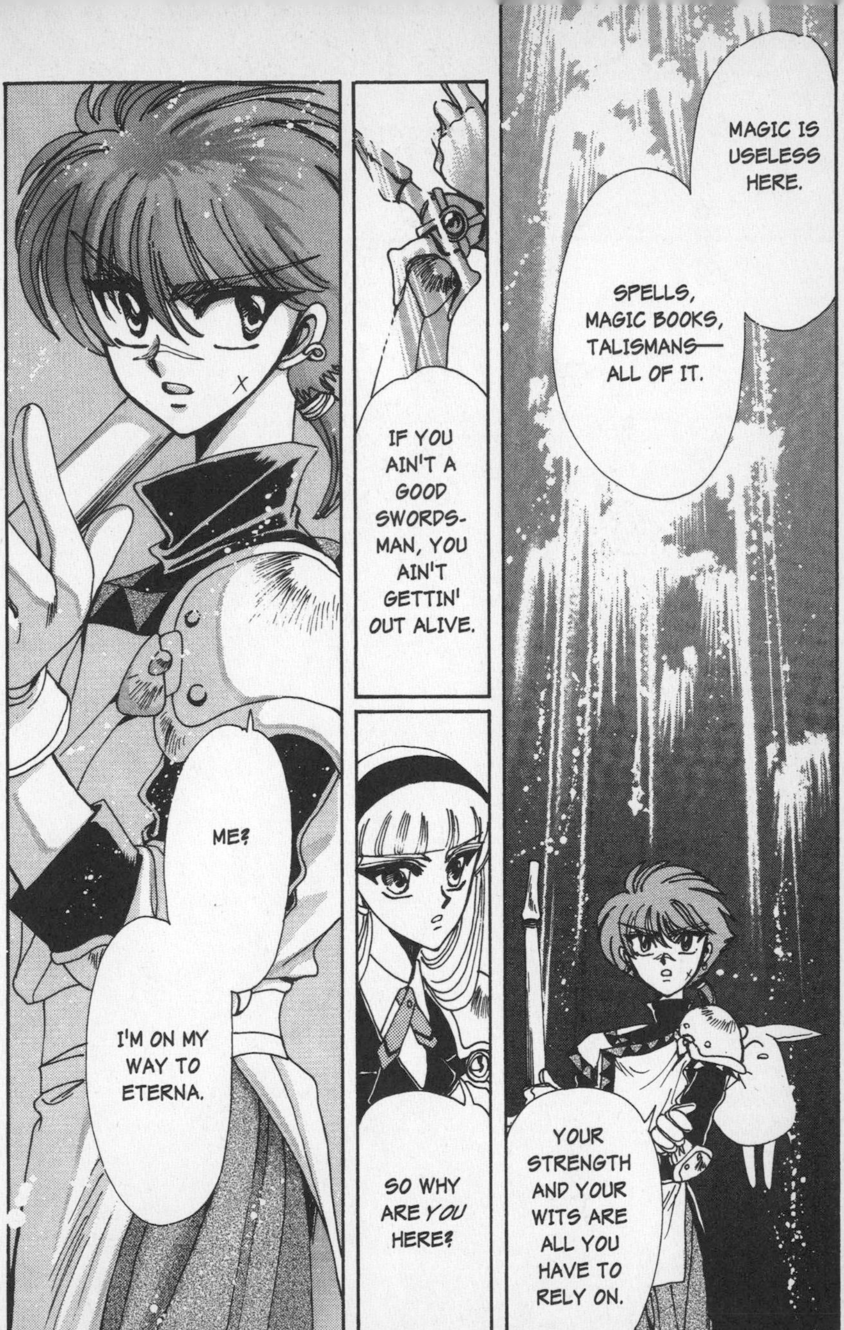
MAGIC IS USELESS HERE.
SPELLS, MAGIC BOOKS, TALISMANS— ALL OF IT.
YOUR STRENGTH AND YOUR WITS ARE ALL YOU HAVE TO RELY ON.
IF YOU AIN'T A GOOD SWORDS-MAN, YOU AIN'T GETTIN' OUT ALIVE.
SO WHY ARE *YOU* HERE?
ME?
I'M ON MY WAY TO ETERNA.

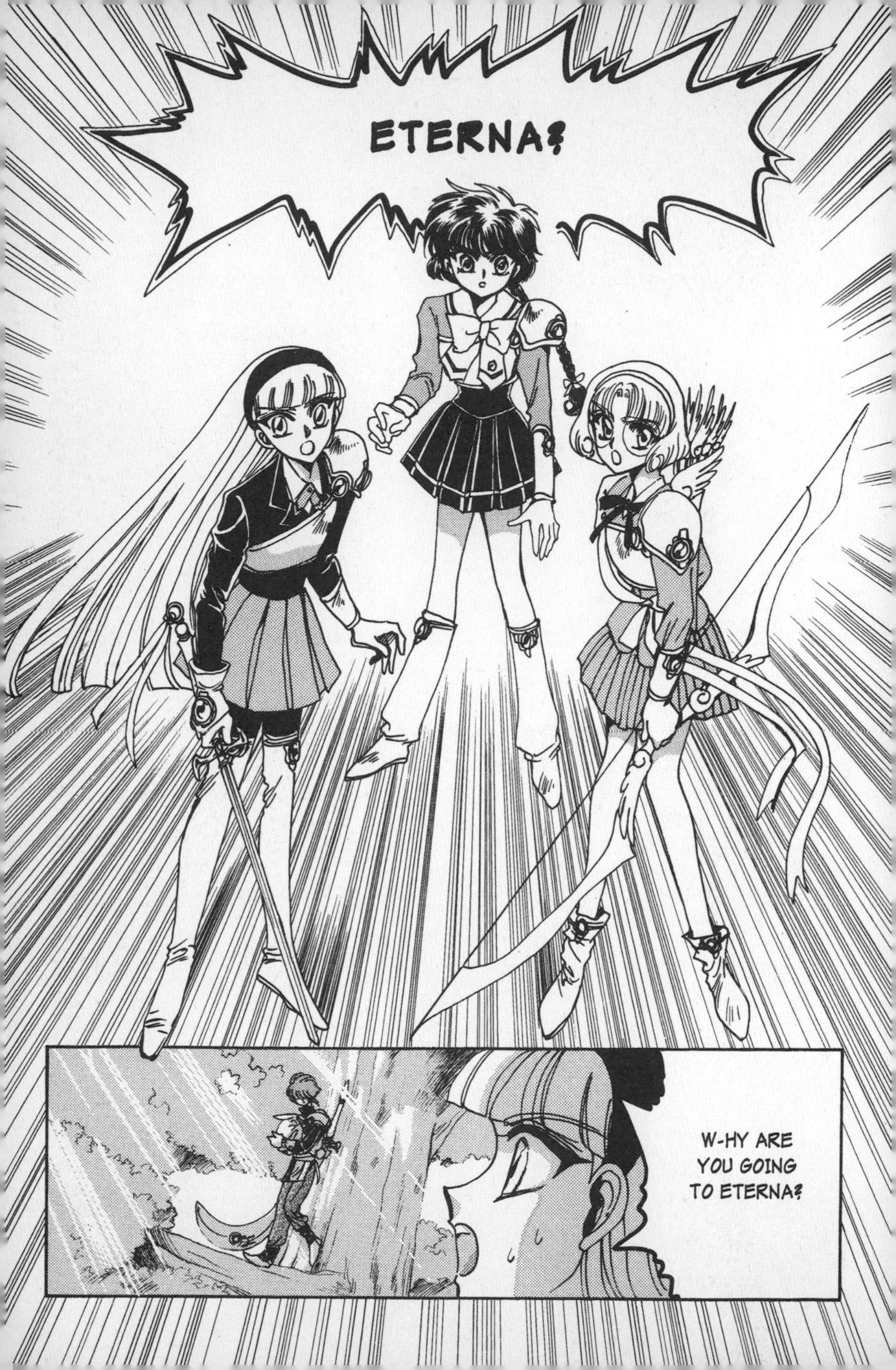
ETERNA?
W-HY ARE
YOU GOING
TO ETERNA?

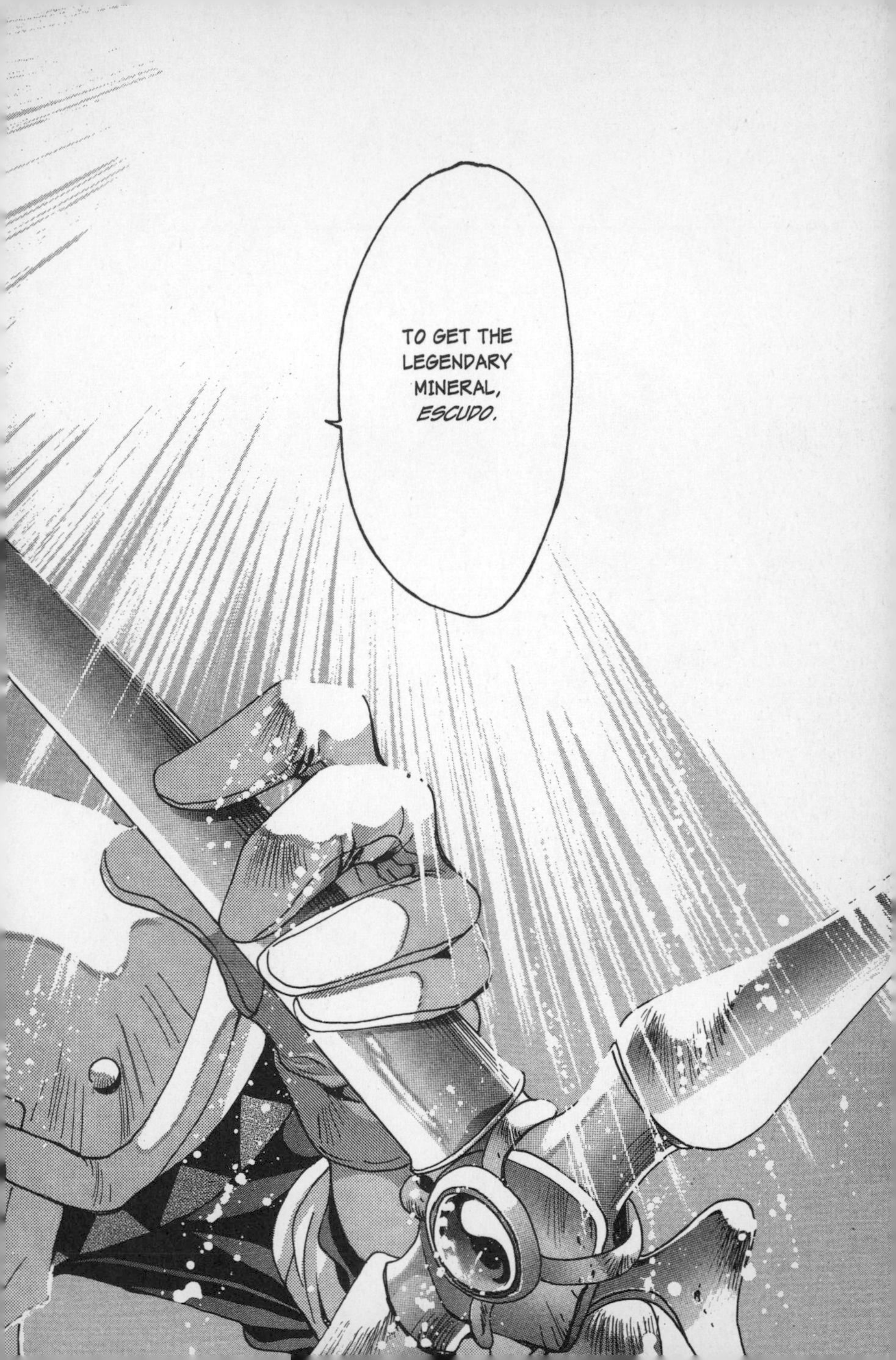
TO GET THE LEGENDARY MINERAL, *ESCUDO*.

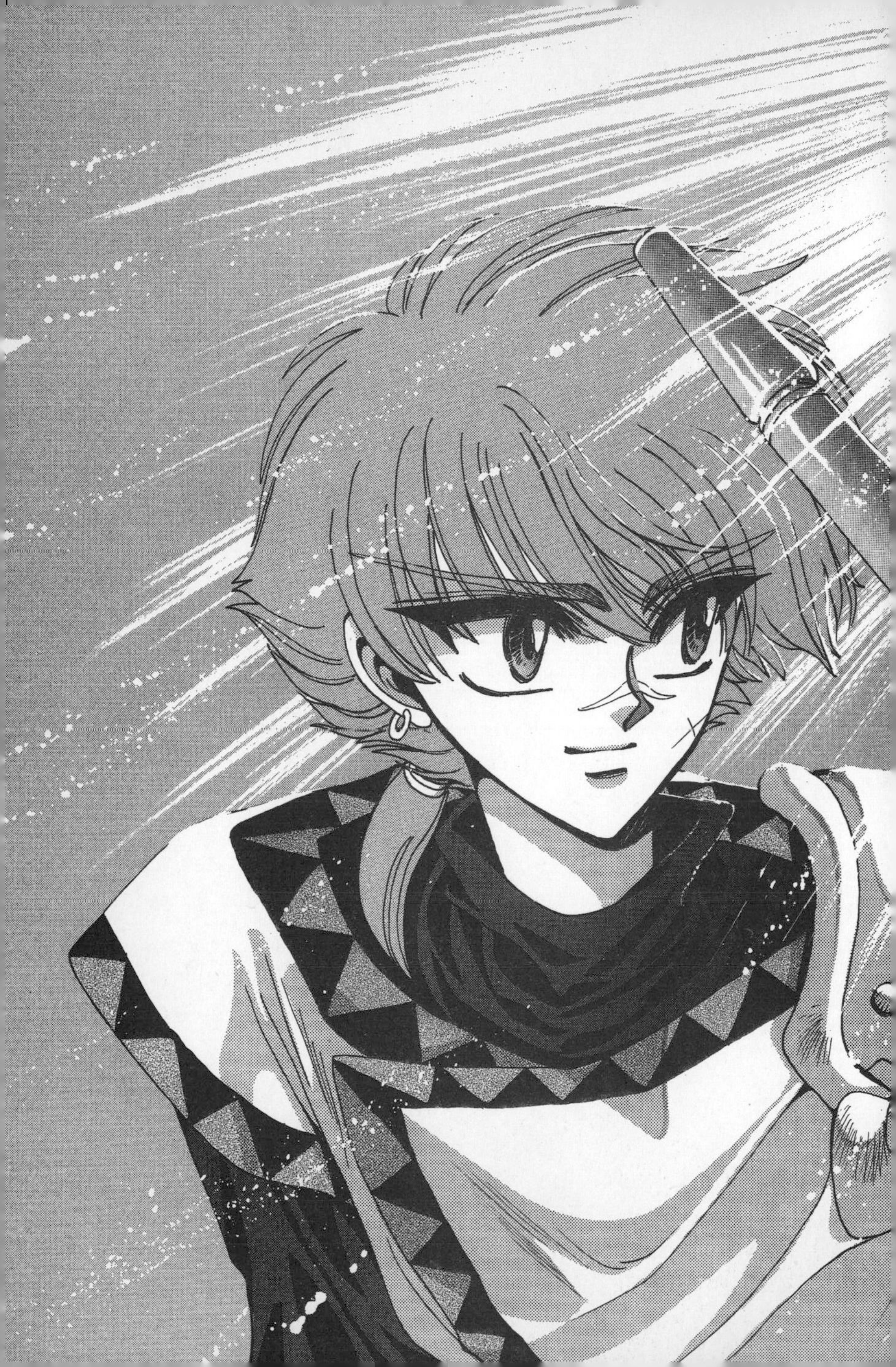

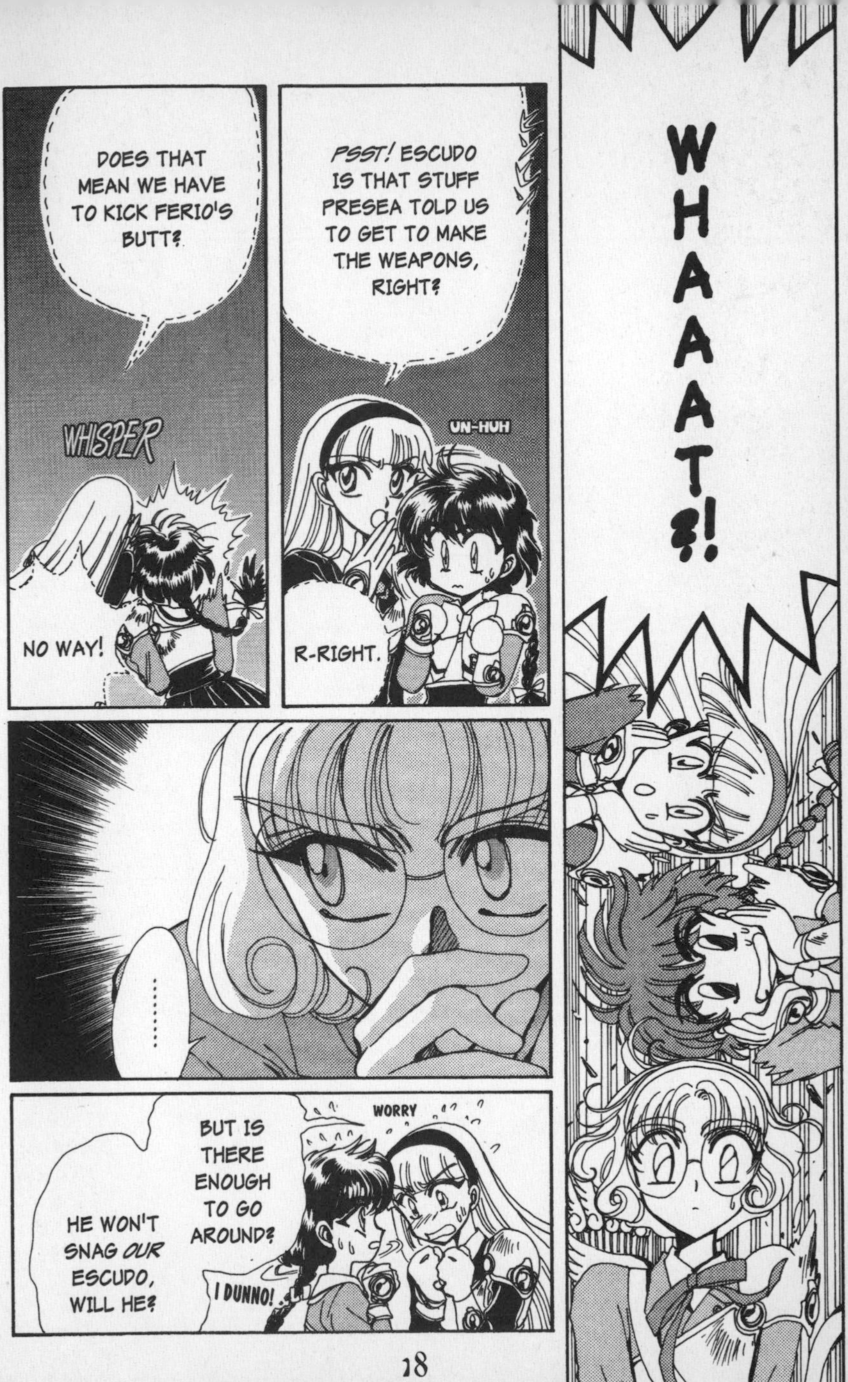
WHAAAT?!
PSST! ESCUDO IS THAT STUFF PRESEA TOLD US TO GET TO MAKE THE WEAPONS, RIGHT?
UN-HUH
R-RIGHT.
DOES THAT MEAN WE HAVE TO KICK FERIO'S BUTT?
WHISPER
NO WAY!
......
WORRY
BUT IS THERE ENOUGH TO GO AROUND?
I DUNNO!
HE WON'T SNAG OUR ESCUDO, WILL HE?

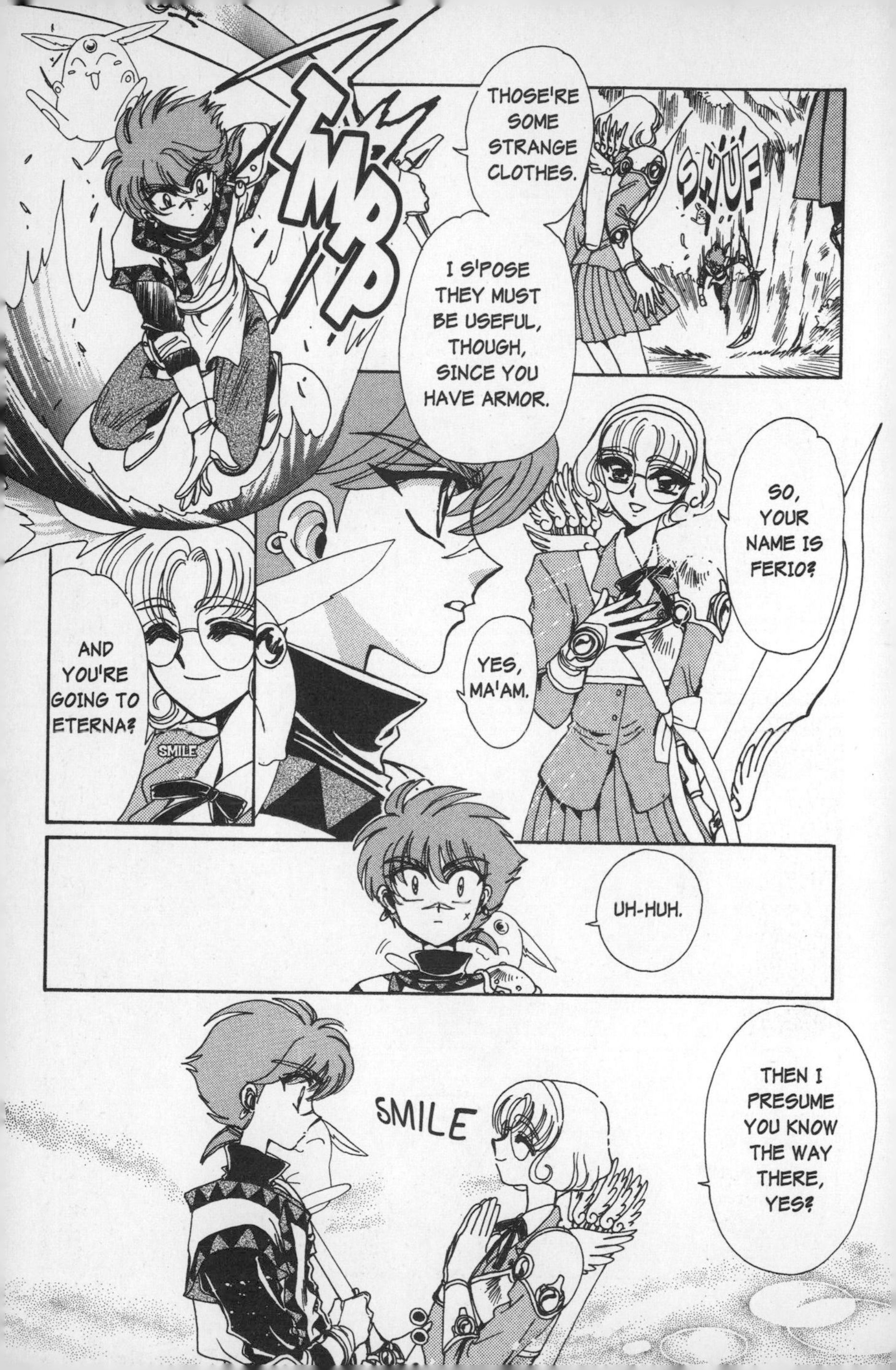
SHUF
TMP
THOSE'RE SOME STRANGE CLOTHES.
I S'POSE THEY MUST BE USEFUL, THOUGH, SINCE YOU HAVE ARMOR.
SO, YOUR NAME IS FERIO?
YES, MA'AM.
AND YOU'RE GOING TO ETERNA?
SMILE
UH-HUH.
THEN I PRESUME YOU KNOW THE WAY THERE, YES?
SMILE

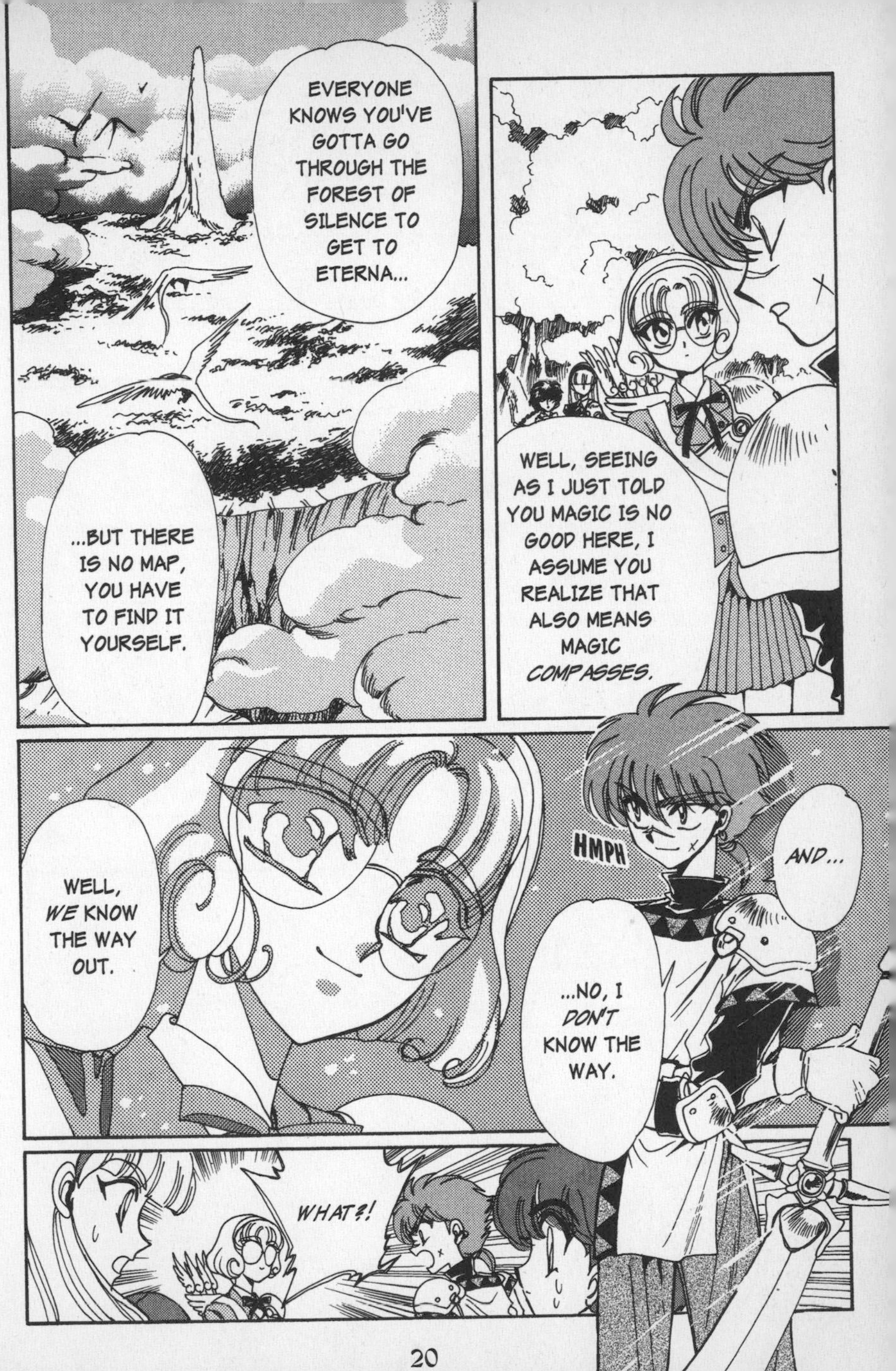
WELL, SEEING AS I JUST TOLD YOU MAGIC IS NO GOOD HERE, I ASSUME YOU REALIZE THAT ALSO MEANS MAGIC *COMPASSES.*
EVERYONE KNOWS YOU'VE GOTTA GO THROUGH THE FOREST OF SILENCE TO GET TO ETERNA...
...BUT THERE IS NO MAP, YOU HAVE TO FIND IT YOURSELF.
AND...
HMPH
...NO, I *DON'T* KNOW THE WAY.
WELL, *WE* KNOW THE WAY OUT.
WHAT?!

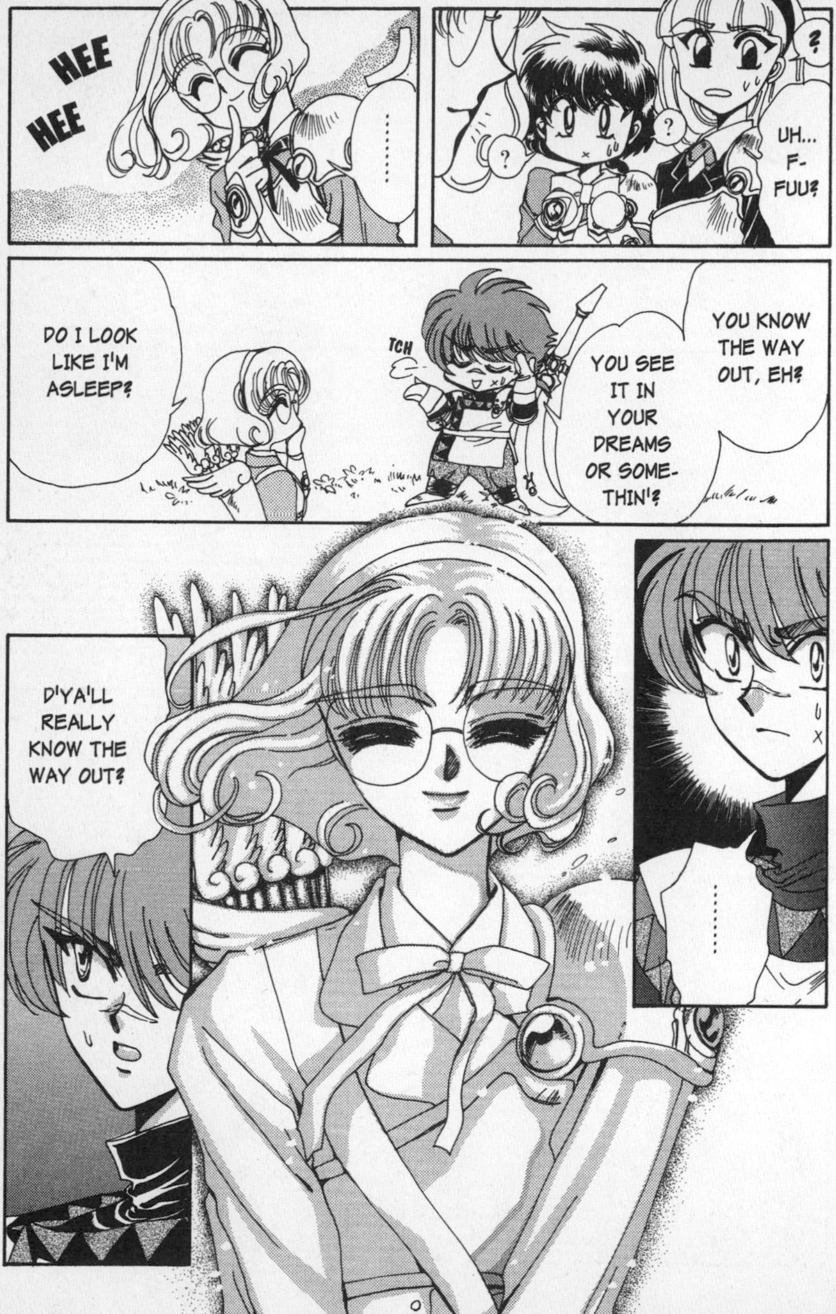
?
?
?
UH... F-FUU?
HEE HEE
......
YOU KNOW THE WAY OUT, EH?
YOU SEE IT IN YOUR DREAMS OR SOME-THIN'?
TCH
DO I LOOK LIKE I'M ASLEEP?
......
D'YA'LL REALLY KNOW THE WAY OUT?

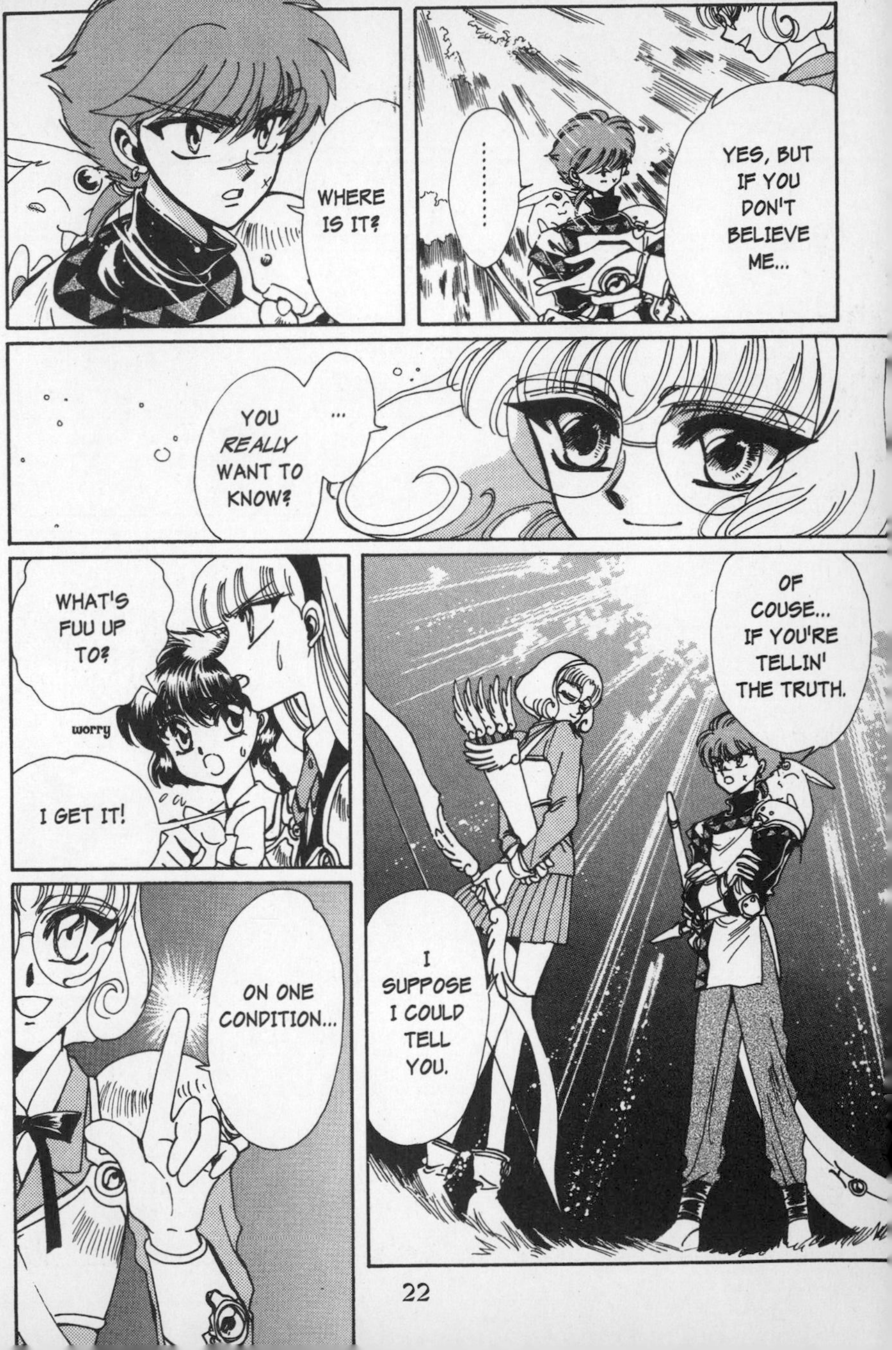
YES, BUT IF YOU DON'T BELIEVE ME...
......
WHERE IS IT?
...
YOU *REALLY* WANT TO KNOW?
OF COUSE... IF YOU'RE TELLIN' THE TRUTH.
I SUPPOSE I COULD TELL YOU.
WHAT'S FUU UP TO?
worry
I GET IT!
ON ONE CONDITION...

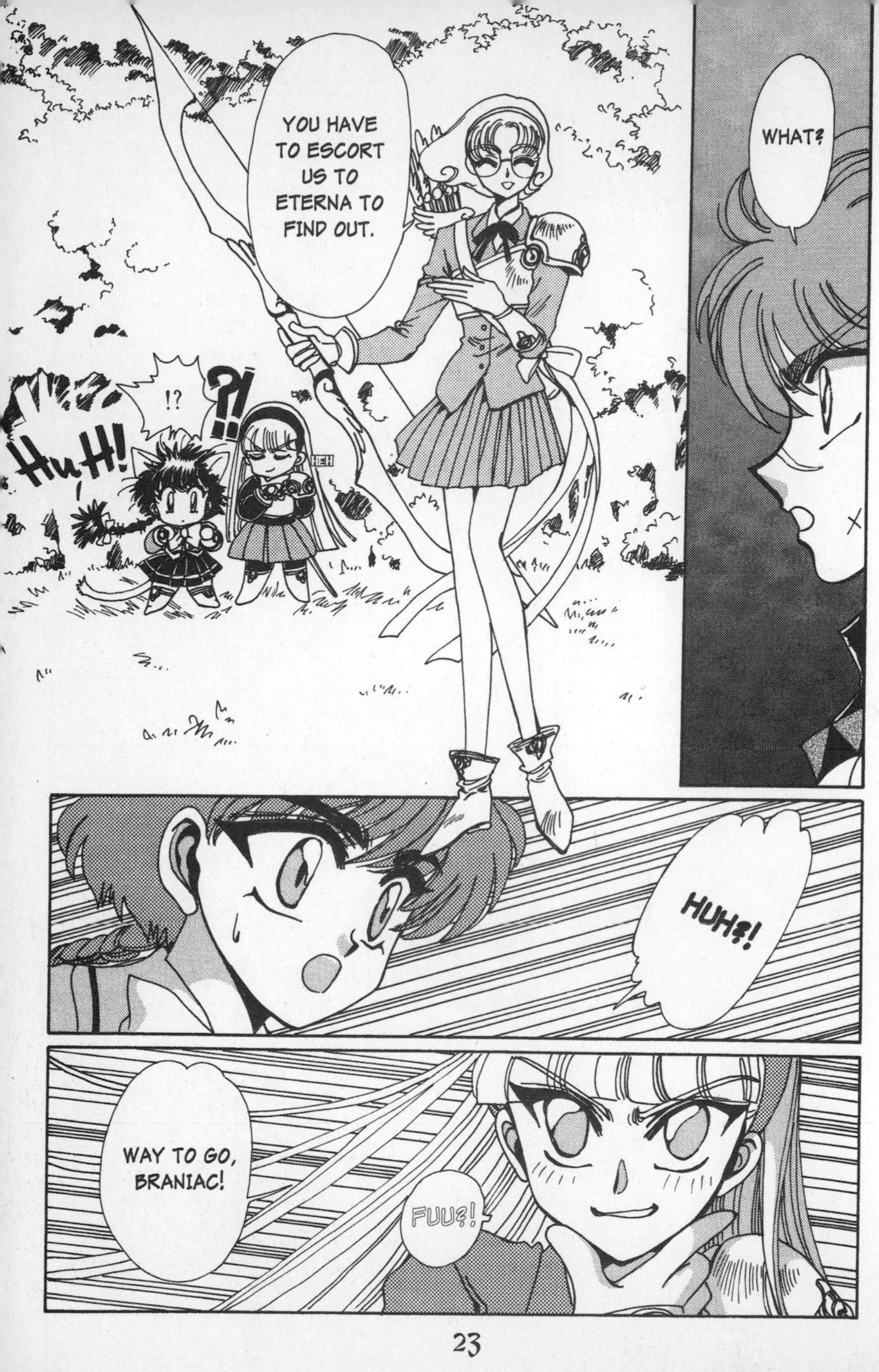
WHAT?
YOU HAVE TO ESCORT US TO ETERNA TO FIND OUT.
?!
!?
HuH!
HEH
HUH?!
WAY TO GO, BRANIAC!
FUU?!

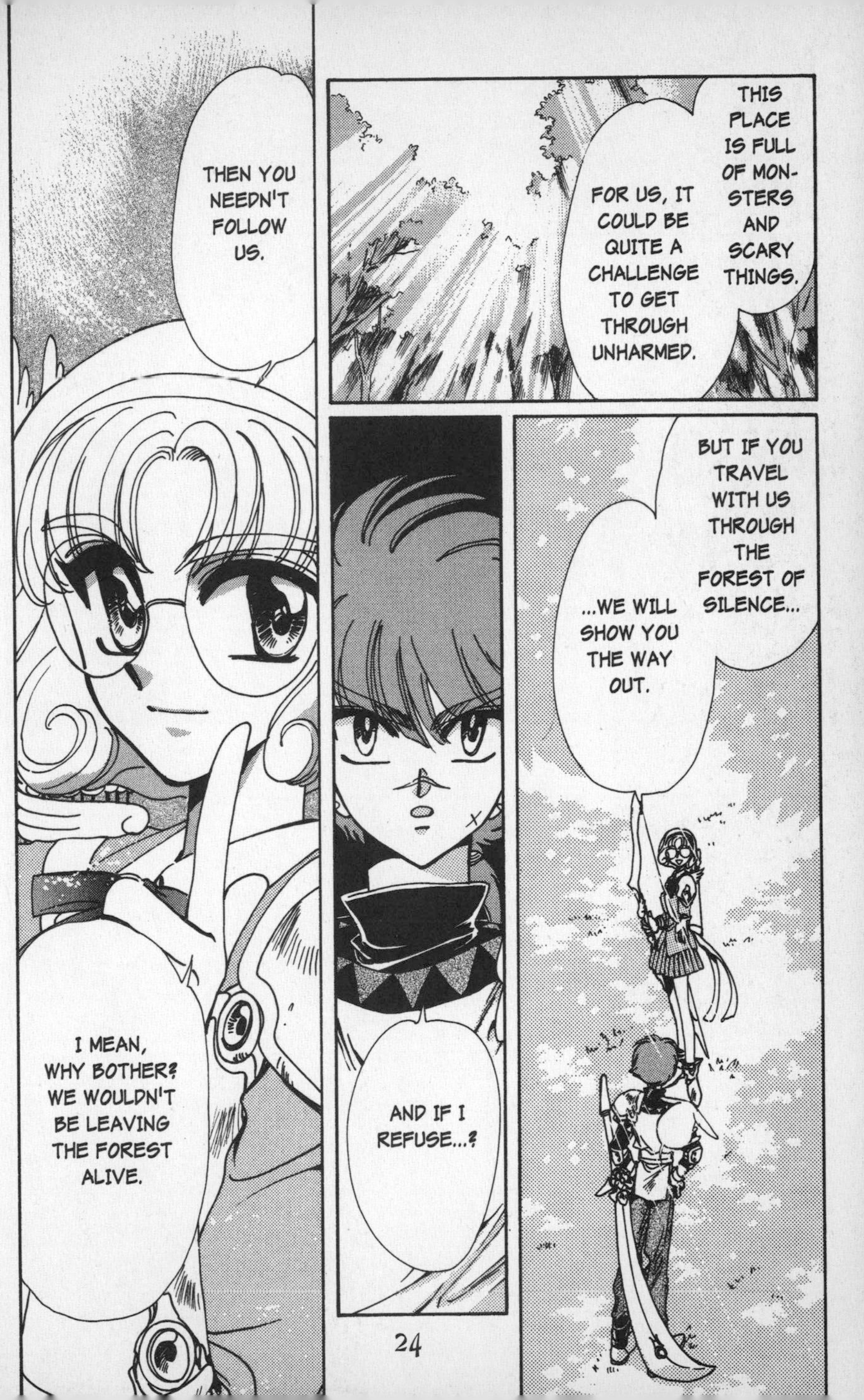
THIS PLACE IS FULL OF MON-STERS AND SCARY THINGS.
FOR US, IT COULD BE QUITE A CHALLENGE TO GET THROUGH UNHARMED.
BUT IF YOU TRAVEL WITH US THROUGH THE FOREST OF SILENCE...
...WE WILL SHOW YOU THE WAY OUT.
AND IF I REFUSE...?
THEN YOU NEEDN'T FOLLOW US.
I MEAN, WHY BOTHER? WE WOULDN'T BE LEAVING THE FOREST ALIVE.

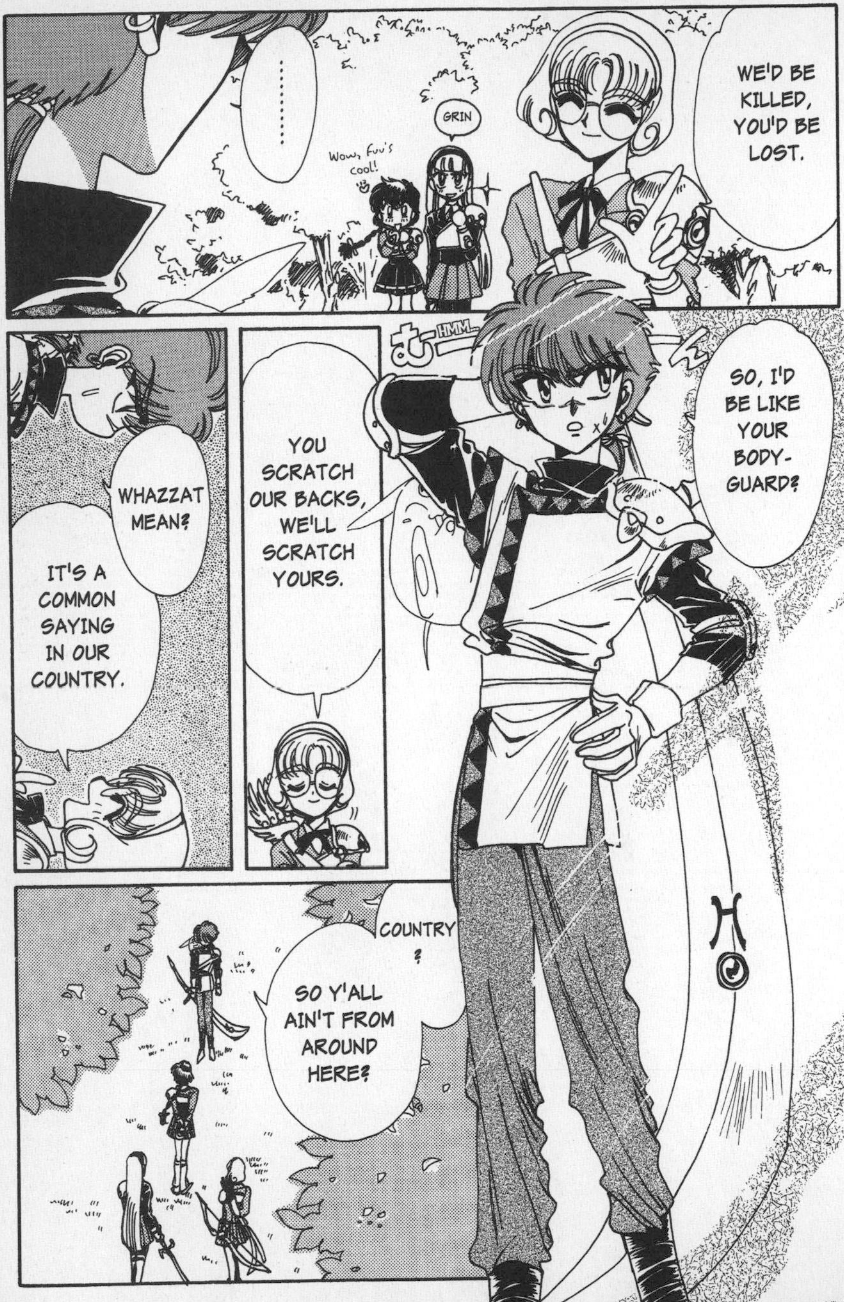
WE'D BE KILLED, YOU'D BE LOST.
GRIN
Wow, Fuu's cool!
......
HMM...
SO, I'D BE LIKE YOUR BODY-GUARD?
YOU SCRATCH OUR BACKS, WE'LL SCRATCH YOURS.
WHAZZAT MEAN?
IT'S A COMMON SAYING IN OUR COUNTRY.
COUNTRY?
SO Y'ALL AIN'T FROM AROUND HERE?

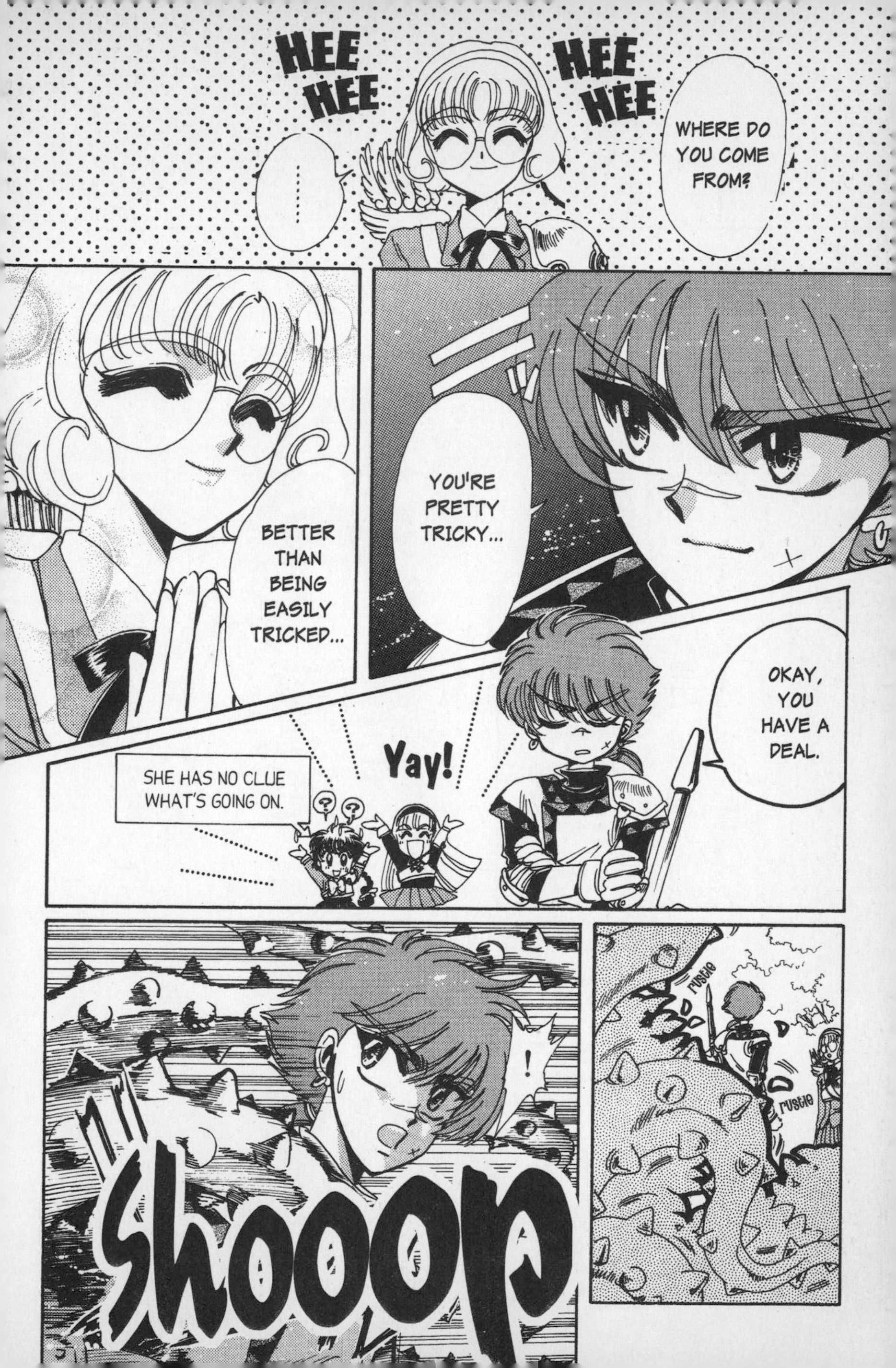
HEE HEE
WHERE DO YOU COME FROM?
HEE HEE
YOU'RE PRETTY TRICKY...
BETTER THAN BEING EASILY TRICKED...
OKAY, YOU HAVE A DEAL.
Yay!
SHE HAS NO CLUE WHAT'S GOING ON.
rustle
rustle
!
shooop

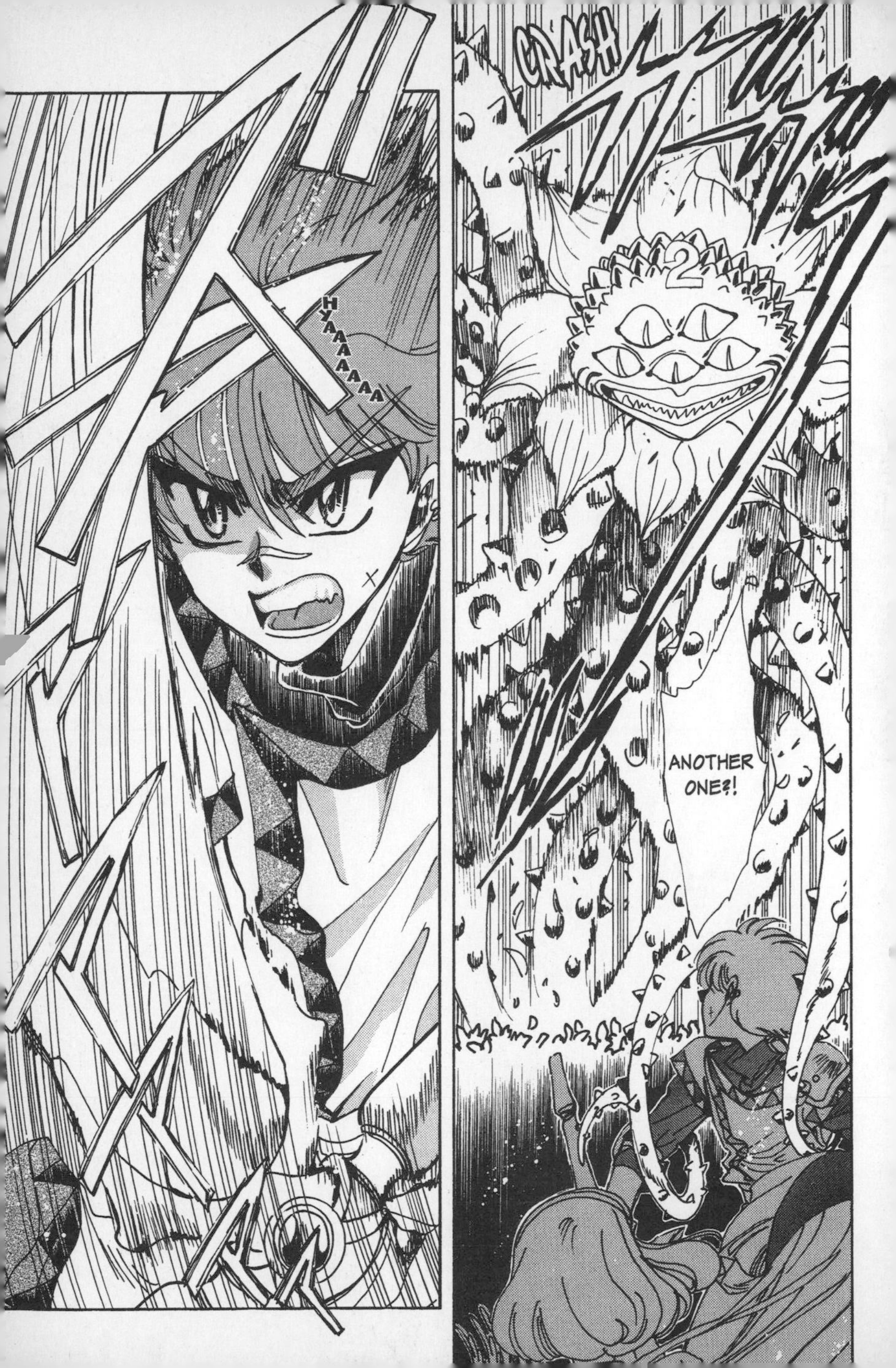
CRASH
ANOTHER ONE?!
HYAAAAAAA

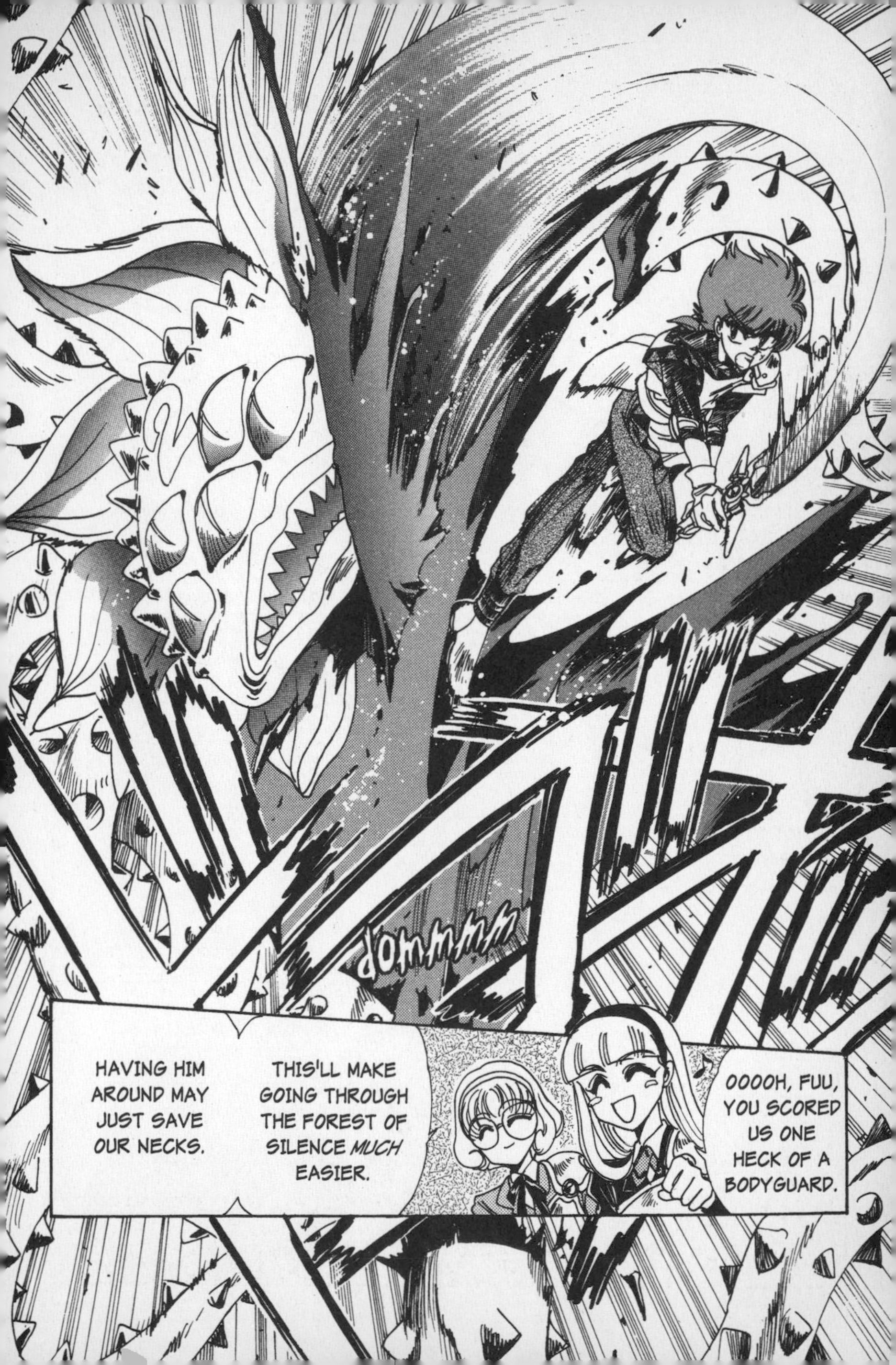
OOOOH, FUU, YOU SCORED US ONE HECK OF A BODYGUARD.
THIS'LL MAKE GOING THROUGH THE FOREST OF SILENCE *MUCH* EASIER.
HAVING HIM AROUND MAY JUST SAVE OUR NECKS.

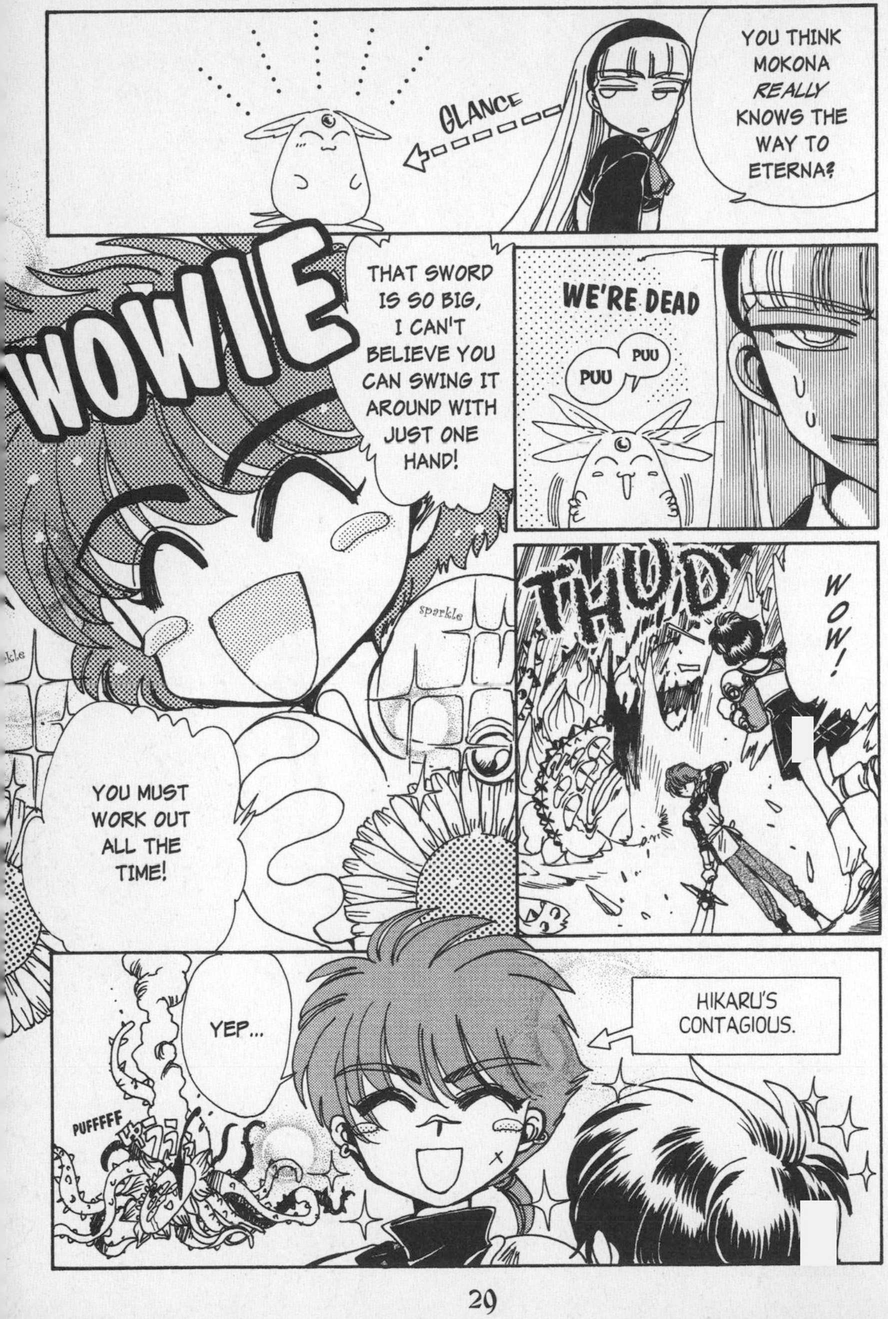
YOU THINK MOKONA *REALLY* KNOWS THE WAY TO ETERNA?
GLANCE
WE'RE DEAD
PUU
PUU
THUD
WOW!
WOWIE
THAT SWORD IS SO BIG, I CAN'T BELIEVE YOU CAN SWING IT AROUND WITH JUST ONE HAND!
sparkle
YOU MUST WORK OUT ALL THE TIME!
HIKARU'S CONTAGIOUS.
YEP...
PUFFFFF

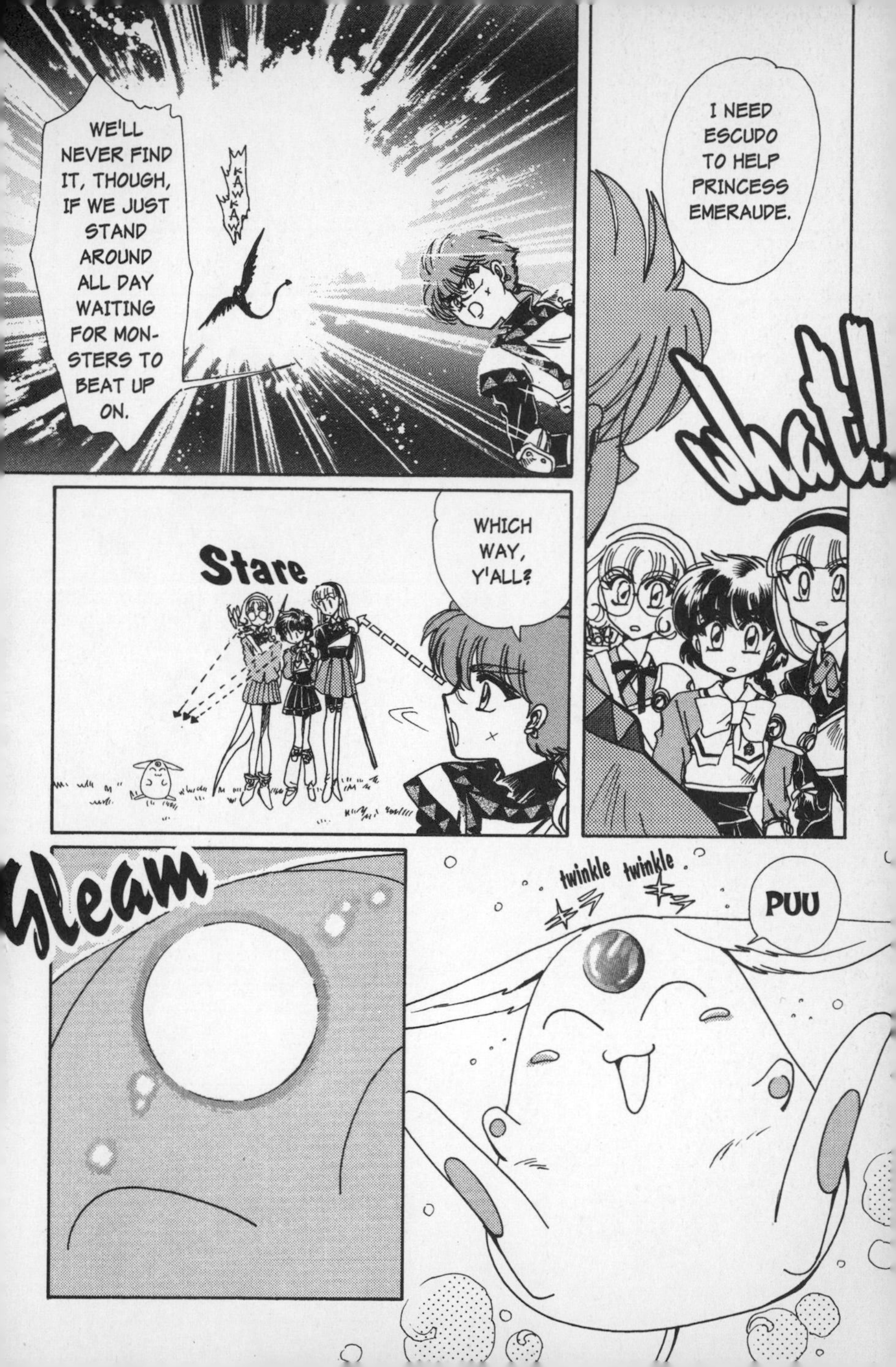
I NEED ESCUDO TO HELP PRINCESS EMERAUDE.
KAWKAW
WE'LL NEVER FIND IT, THOUGH, IF WE JUST STAND AROUND ALL DAY WAITING FOR MON-STERS TO BEAT UP ON.
What!
WHICH WAY, Y'ALL?
Stare
PUU
twinkle twinkle
Gleam

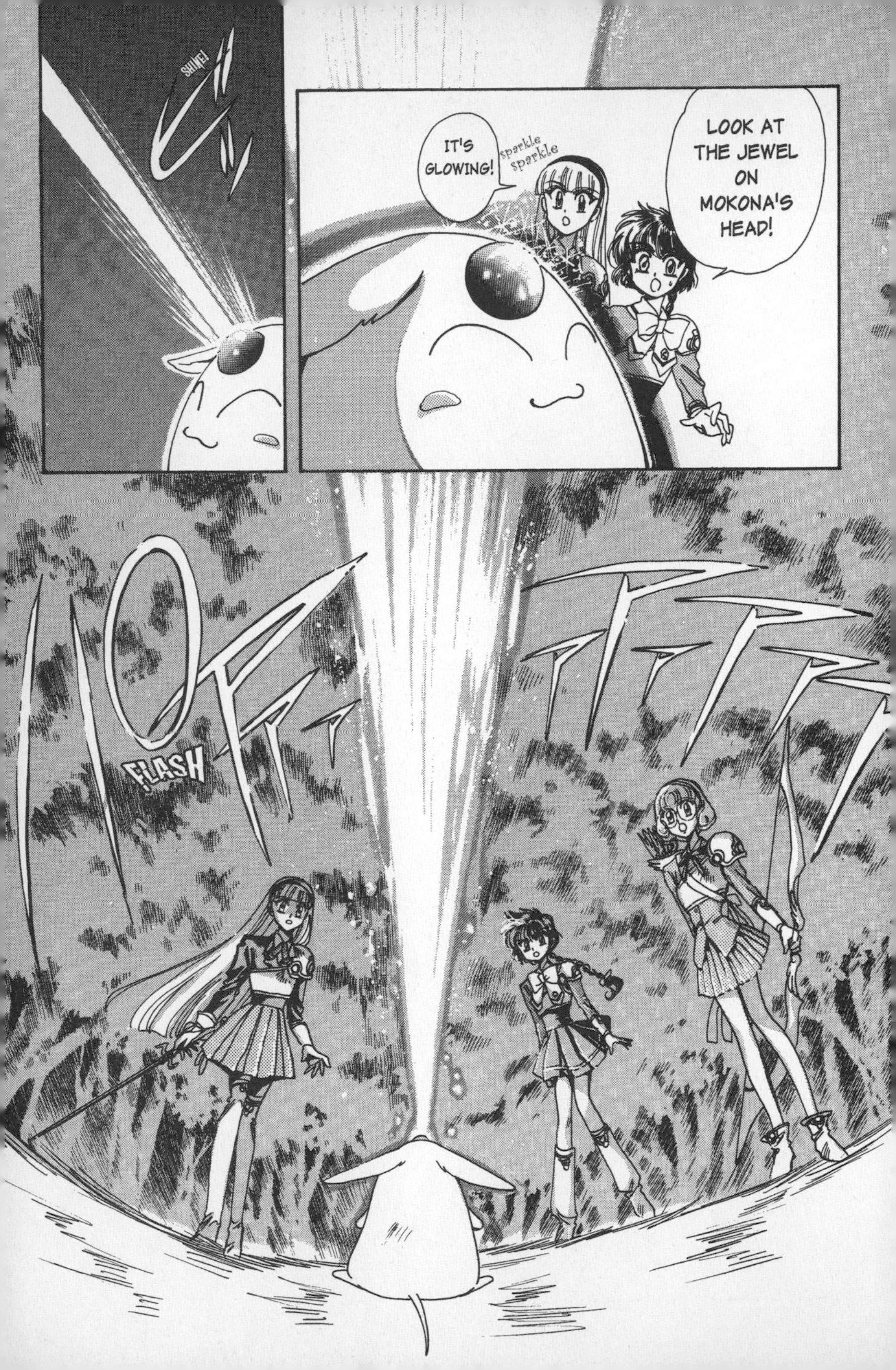
LOOK AT THE JEWEL ON MOKONA'S HEAD!
sparkle sparkle
IT'S GLOWING!
SHINE!
FLASH

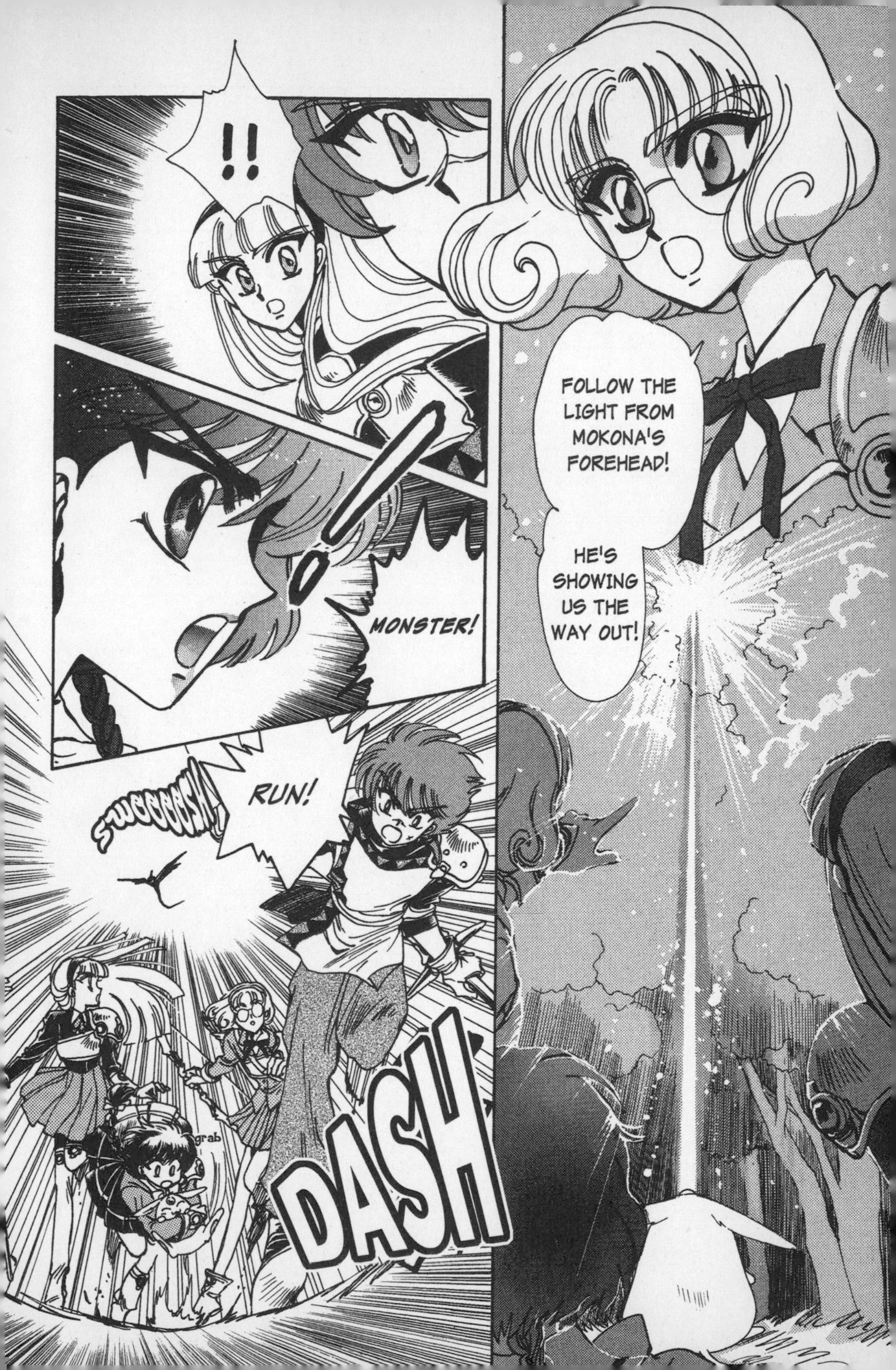
FOLLOW THE LIGHT FROM MOKONA'S FOREHEAD!
HE'S SHOWING US THE WAY OUT!
!!
MONSTER!
RUN!
SWEEEESH
grab
DASH

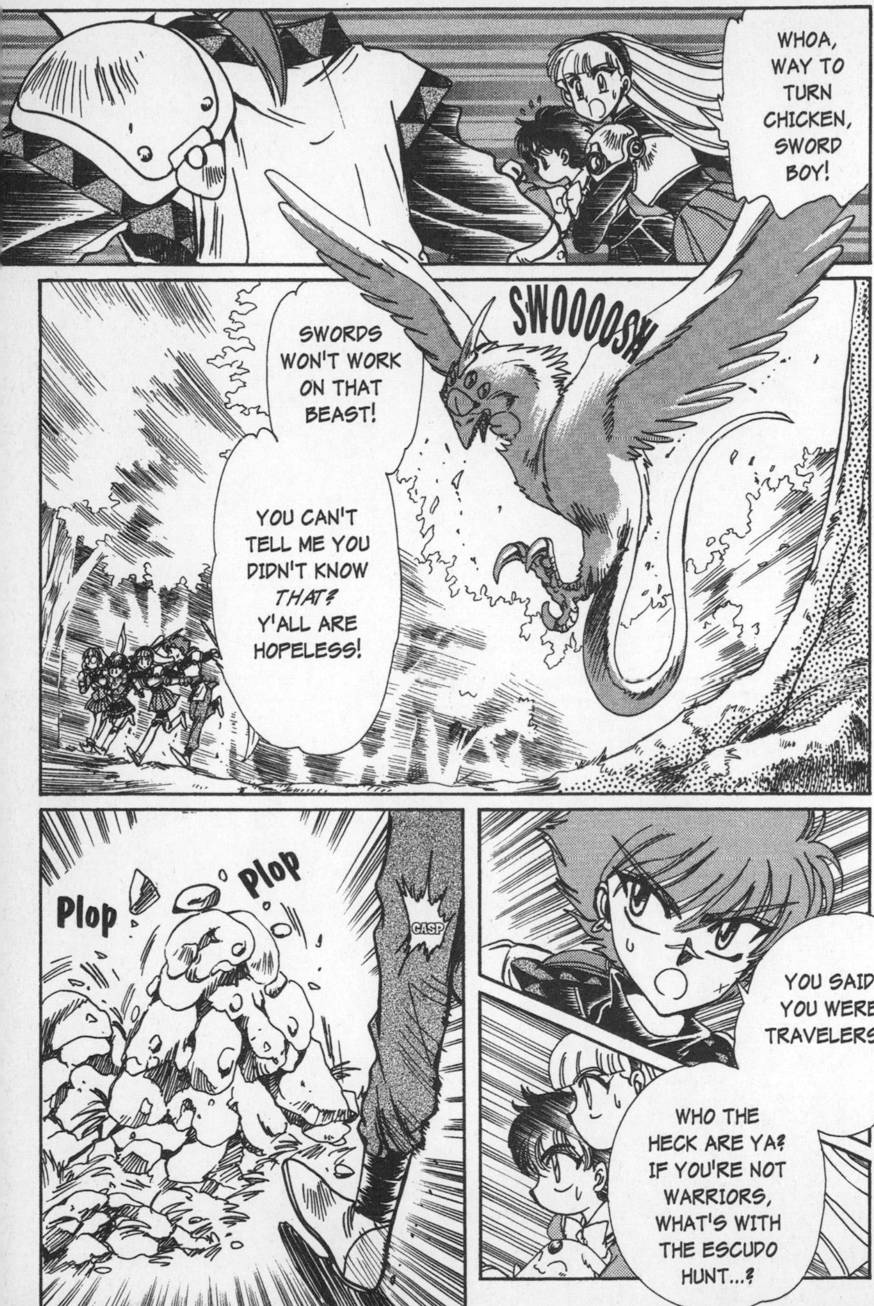
WHOA, WAY TO TURN CHICKEN, SWORD BOY!
SWOOOOSH
SWORDS WON'T WORK ON THAT BEAST!
YOU CAN'T TELL ME YOU DIDN'T KNOW *THAT*? Y'ALL ARE HOPELESS!
YOU SAID YOU WERE TRAVELERS...
WHO THE HECK ARE YA? IF YOU'RE NOT WARRIORS, WHAT'S WITH THE ESCUDO HUNT...?
Plop
Plop
GASP

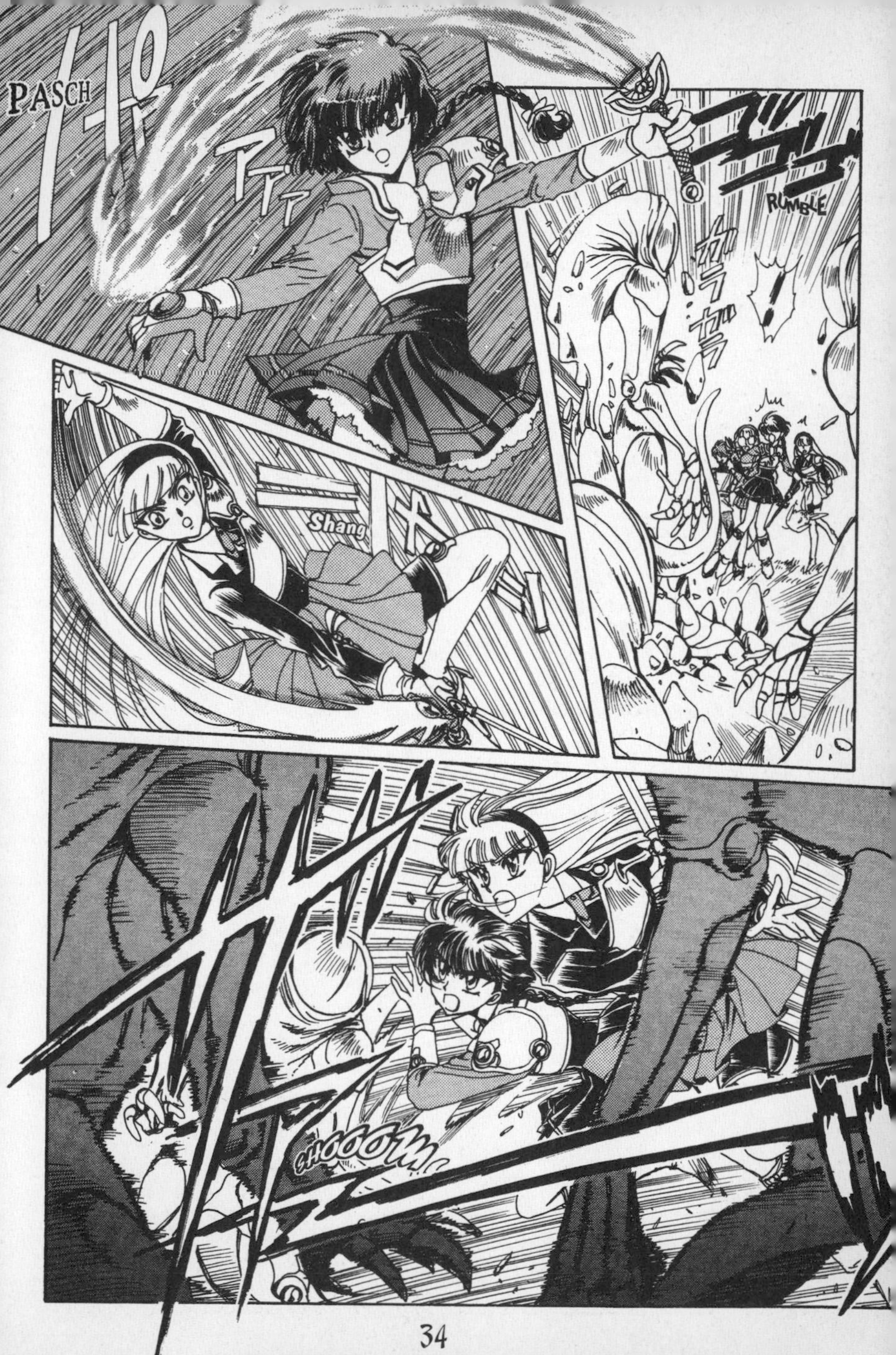
RUMBLE
PASCH
Shang
WHOOOM!

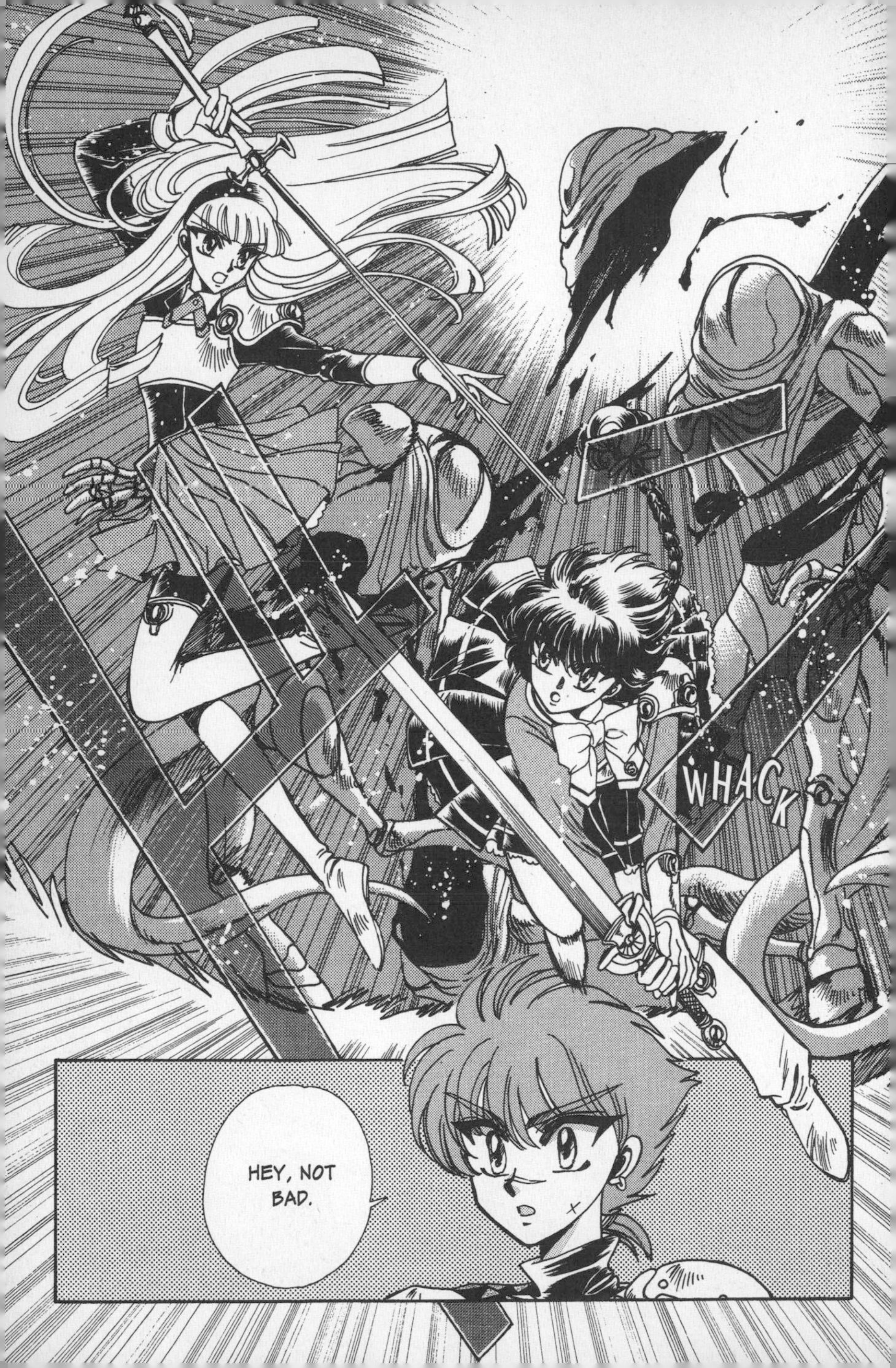
WHACK
HEY, NOT BAD.

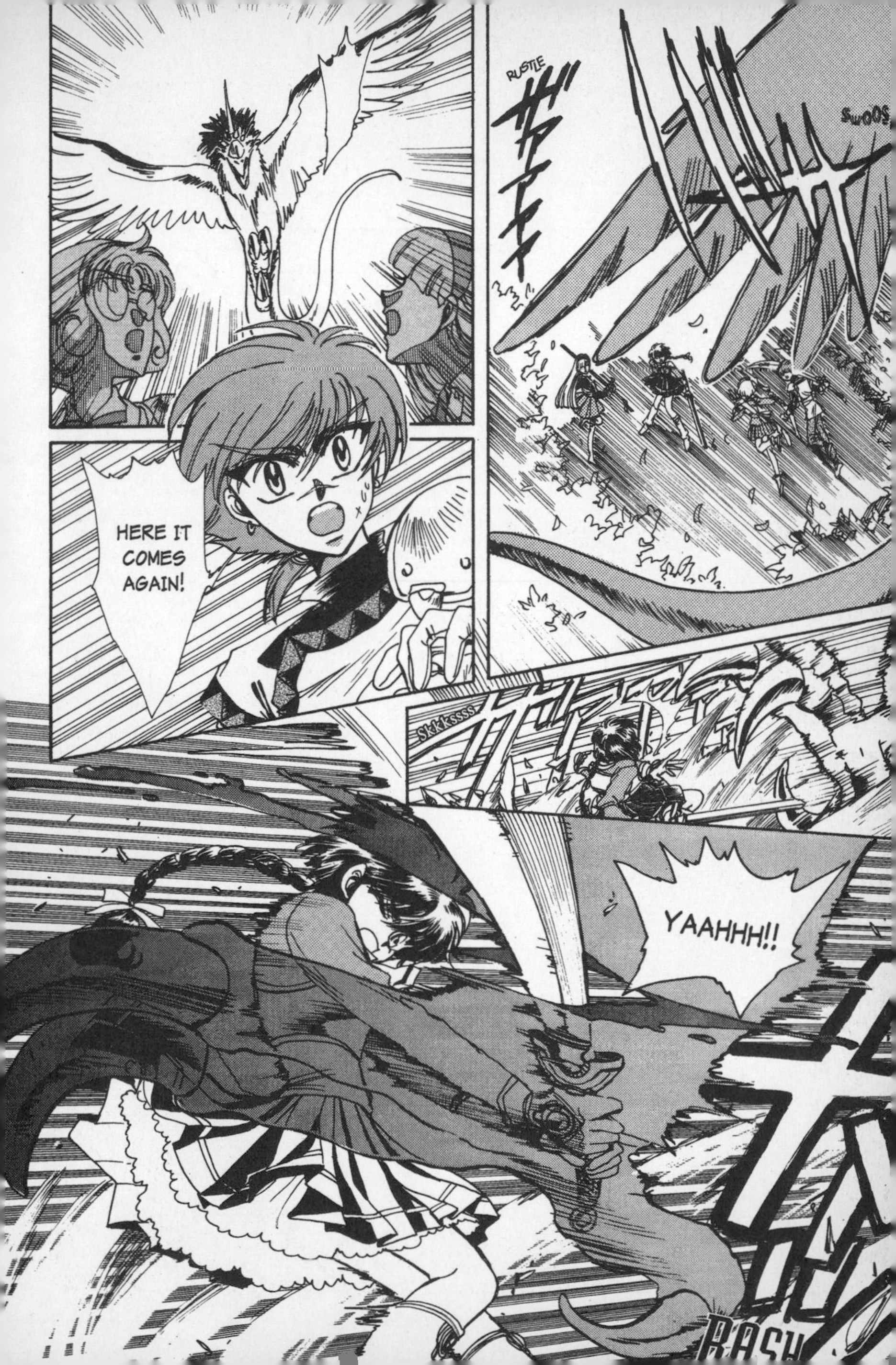
RUSTLE
SWOOS
HERE IT COMES AGAIN!
Skkkssss
YAAHHH!!
BASH

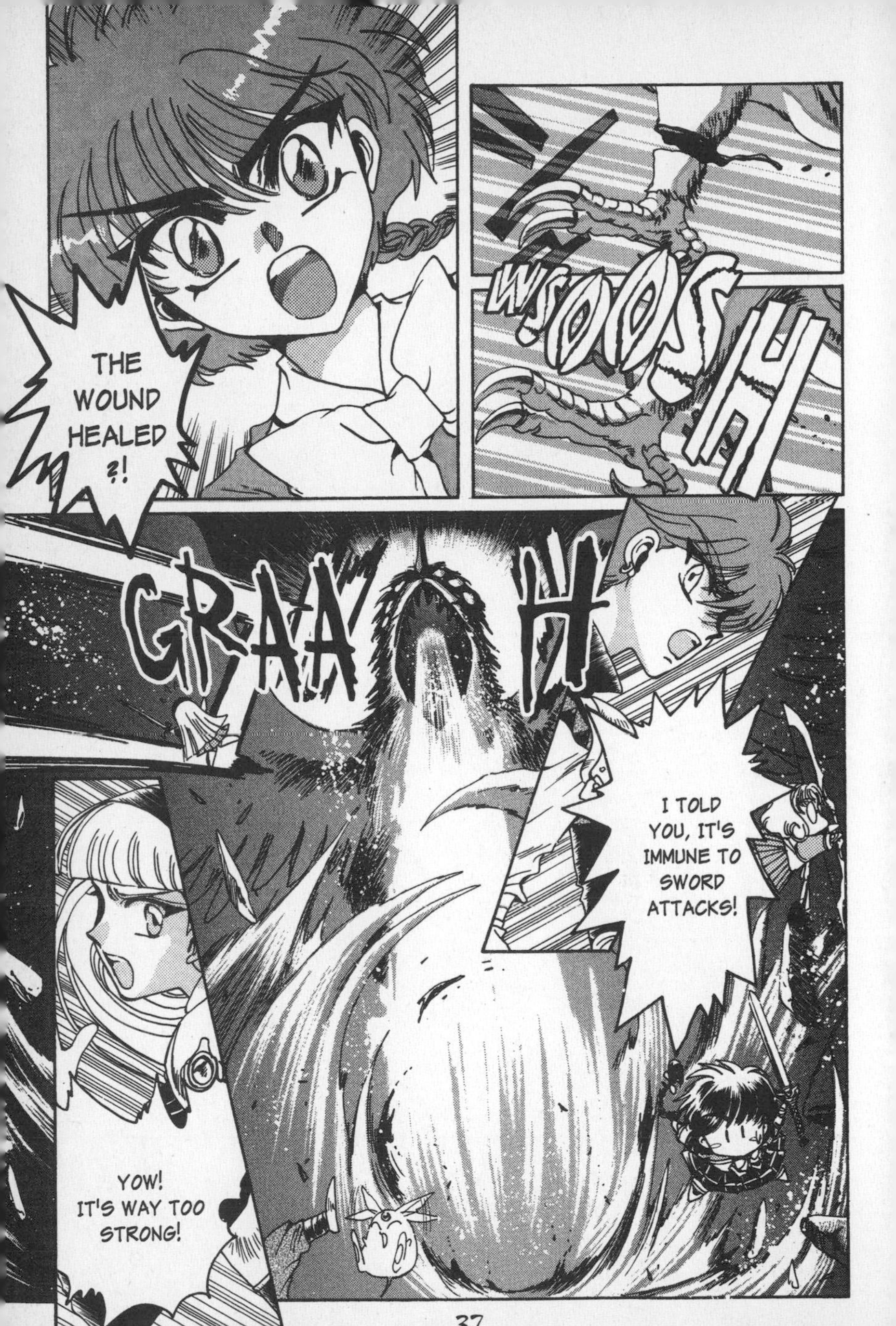
WSOOOSH
THE WOUND HEALED ?!
GRAAAH
I TOLD YOU, IT'S IMMUNE TO SWORD ATTACKS!
YOW! IT'S WAY TOO STRONG!

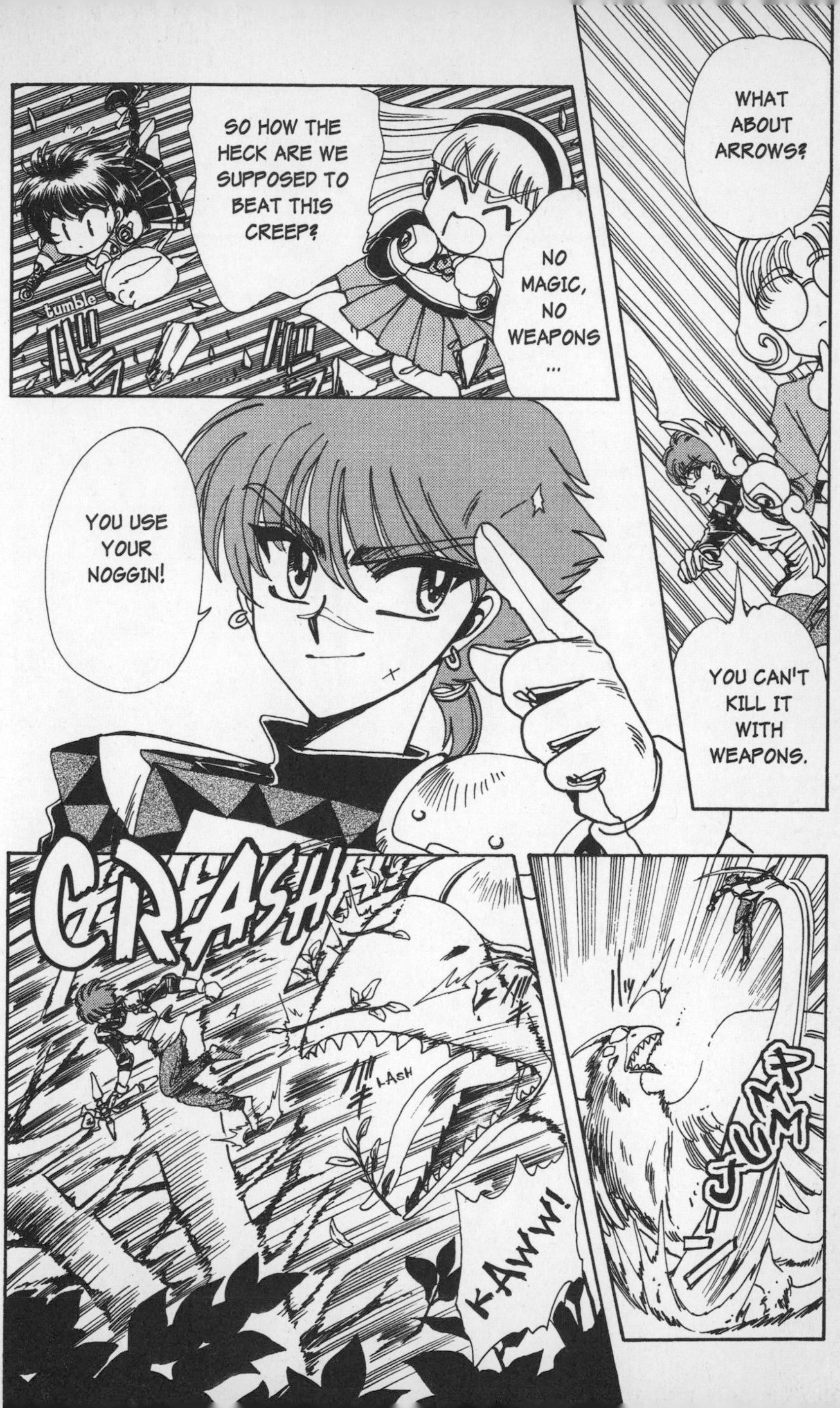
WHAT ABOUT ARROWS?
YOU CAN'T KILL IT WITH WEAPONS.
SO HOW THE HECK ARE WE SUPPOSED TO BEAT THIS CREEP?
NO MAGIC, NO WEAPONS ...
tumble
YOU USE YOUR NOGGIN!
JUMP
CRASH
LASH
KAWW!

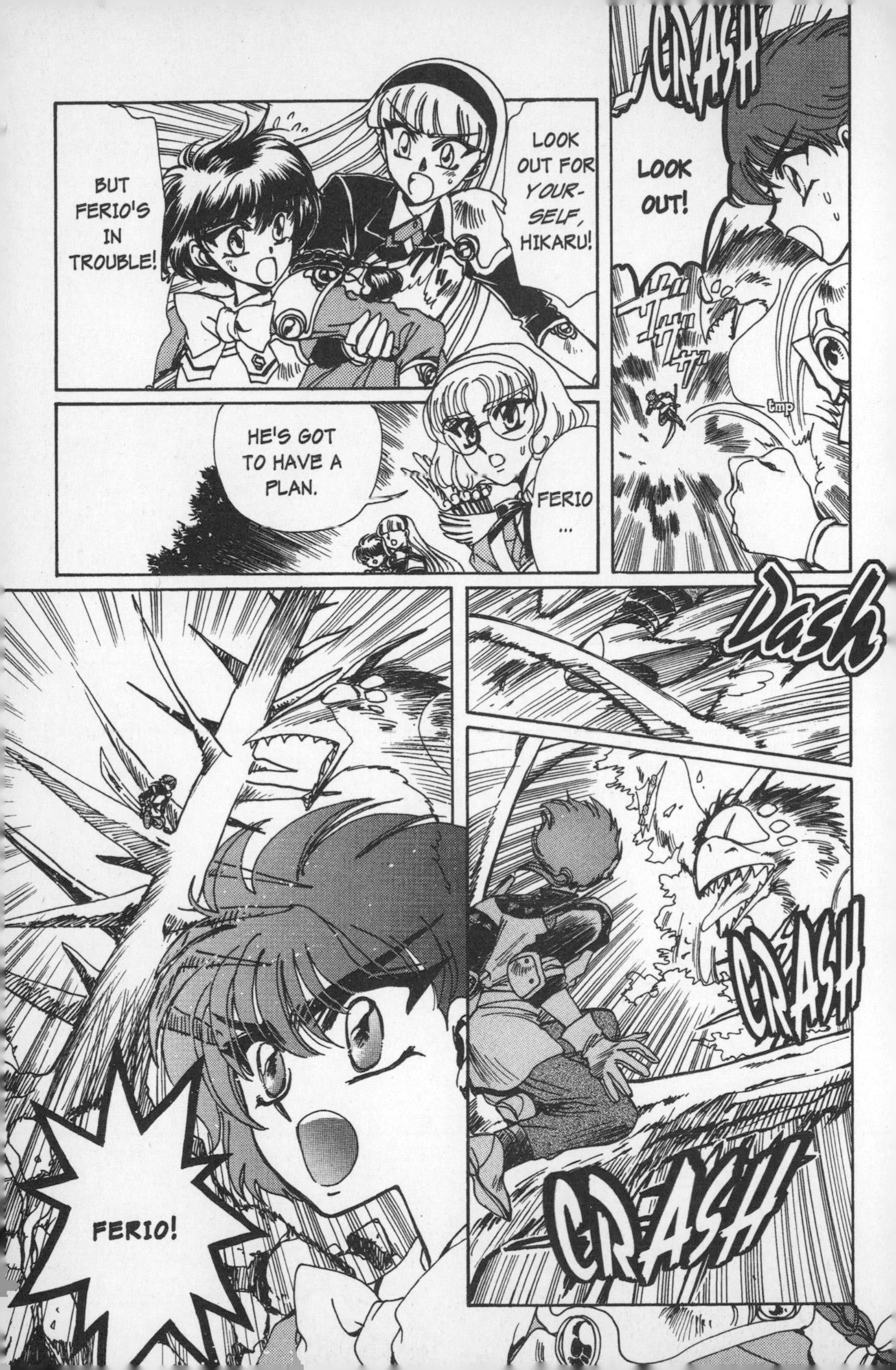
CRASH
LOOK OUT!
tmp
LOOK OUT FOR YOUR-SELF, HIKARU!
BUT FERIO'S IN TROUBLE!
FERIO ...
HE'S GOT TO HAVE A PLAN.
Dash
CRASH
CRASH
FERIO!

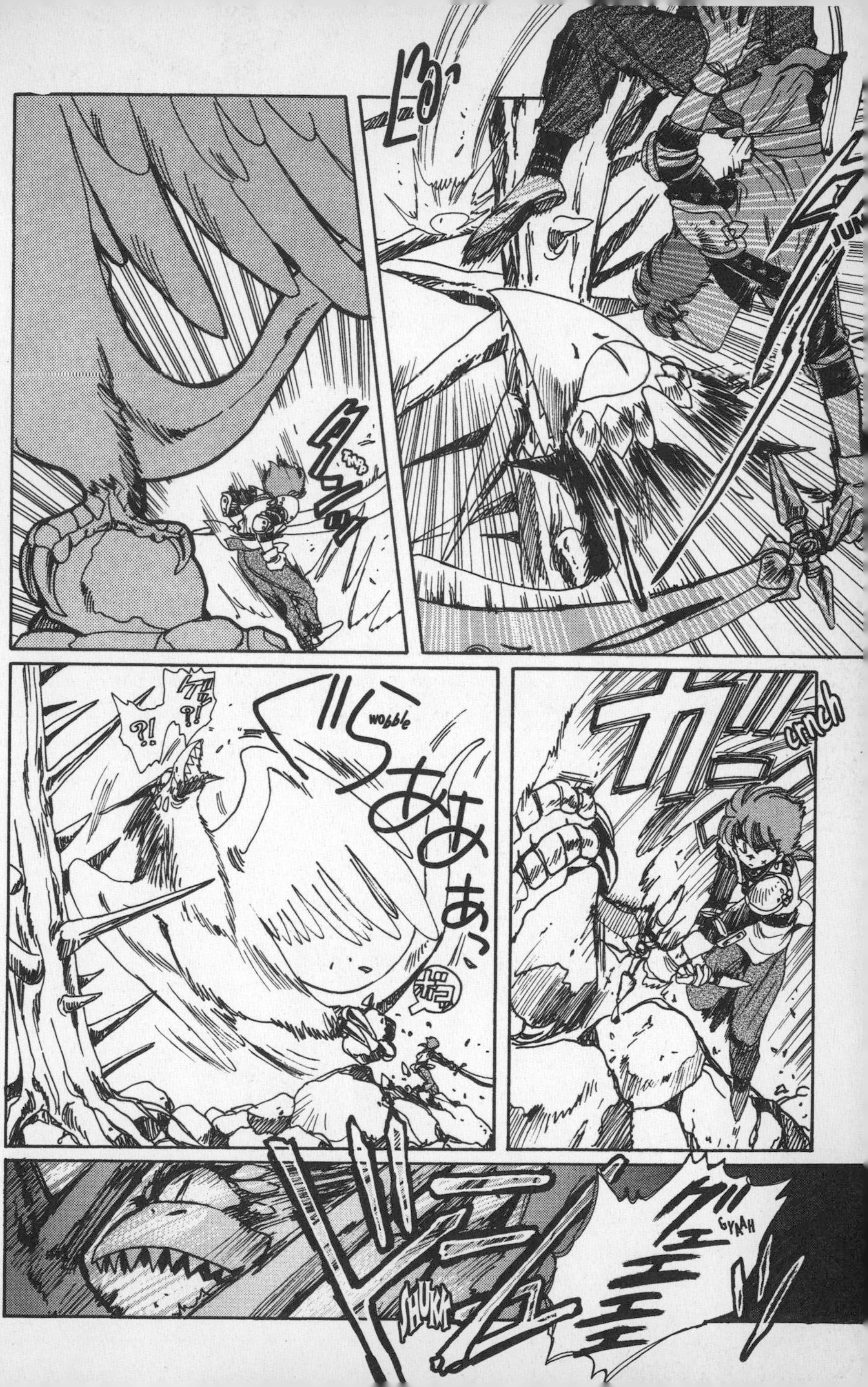

JUM
TMP
crnch
?!
?!
ぐらあああっ
wobble
GYAAH
SHUKK

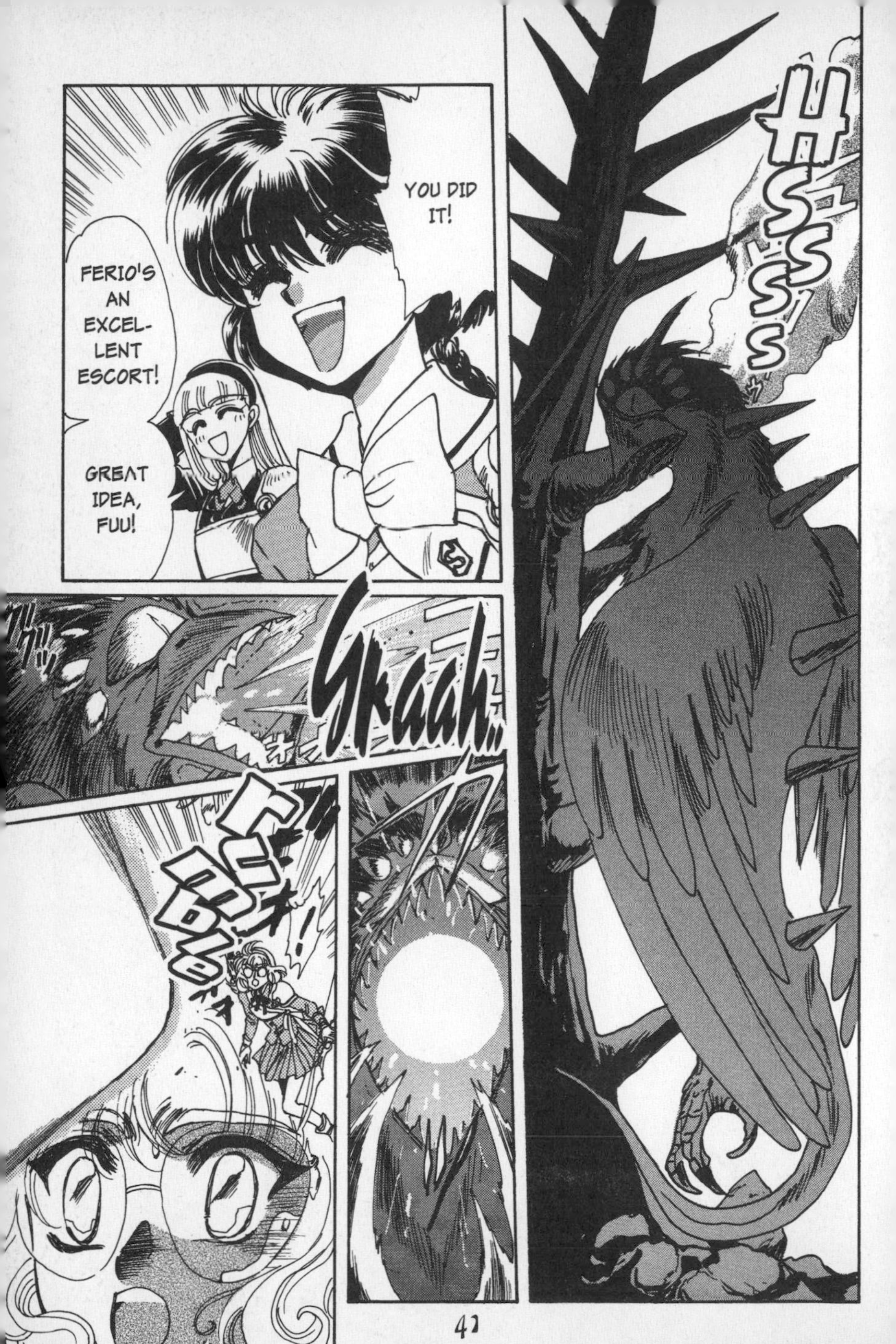
HSSSS
YOU DID IT!
FERIO'S AN EXCEL-LENT ESCORT!
GREAT IDEA, FUU!
Graah...
rumble

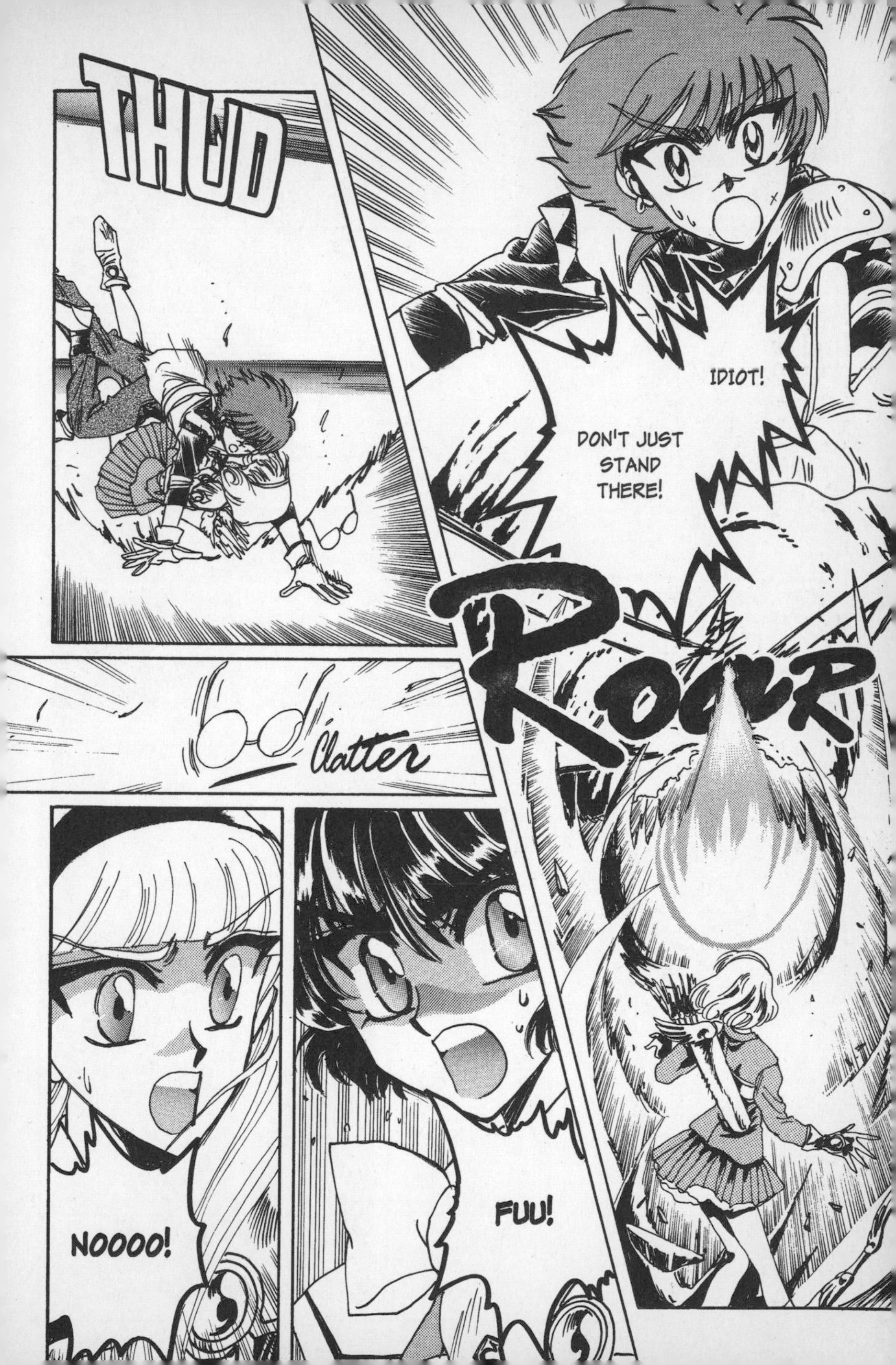
IDIOT!
DON'T JUST STAND THERE!
ROOAR
THUD
Clatter
FUU!
NOOOO!

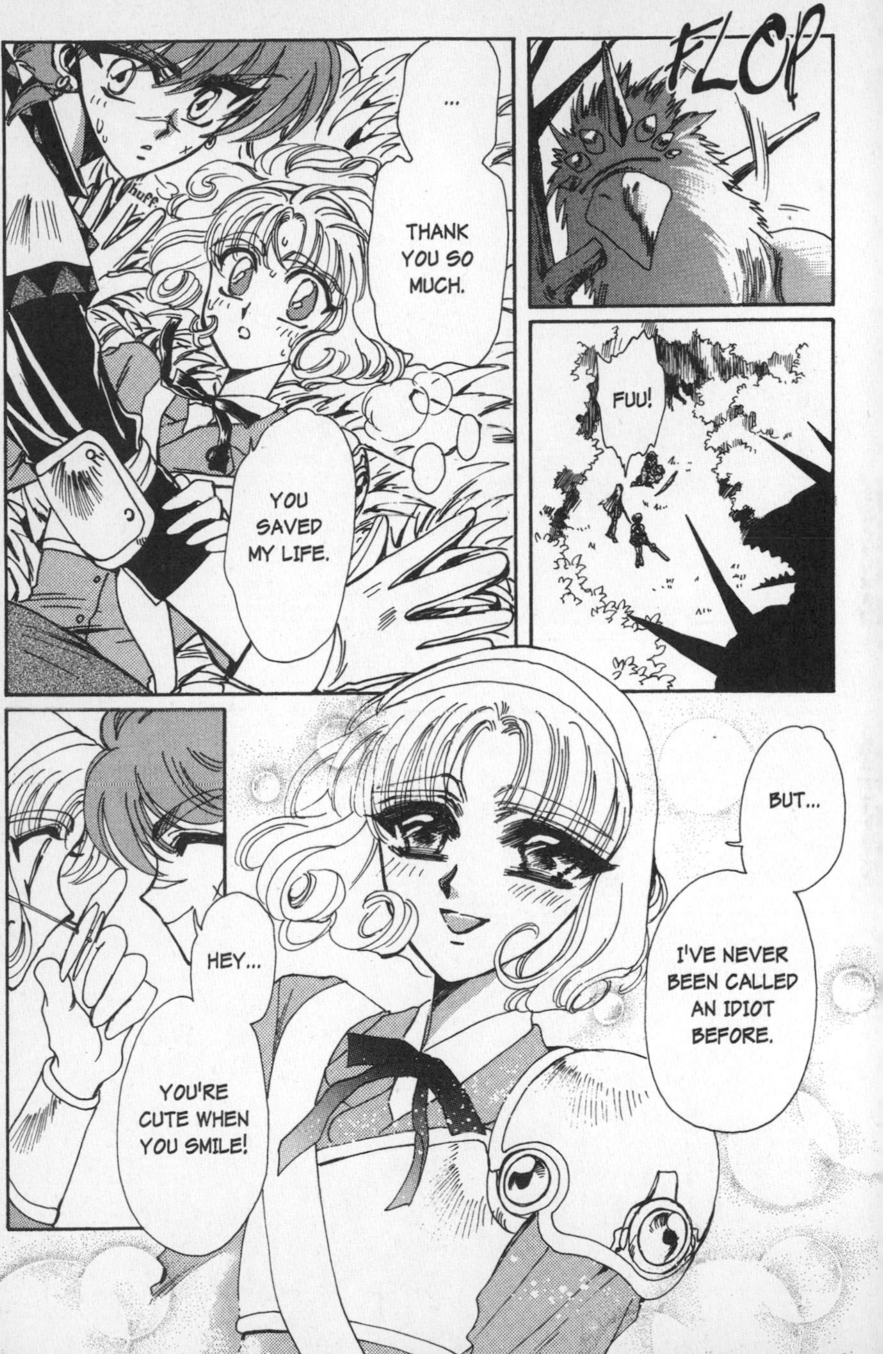
FLOP
FUU!
...
huff
THANK YOU SO MUCH.
YOU SAVED MY LIFE.
BUT...
I'VE NEVER BEEN CALLED AN IDIOT BEFORE.
HEY...
YOU'RE CUTE WHEN YOU SMILE!

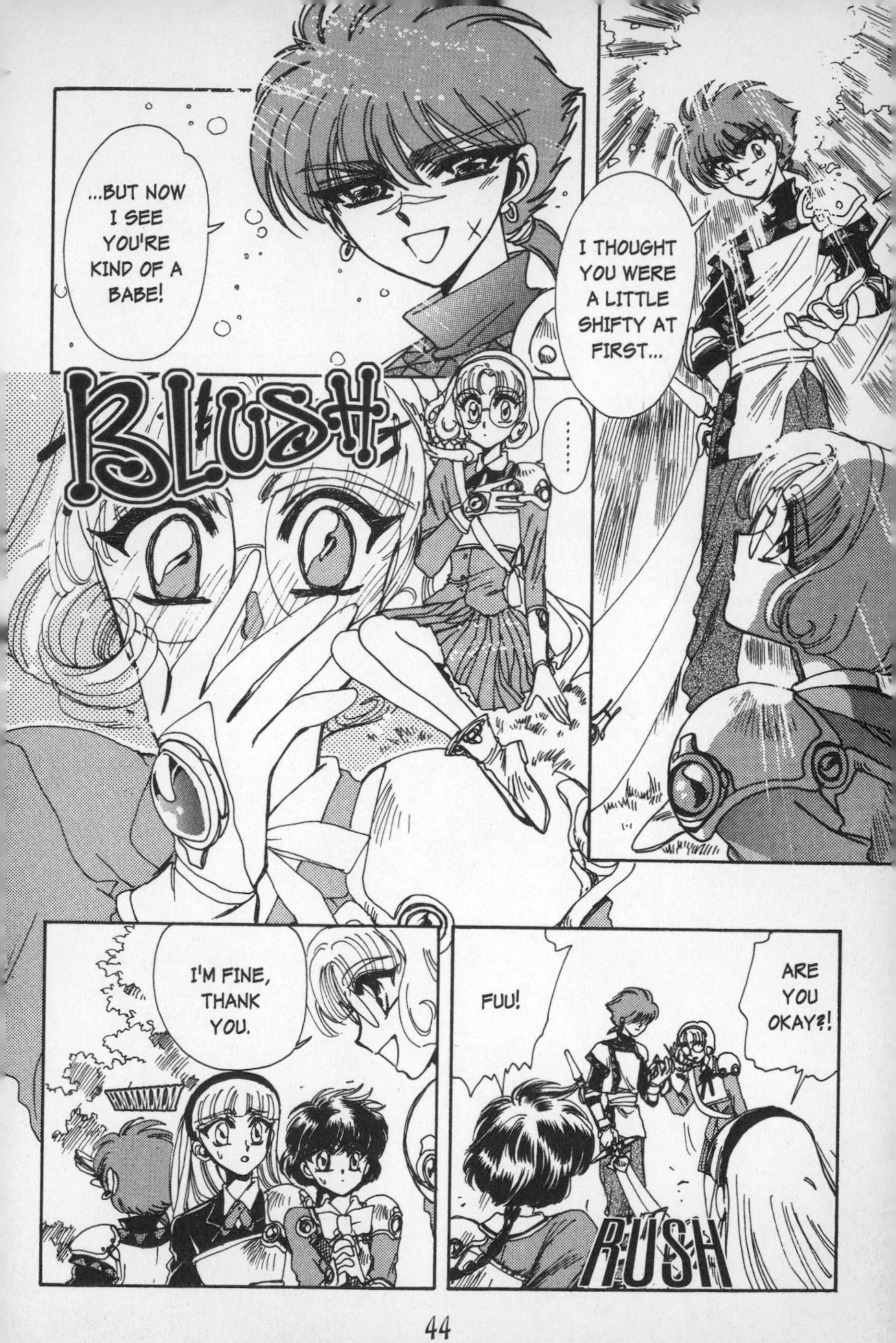
I THOUGHT YOU WERE A LITTLE SHIFTY AT FIRST...
...BUT NOW I SEE YOU'RE KIND OF A BABE!
BLUSH
......
ARE YOU OKAY?!
FUU!
RUSH
I'M FINE, THANK YOU.

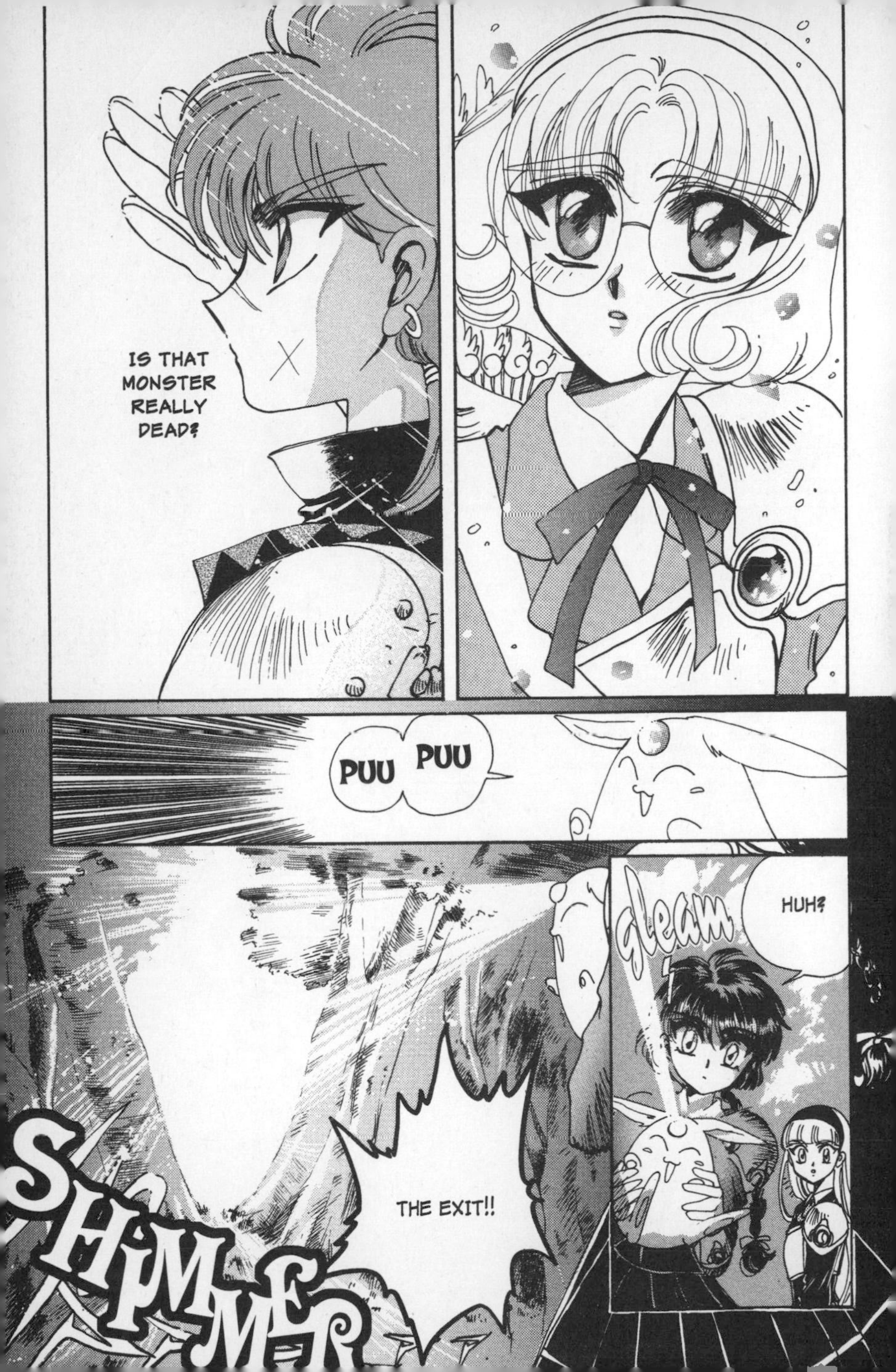
IS THAT MONSTER REALLY DEAD?
PUU PUU
gleam
HUH?
SHIMMER
THE EXIT!!

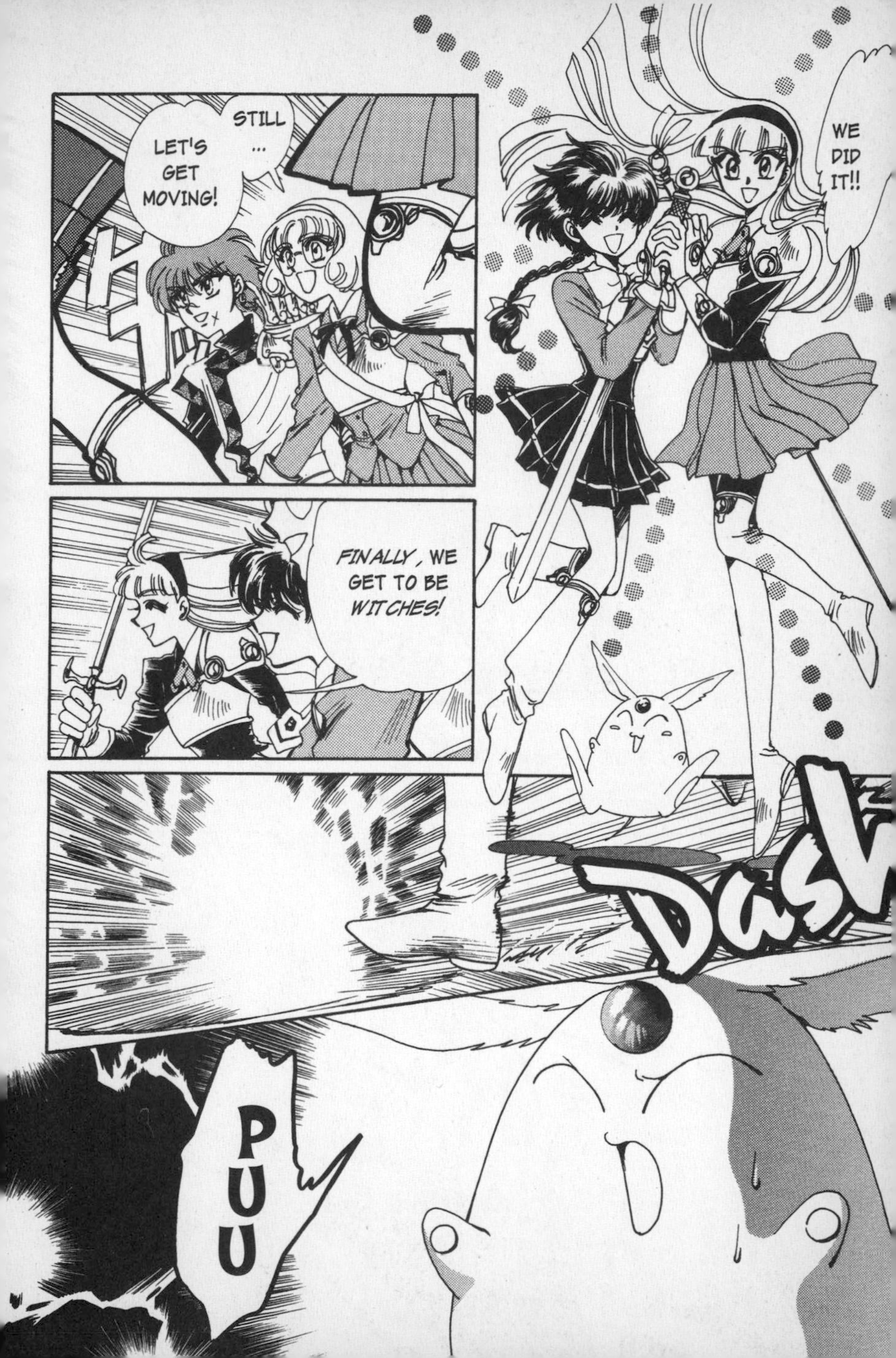
WE DID IT!!
STILL ...
LET'S GET MOVING!
FINALLY, WE GET TO BE WITCHES!
PUU

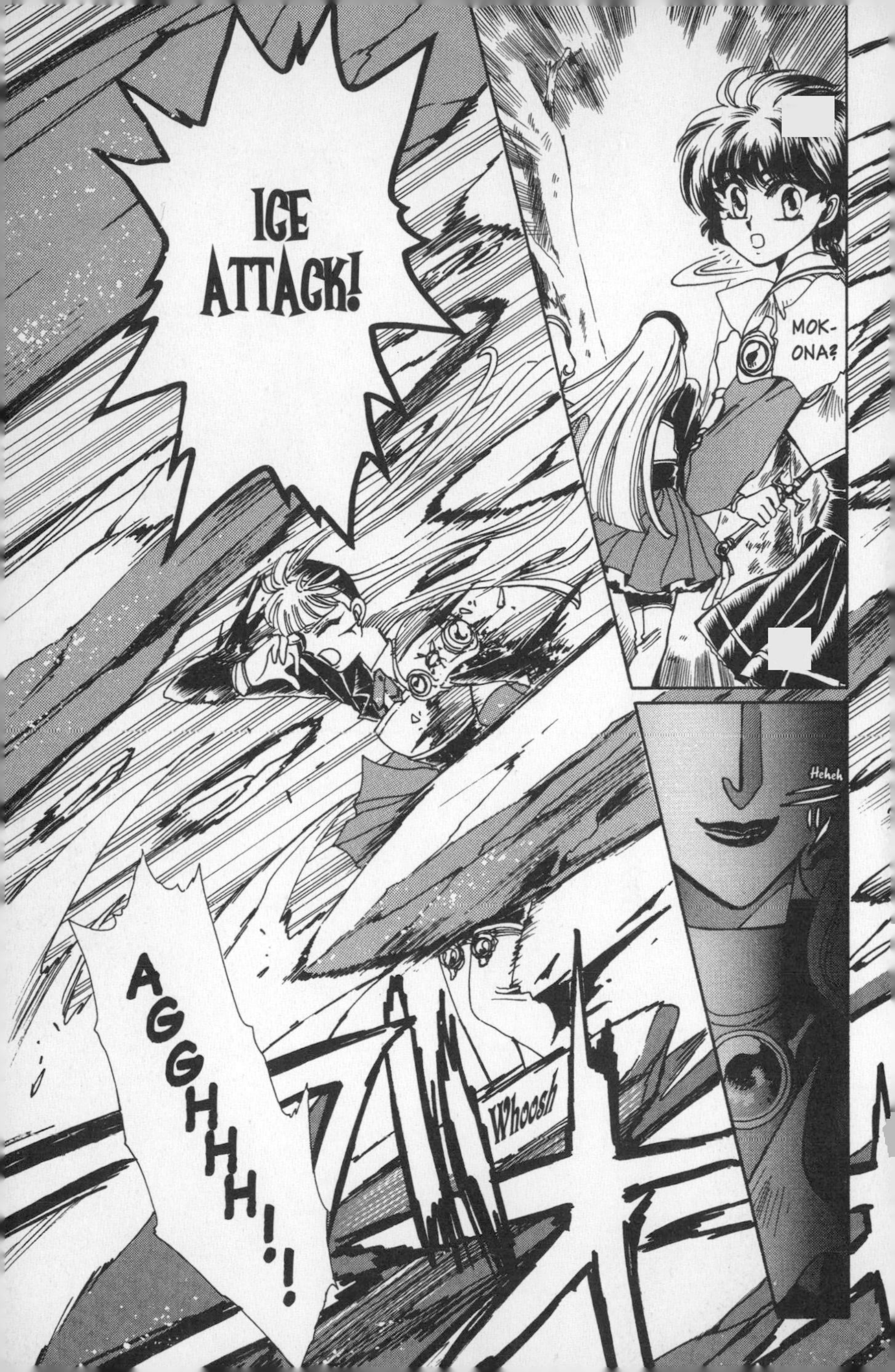
MOK-ONA?
Heheh
ICE ATTACK!
Whoosh
AGGHHH!!

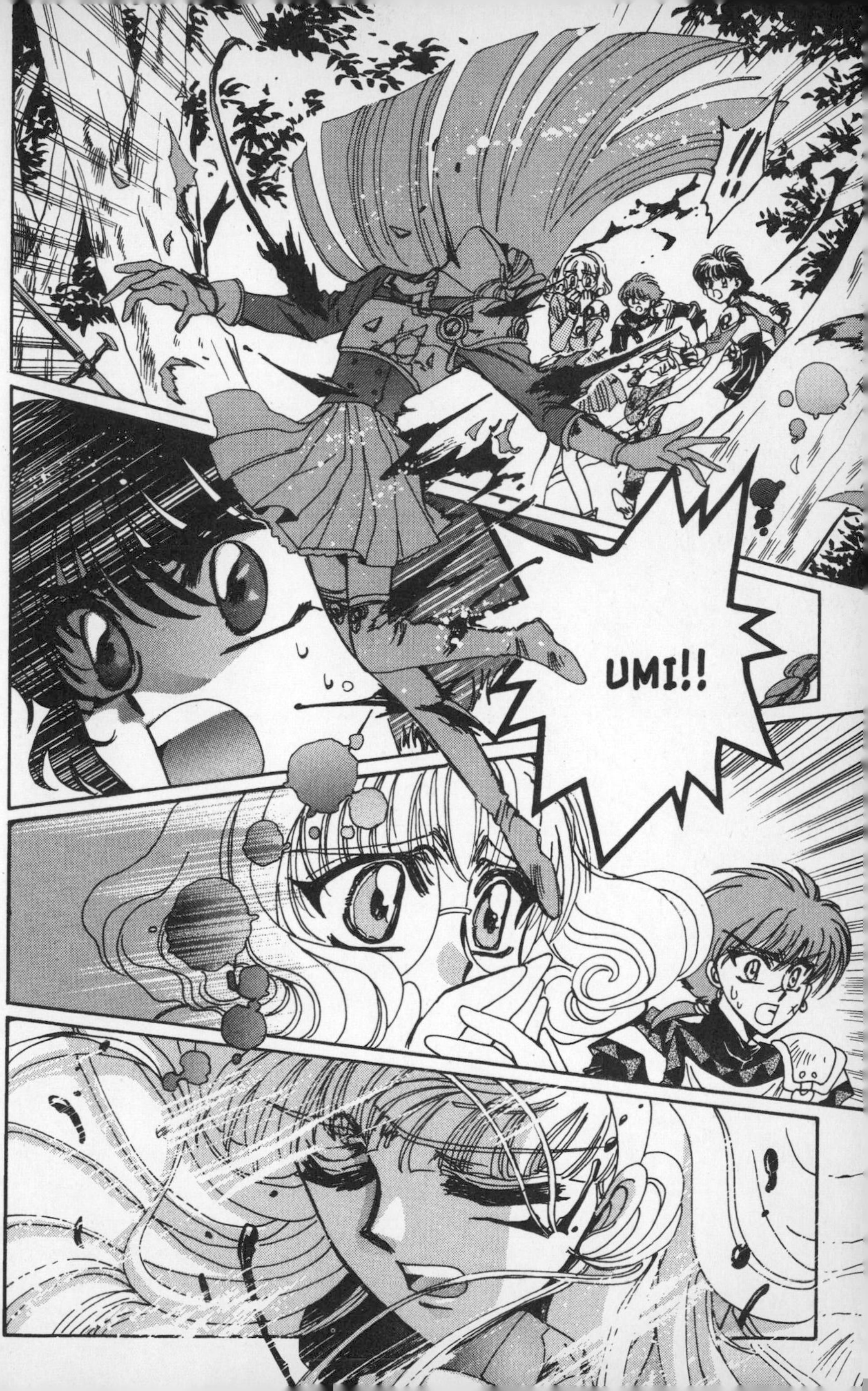
UMI!!

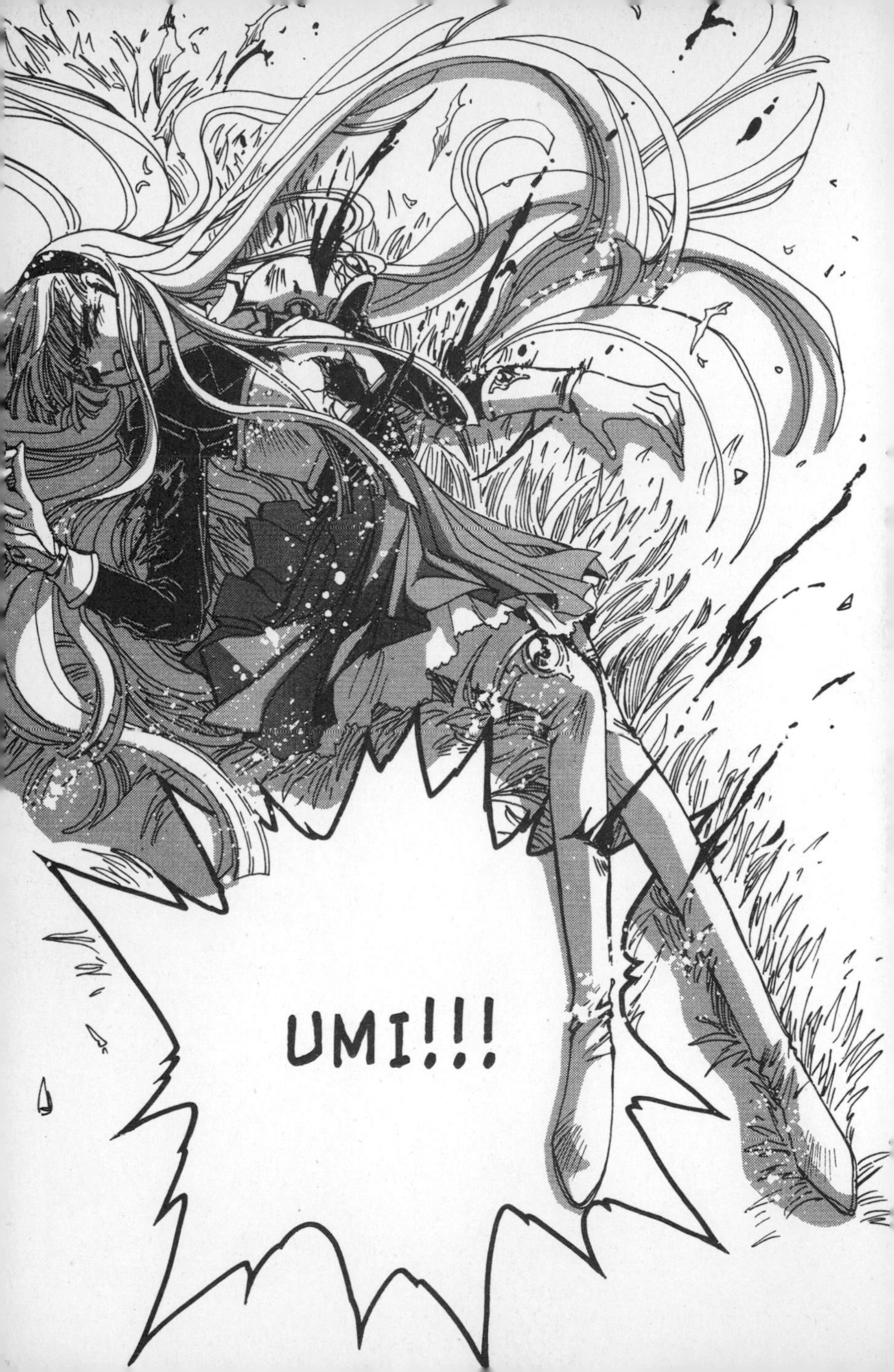
UMI!!!

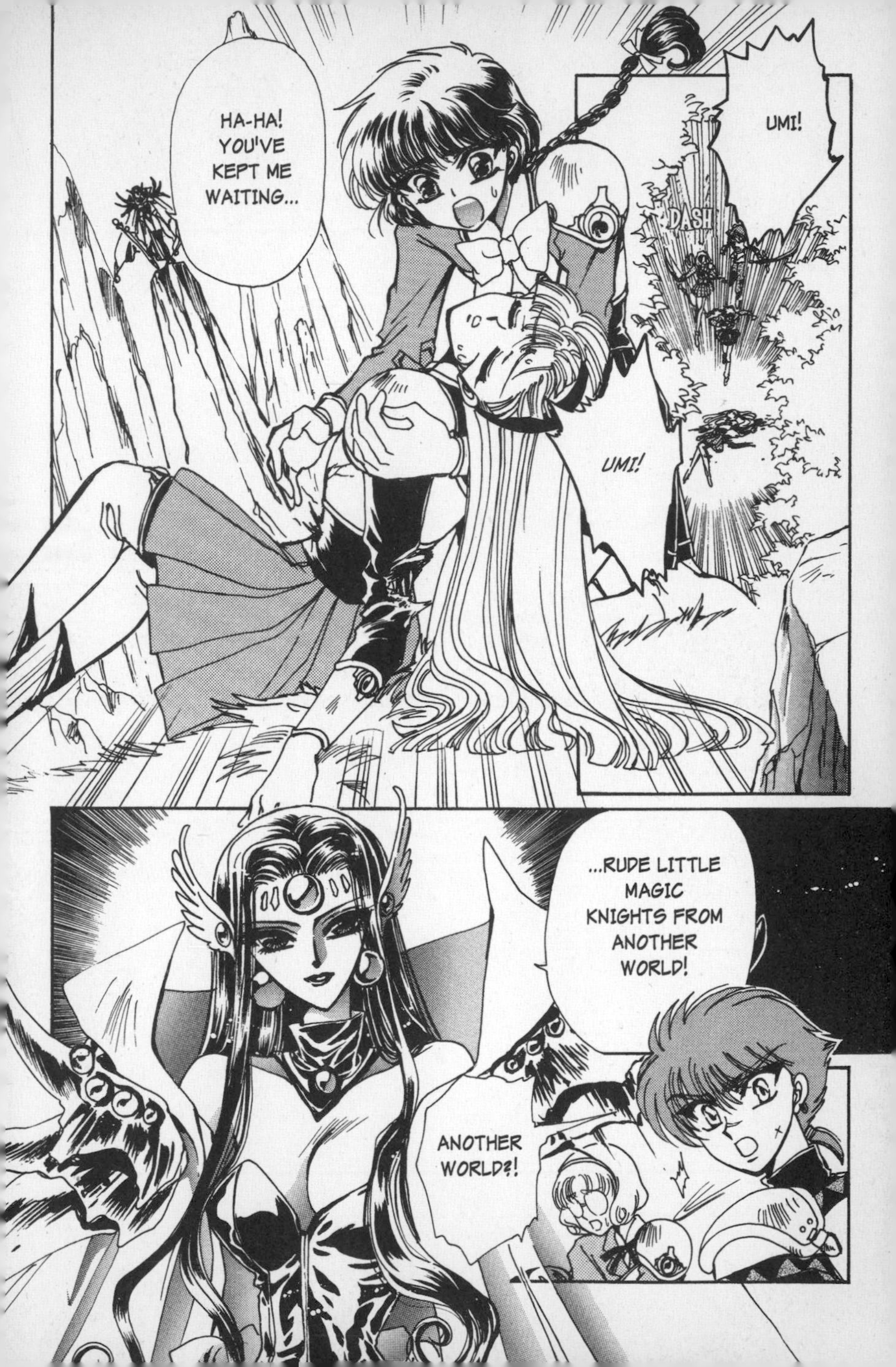
UMI!
DASH
UMI!
HA-HA! YOU'VE KEPT ME WAITING...
...RUDE LITTLE MAGIC KNIGHTS FROM ANOTHER WORLD!
ANOTHER WORLD?!

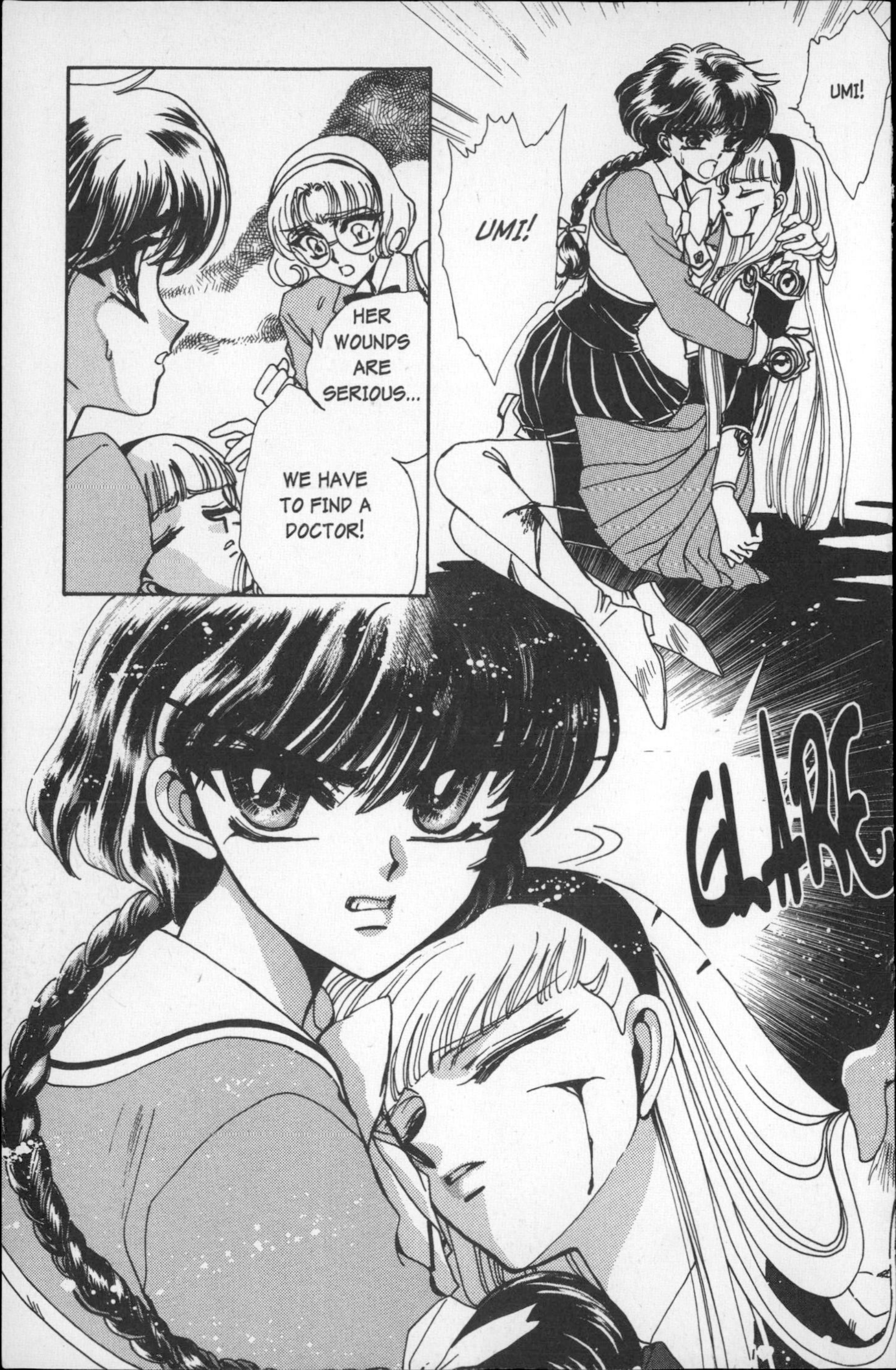
UMI!
UMI!
HER WOUNDS ARE SERIOUS...
WE HAVE TO FIND A DOCTOR!
GLARE

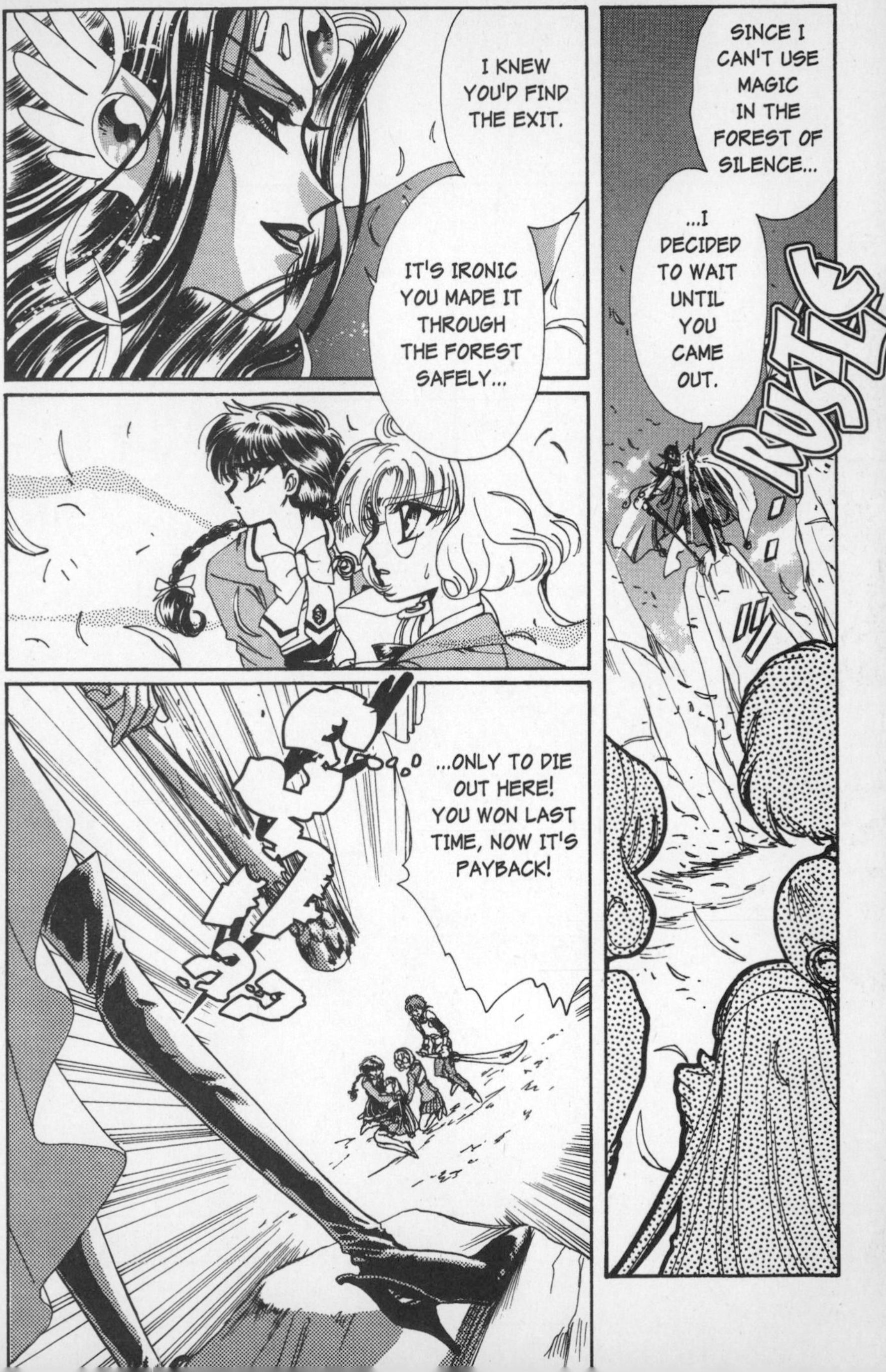
SINCE I CAN'T USE MAGIC IN THE FOREST OF SILENCE...
...I DECIDED TO WAIT UNTIL YOU CAME OUT.
RUSTLE
I KNEW YOU'D FIND THE EXIT.
IT'S IRONIC YOU MADE IT THROUGH THE FOREST SAFELY...
...ONLY TO DIE OUT HERE! YOU WON LAST TIME, NOW IT'S PAYBACK!

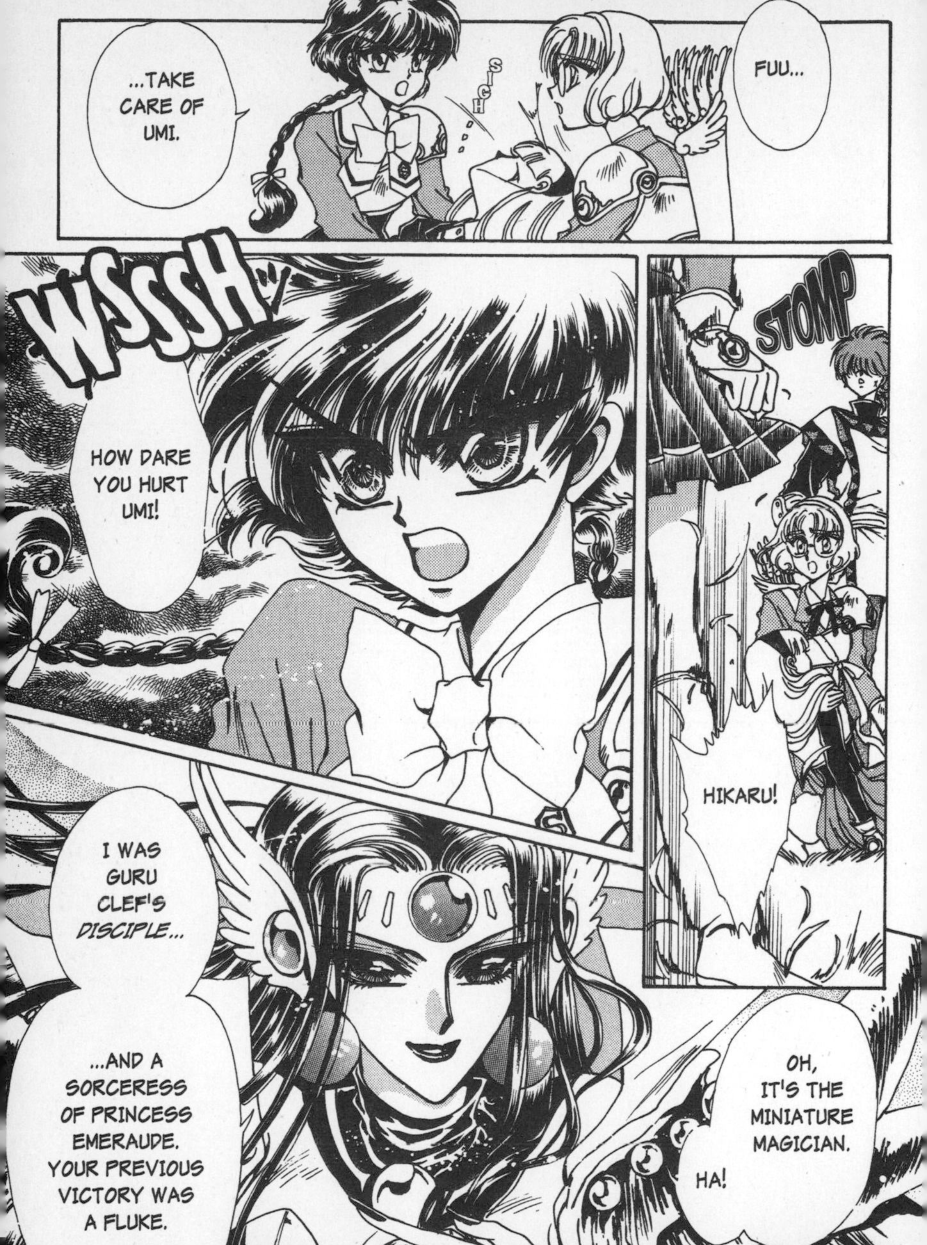
FUU...
SIGH
...TAKE CARE OF UMI.
STOMP
HIKARU!
WSSSH
HOW DARE YOU HURT UMI!
OH, IT'S THE MINIATURE MAGICIAN.
HA!
I WAS GURU CLEF'S *DISCIPLE*...
...AND A SORCERESS OF PRINCESS EMERAUDE. YOUR PREVIOUS VICTORY WAS A FLUKE.

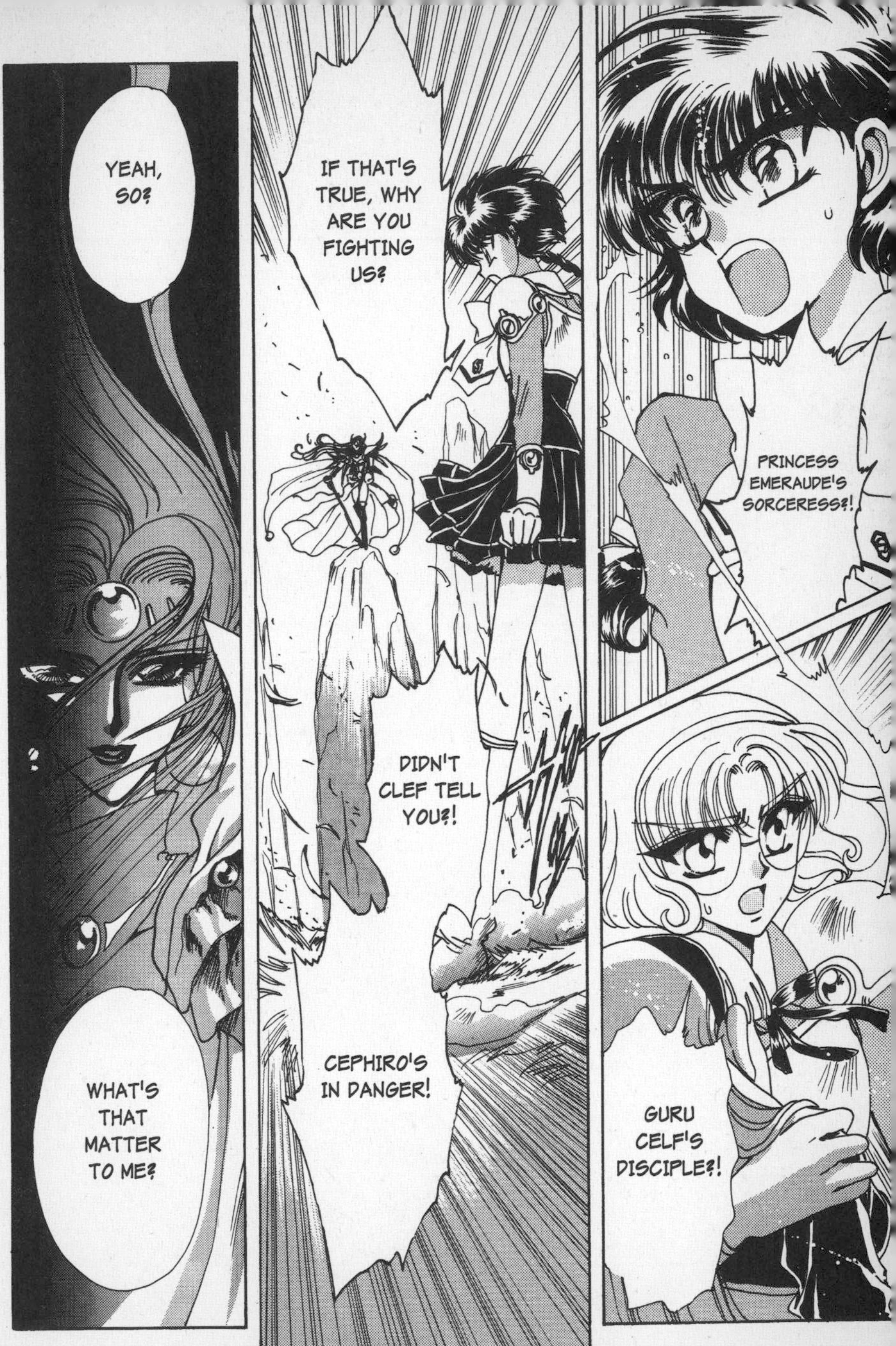
PRINCESS EMERAUDE'S SORCERESS?!
GURU CELF'S DISCIPLE?!
IF THAT'S TRUE, WHY ARE YOU FIGHTING US?
DIDN'T CLEF TELL YOU?!
CEPHIRO'S IN DANGER!
YEAH, SO?
WHAT'S THAT MATTER TO ME?

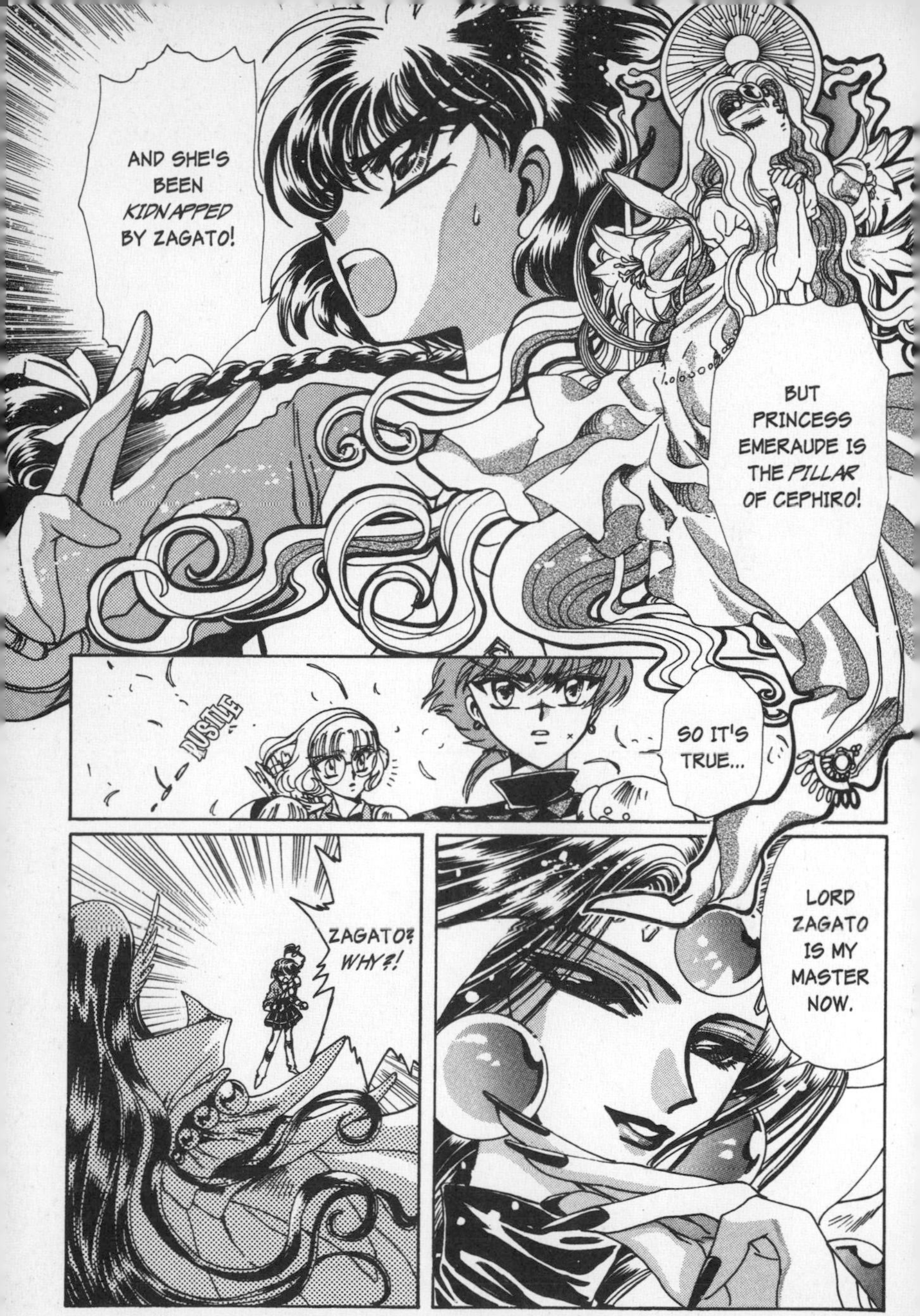
BUT PRINCESS EMERAUDE IS THE *PILLAR* OF CEPHIRO!
AND SHE'S BEEN *KIDNAPPED* BY ZAGATO!
SO IT'S TRUE...
RUSTLE
LORD ZAGATO IS MY MASTER NOW.
ZAGATO?! *WHY?!*

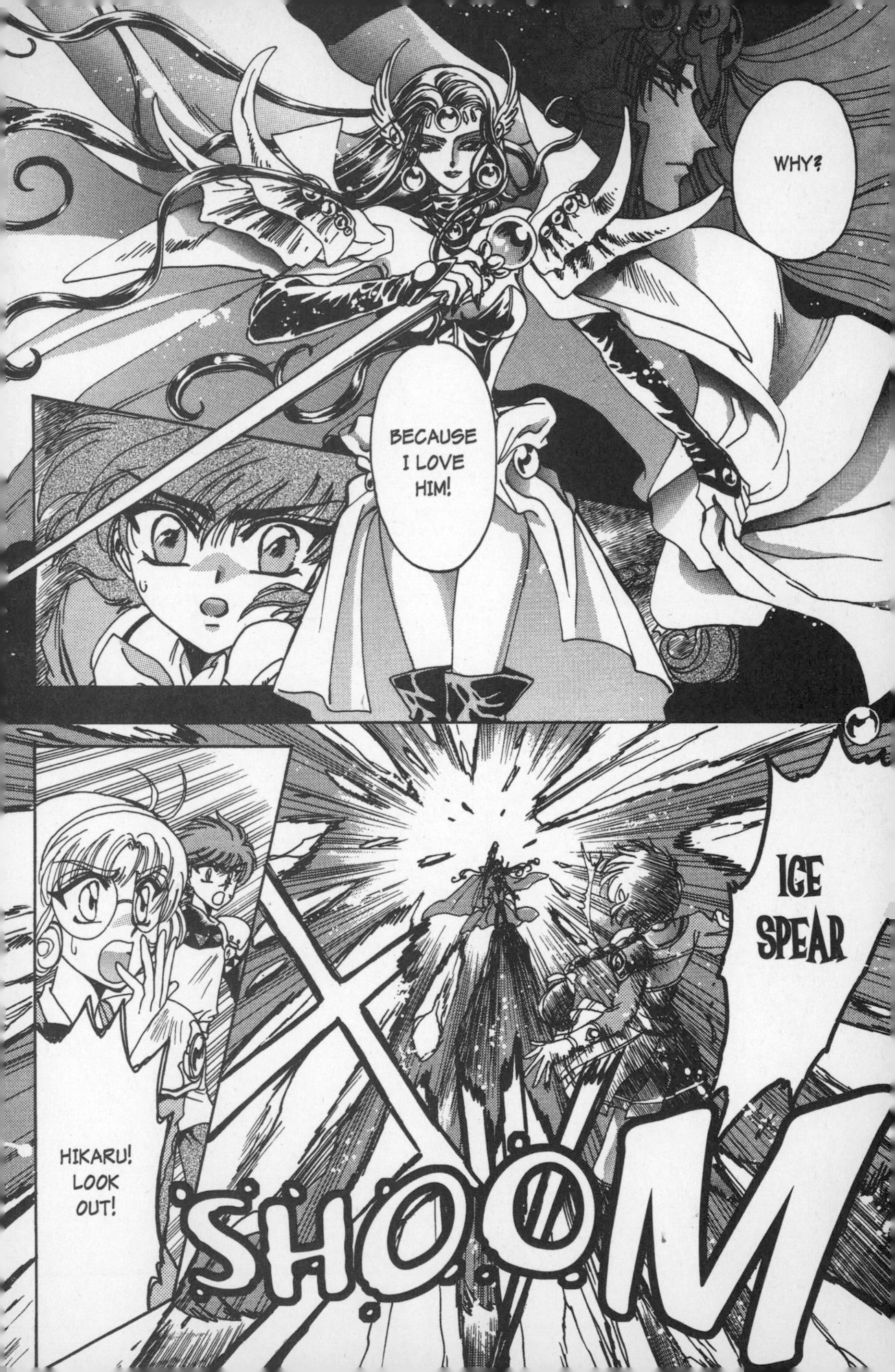
WHY?
BECAUSE I LOVE HIM!
ICE SPEAR
SHOOM
HIKARU! LOOK OUT!

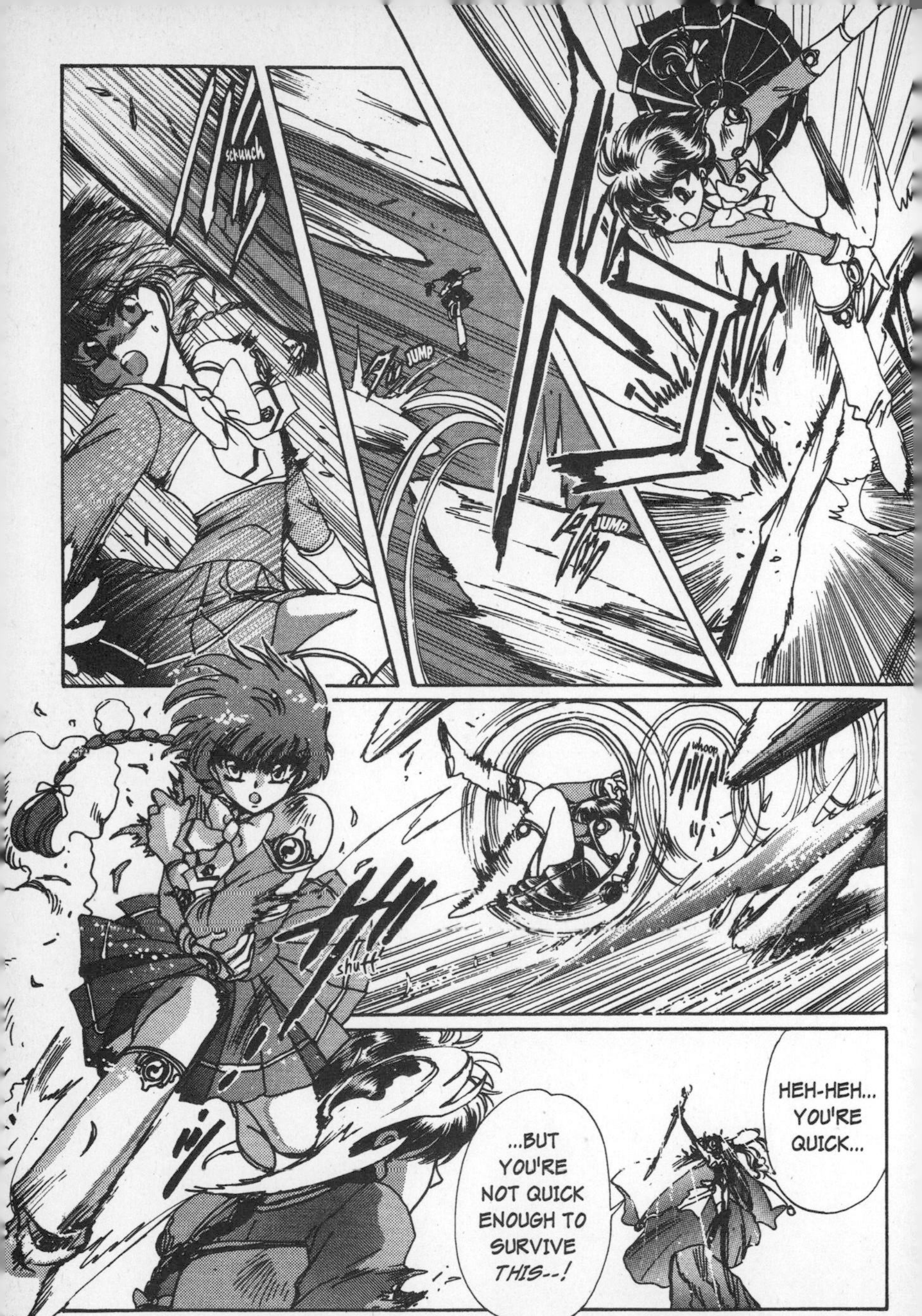
JUMP
JUMP
scrunch
whoop
shutt
HEH-HEH... YOU'RE QUICK...
...BUT YOU'RE NOT QUICK ENOUGH TO SURVIVE THIS--!

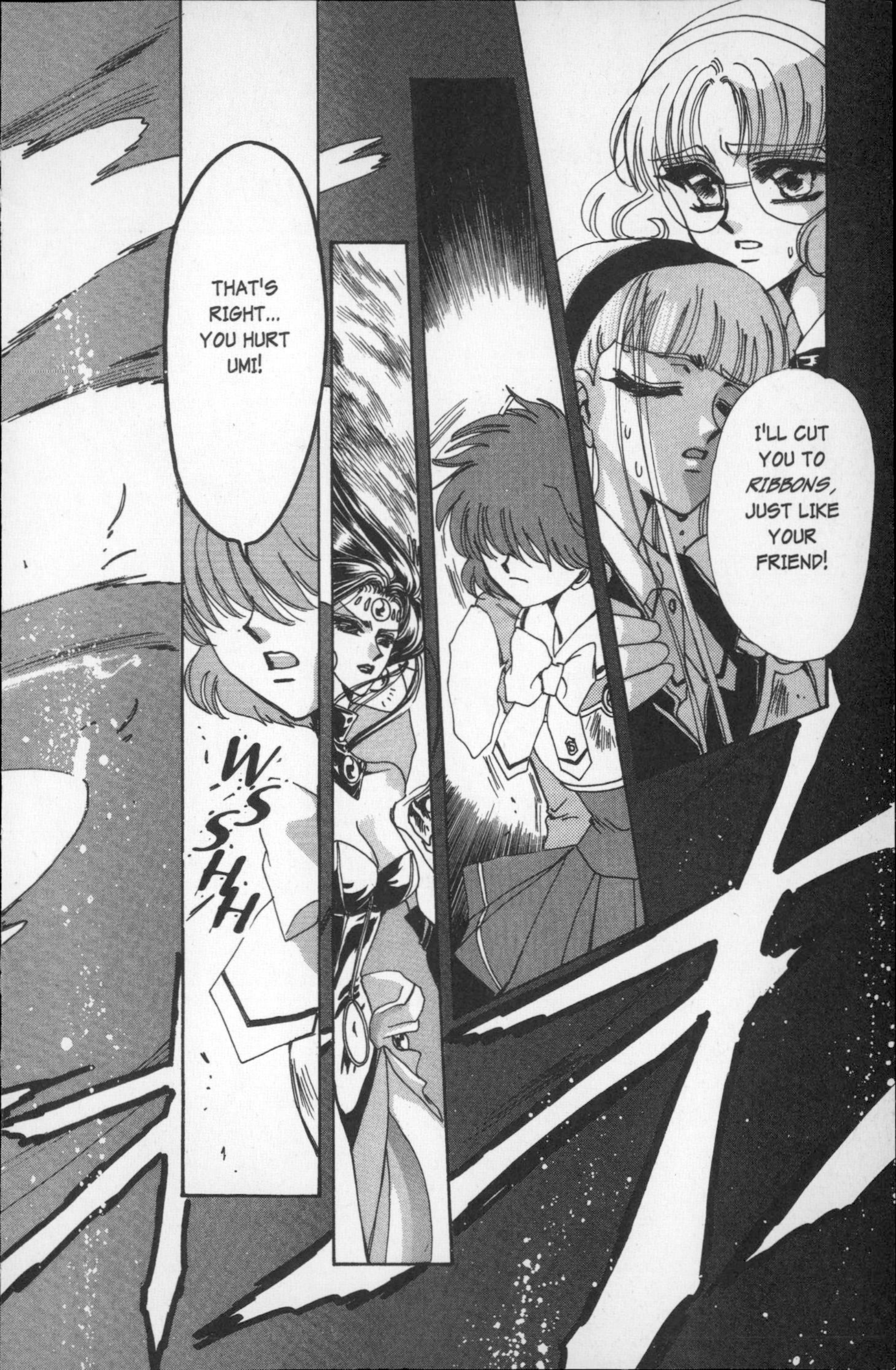
I'LL CUT YOU TO RIBBONS, JUST LIKE YOUR FRIEND!
THAT'S RIGHT... YOU HURT UMI!
WSSHH

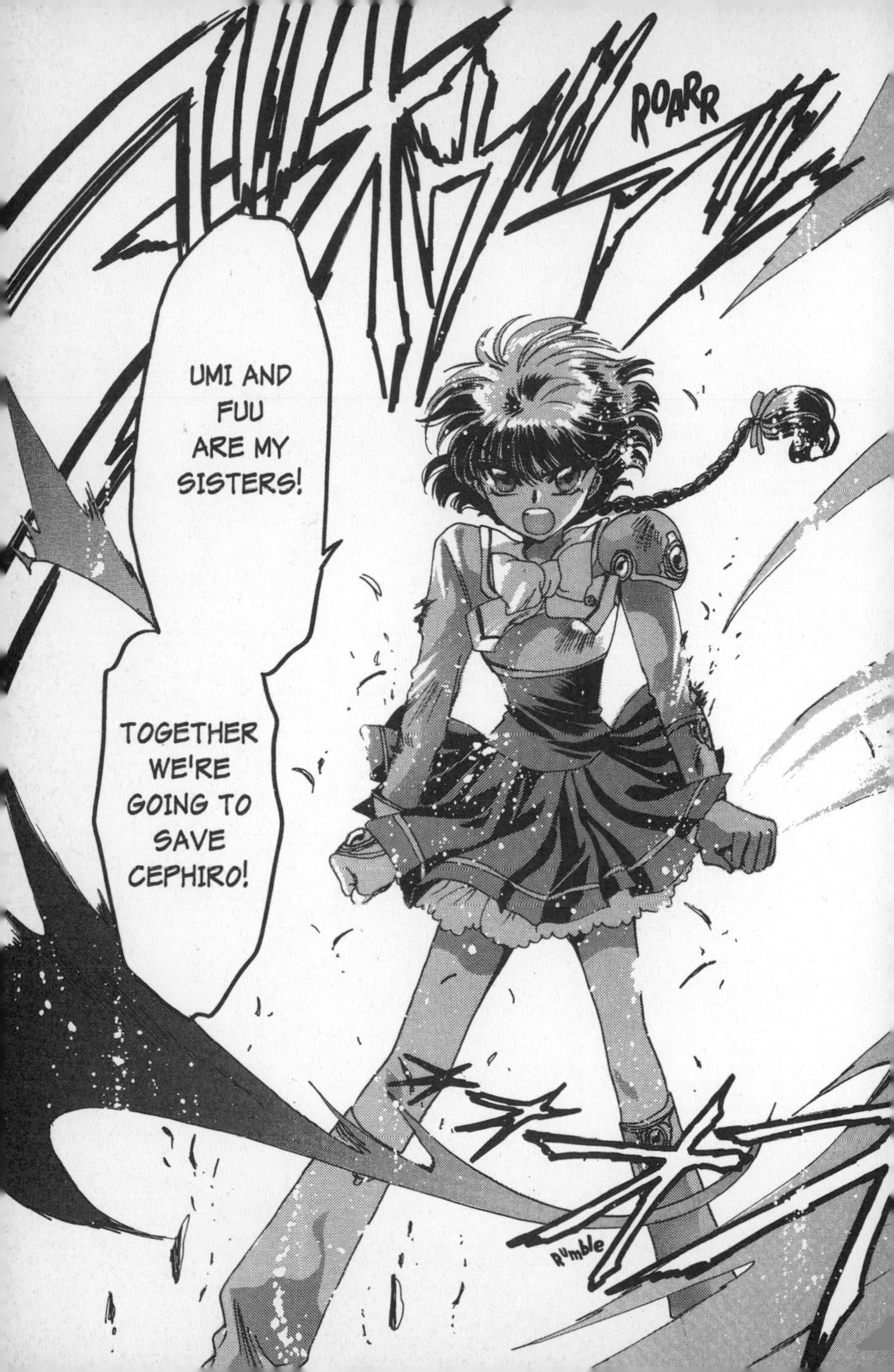
ROARR
UMI AND FUU ARE MY SISTERS!
TOGETHER WE'RE GOING TO SAVE CEPHIRO!
RUMBLE

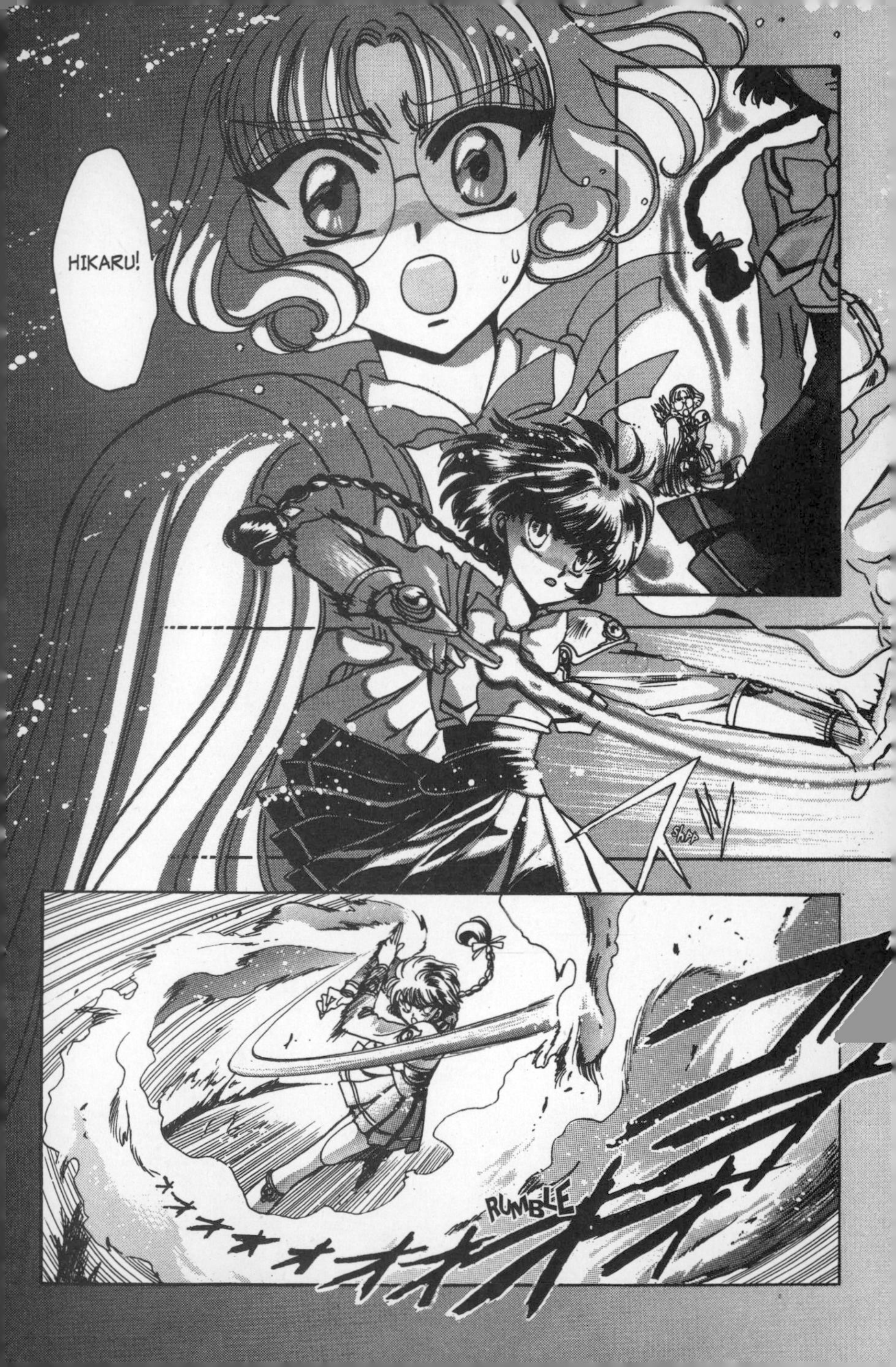
HIKARU!
SHPP
RUMBLE

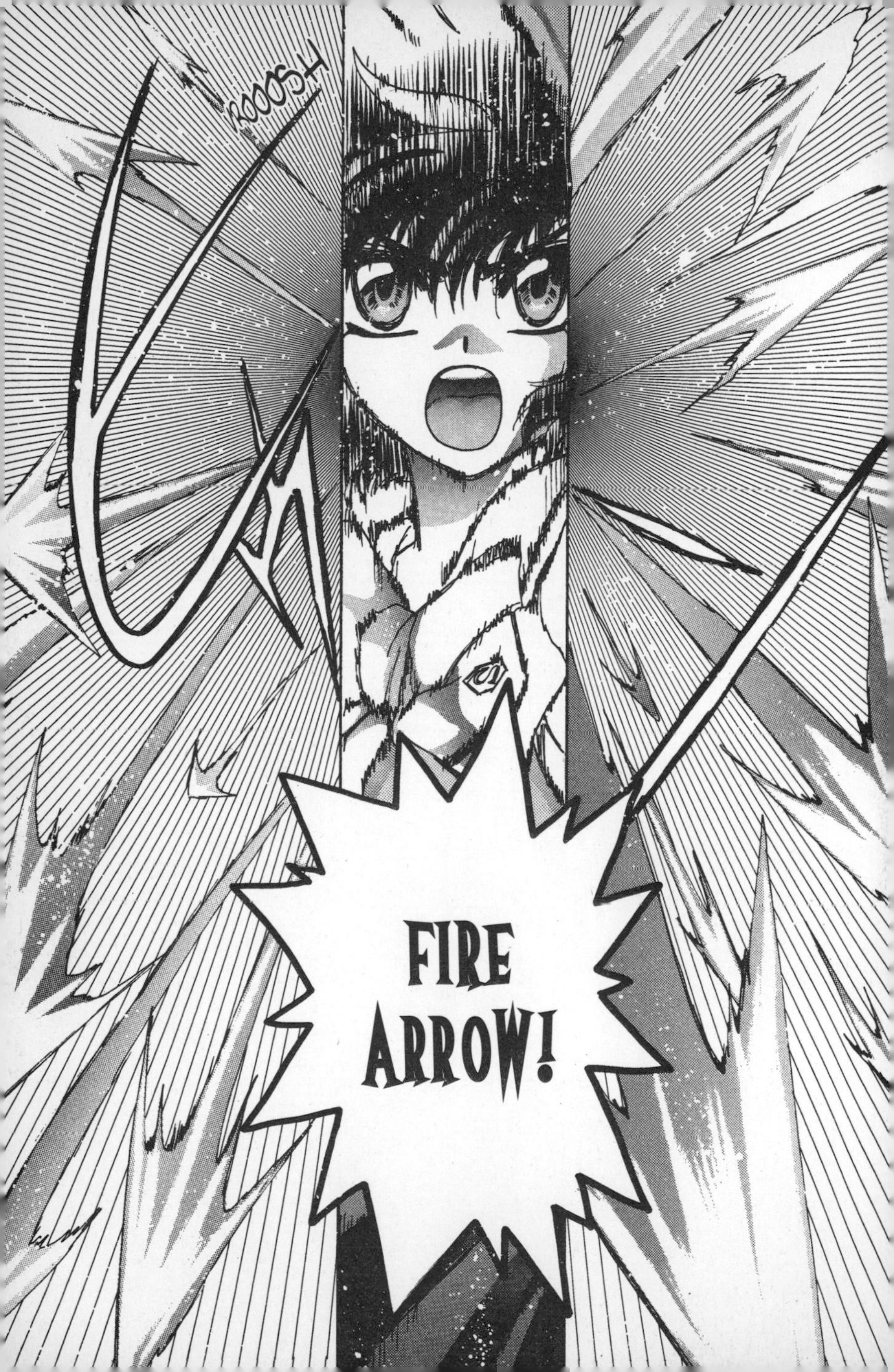
ROOOSH
FIRE ARROW!

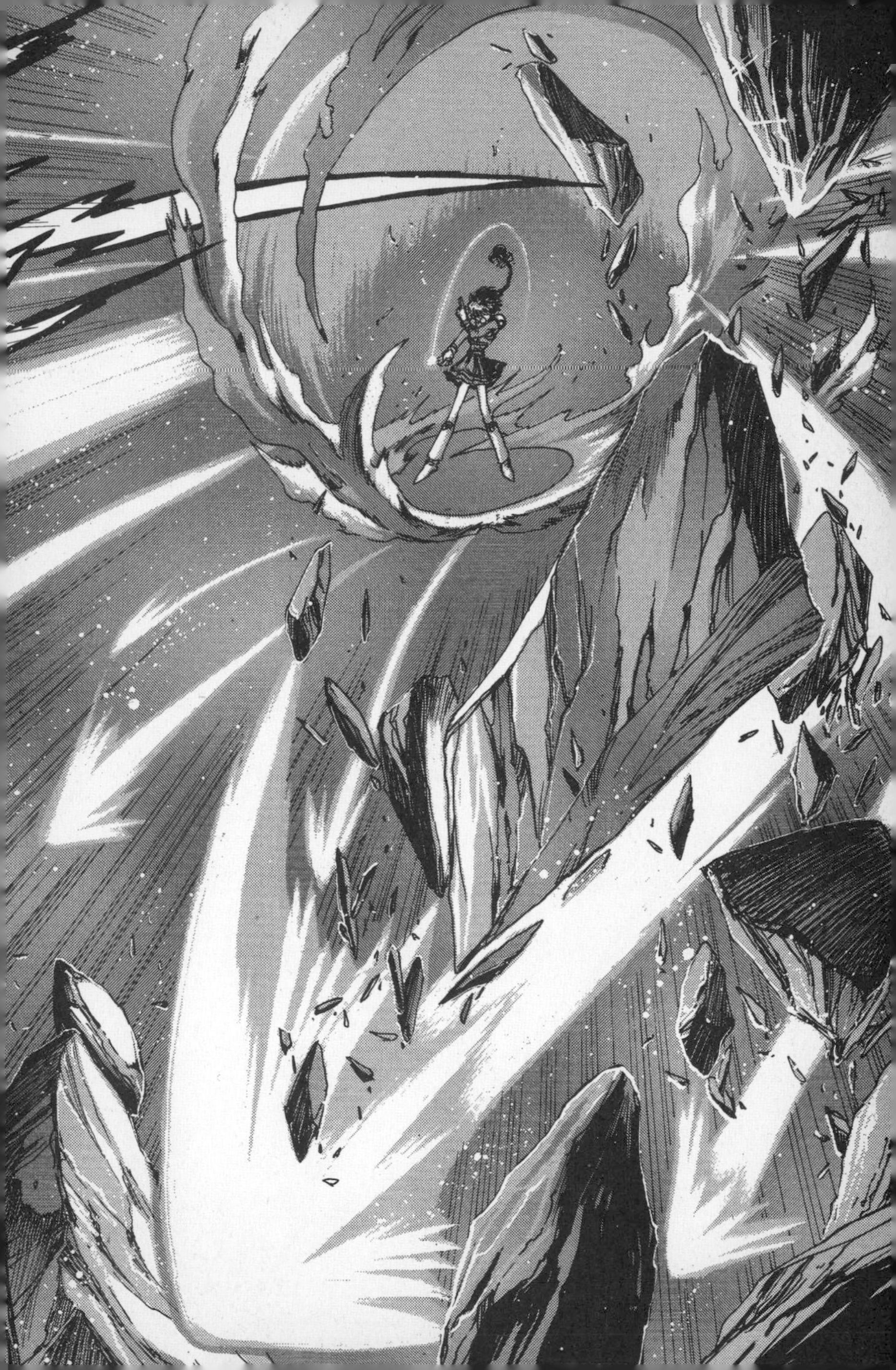

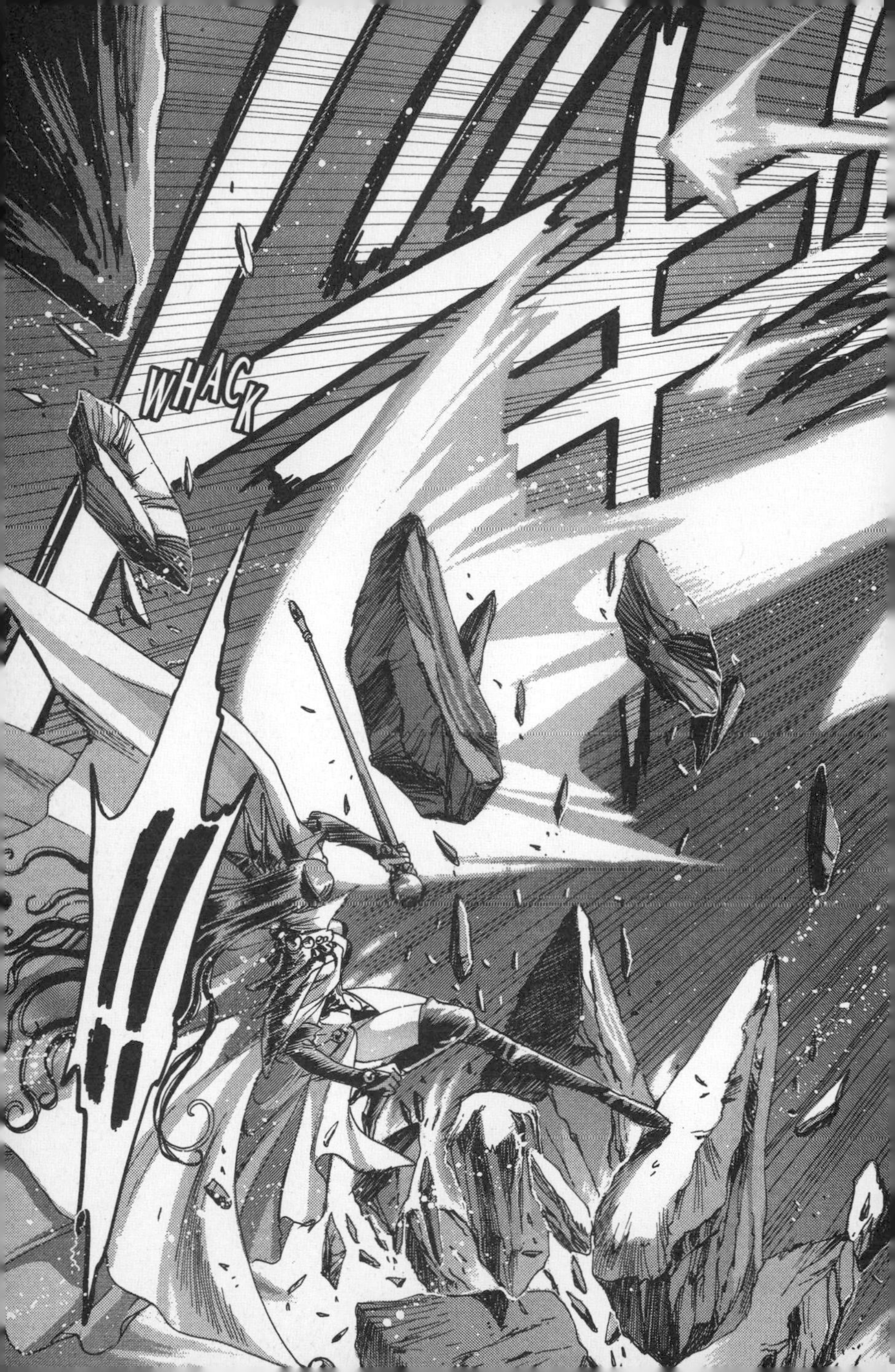
WHACK

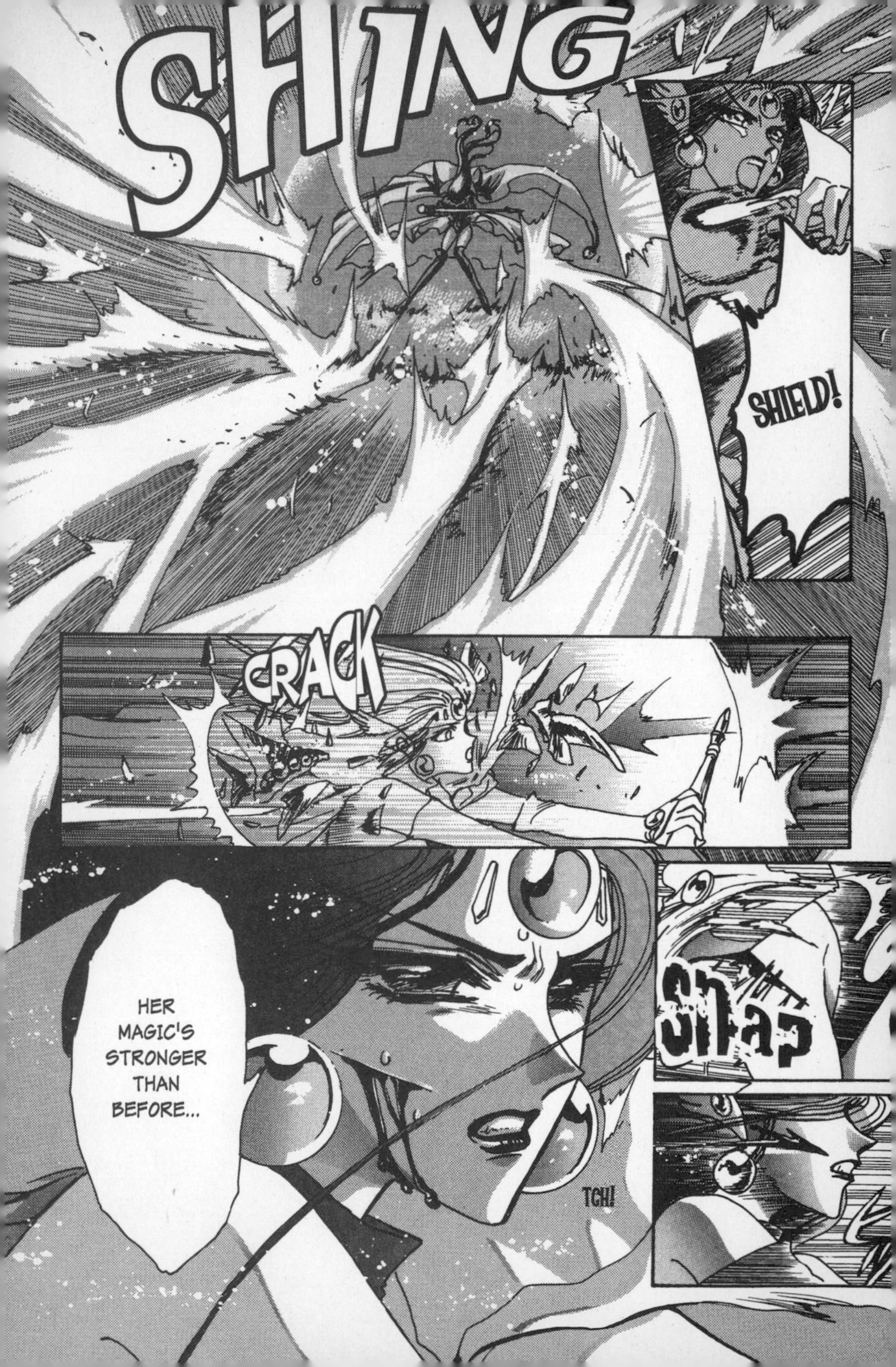
SHIELD!
SHING
CRACK
SNAP
TCH!
HER MAGIC'S STRONGER THAN BEFORE...

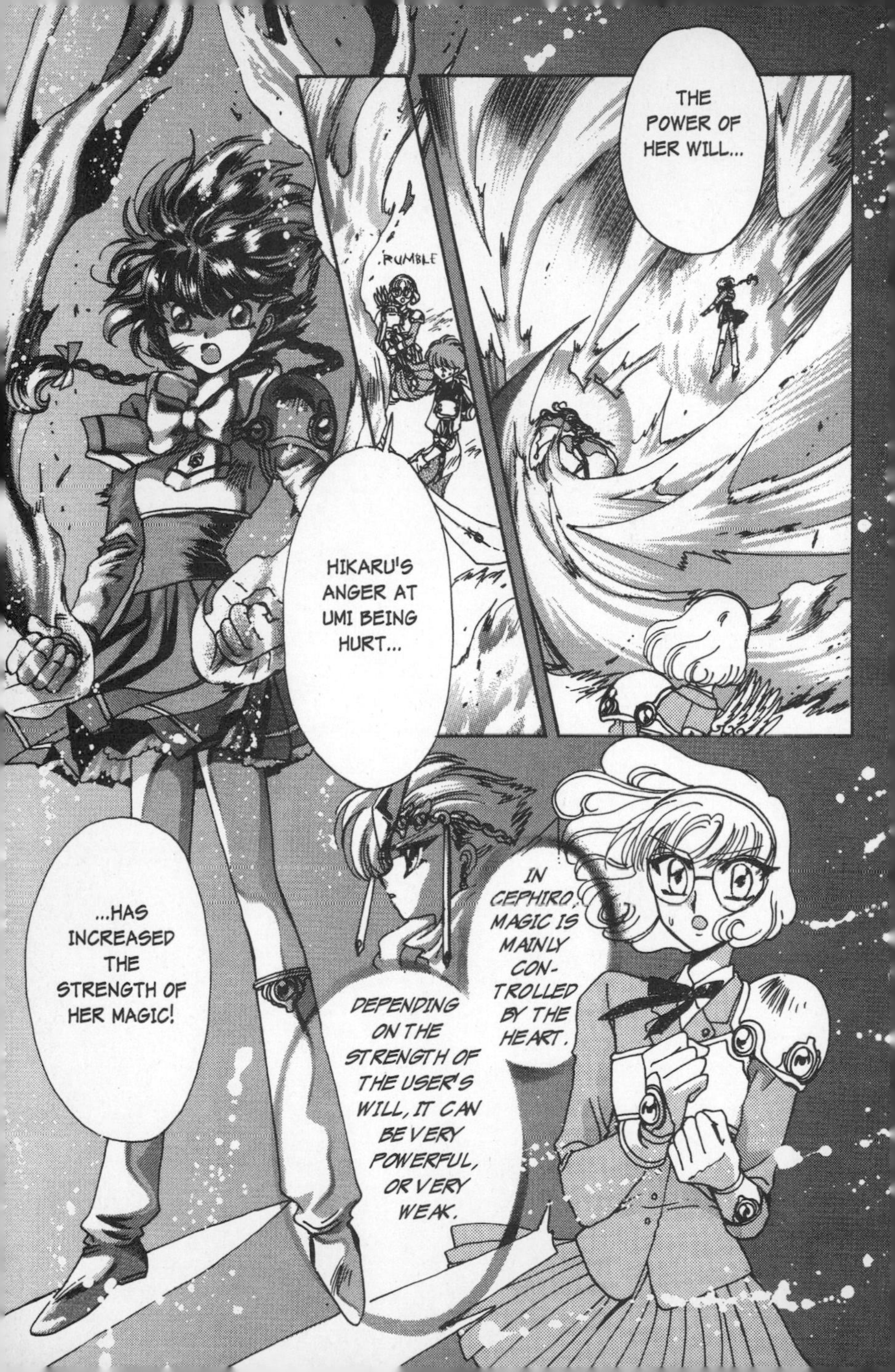
THE POWER OF HER WILL...
RUMBLE
HIKARU'S ANGER AT UMI BEING HURT...
...HAS INCREASED THE STRENGTH OF HER MAGIC!
IN CEPHIRO, MAGIC IS MAINLY CON-TROLLED BY THE HEART.
DEPENDING ON THE STRENGTH OF THE USER'S WILL, IT CAN BE VERY POWERFUL, OR VERY WEAK.

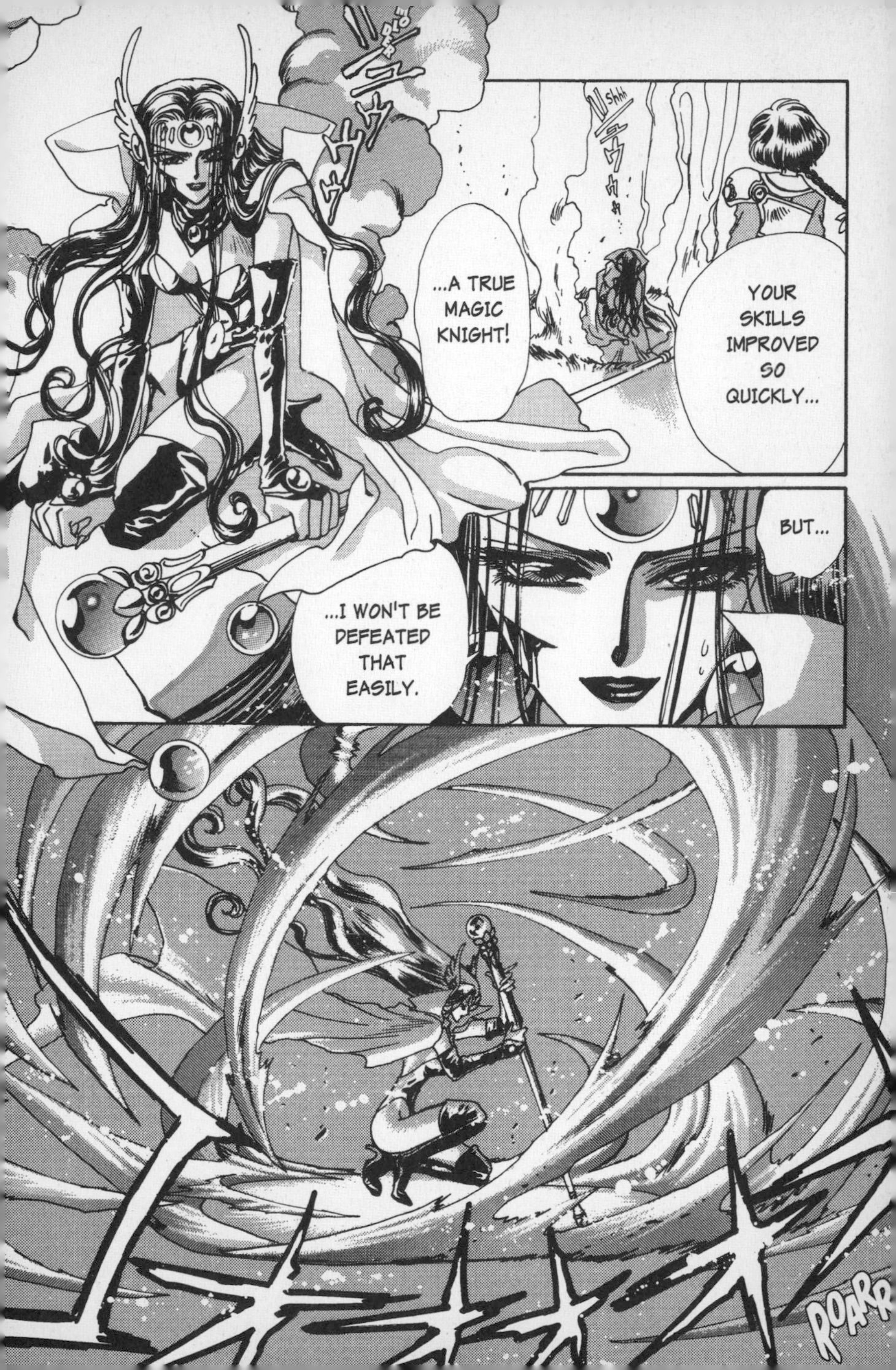
Shhh
YOUR SKILLS IMPROVED SO QUICKLY...
...A TRUE MAGIC KNIGHT!
MOLDER
BUT...
...I WON'T BE DEFEATED THAT EASILY.
ROARR

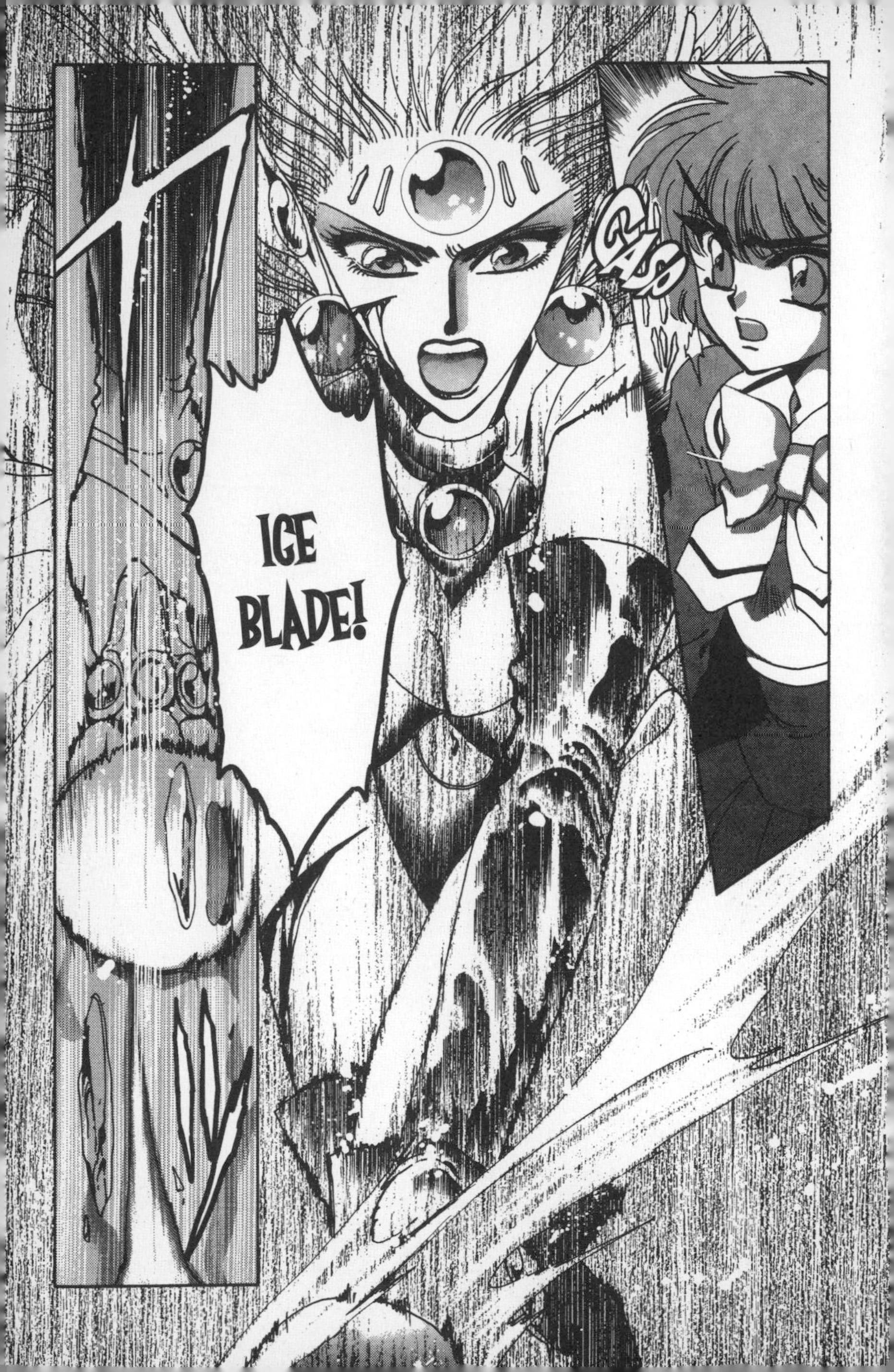
GASP
ICE BLADE!

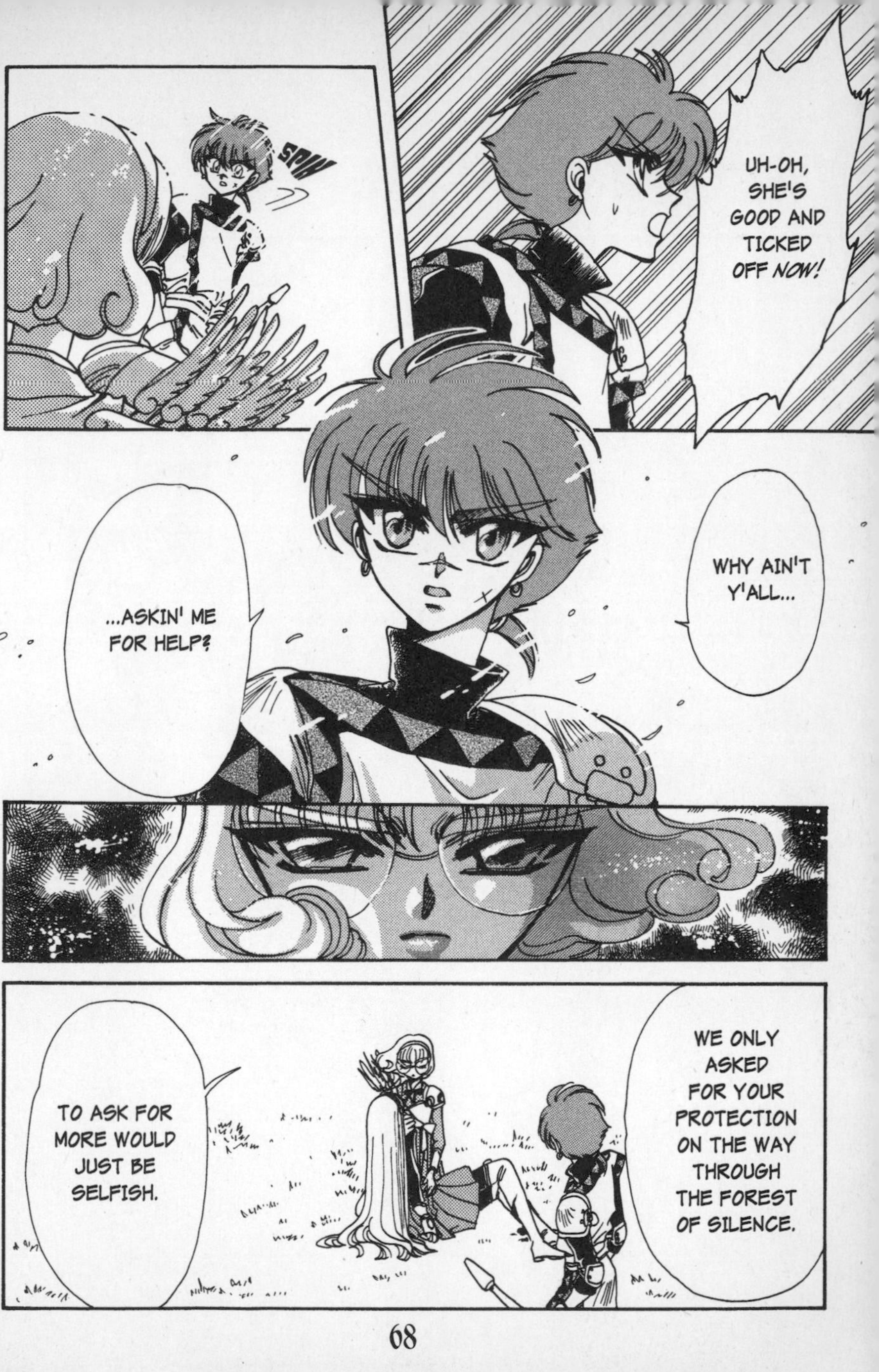
UH-OH, SHE'S GOOD AND TICKED OFF *NOW!*
SPIN
WHY AIN'T Y'ALL...
...ASKIN' ME FOR HELP?
WE ONLY ASKED FOR YOUR PROTECTION ON THE WAY THROUGH THE FOREST OF SILENCE.
TO ASK FOR MORE WOULD JUST BE SELFISH.

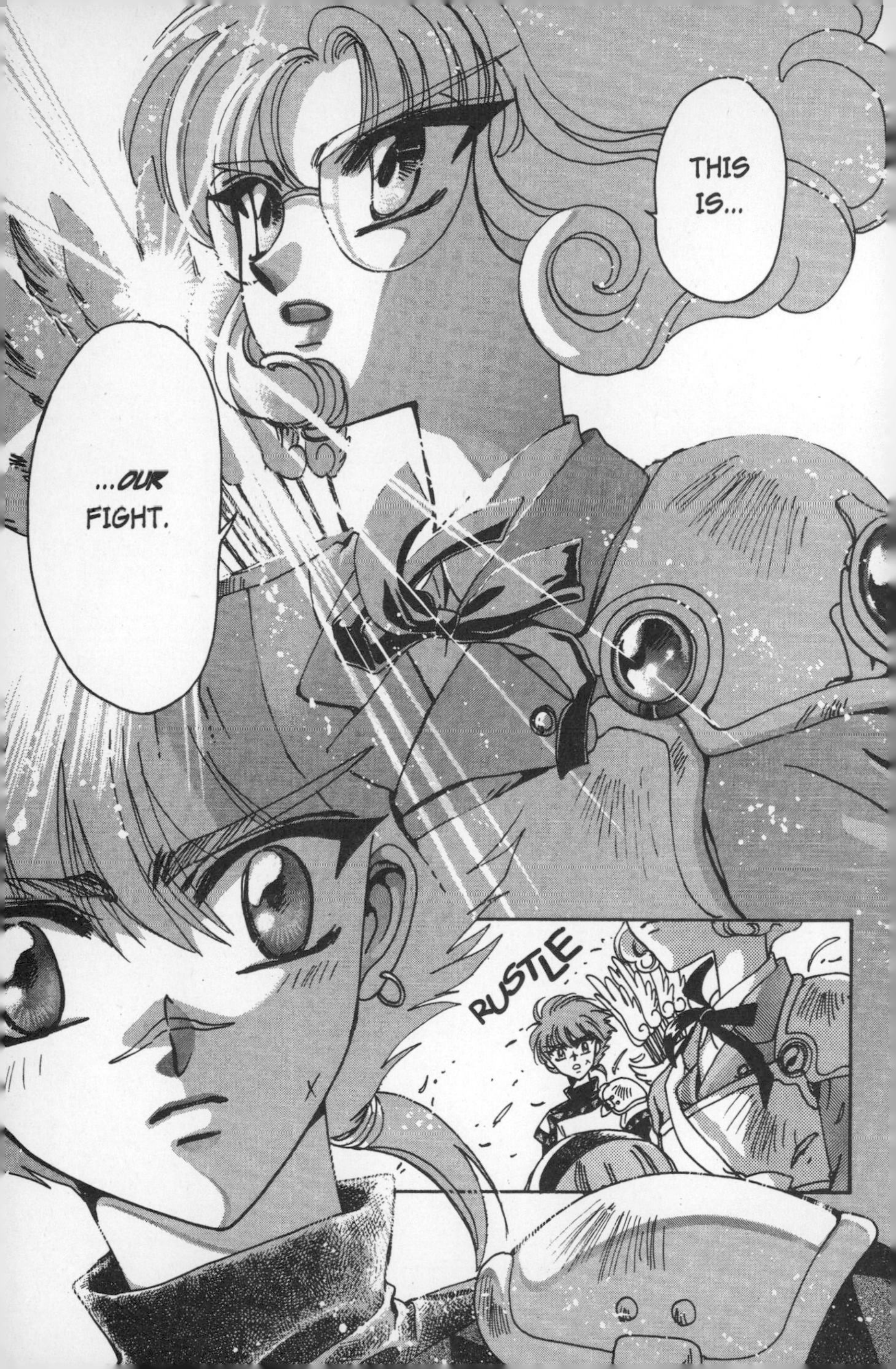
THIS IS...
...OUR FIGHT.
RUSTLE

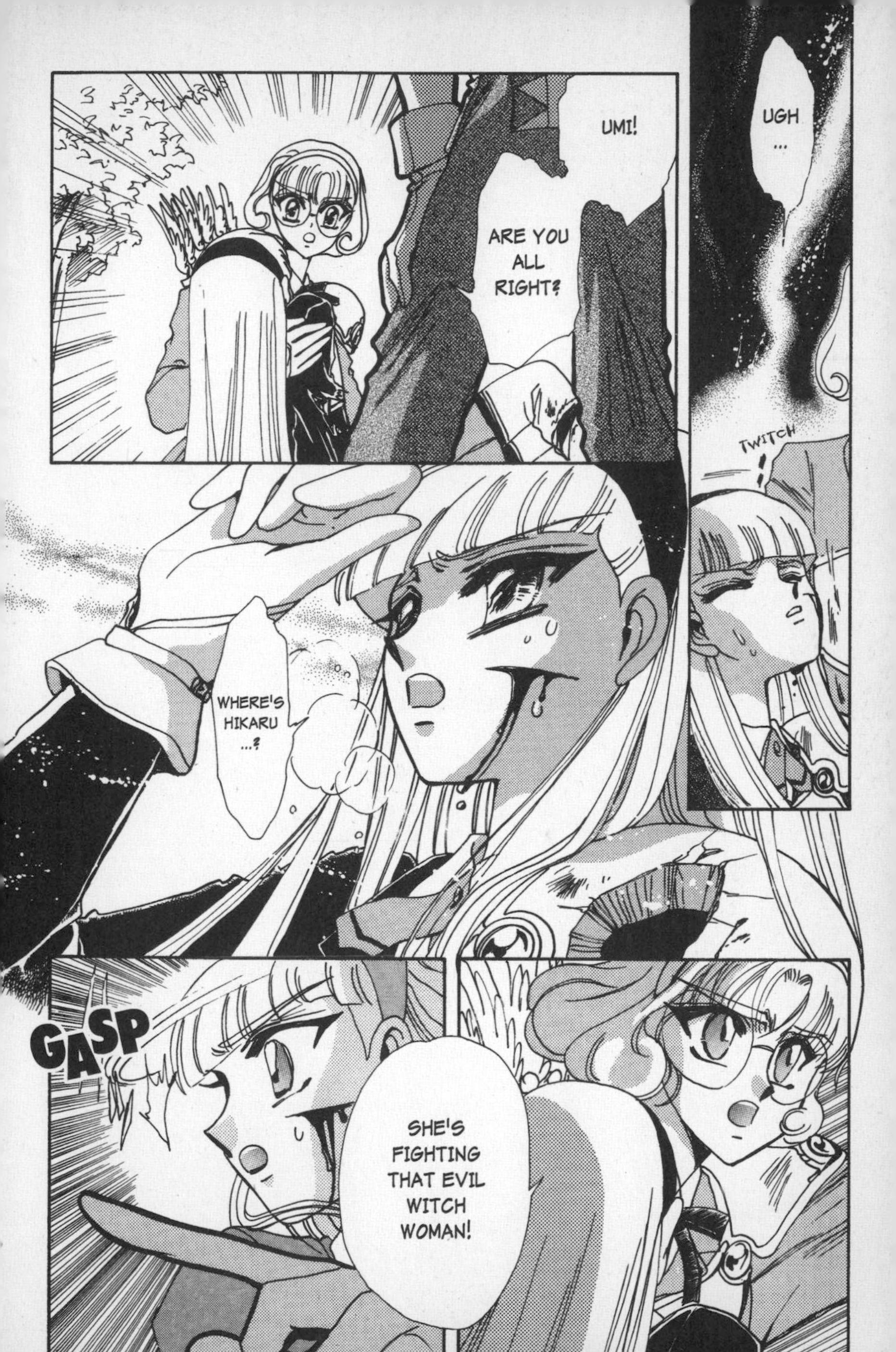
UGH ...
UMI!
ARE YOU ALL RIGHT?
TWITCH
WHERE'S HIKARU ...?
SHE'S FIGHTING THAT EVIL WITCH WOMAN!
GASP

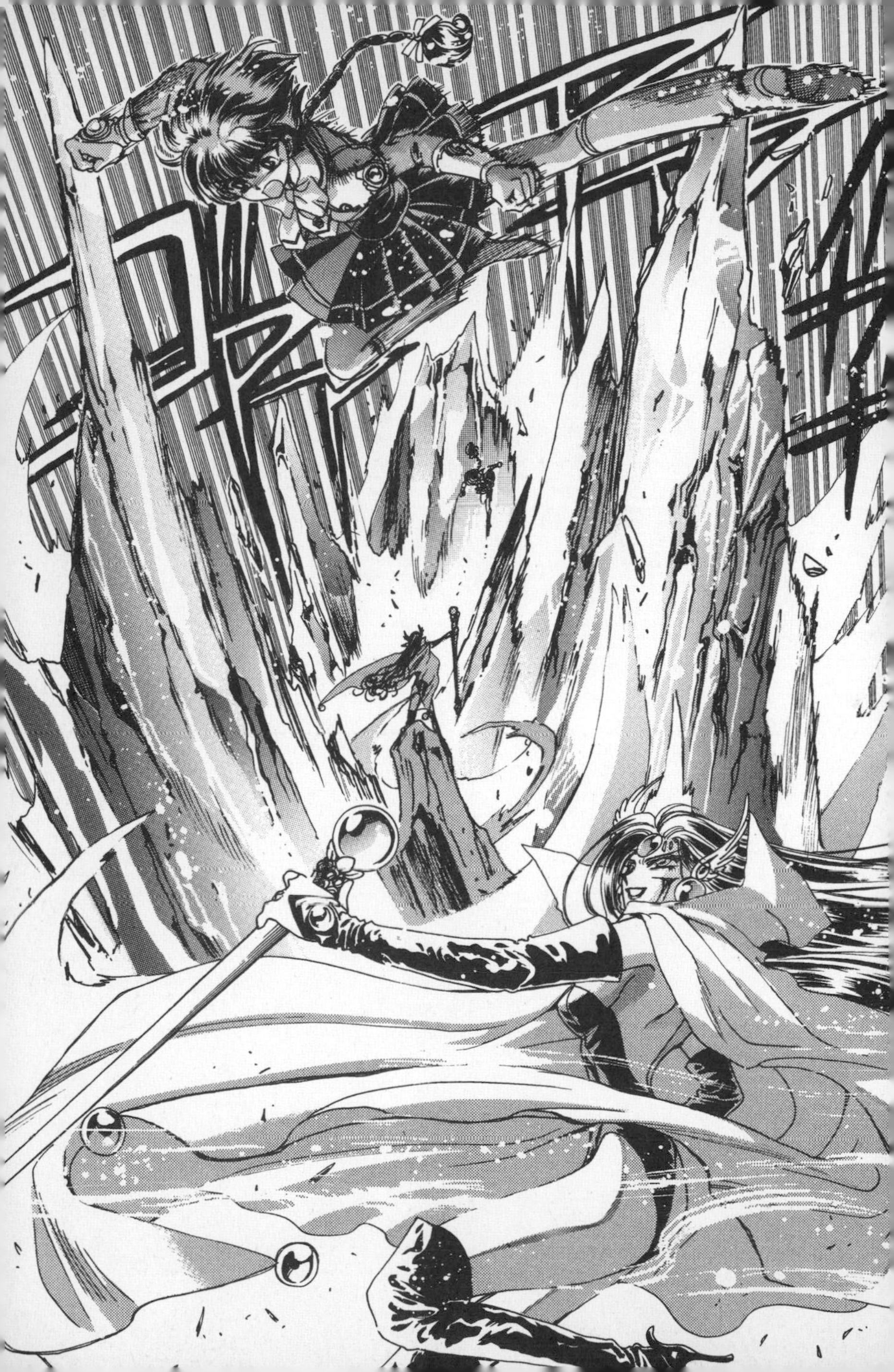

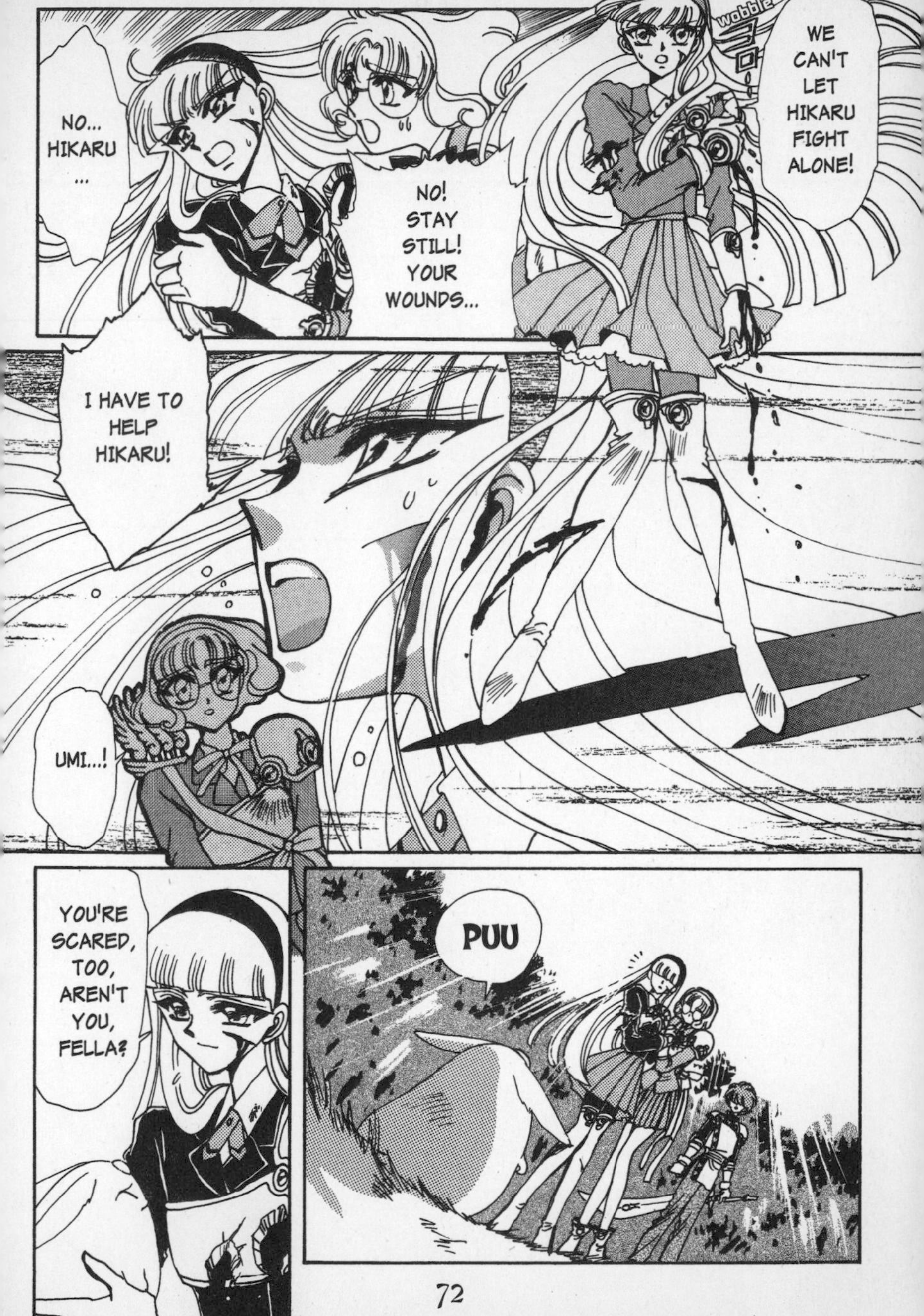
NO... HIKARU ...
NO! STAY STILL! YOUR WOUNDS...
wobble
WE CAN'T LET HIKARU FIGHT ALONE!
I HAVE TO HELP HIKARU!
UMI...!
PUU
YOU'RE SCARED, TOO, AREN'T YOU, FELLA?

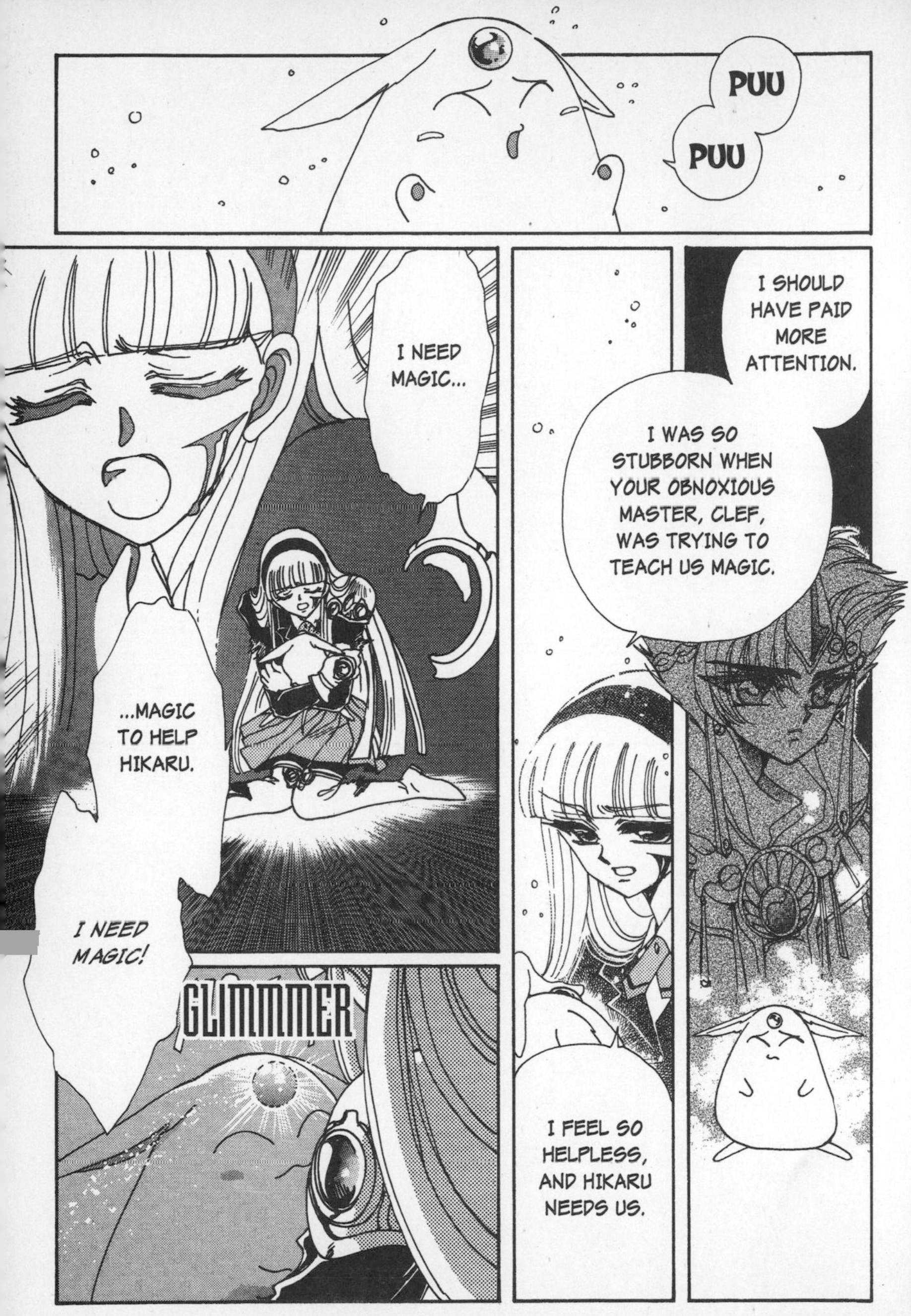
PUU
PUU
I SHOULD HAVE PAID MORE ATTENTION.
I WAS SO STUBBORN WHEN YOUR OBNOXIOUS MASTER, CLEF, WAS TRYING TO TEACH US MAGIC.
I FEEL SO HELPLESS, AND HIKARU NEEDS US.
I NEED MAGIC...
...MAGIC TO HELP HIKARU.
I NEED MAGIC!
GLIMMMER

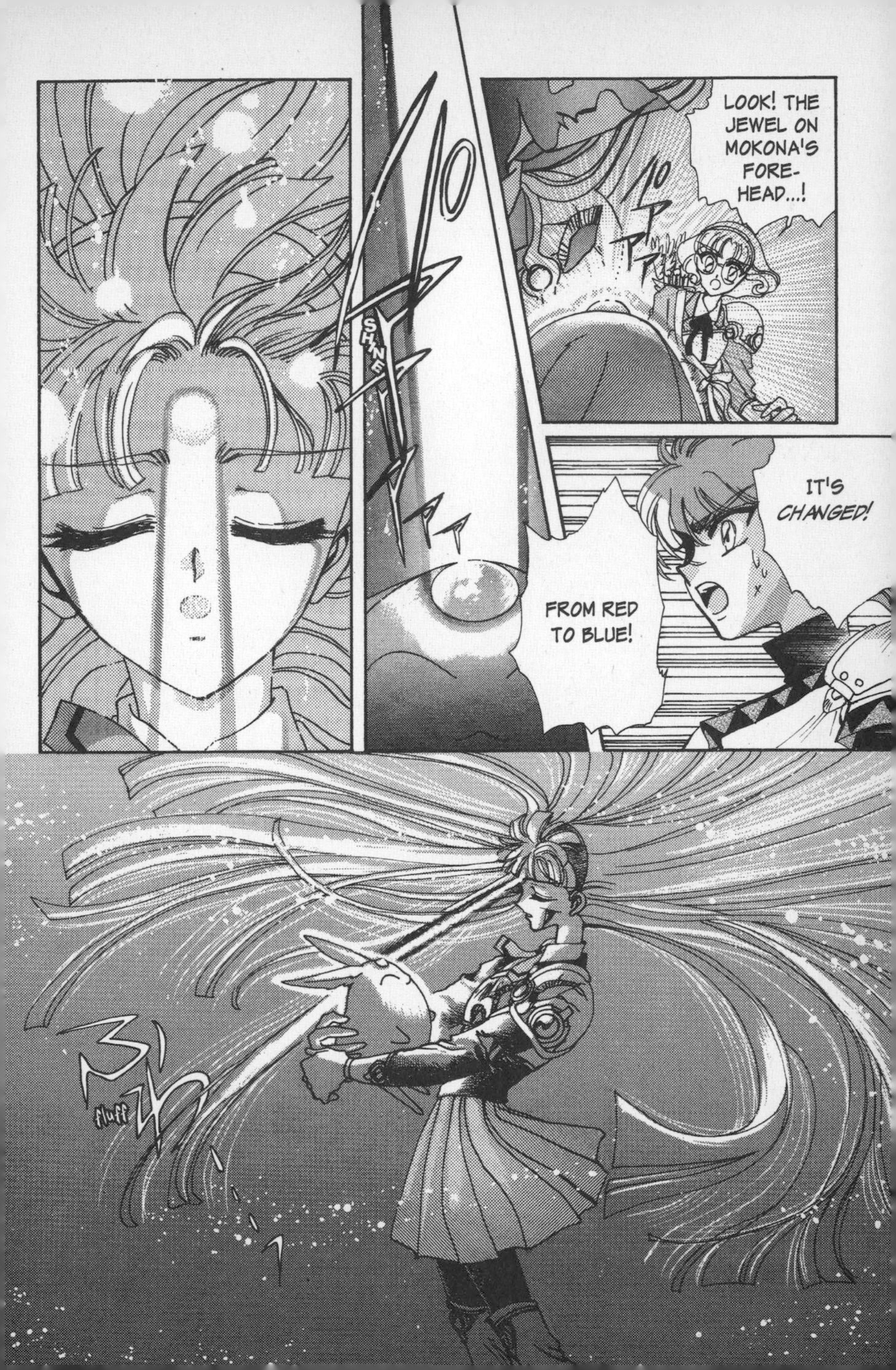
LOOK! THE JEWEL ON MOKONA'S FORE-HEAD...!
IT'S CHANGED!
FROM RED TO BLUE!
SHINE
fluff

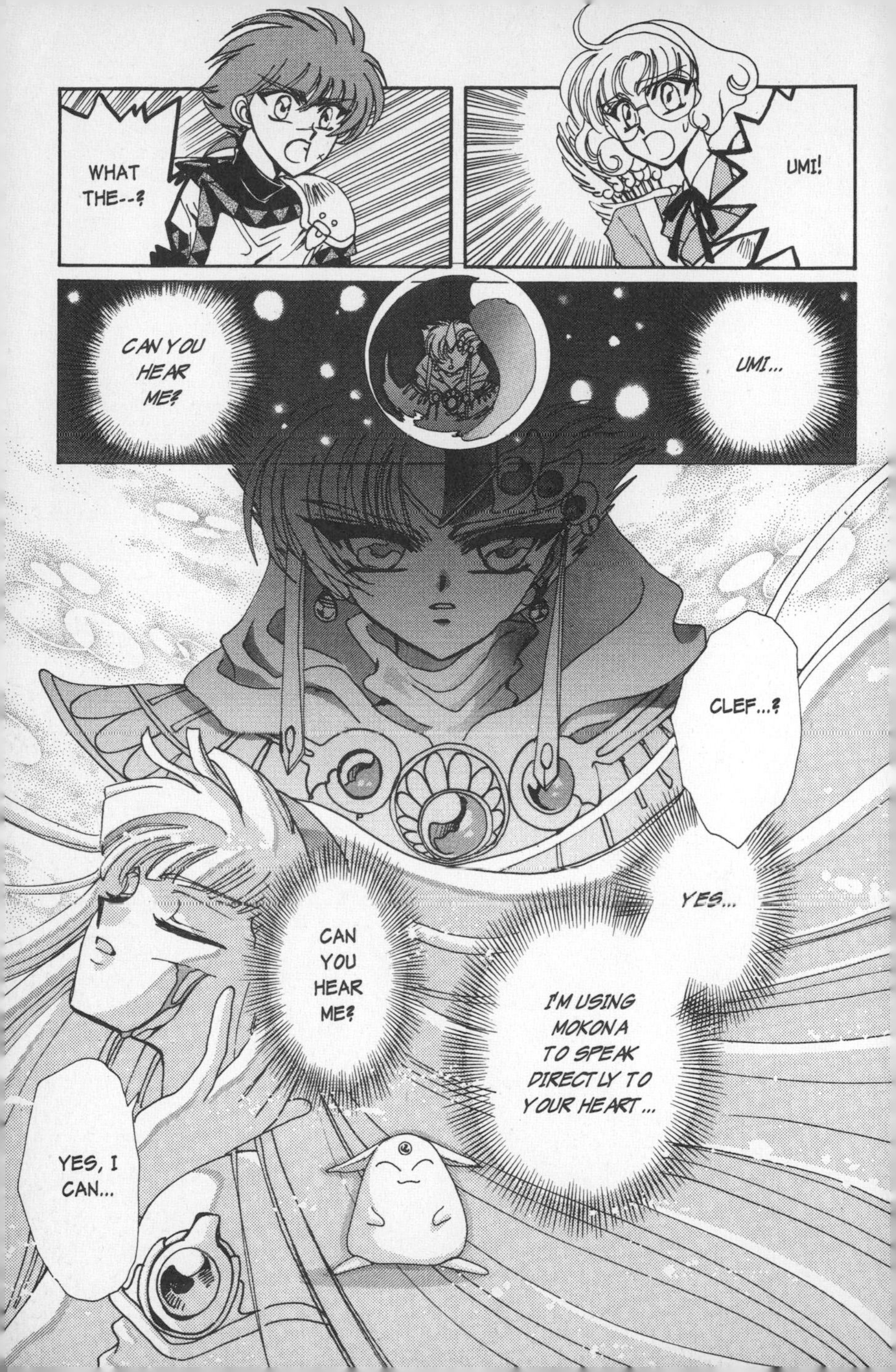
UMI!
WHAT THE--?
UMI...
CAN YOU HEAR ME?
CLEF...?
YES...
I'M USING MOKONA TO SPEAK DIRECTLY TO YOUR HEART...
CAN YOU HEAR ME?
YES, I CAN...

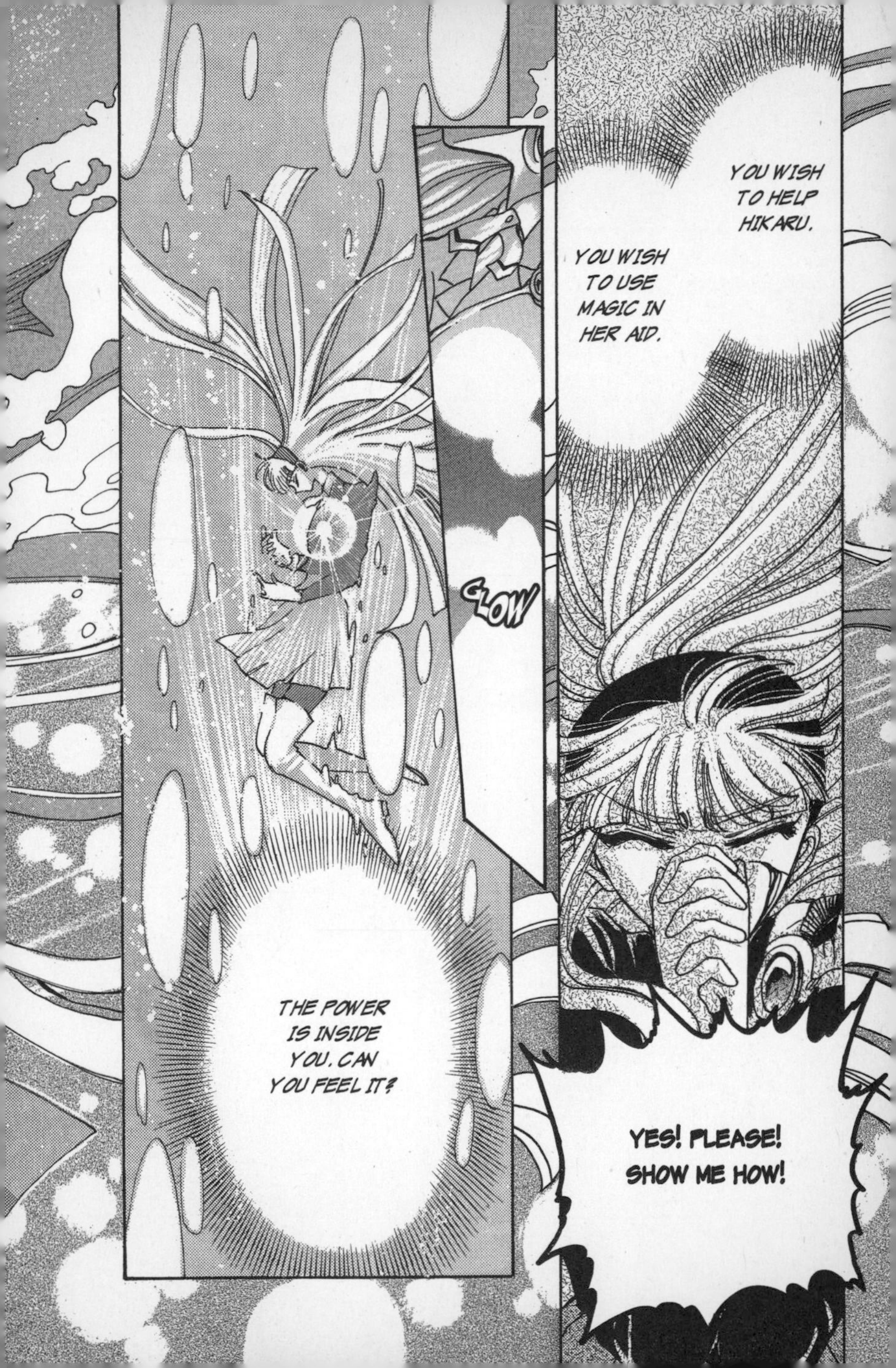
YOU WISH TO HELP HIKARU.
YOU WISH TO USE MAGIC IN HER AID.
GLOW
THE POWER IS INSIDE YOU. CAN YOU FEEL IT?
YES! PLEASE! SHOW ME HOW!

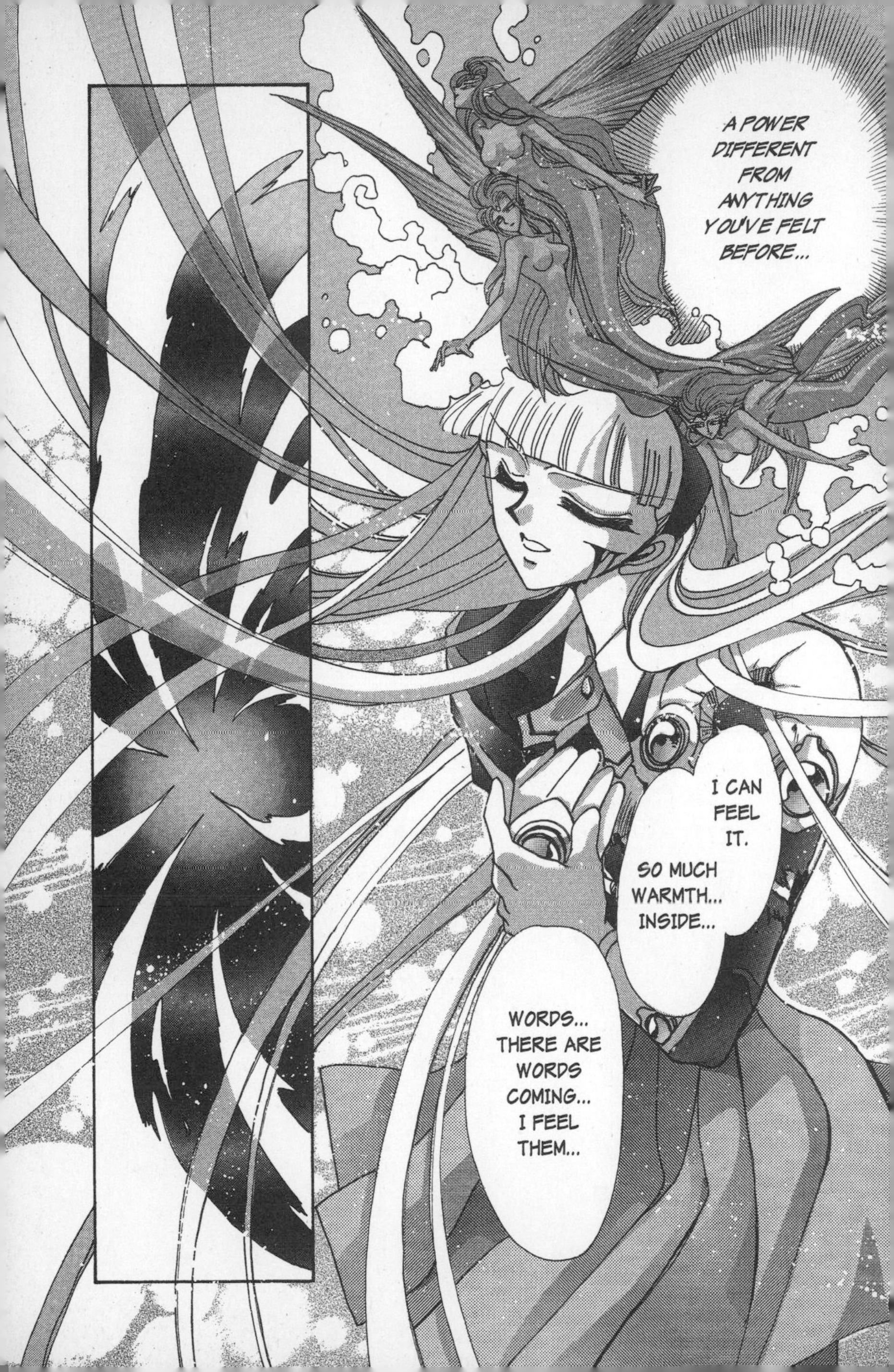
A POWER DIFFERENT FROM ANYTHING YOU'VE FELT BEFORE...
I CAN FEEL IT. SO MUCH WARMTH... INSIDE...
WORDS... THERE ARE WORDS COMING... I FEEL THEM...

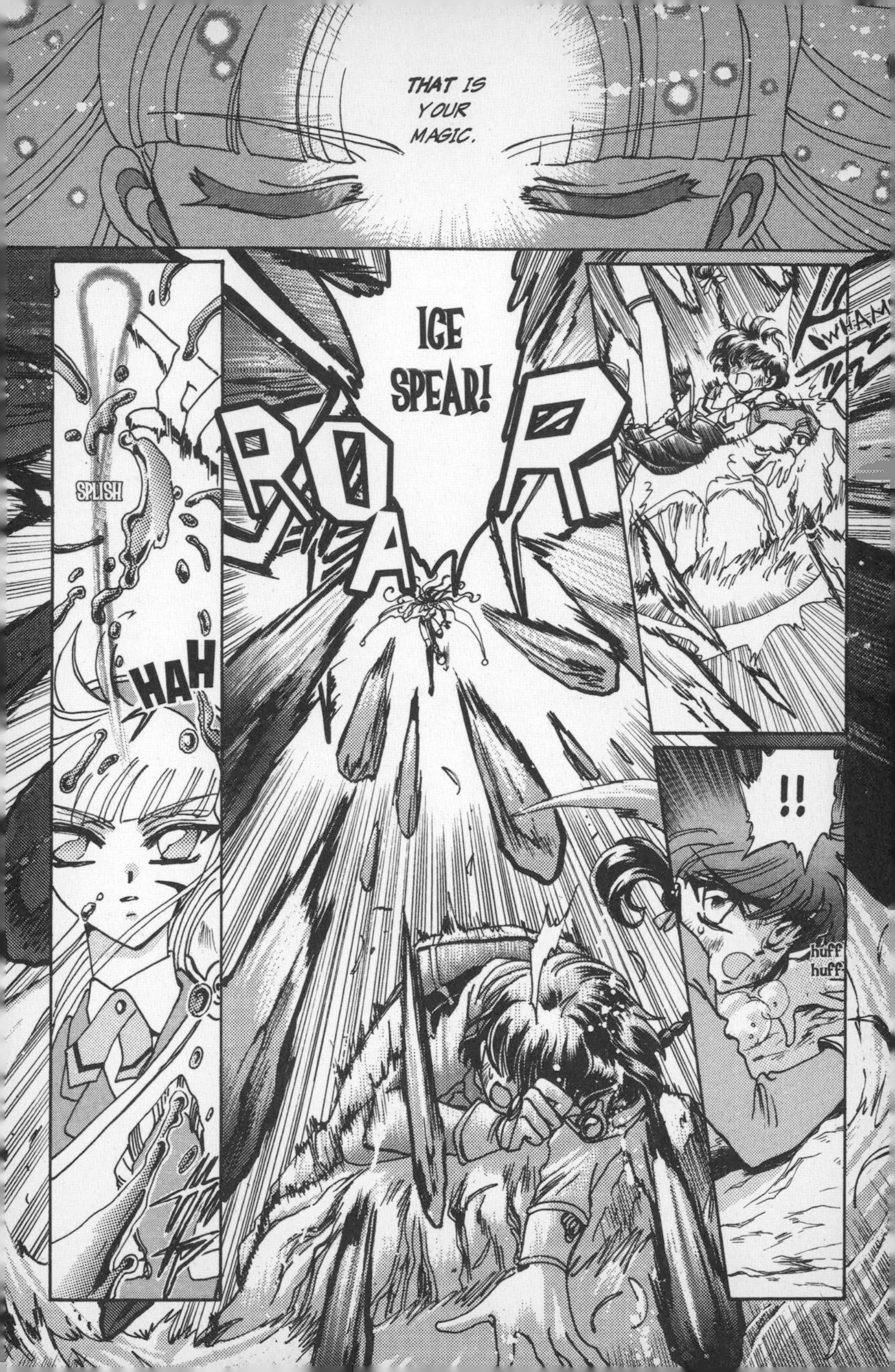
THAT IS YOUR MAGIC.
WHAM
!!
huff huff
ICE SPEAR!
ROAR
SPLISH
HAH

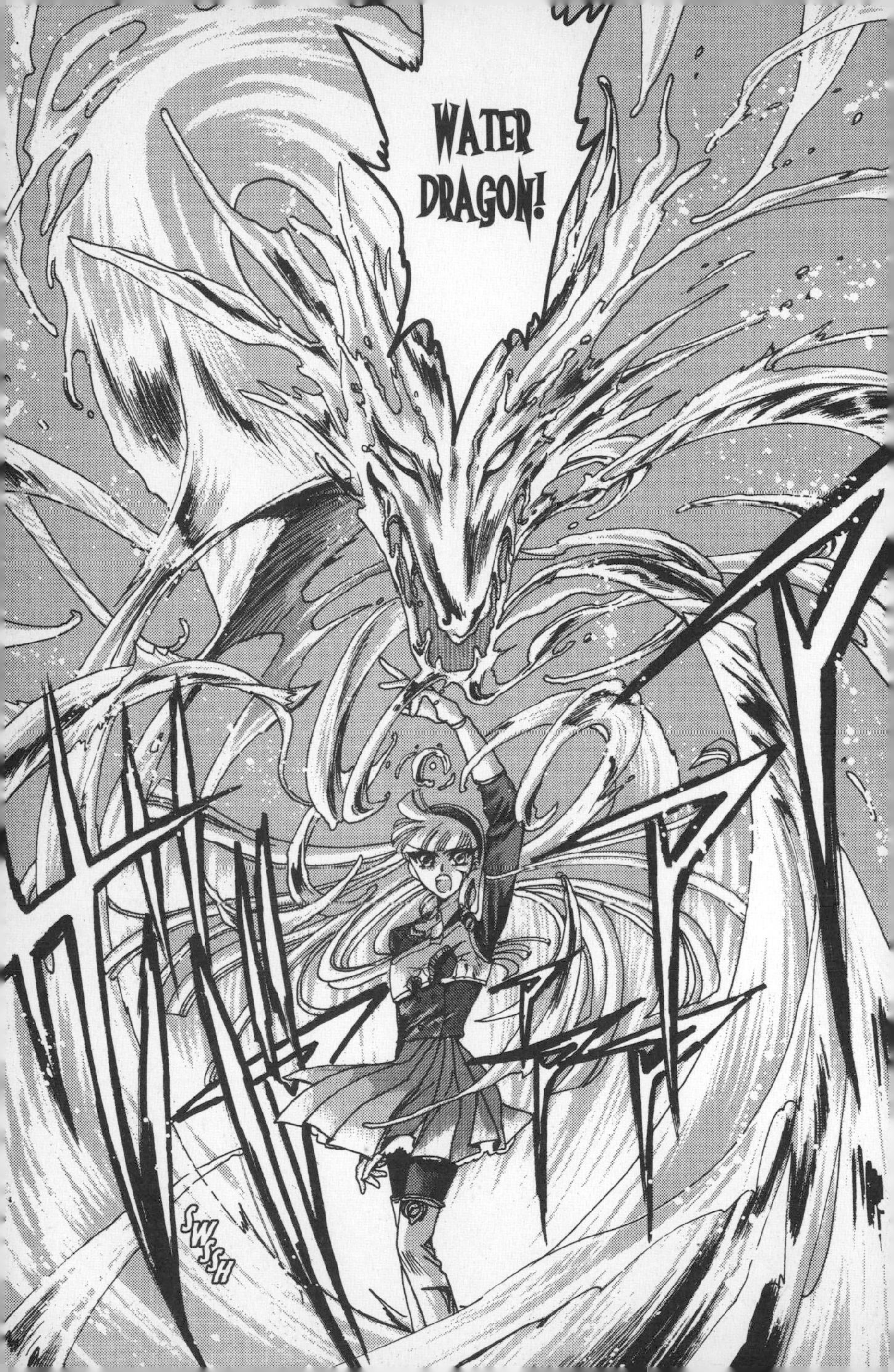
WATER DRAGON!
SWSSH

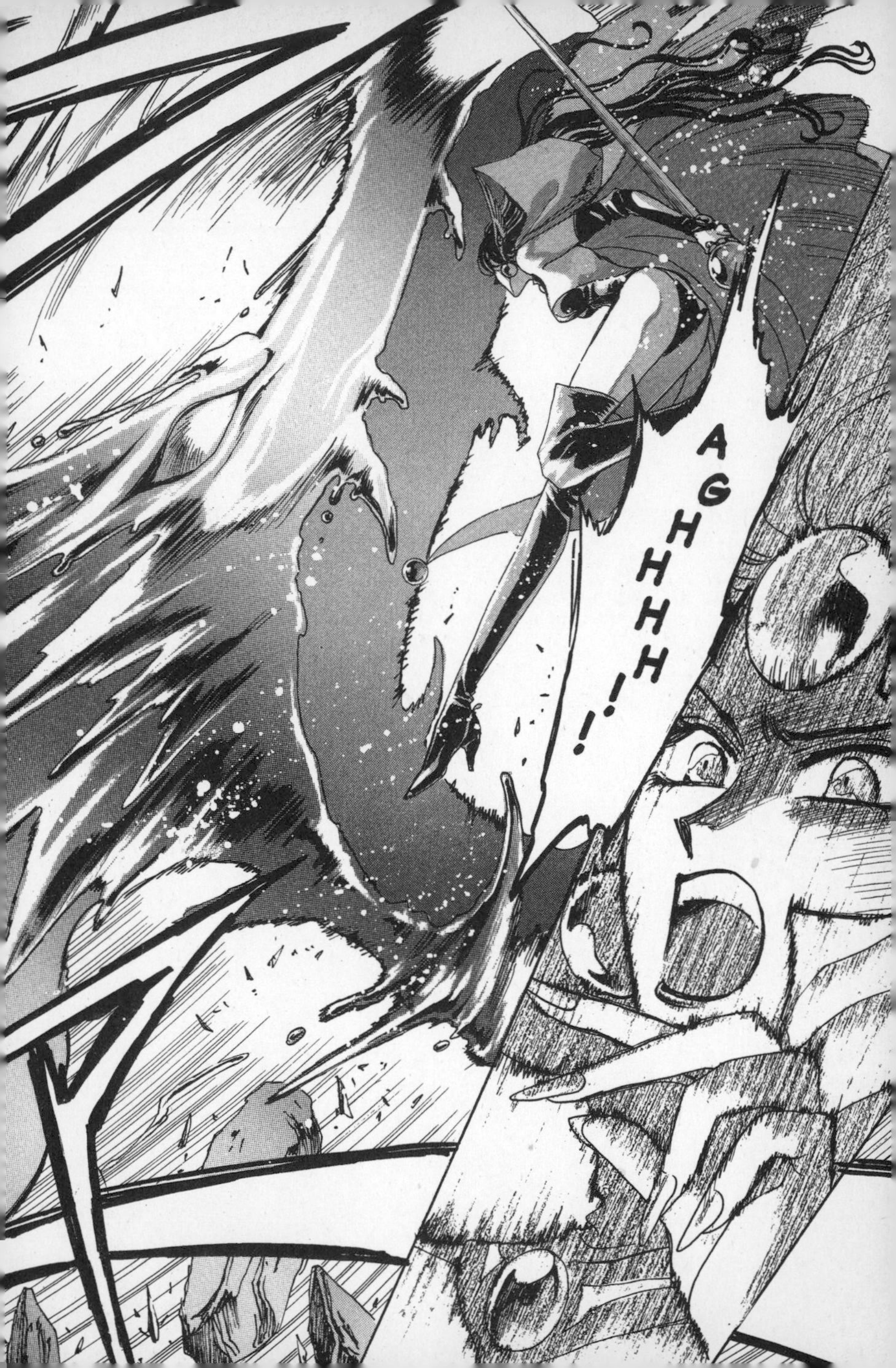
AGHHHH!!

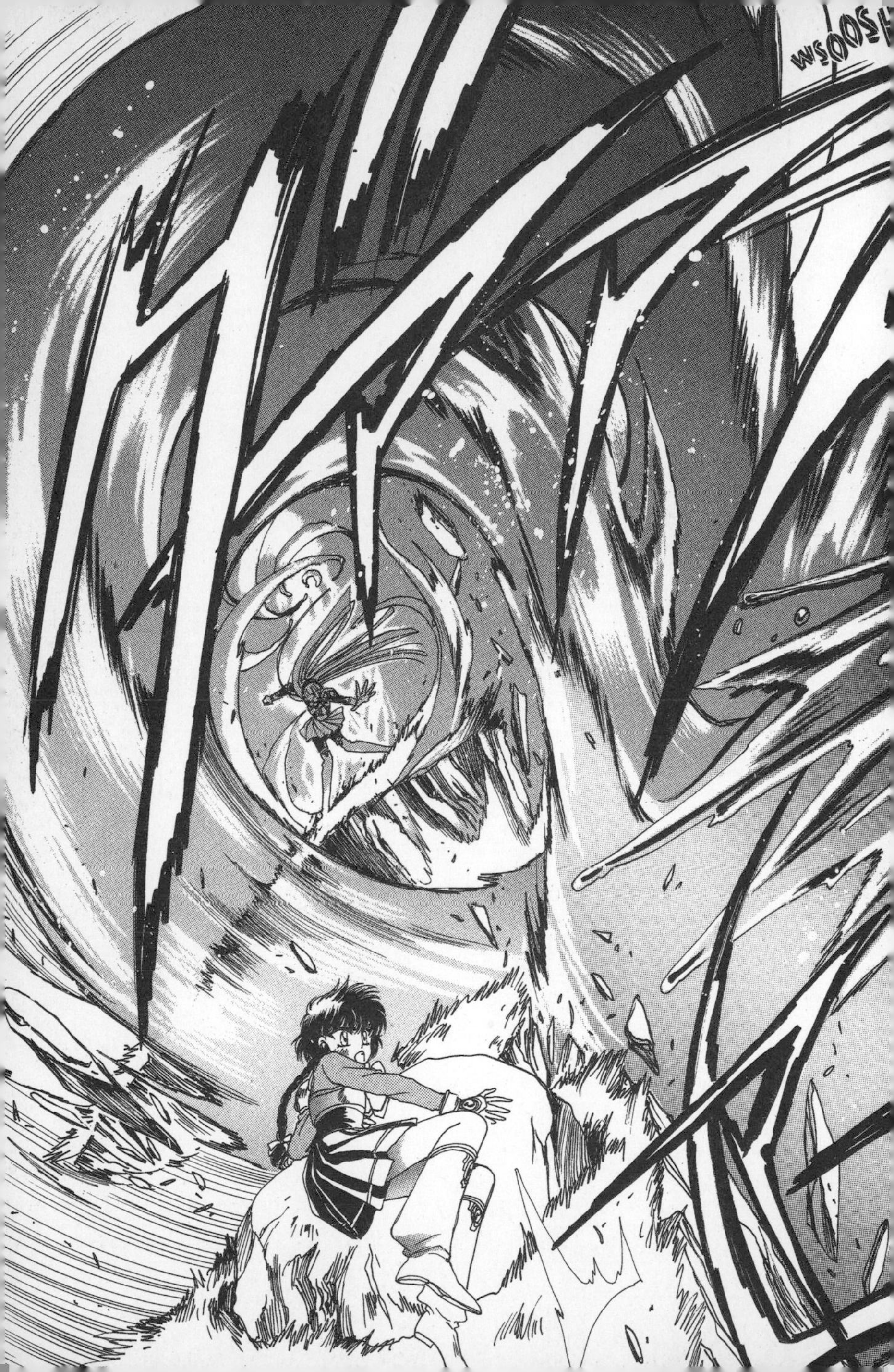

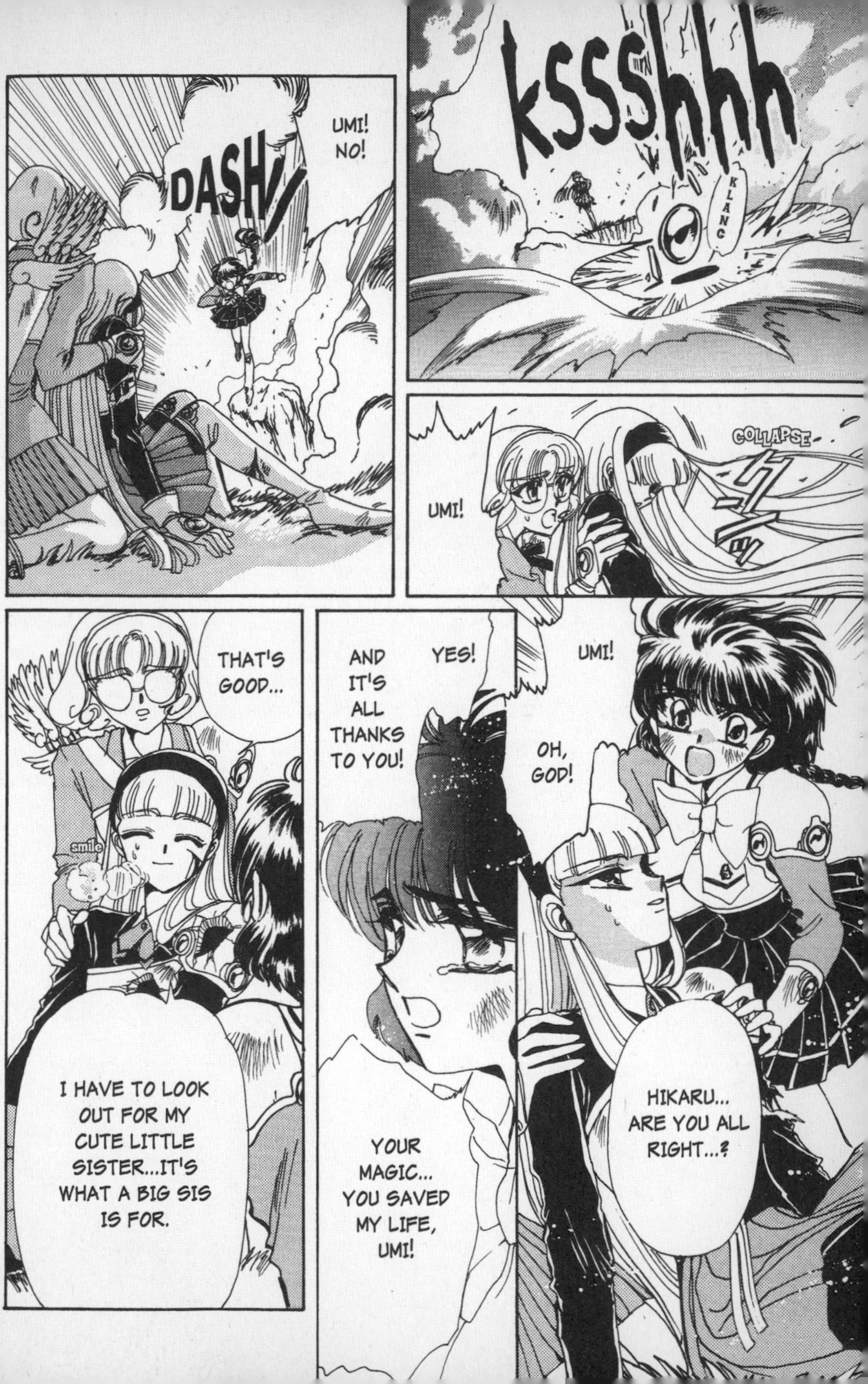

ksssshhh
KLANG
COLLAPSE
UMI!
UMI!
NO!
DASH
UMI!
OH, GOD!
HIKARU... ARE YOU ALL RIGHT...?
YES!
AND IT'S ALL THANKS TO YOU!
YOUR MAGIC... YOU SAVED MY LIFE, UMI!
THAT'S GOOD...
smile
I HAVE TO LOOK OUT FOR MY CUTE LITTLE SISTER...IT'S WHAT A BIG SIS IS FOR.

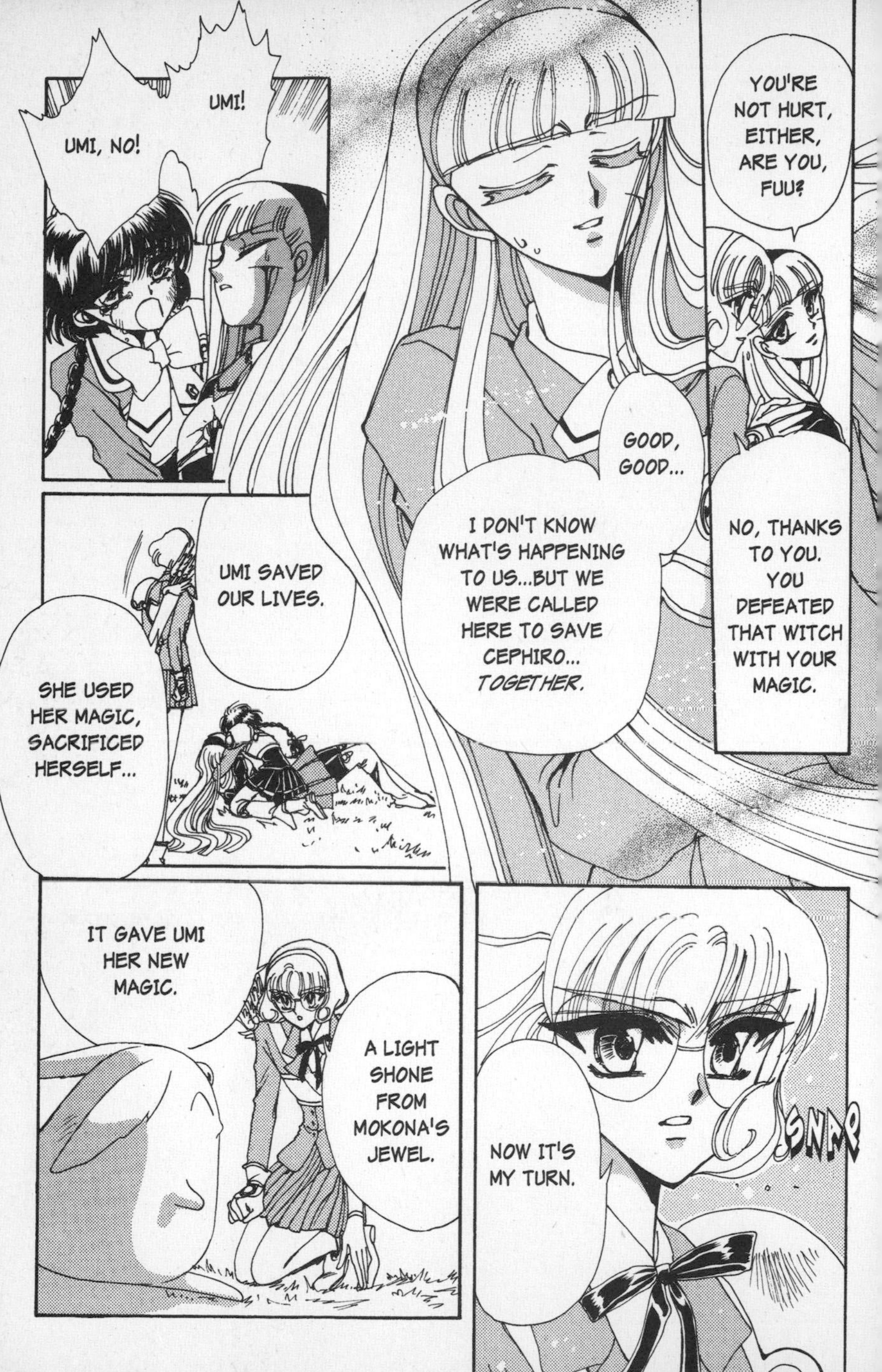
YOU'RE NOT HURT, EITHER, ARE YOU, FUU?
NO, THANKS TO YOU. YOU DEFEATED THAT WITCH WITH YOUR MAGIC.
GOOD, GOOD...
I DON'T KNOW WHAT'S HAPPENING TO US...BUT WE WERE CALLED HERE TO SAVE CEPHIRO... *TOGETHER.*
UMI!
UMI, NO!
UMI SAVED OUR LIVES.
SHE USED HER MAGIC, SACRIFICED HERSELF...
NOW IT'S MY TURN.
SNAP
A LIGHT SHONE FROM MOKONA'S JEWEL.
IT GAVE UMI HER NEW MAGIC.

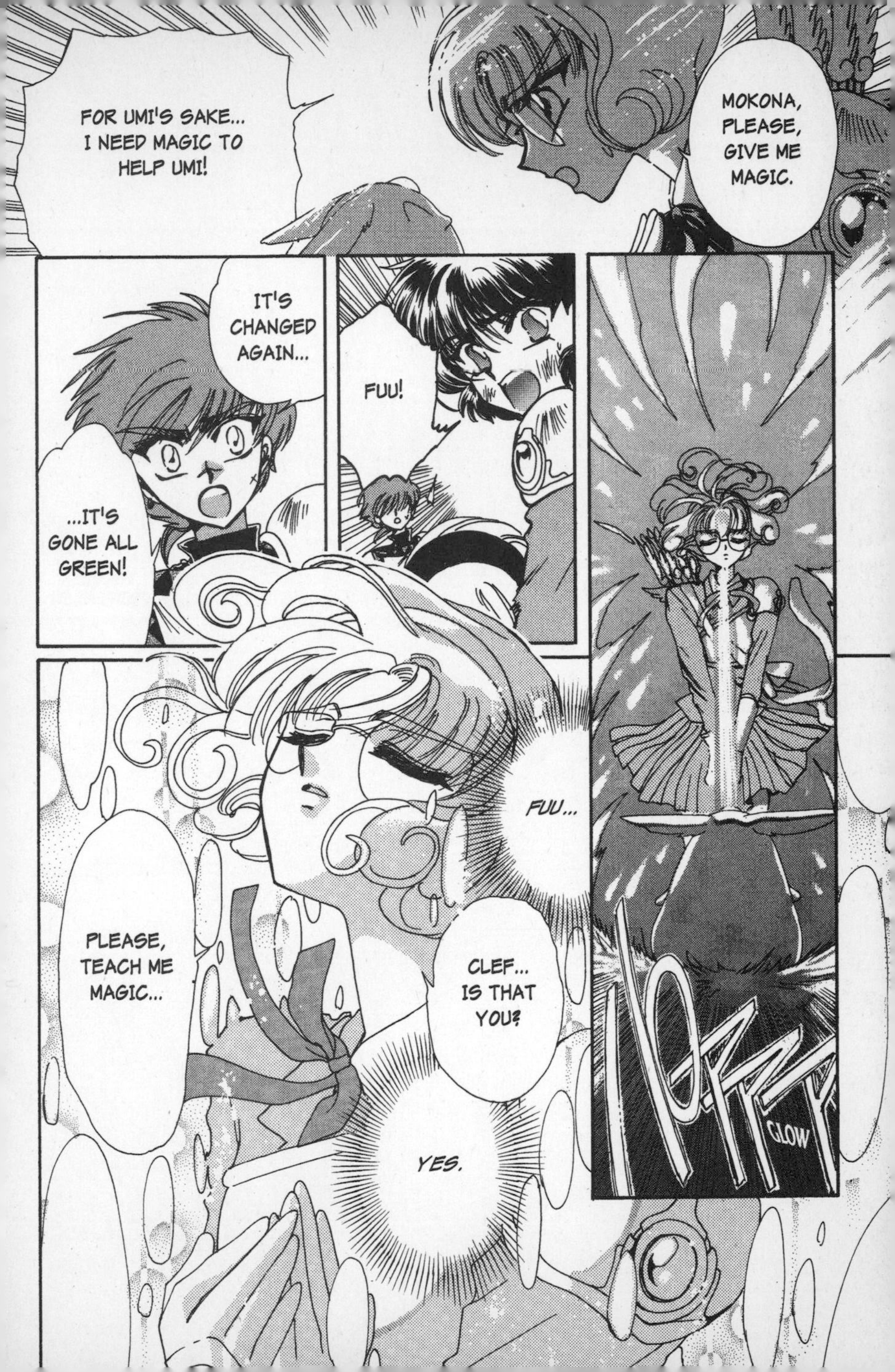
MOKONA, PLEASE, GIVE ME MAGIC.
FOR UMI'S SAKE... I NEED MAGIC TO HELP UMI!
GLOW
FUU!
IT'S CHANGED AGAIN...
...IT'S GONE ALL GREEN!
FUU...
CLEF... IS THAT YOU?
YES.
PLEASE, TEACH ME MAGIC...

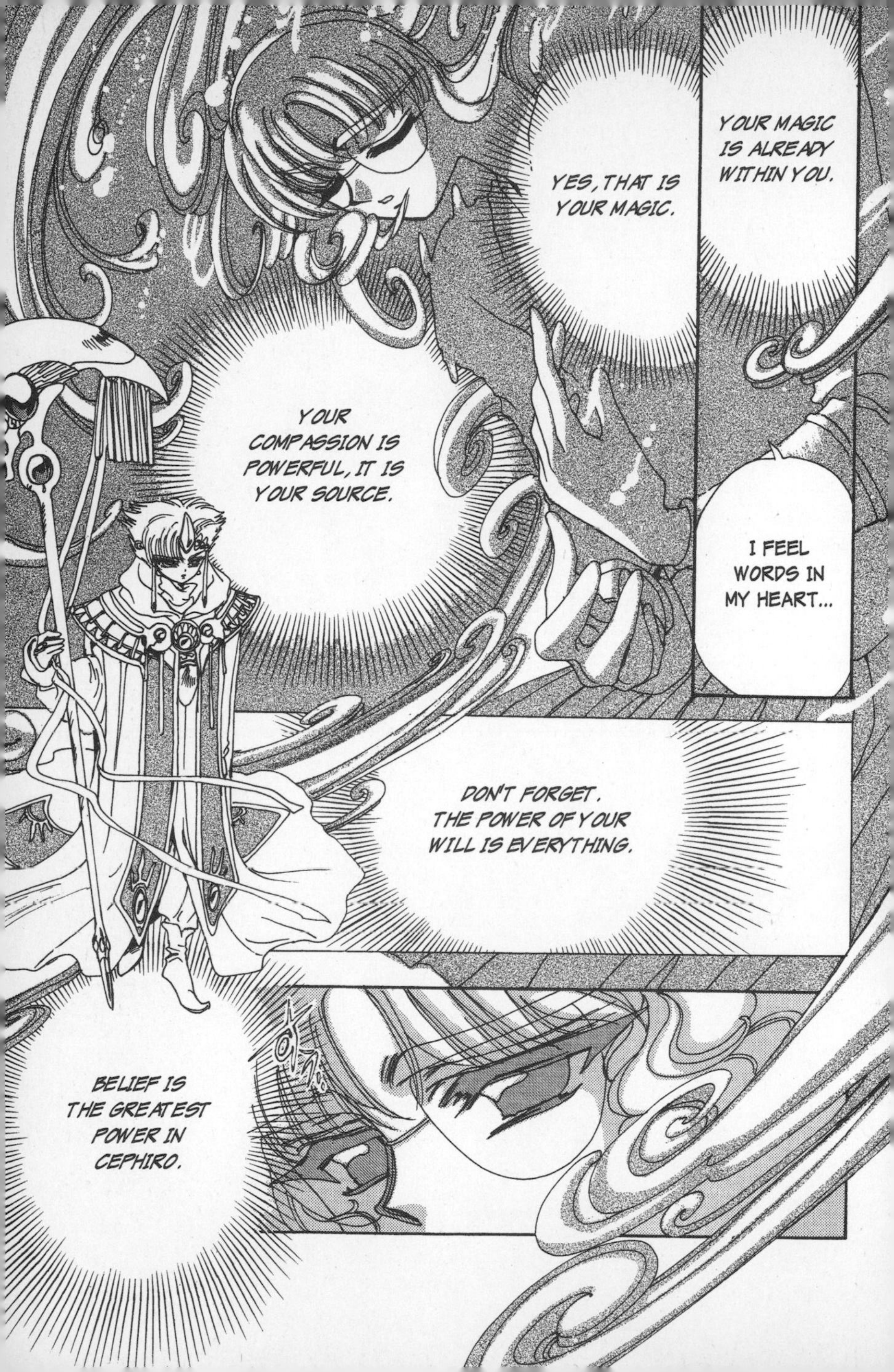
YOUR MAGIC IS ALREADY WITHIN YOU.
I FEEL WORDS IN MY HEART...
YES, THAT IS YOUR MAGIC.
YOUR COMPASSION IS POWERFUL, IT IS YOUR SOURCE.
DON'T FORGET. THE POWER OF YOUR WILL IS EVERYTHING.
BELIEF IS THE GREATEST POWER IN CEPHIRO.

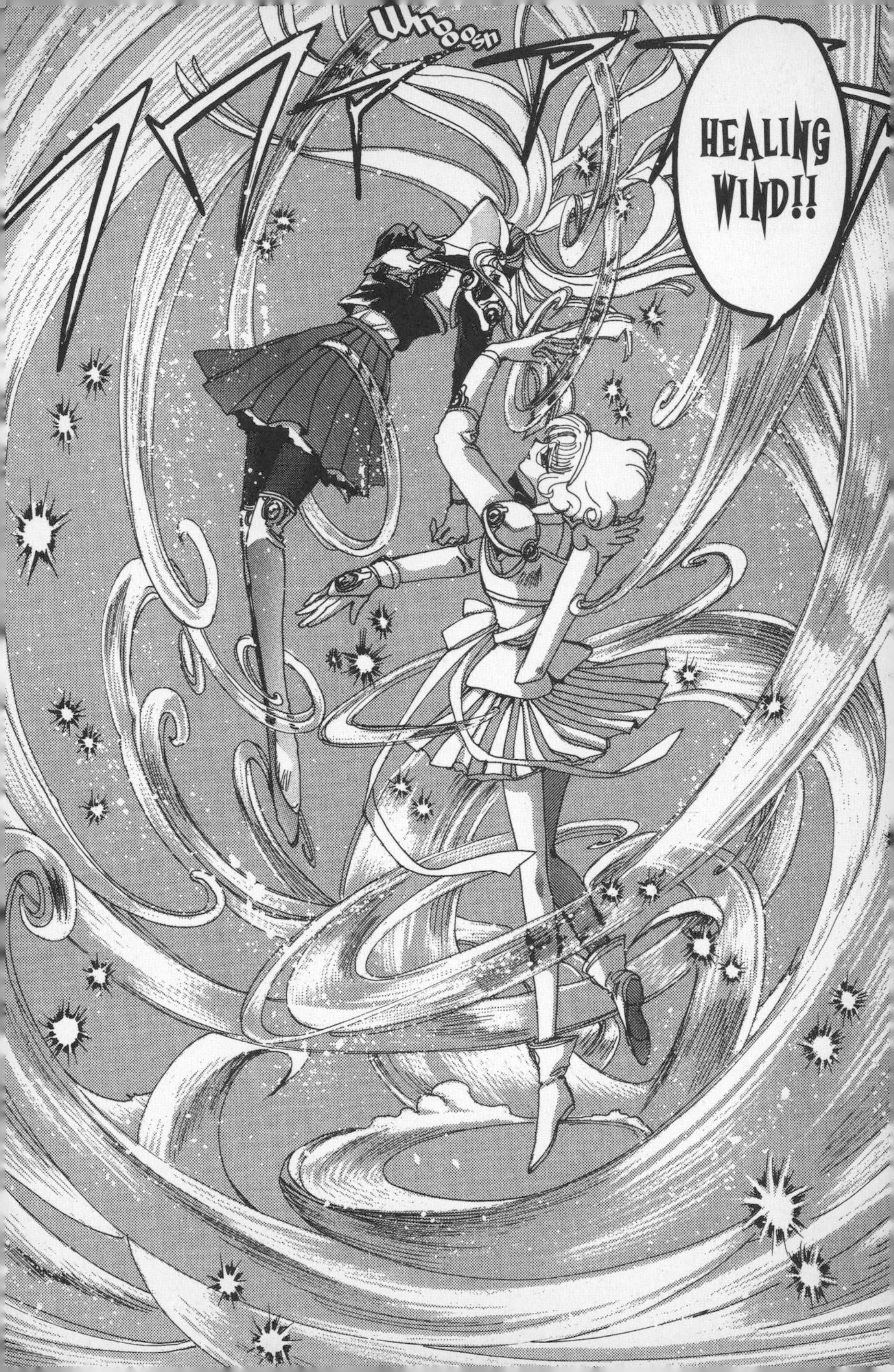
HEALING WIND!!
Whoosh

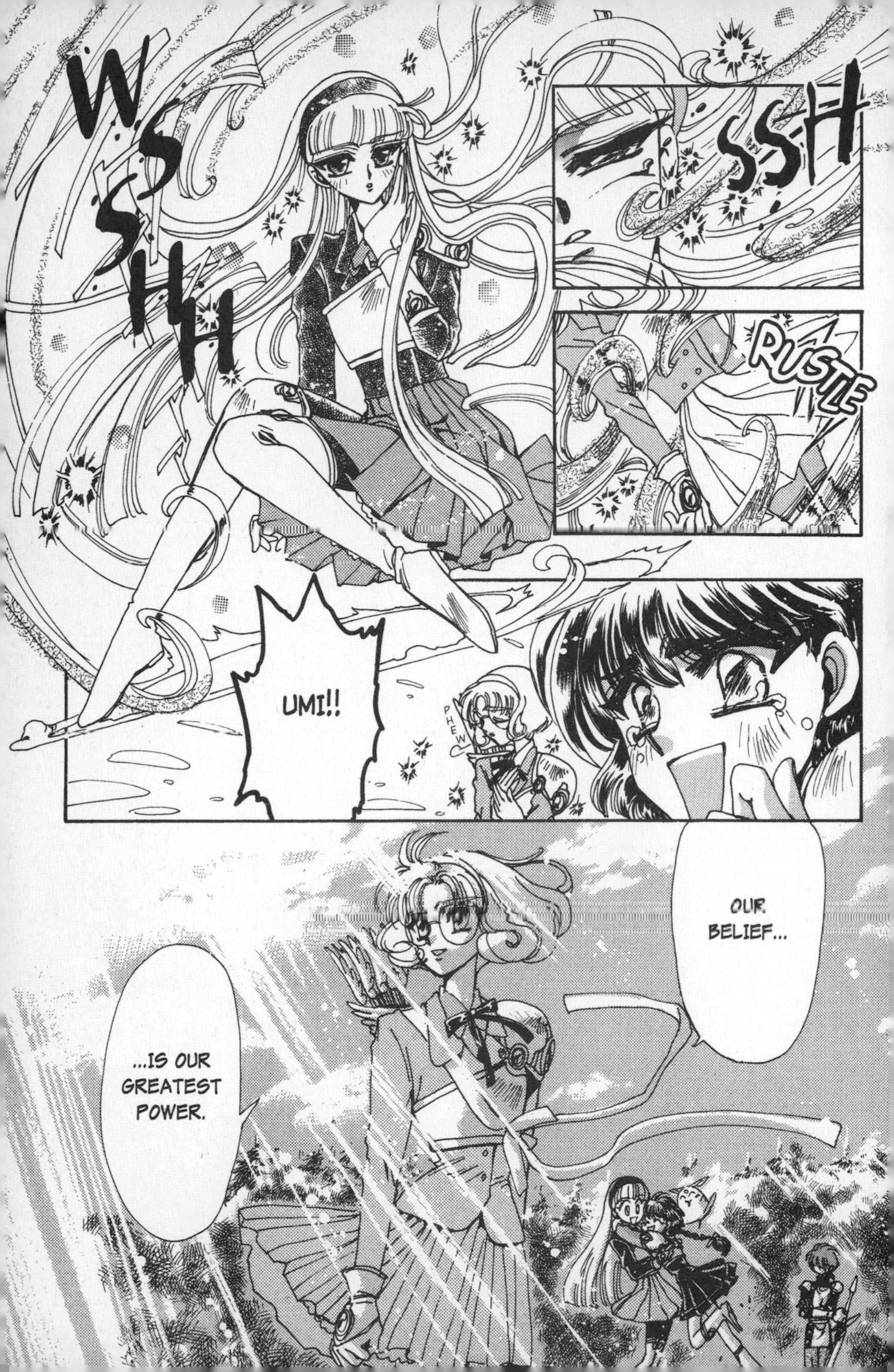
SSH
RUSTLE
WSSHH
PHEW
UMI!!
OUR BELIEF...
...IS OUR GREATEST POWER.

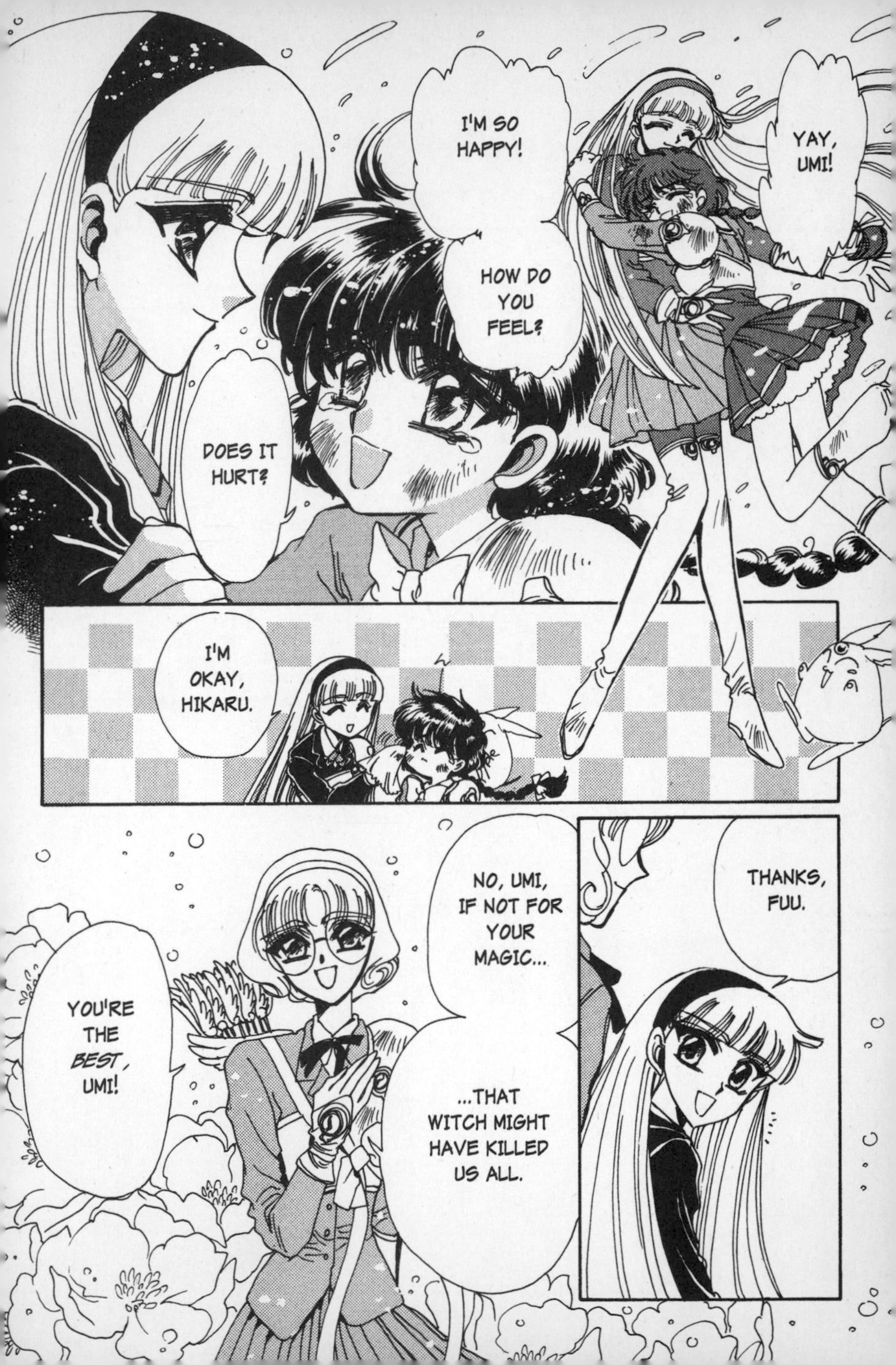
YAY, UMI!
I'M SO HAPPY!
HOW DO YOU FEEL?
DOES IT HURT?
I'M OKAY, HIKARU.
THANKS, FUU.
NO, UMI, IF NOT FOR YOUR MAGIC...
...THAT WITCH MIGHT HAVE KILLED US ALL.
YOU'RE THE *BEST*, UMI!

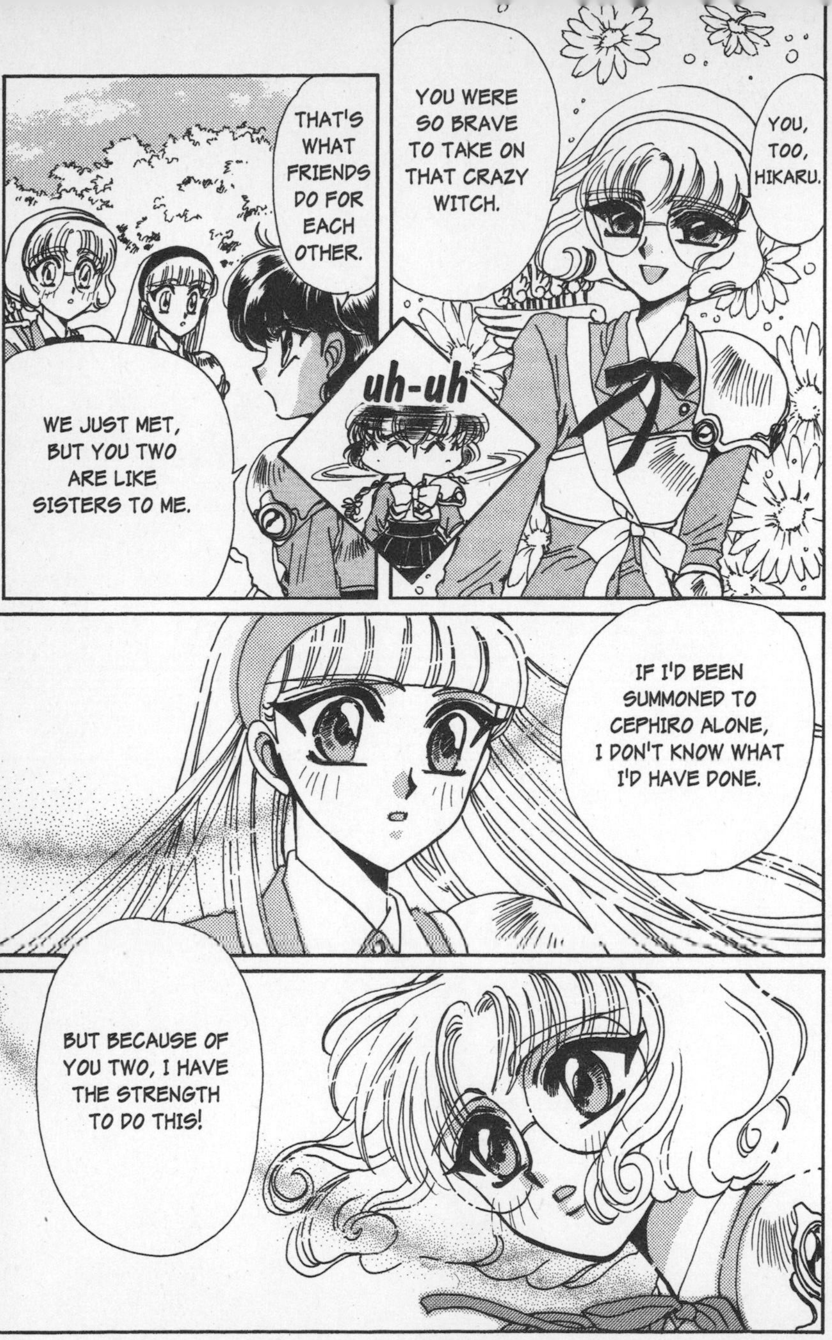

YOU, TOO, HIKARU.
YOU WERE SO BRAVE TO TAKE ON THAT CRAZY WITCH.
uh-uh
THAT'S WHAT FRIENDS DO FOR EACH OTHER.
WE JUST MET, BUT YOU TWO ARE LIKE SISTERS TO ME.
IF I'D BEEN SUMMONED TO CEPHIRO ALONE, I DON'T KNOW WHAT I'D HAVE DONE.
BUT BECAUSE OF YOU TWO, I HAVE THE STRENGTH TO DO THIS!

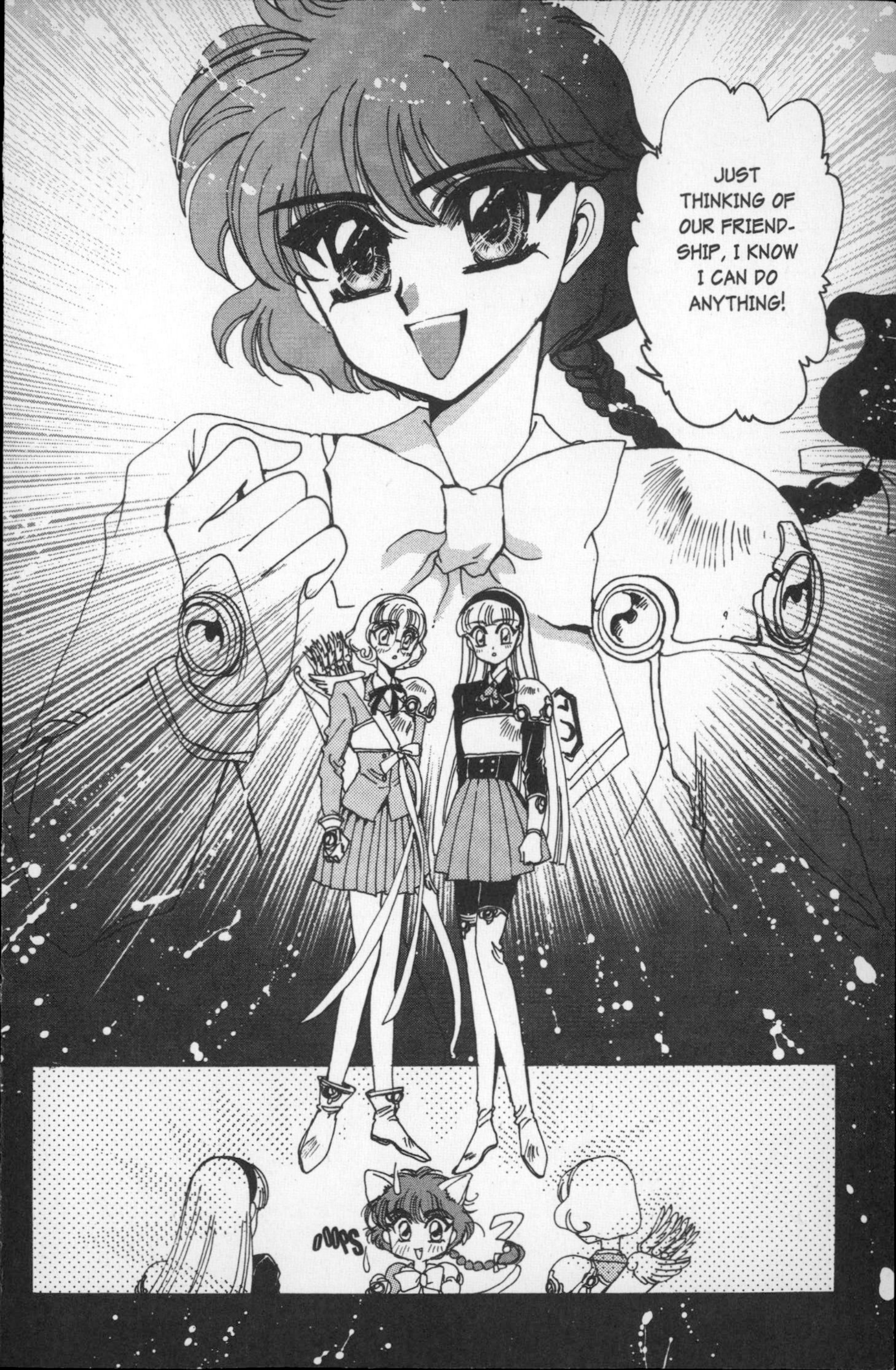
JUST THINKING OF OUR FRIEND-SHIP, I KNOW I CAN DO ANYTHING!
OOPS

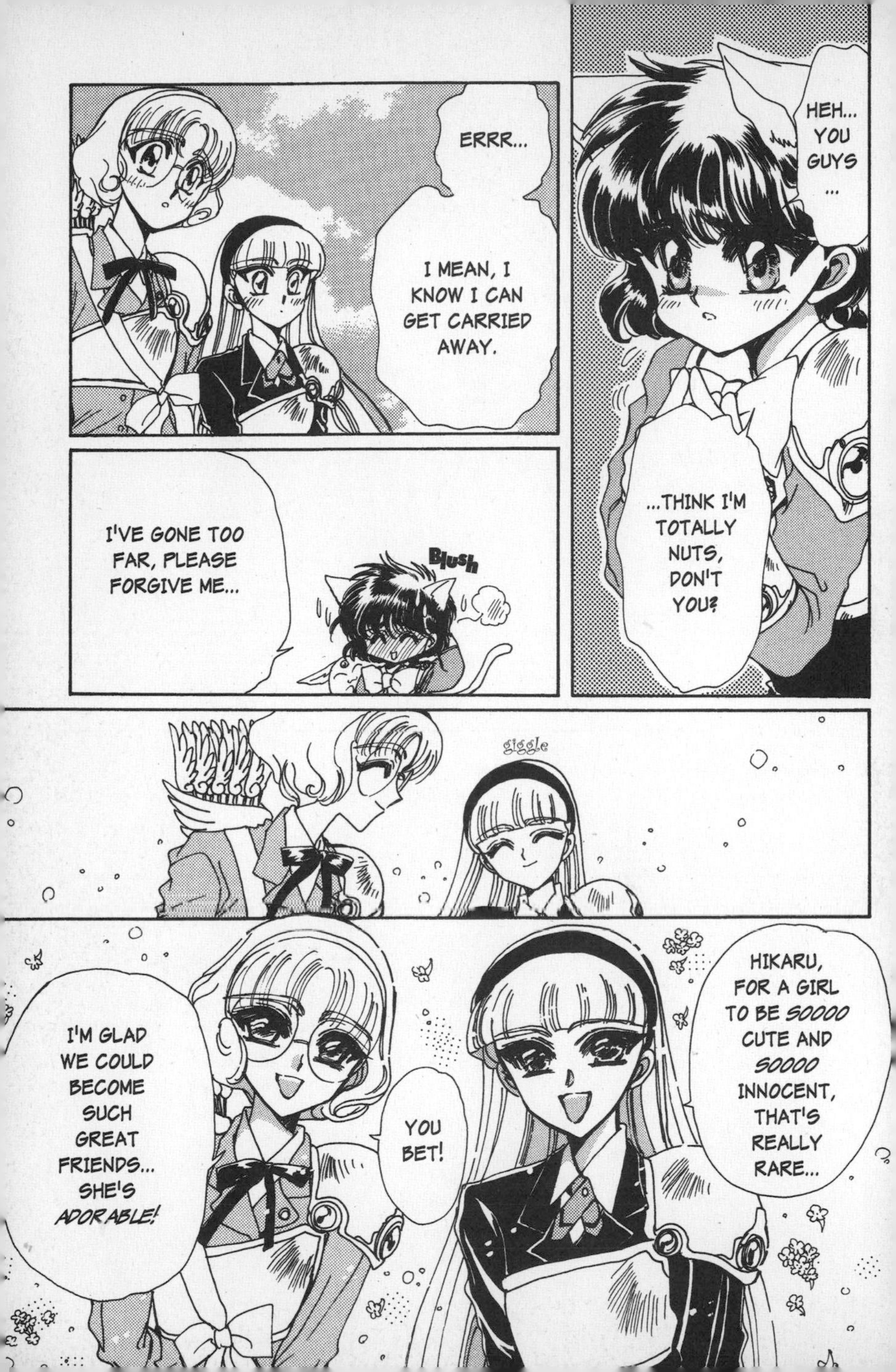
HEH... YOU GUYS ...
...THINK I'M TOTALLY NUTS, DON'T YOU?
ERRR...
I MEAN, I KNOW I CAN GET CARRIED AWAY.
I'VE GONE TOO FAR, PLEASE FORGIVE ME...
Blush
giggle
HIKARU, FOR A GIRL TO BE *SOOOO* CUTE AND *SOOOO* INNOCENT, THAT'S REALLY RARE...
YOU BET!
I'M GLAD WE COULD BECOME SUCH GREAT FRIENDS... SHE'S *ADORABLE!*

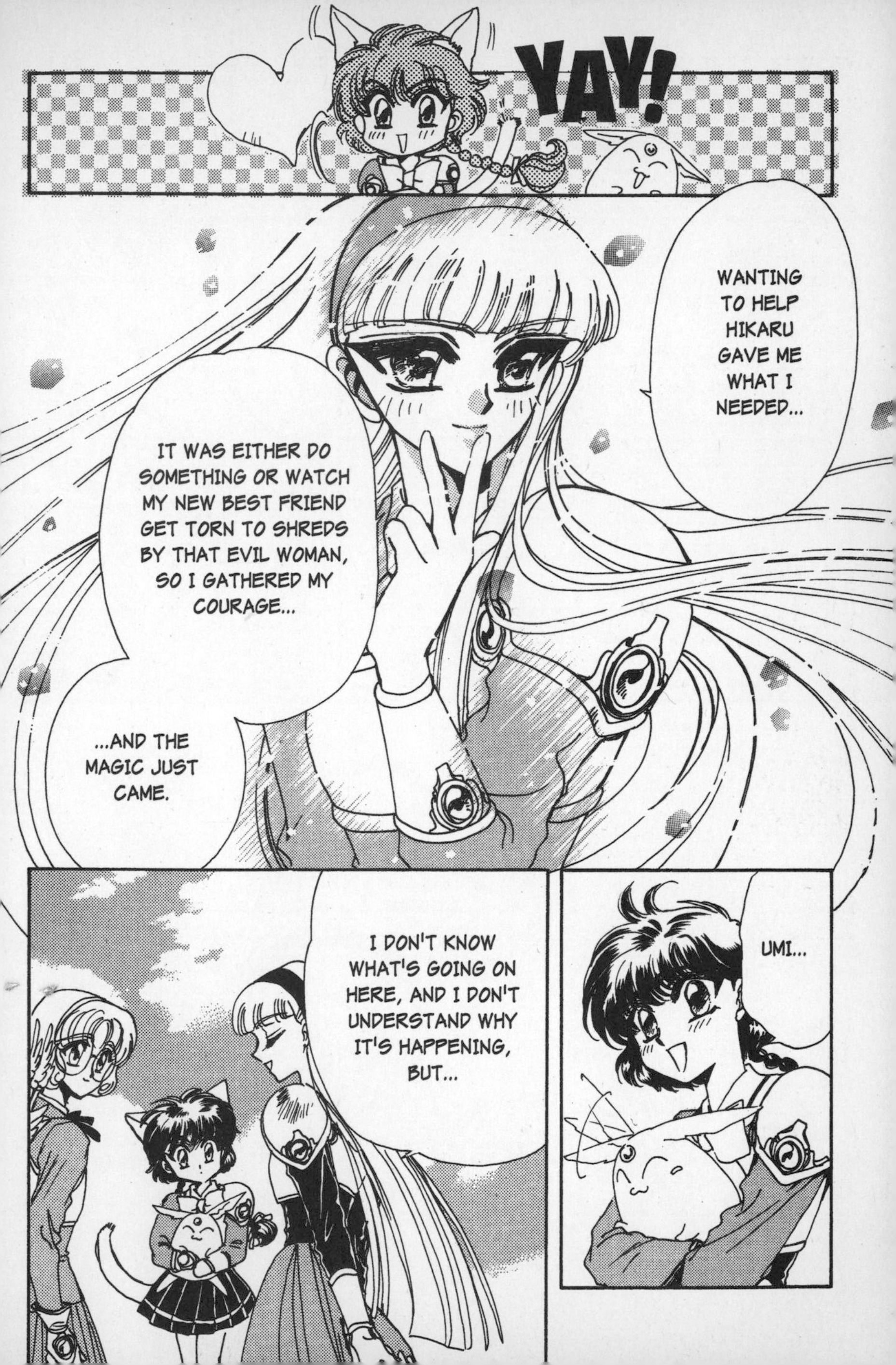
YAY!
WANTING TO HELP HIKARU GAVE ME WHAT I NEEDED...
IT WAS EITHER DO SOMETHING OR WATCH MY NEW BEST FRIEND GET TORN TO SHREDS BY THAT EVIL WOMAN, SO I GATHERED MY COURAGE...
...AND THE MAGIC JUST CAME.
UMI...
I DON'T KNOW WHAT'S GOING ON HERE, AND I DON'T UNDERSTAND WHY IT'S HAPPENING, BUT...

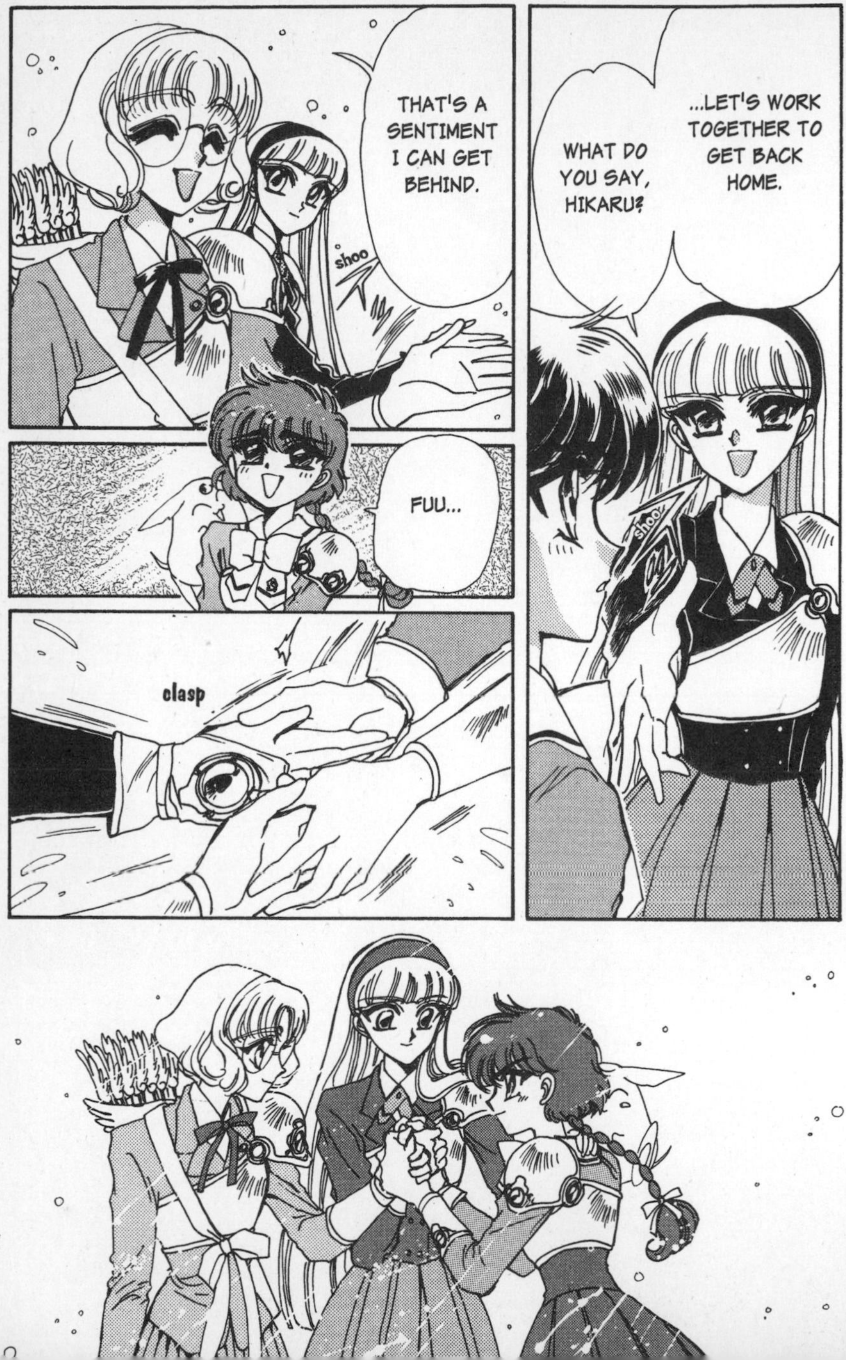
...LET'S WORK TOGETHER TO GET BACK HOME.
WHAT DO YOU SAY, HIKARU?
shoo
THAT'S A SENTIMENT I CAN GET BEHIND.
shoo
FUU...
clasp

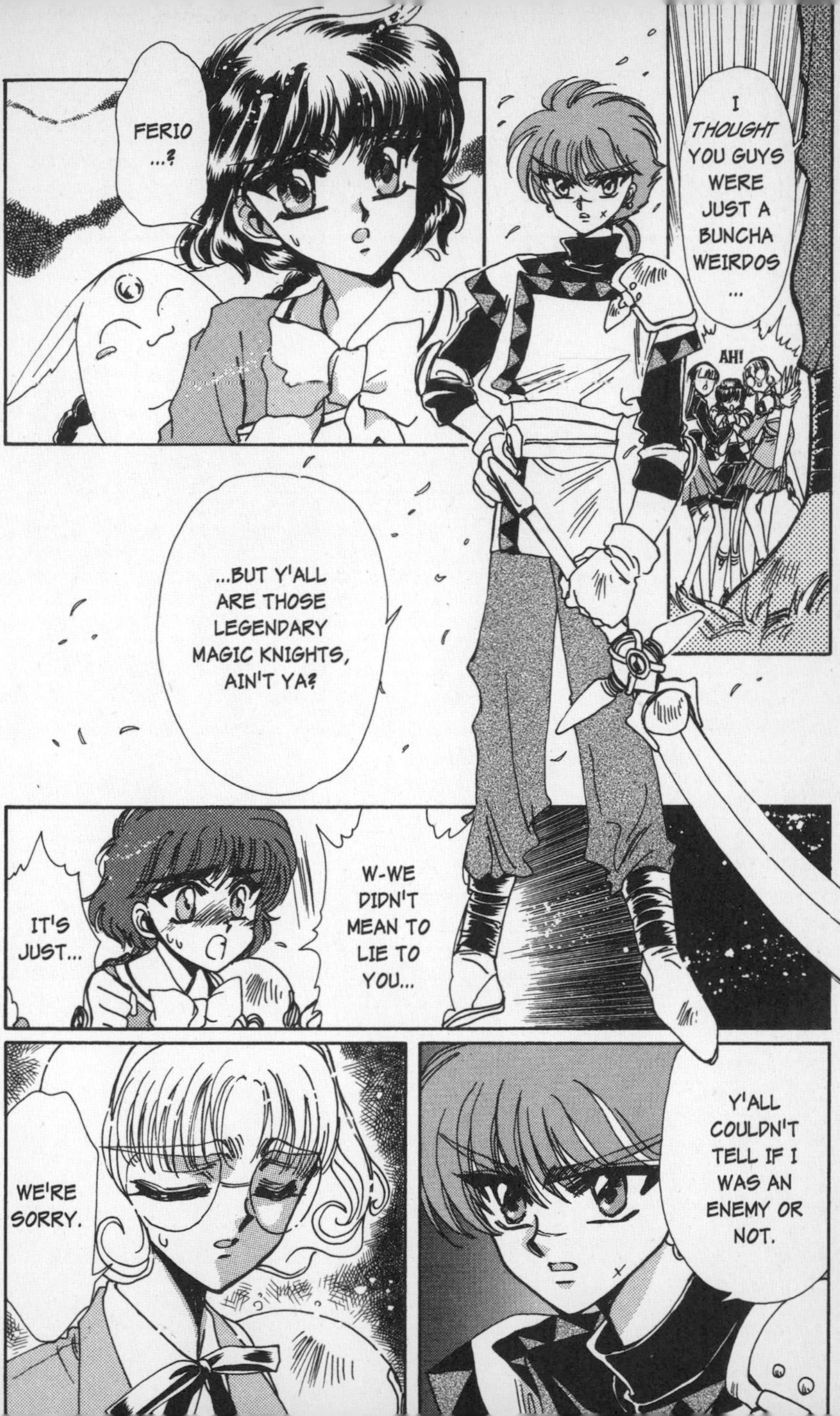
I *THOUGHT* YOU GUYS WERE JUST A BUNCHA WEIRDOS...
AH!
FERIO ...?
...BUT Y'ALL ARE THOSE LEGENDARY MAGIC KNIGHTS, AIN'T YA?
W-WE DIDN'T MEAN TO LIE TO YOU...
IT'S JUST...
Y'ALL COULDN'T TELL IF I WAS AN ENEMY OR NOT.
WE'RE SORRY.

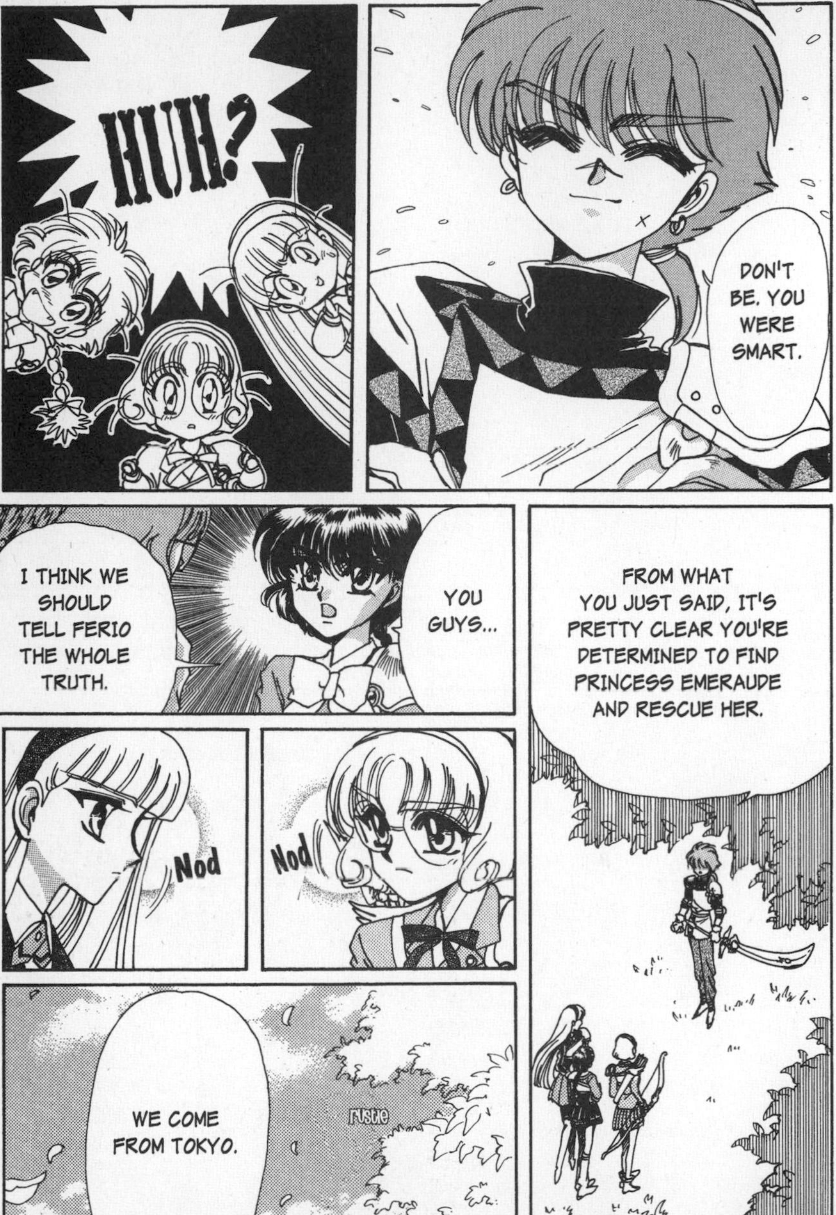
DON'T BE. YOU WERE SMART.
HUH?
FROM WHAT YOU JUST SAID, IT'S PRETTY CLEAR YOU'RE DETERMINED TO FIND PRINCESS EMERAUDE AND RESCUE HER.
YOU GUYS...
I THINK WE SHOULD TELL FERIO THE WHOLE TRUTH.
Nod
Nod
rustle
WE COME FROM TOKYO.

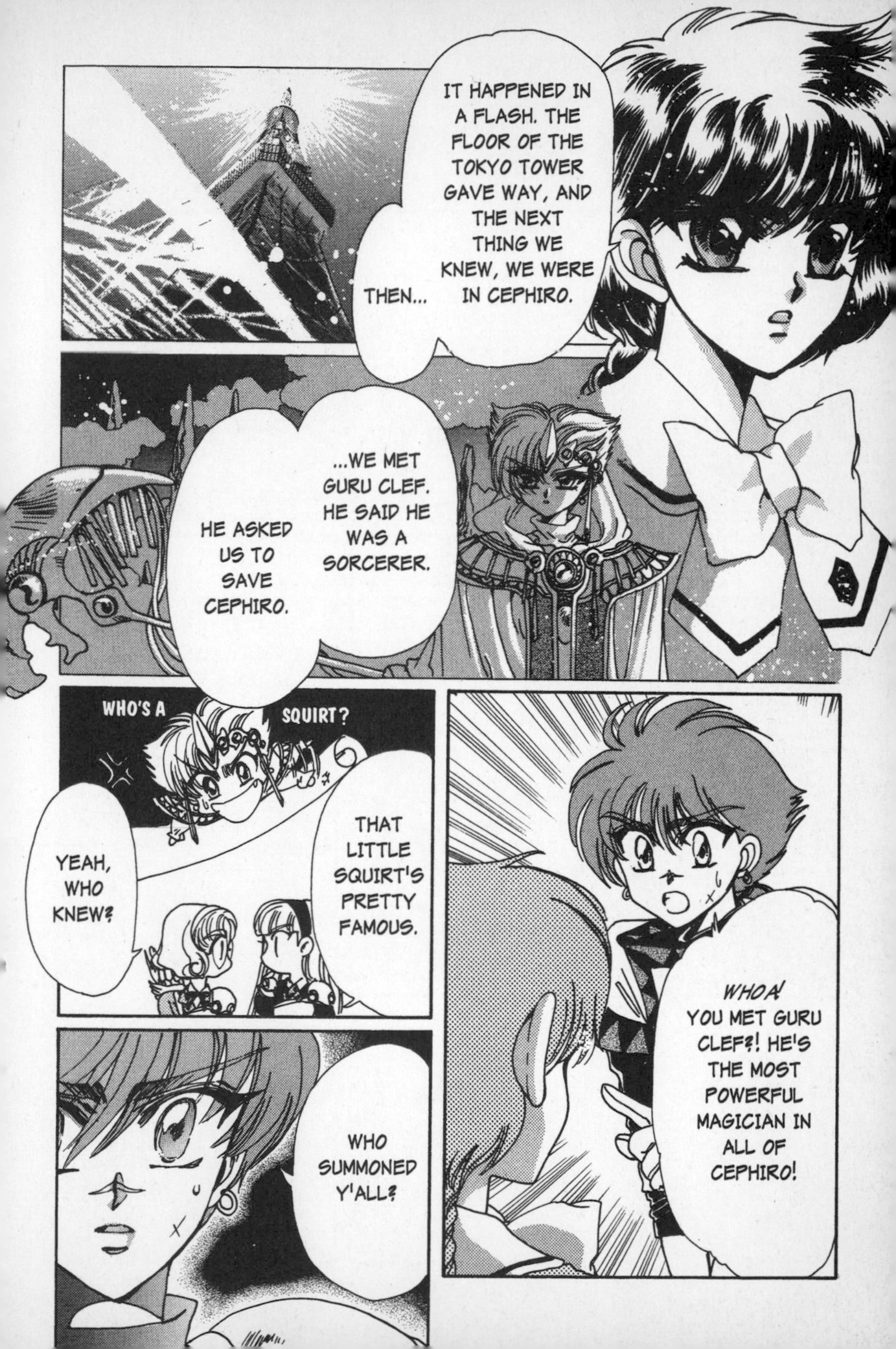
IT HAPPENED IN A FLASH. THE FLOOR OF THE TOKYO TOWER GAVE WAY, AND THE NEXT THING WE KNEW, WE WERE IN CEPHIRO.
THEN...
...WE MET GURU CLEF. HE SAID HE WAS A SORCERER.
HE ASKED US TO SAVE CEPHIRO.
WHOA! YOU MET GURU CLEF?! HE'S THE MOST POWERFUL MAGICIAN IN ALL OF CEPHIRO!
THAT LITTLE SQUIRT'S PRETTY FAMOUS.
YEAH, WHO KNEW?
WHO'S A SQUIRT?
WHO SUMMONED Y'ALL?

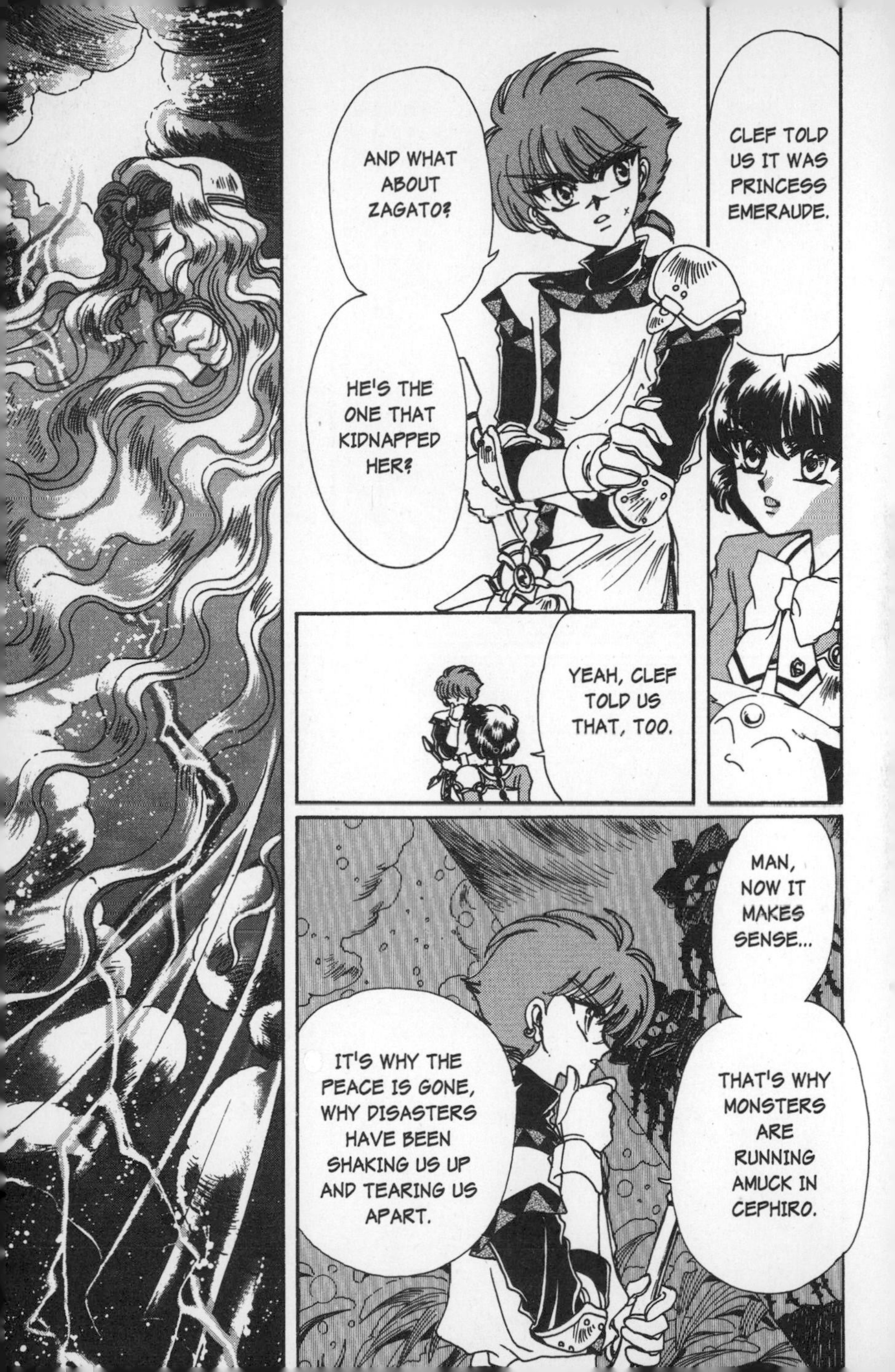
CLEF TOLD US IT WAS PRINCESS EMERAUDE.
AND WHAT ABOUT ZAGATO?
HE'S THE ONE THAT KIDNAPPED HER?
YEAH, CLEF TOLD US THAT, TOO.
MAN, NOW IT MAKES SENSE...
THAT'S WHY MONSTERS ARE RUNNING AMUCK IN CEPHIRO.
IT'S WHY THE PEACE IS GONE, WHY DISASTERS HAVE BEEN SHAKING US UP AND TEARING US APART.

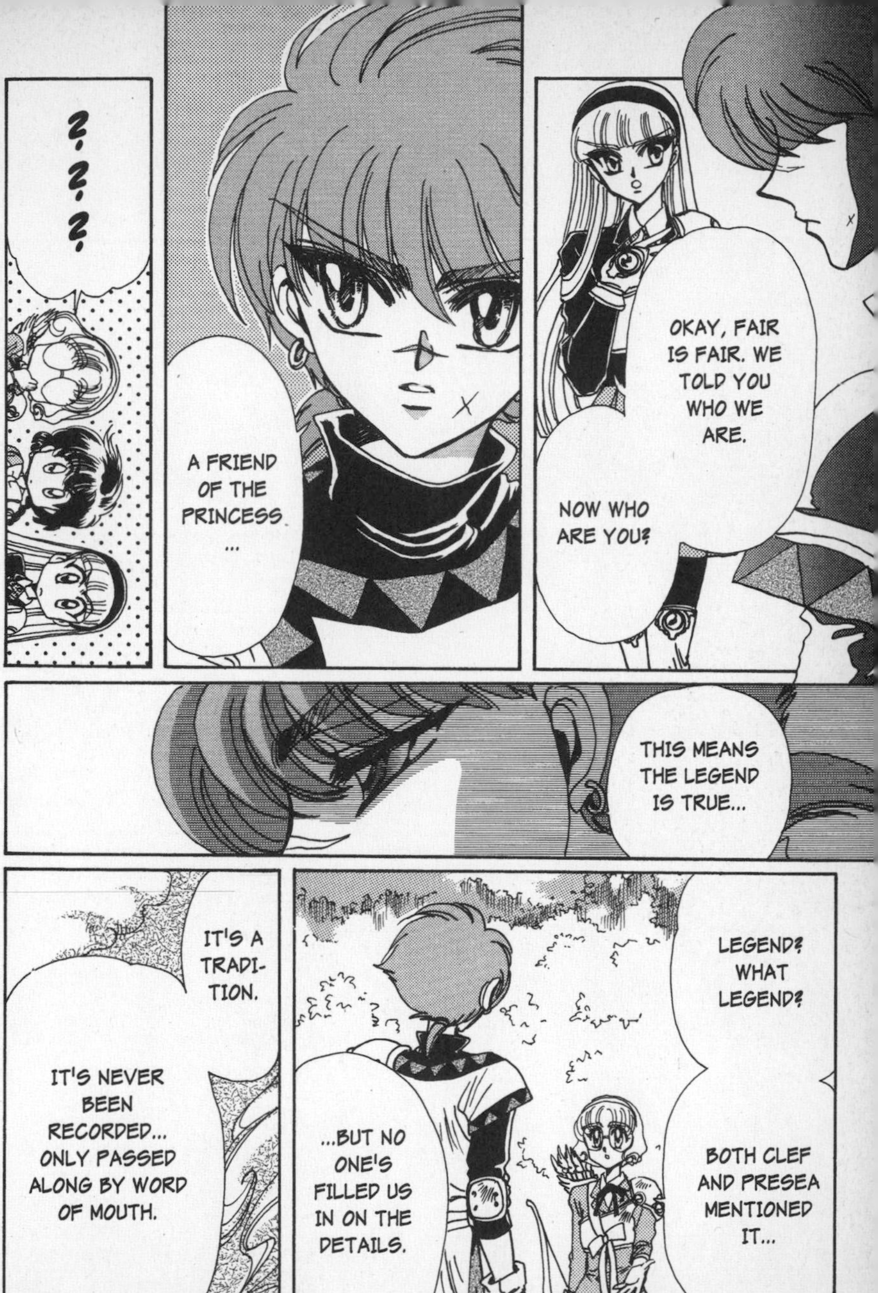
OKAY, FAIR IS FAIR. WE TOLD YOU WHO WE ARE.
NOW WHO ARE YOU?
A FRIEND OF THE PRINCESS ...
???
THIS MEANS THE LEGEND IS TRUE...
LEGEND? WHAT LEGEND?
BOTH CLEF AND PRESEA MENTIONED IT...
...BUT NO ONE'S FILLED US IN ON THE DETAILS.
IT'S A TRADI- TION.
IT'S NEVER BEEN RECORDED... ONLY PASSED ALONG BY WORD OF MOUTH.

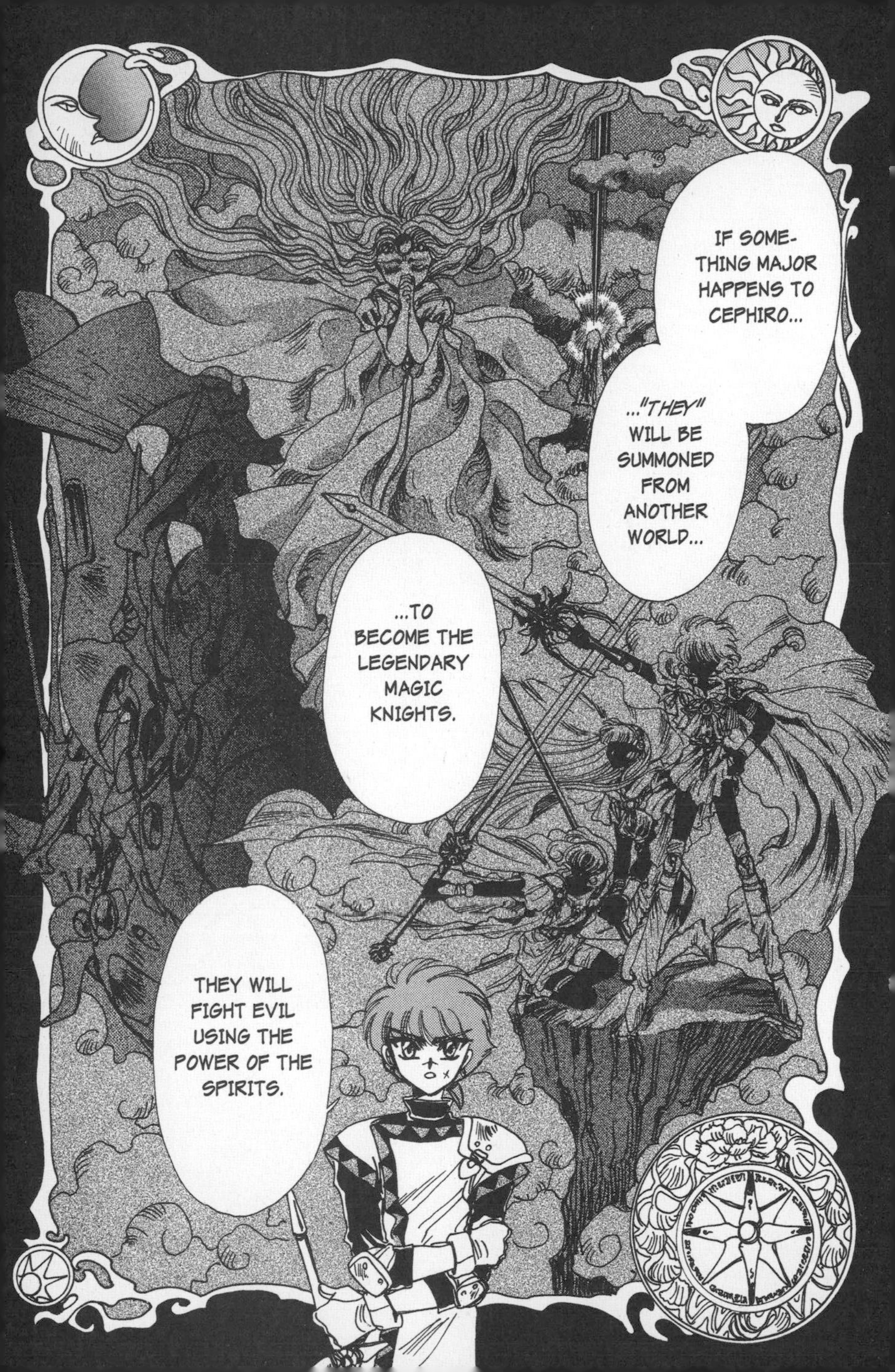
IF SOME-THING MAJOR HAPPENS TO CEPHIRO...
..."THEY" WILL BE SUMMONED FROM ANOTHER WORLD...
...TO BECOME THE LEGENDARY MAGIC KNIGHTS.
THEY WILL FIGHT EVIL USING THE POWER OF THE SPIRITS.

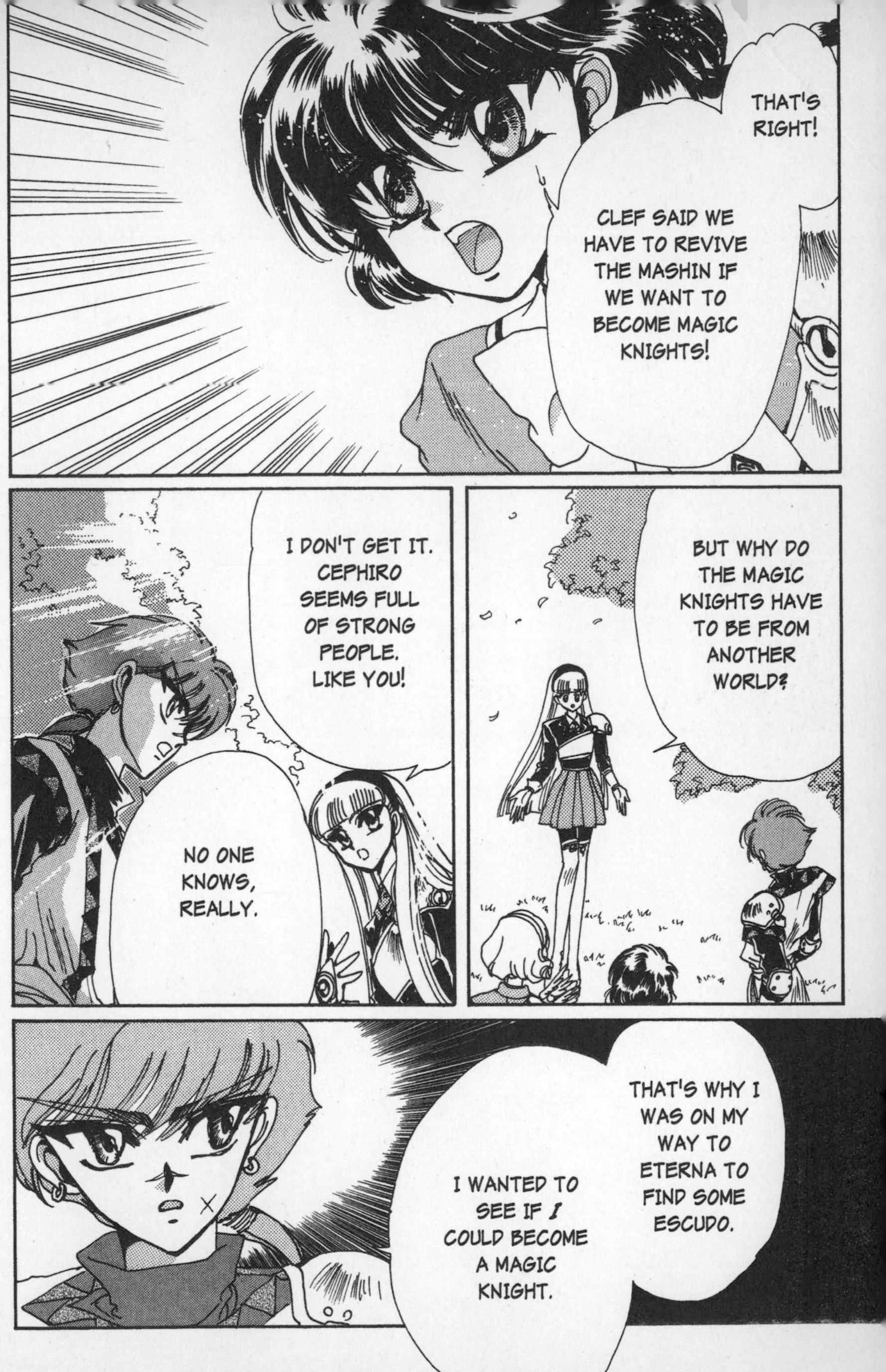
THAT'S RIGHT!
CLEF SAID WE HAVE TO REVIVE THE MASHIN IF WE WANT TO BECOME MAGIC KNIGHTS!
BUT WHY DO THE MAGIC KNIGHTS HAVE TO BE FROM ANOTHER WORLD?
I DON'T GET IT. CEPHIRO SEEMS FULL OF STRONG PEOPLE. LIKE YOU!
NO ONE KNOWS, REALLY.
THAT'S WHY I WAS ON MY WAY TO ETERNA TO FIND SOME ESCUDO.
I WANTED TO SEE IF *I* COULD BECOME A MAGIC KNIGHT.

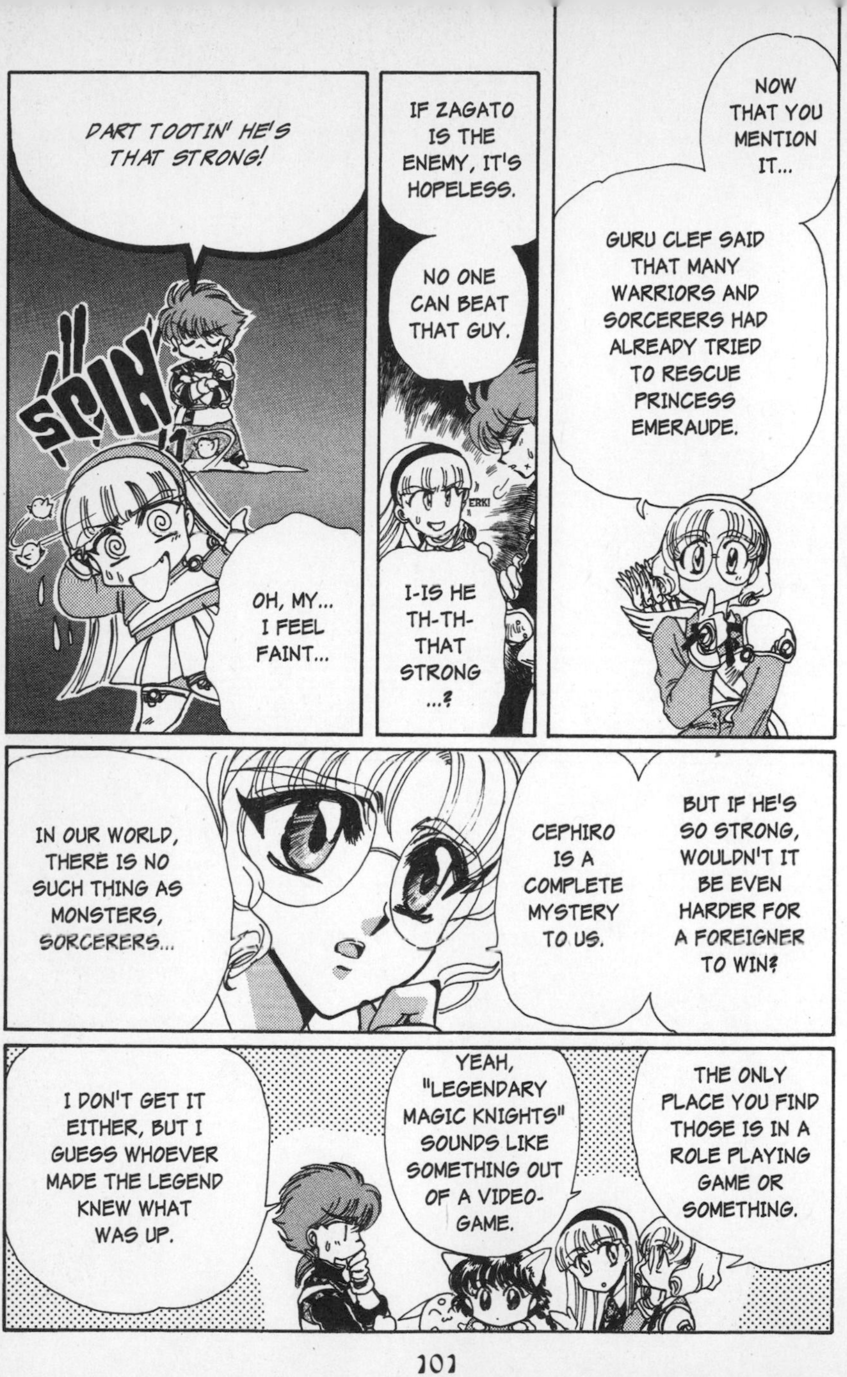
NOW THAT YOU MENTION IT...
GURU CLEF SAID THAT MANY WARRIORS AND SORCERERS HAD ALREADY TRIED TO RESCUE PRINCESS EMERAUDE.
IF ZAGATO IS THE ENEMY, IT'S HOPELESS.
NO ONE CAN BEAT THAT GUY.
ERK!
I-IS HE TH-TH-THAT STRONG ...?
DART TOOTIN' HE'S THAT STRONG!
SPIN
OH, MY... I FEEL FAINT...
BUT IF HE'S SO STRONG, WOULDN'T IT BE EVEN HARDER FOR A FOREIGNER TO WIN?
CEPHIRO IS A COMPLETE MYSTERY TO US.
IN OUR WORLD, THERE IS NO SUCH THING AS MONSTERS, SORCERERS...
THE ONLY PLACE YOU FIND THOSE IS IN A ROLE PLAYING GAME OR SOMETHING.
YEAH, "LEGENDARY MAGIC KNIGHTS" SOUNDS LIKE SOMETHING OUT OF A VIDEO-GAME.
I DON'T GET IT EITHER, BUT I GUESS WHOEVER MADE THE LEGEND KNEW WHAT WAS UP.

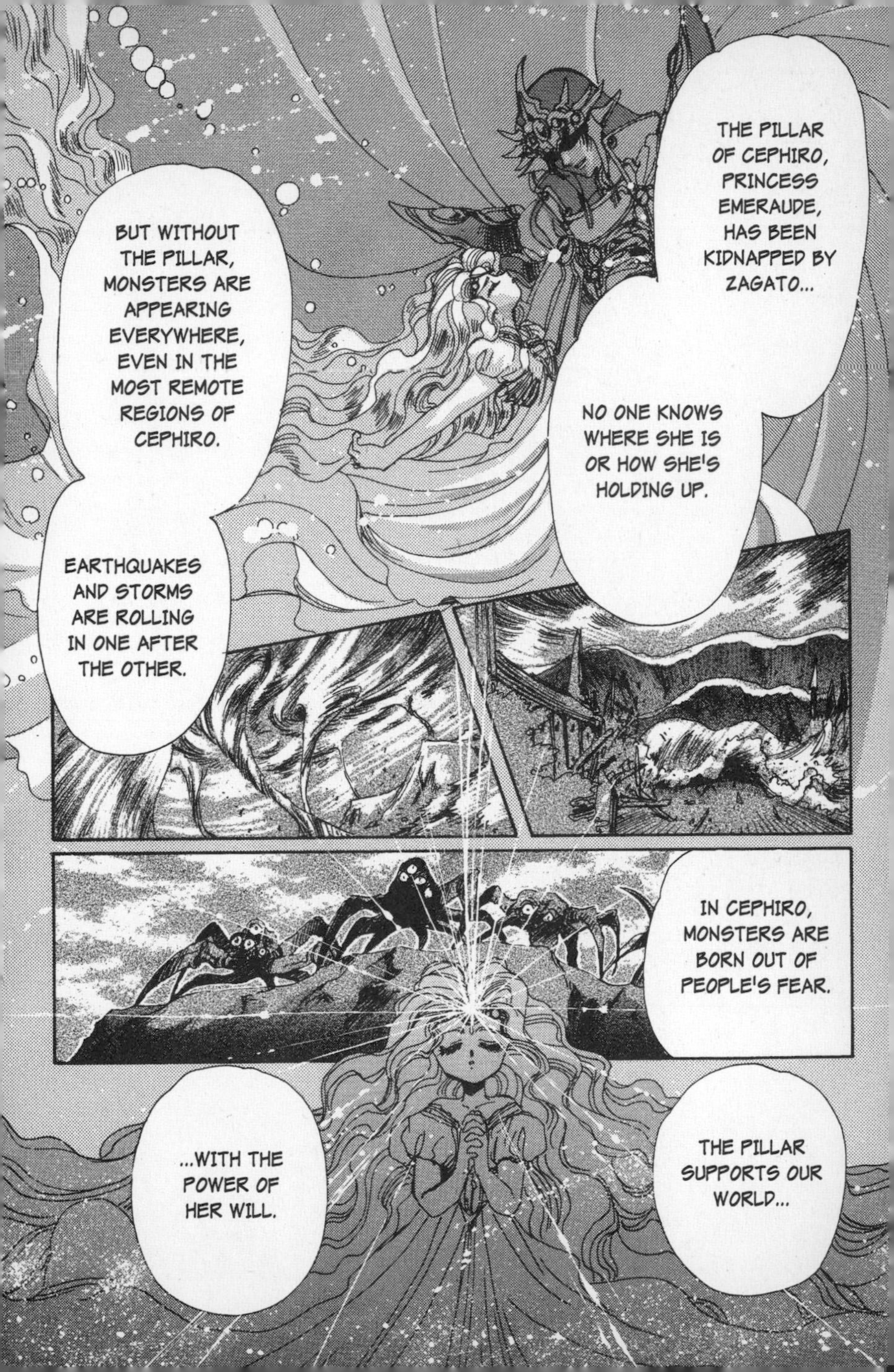
THE PILLAR OF CEPHIRO, PRINCESS EMERAUDE, HAS BEEN KIDNAPPED BY ZAGATO...
NO ONE KNOWS WHERE SHE IS OR HOW SHE'S HOLDING UP.
BUT WITHOUT THE PILLAR, MONSTERS ARE APPEARING EVERYWHERE, EVEN IN THE MOST REMOTE REGIONS OF CEPHIRO.
EARTHQUAKES AND STORMS ARE ROLLING IN ONE AFTER THE OTHER.
IN CEPHIRO, MONSTERS ARE BORN OUT OF PEOPLE'S FEAR.
THE PILLAR SUPPORTS OUR WORLD...
...WITH THE POWER OF HER WILL.

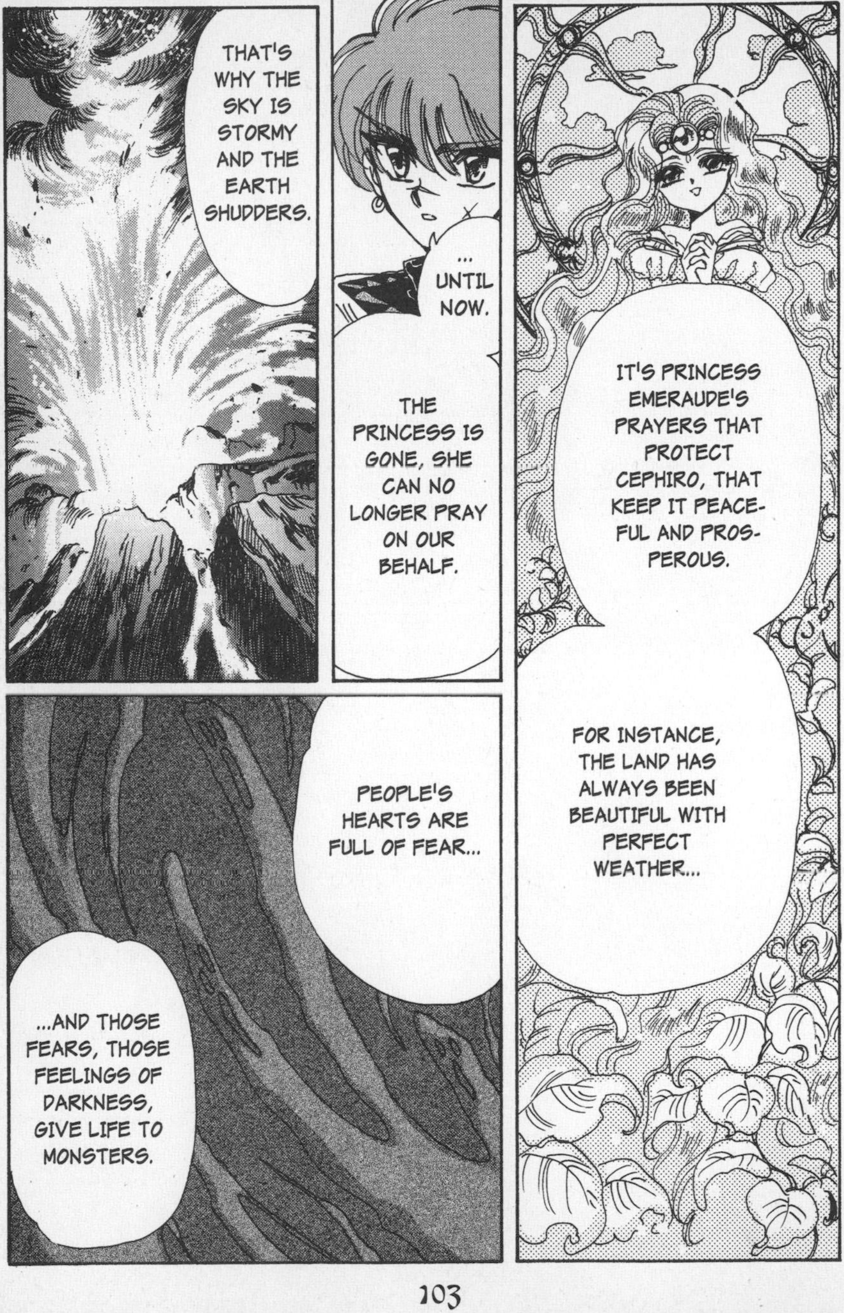
IT'S PRINCESS EMERAUDE'S PRAYERS THAT PROTECT CEPHIRO, THAT KEEP IT PEACE-FUL AND PROS-PEROUS.
FOR INSTANCE, THE LAND HAS ALWAYS BEEN BEAUTIFUL WITH PERFECT WEATHER...
... UNTIL NOW.
THE PRINCESS IS GONE, SHE CAN NO LONGER PRAY ON OUR BEHALF.
THAT'S WHY THE SKY IS STORMY AND THE EARTH SHUDDERS.
PEOPLE'S HEARTS ARE FULL OF FEAR...
...AND THOSE FEARS, THOSE FEELINGS OF DARKNESS, GIVE LIFE TO MONSTERS.

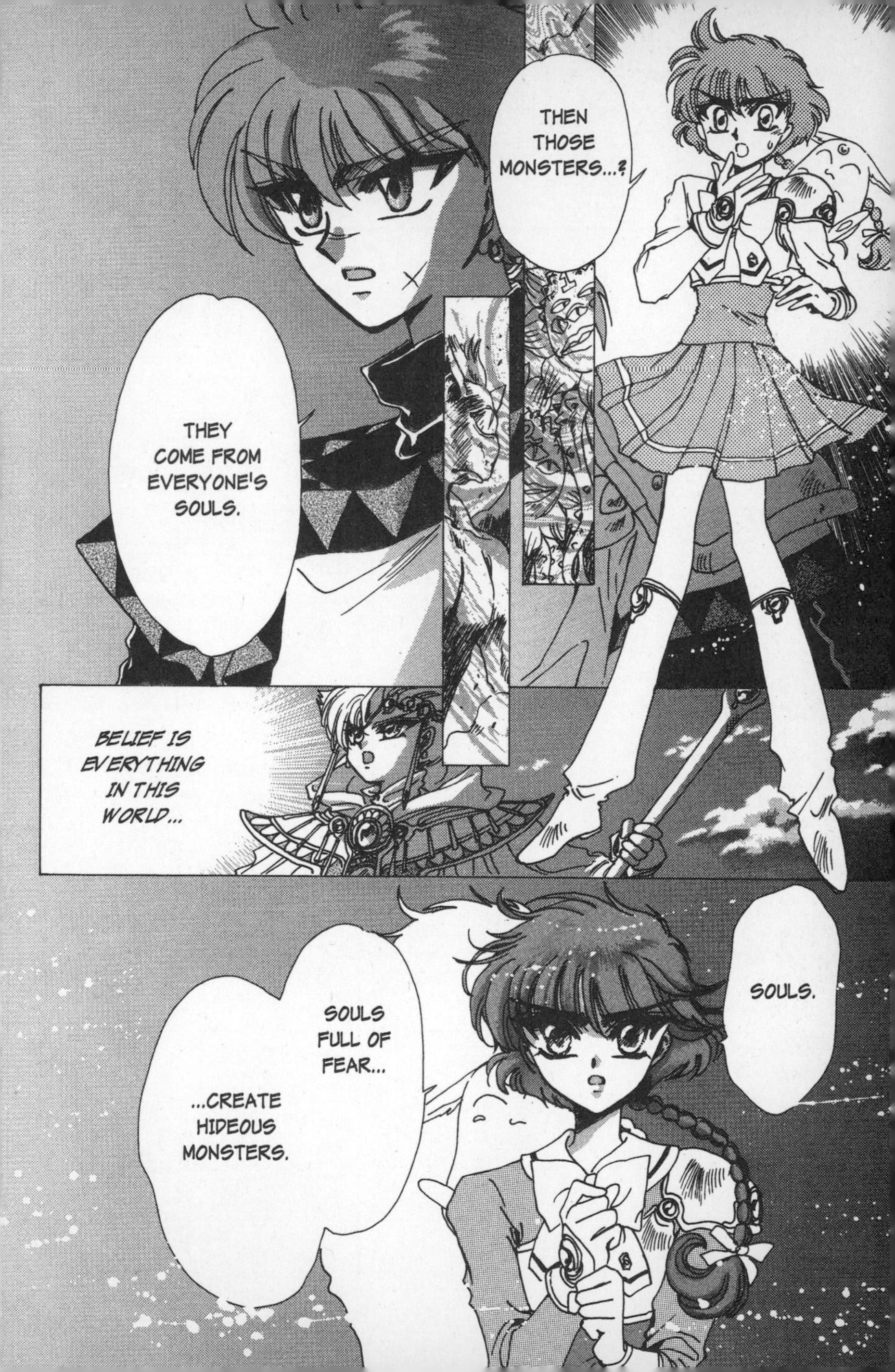
THEN THOSE MONSTERS...?
THEY COME FROM EVERYONE'S SOULS.
BELIEF IS EVERYTHING IN THIS WORLD...
SOULS.
SOULS FULL OF FEAR...
...CREATE HIDEOUS MONSTERS.

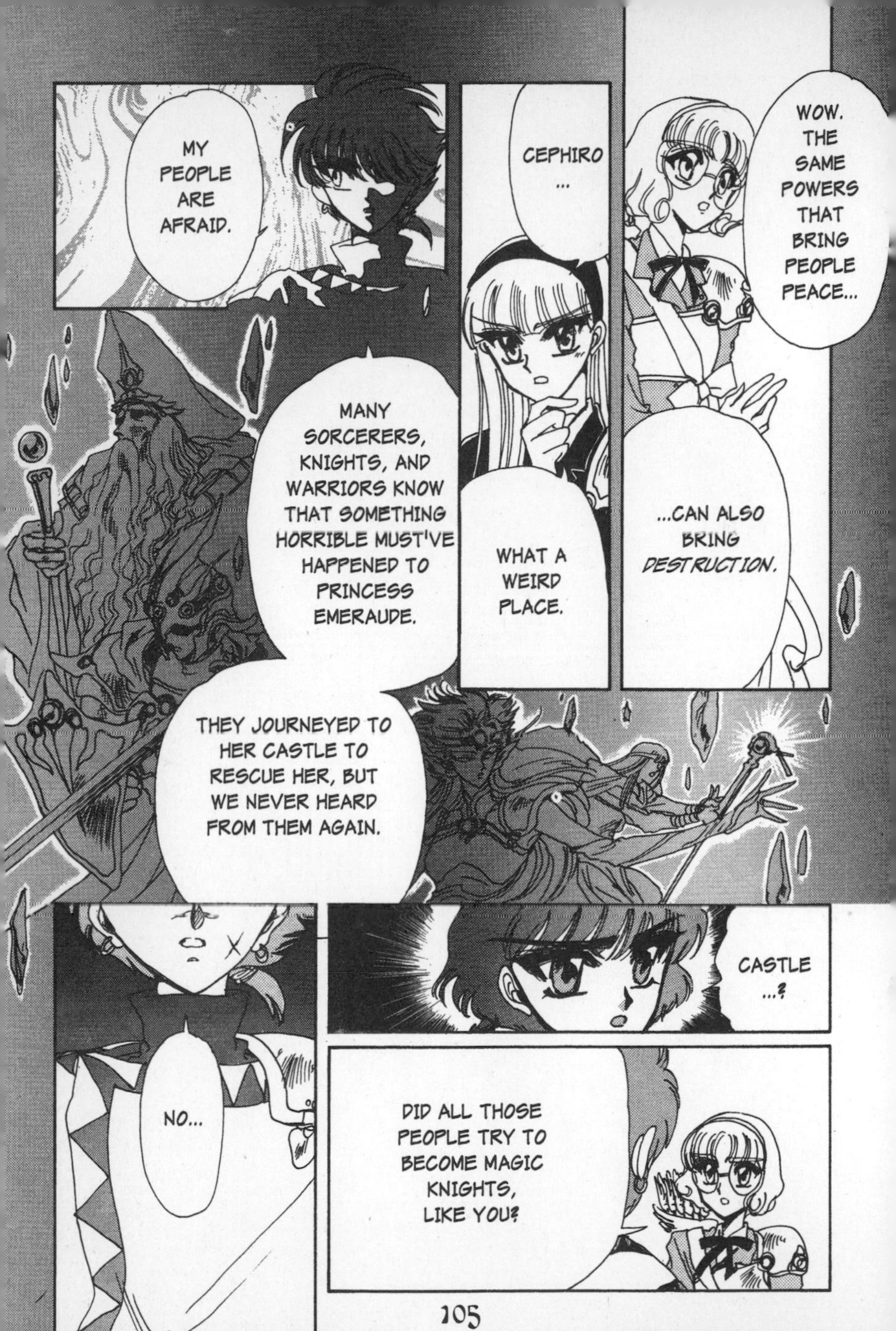
WOW. THE SAME POWERS THAT BRING PEOPLE PEACE...
...CAN ALSO BRING *DESTRUCTION*.
CEPHIRO ...
WHAT A WEIRD PLACE.
MY PEOPLE ARE AFRAID.
MANY SORCERERS, KNIGHTS, AND WARRIORS KNOW THAT SOMETHING HORRIBLE MUST'VE HAPPENED TO PRINCESS EMERAUDE.
THEY JOURNEYED TO HER CASTLE TO RESCUE HER, BUT WE NEVER HEARD FROM THEM AGAIN.
CASTLE ...?
DID ALL THOSE PEOPLE TRY TO BECOME MAGIC KNIGHTS, LIKE YOU?
NO...

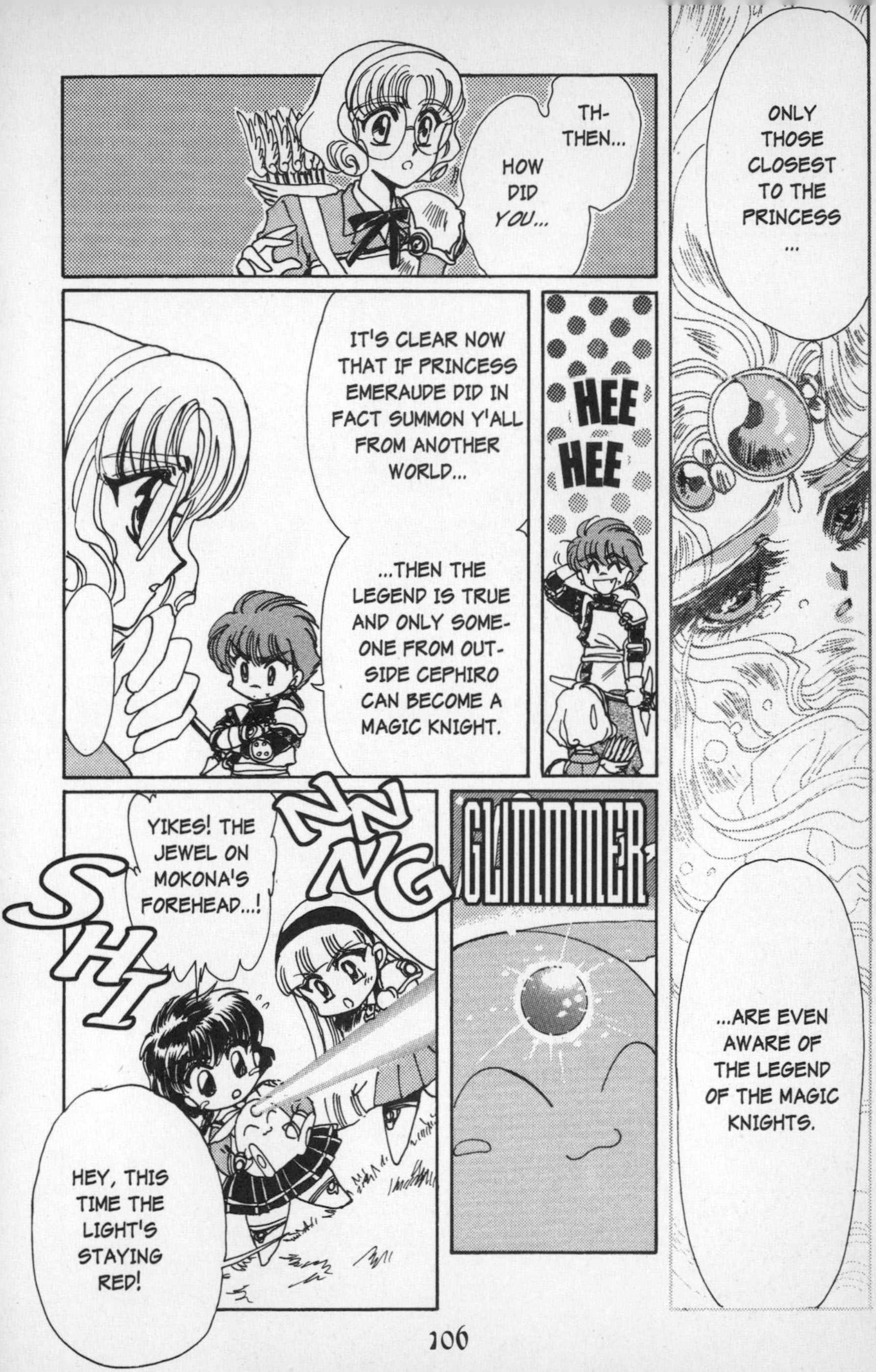
ONLY THOSE CLOSEST TO THE PRINCESS ...
...ARE EVEN AWARE OF THE LEGEND OF THE MAGIC KNIGHTS.
TH- THEN...
HOW DID YOU...
HEE HEE
IT'S CLEAR NOW THAT IF PRINCESS EMERAUDE DID IN FACT SUMMON Y'ALL FROM ANOTHER WORLD...
...THEN THE LEGEND IS TRUE AND ONLY SOME-ONE FROM OUT-SIDE CEPHIRO CAN BECOME A MAGIC KNIGHT.
GLIMMMER
NNNG
YIKES! THE JEWEL ON MOKONA'S FOREHEAD...!
SHI
HEY, THIS TIME THE LIGHT'S STAYING RED!

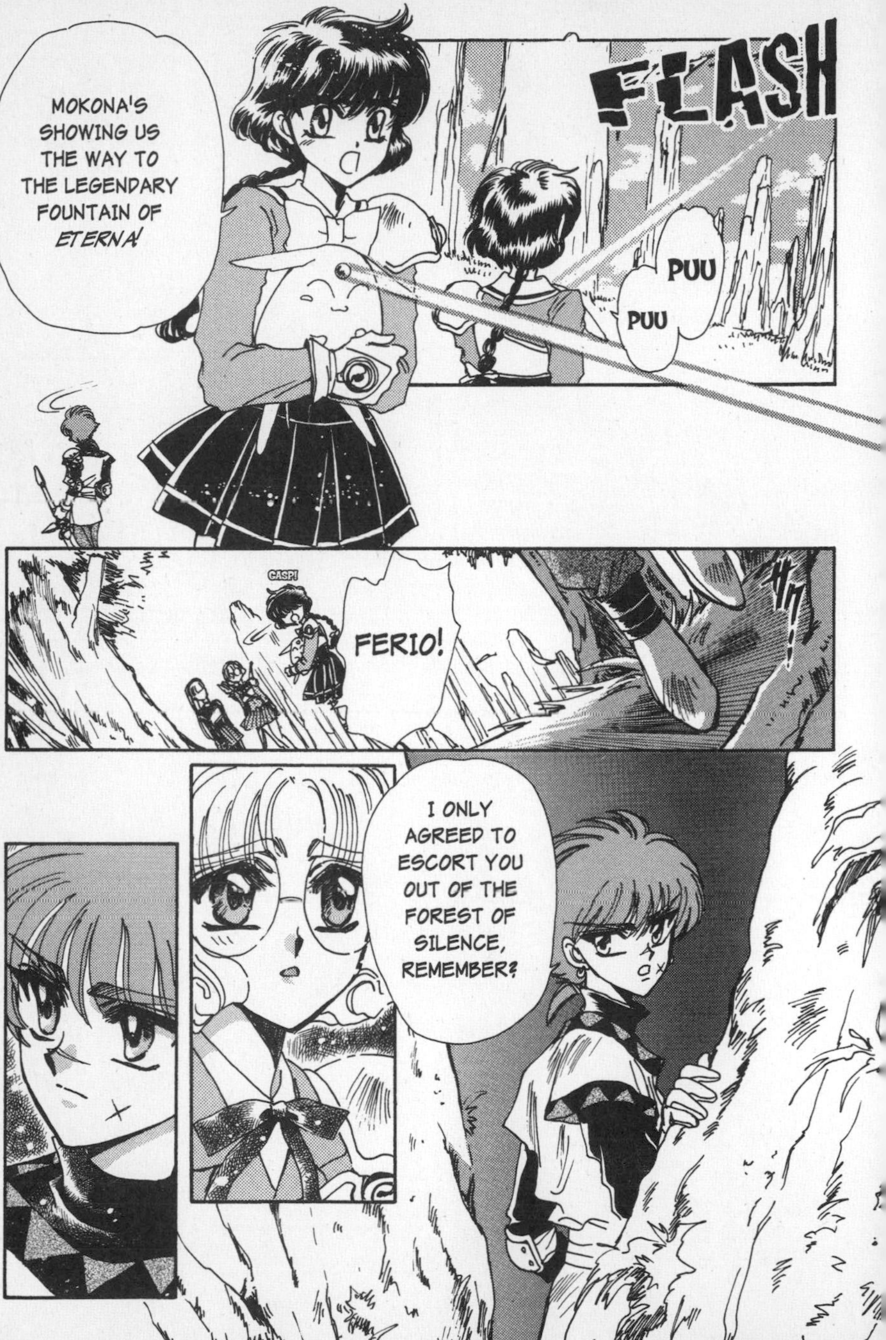
FLASH
PUU
PUU
MOKONA'S SHOWING US THE WAY TO THE LEGENDARY FOUNTAIN OF ETERNA!
GASP!
FERIO!
I ONLY AGREED TO ESCORT YOU OUT OF THE FOREST OF SILENCE, REMEMBER?

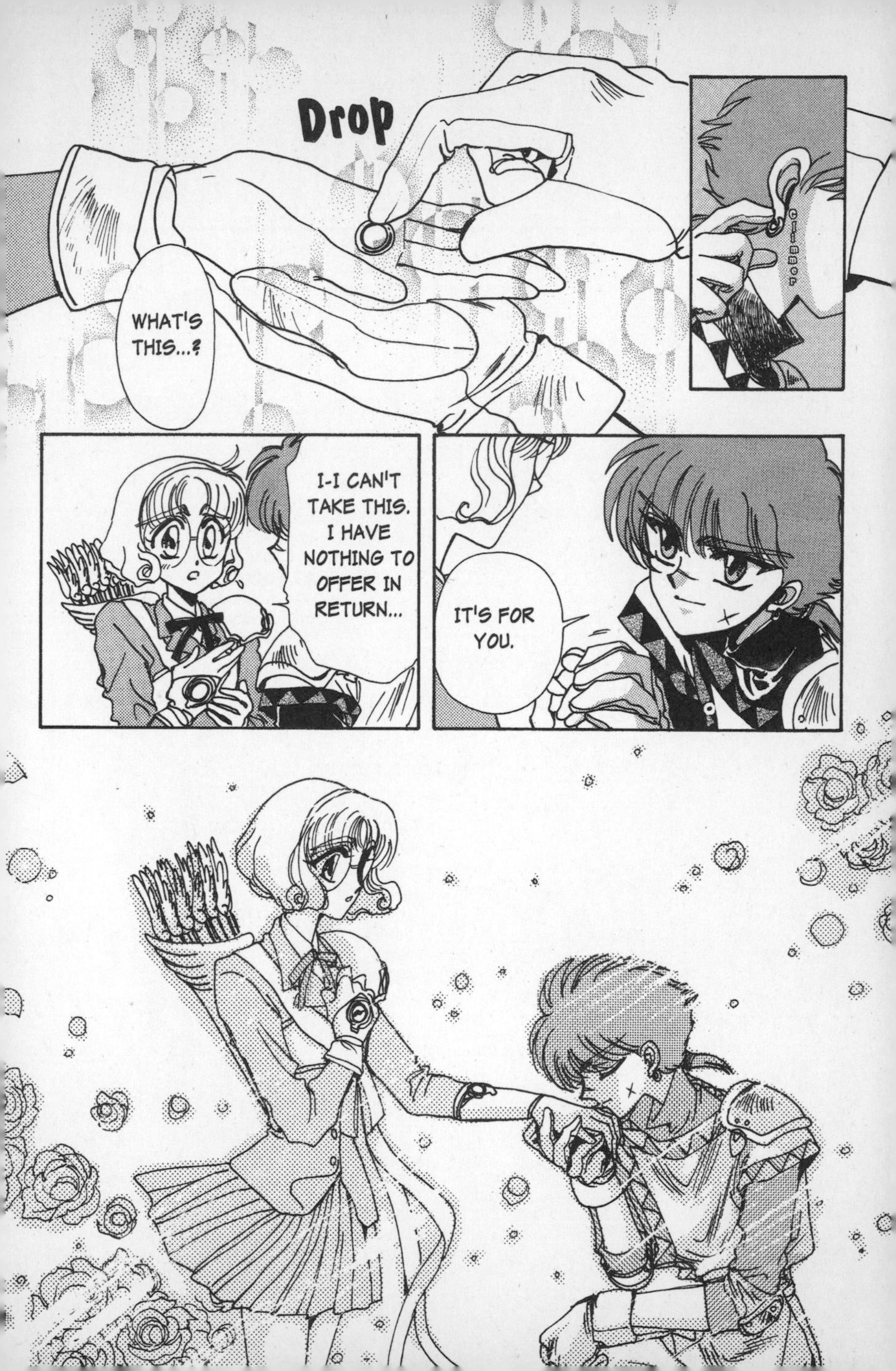
Glimmer
Drop
WHAT'S THIS...?
IT'S FOR YOU.
I-I CAN'T TAKE THIS. I HAVE NOTHING TO OFFER IN RETURN...

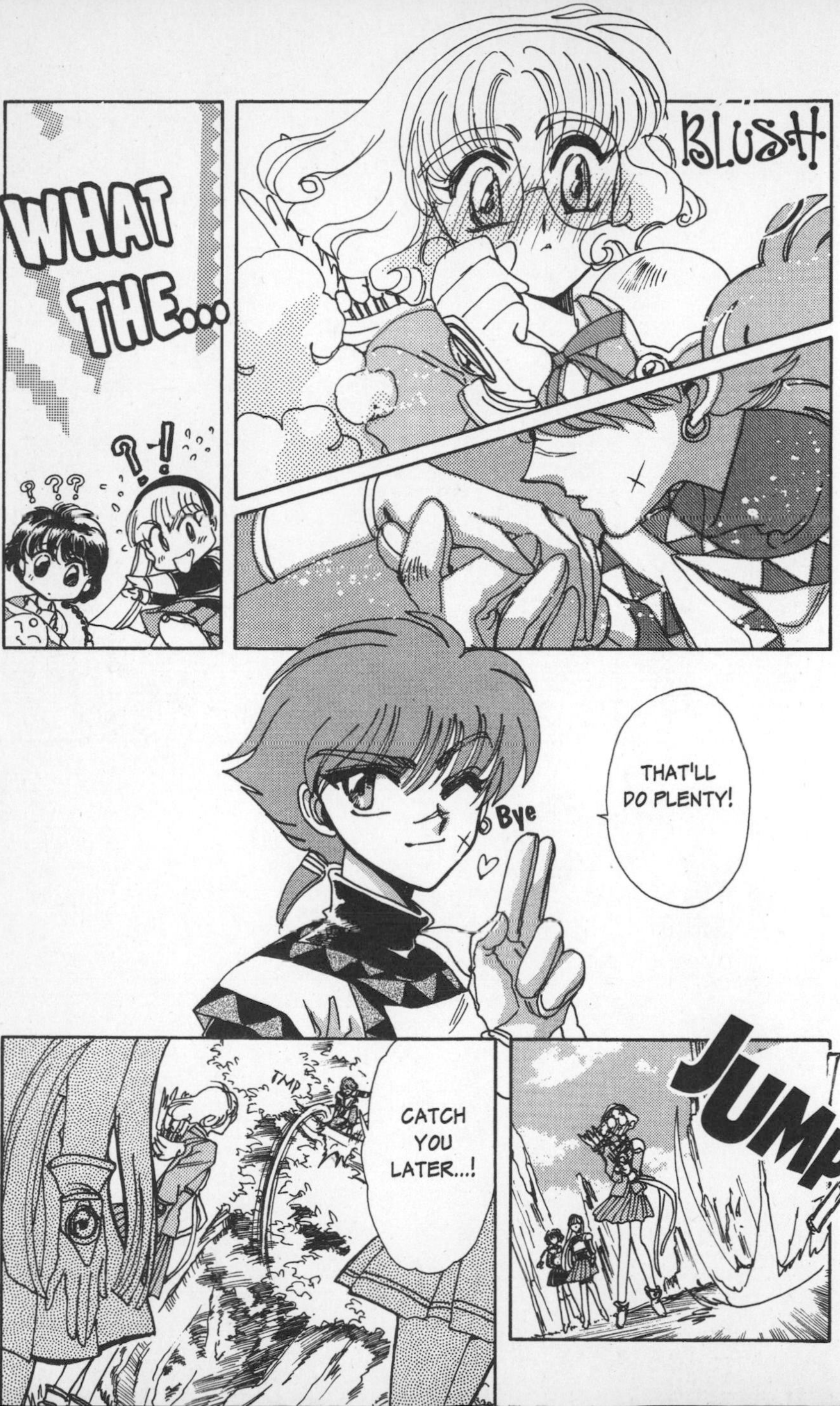
BLUSH
WHAT THE...
?!
THAT'LL DO PLENTY!
Bye
JUMP
CATCH YOU LATER...!
TMP

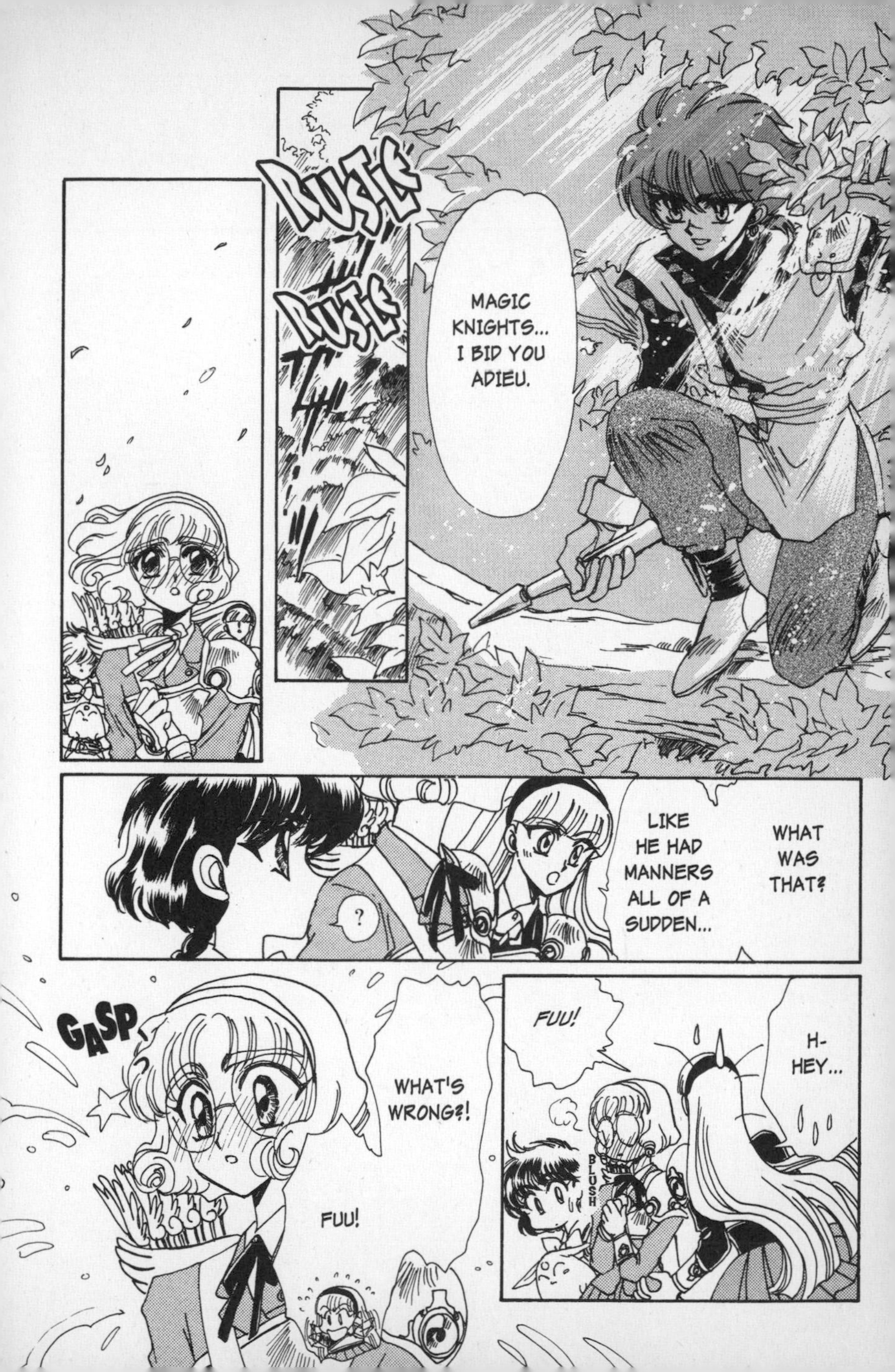
MAGIC KNIGHTS... I BID YOU ADIEU.
RUSTLE
RUSTLE
WHAT WAS THAT?
LIKE HE HAD MANNERS ALL OF A SUDDEN...
?
H- HEY...
FUU!
BLUSH
WHAT'S WRONG?!
FUU!
GASP

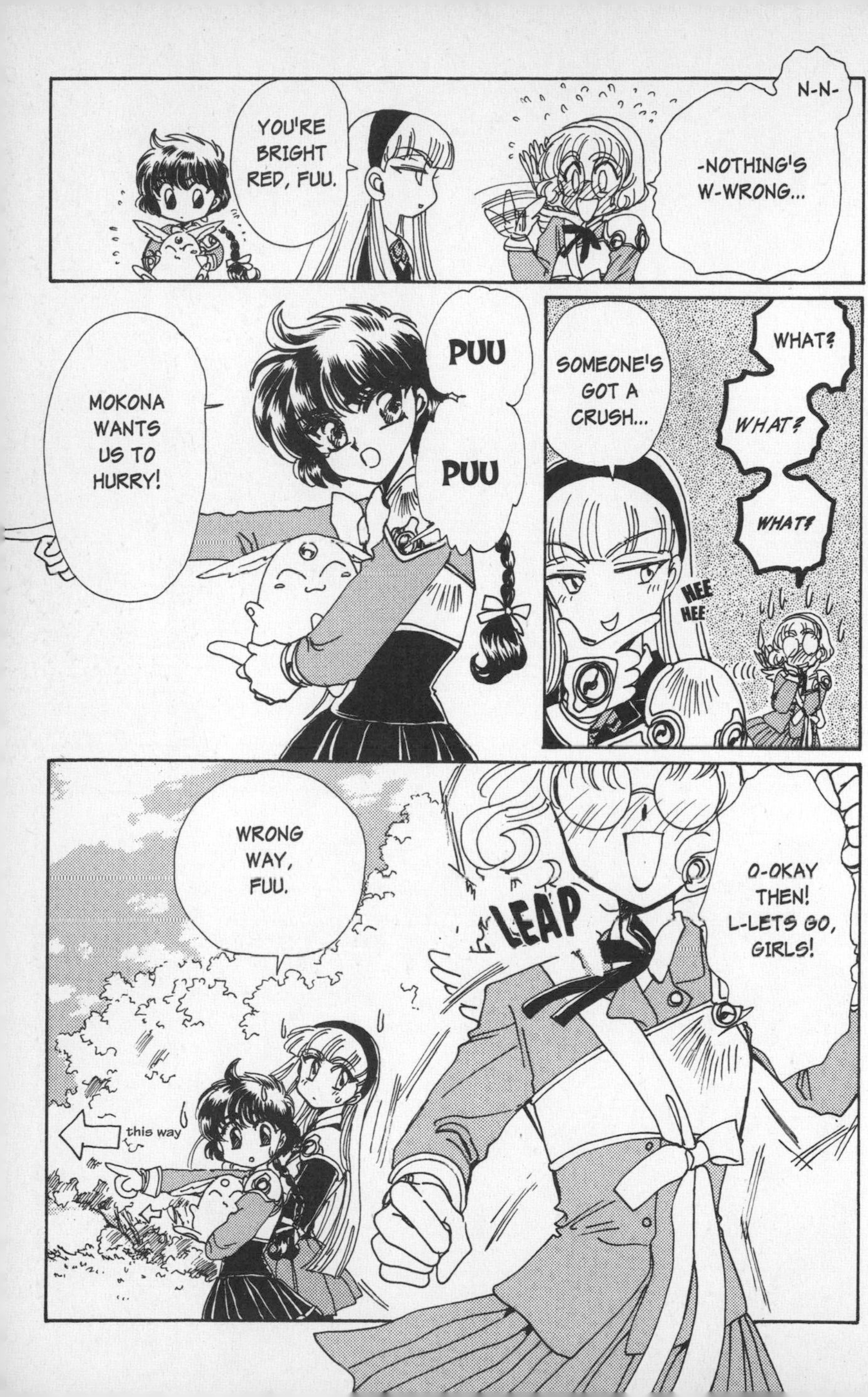
N-N-
-NOTHING'S W-WRONG...
YOU'RE BRIGHT RED, FUU.
SOMEONE'S GOT A CRUSH...
WHAT?
WHAT?
WHAT?
HEE HEE
PUU
PUU
MOKONA WANTS US TO HURRY!
O-OKAY THEN! L-LETS GO, GIRLS!
LEAP
WRONG WAY, FUU.
this way

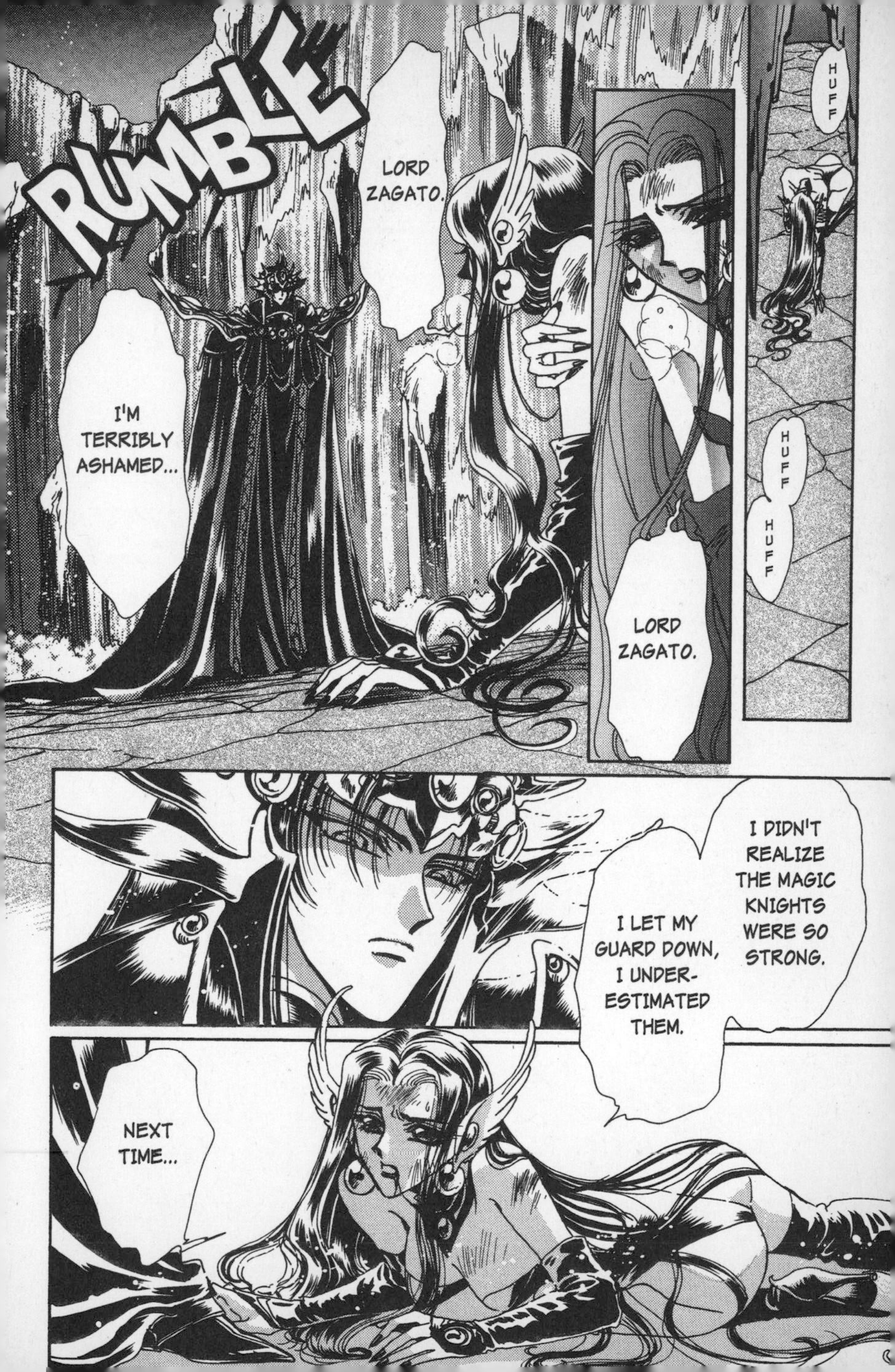
HUFF
HUFF HUFF
LORD ZAGATO.
RUMBLE
LORD ZAGATO.
I'M TERRIBLY ASHAMED...
I DIDN'T REALIZE THE MAGIC KNIGHTS WERE SO STRONG.
I LET MY GUARD DOWN, I UNDER-ESTIMATED THEM.
NEXT TIME...

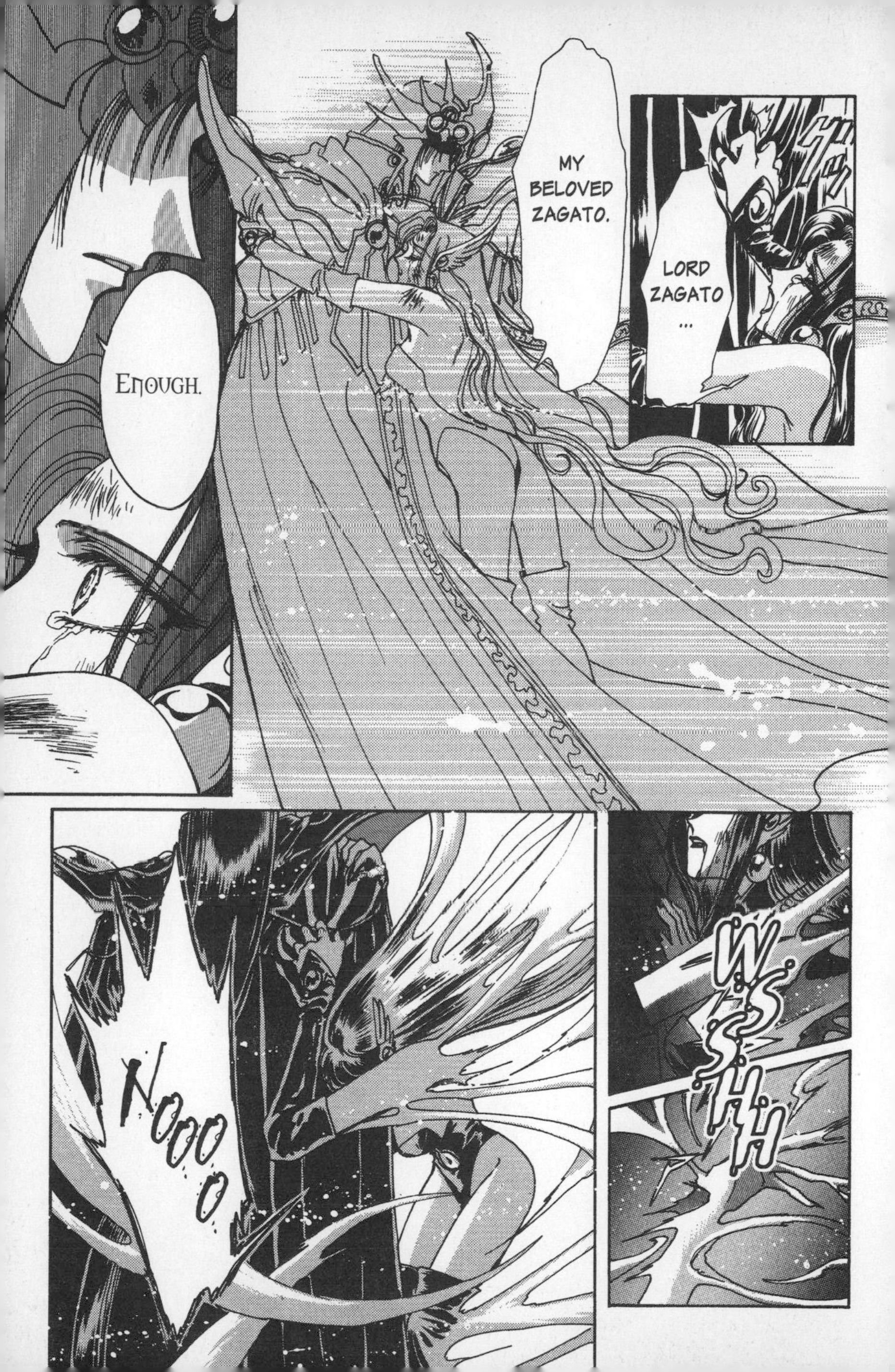
LORD ZAGATO ...
MY BELOVED ZAGATO.
ENOUGH.
WHSSH
NOOOOO

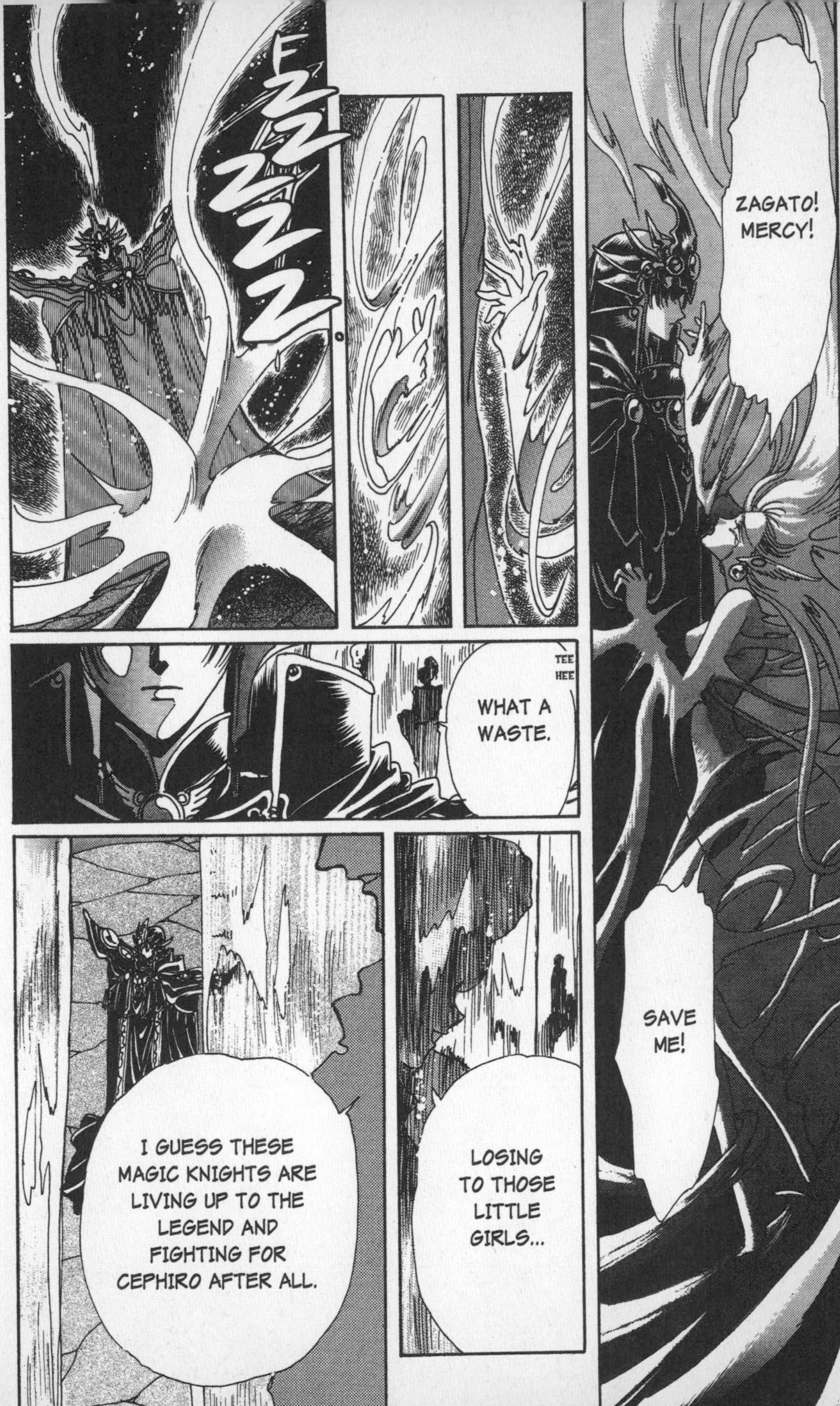
ZAGATO! MERCY!
SAVE ME!
FZZZZZZZ
TEE HEE
WHAT A WASTE.
LOSING TO THOSE LITTLE GIRLS...
I GUESS THESE MAGIC KNIGHTS ARE LIVING UP TO THE LEGEND AND FIGHTING FOR CEPHIRO AFTER ALL.

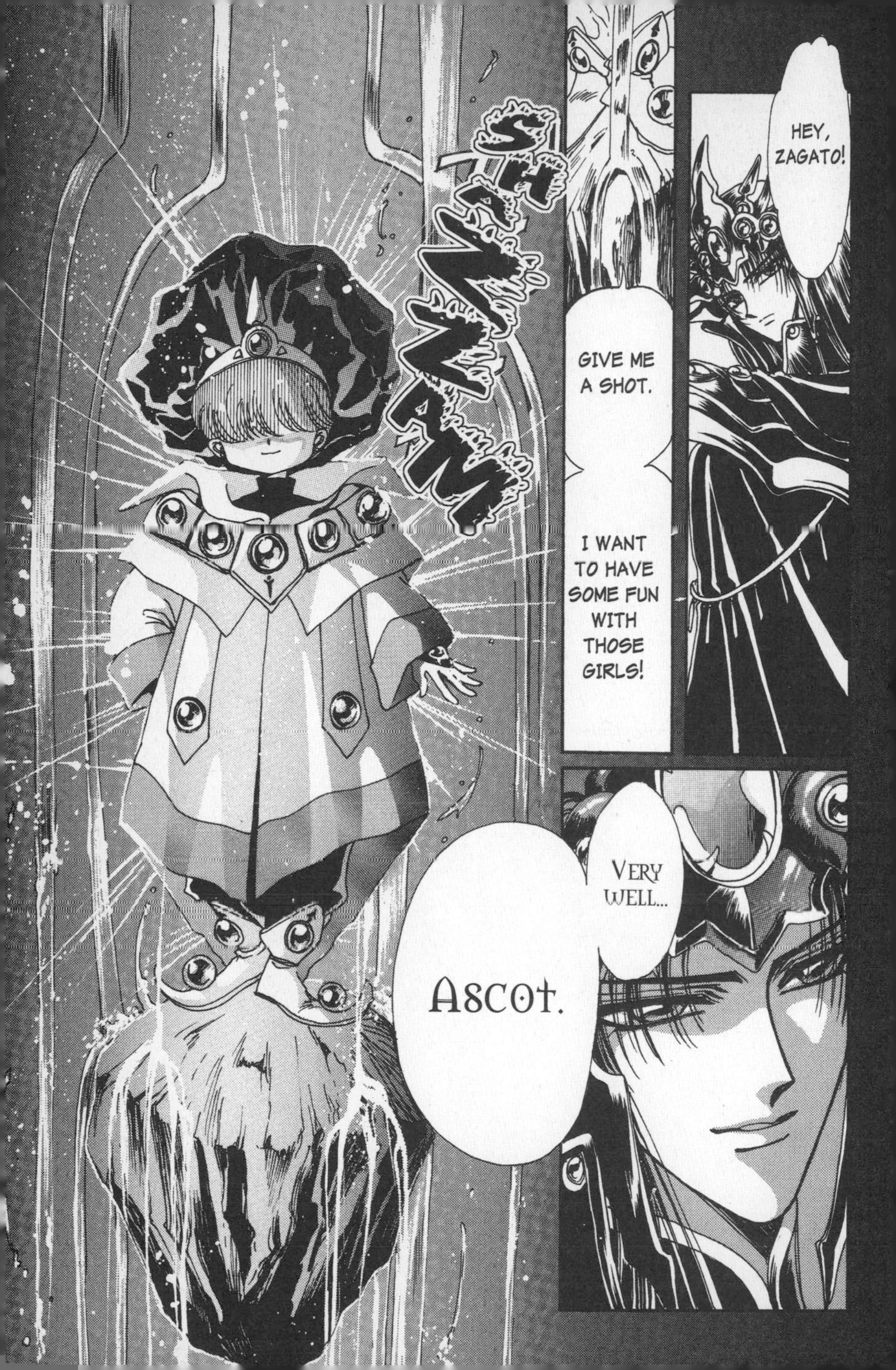
HEY, ZAGATO!
GIVE ME A SHOT.
I WANT TO HAVE SOME FUN WITH THOSE GIRLS!
VERY WELL...
Ascot.
SHAZAM!

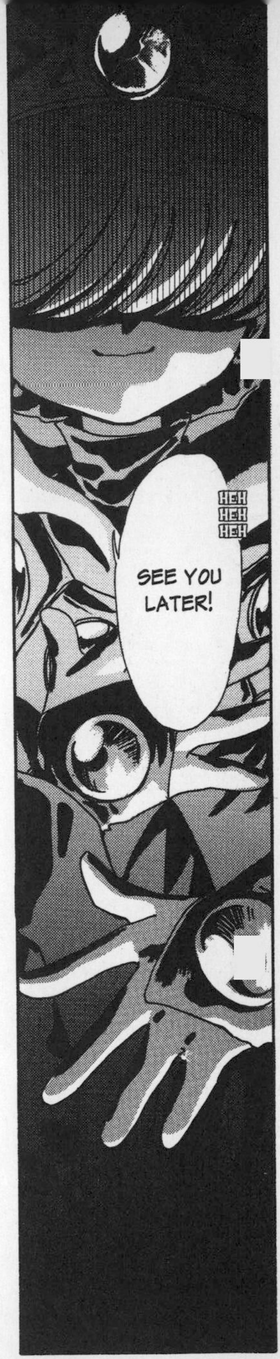
HEH HEH HEH
SEE YOU LATER!

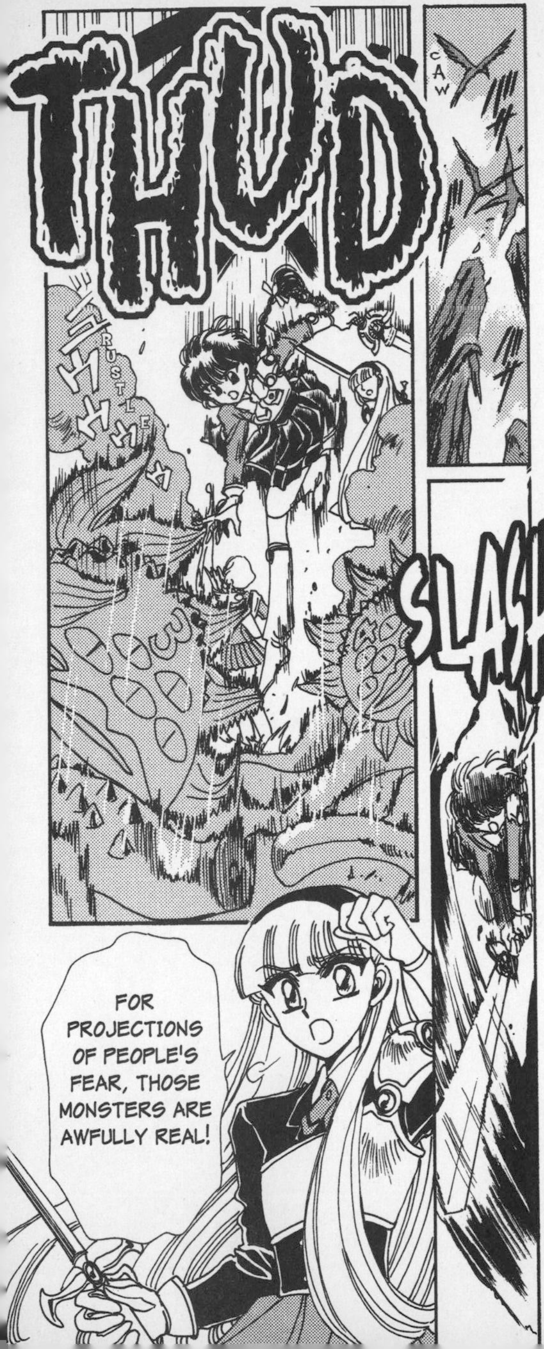
CAW
THUD
RUSTLE
SLASH
FOR PROJECTIONS OF PEOPLE'S FEAR, THOSE MONSTERS ARE AWFULLY REAL!

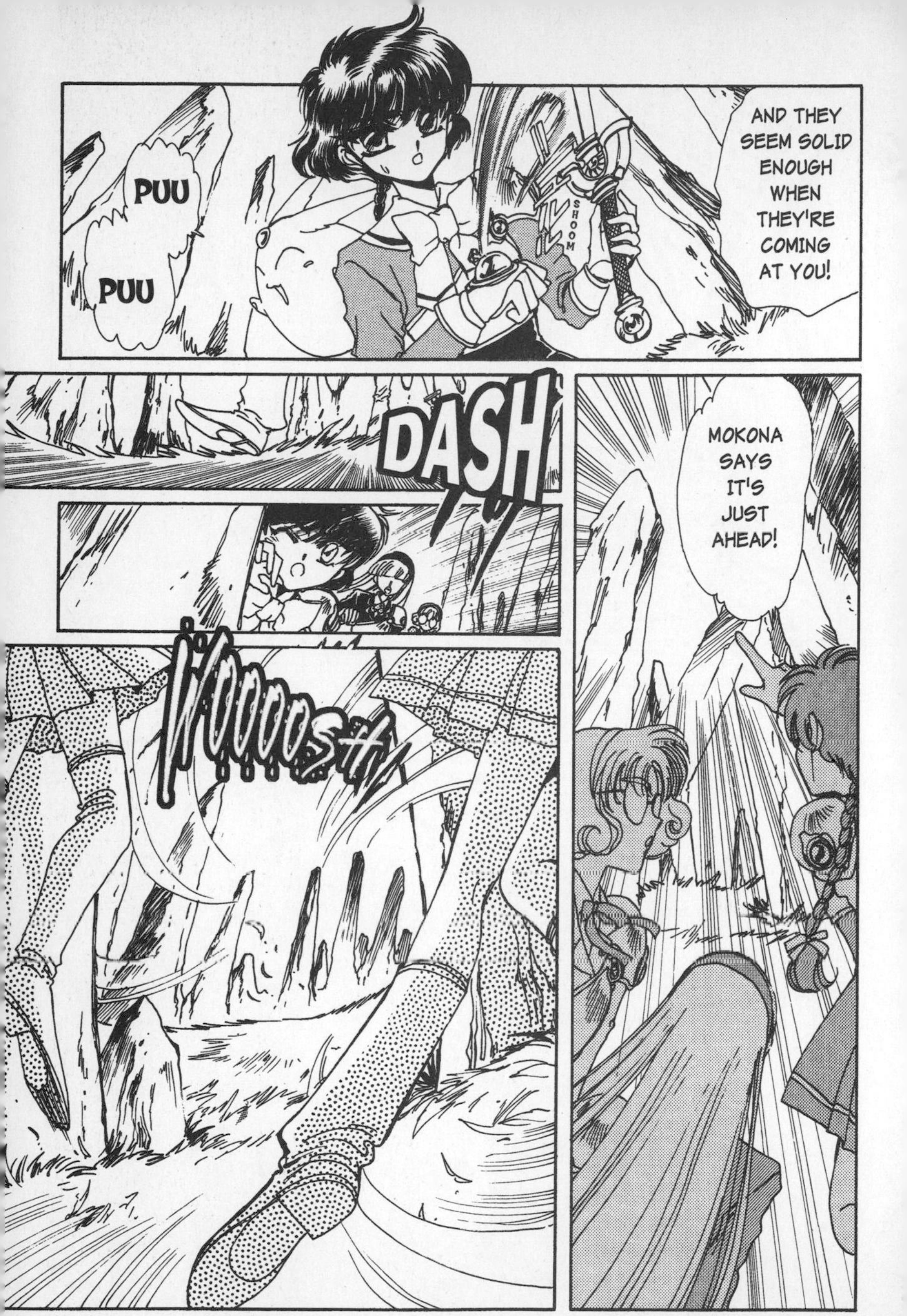
AND THEY SEEM SOLID ENOUGH WHEN THEY'RE COMING AT YOU!
SHOOM
PUU
PUU
MOKONA SAYS IT'S JUST AHEAD!
DASH

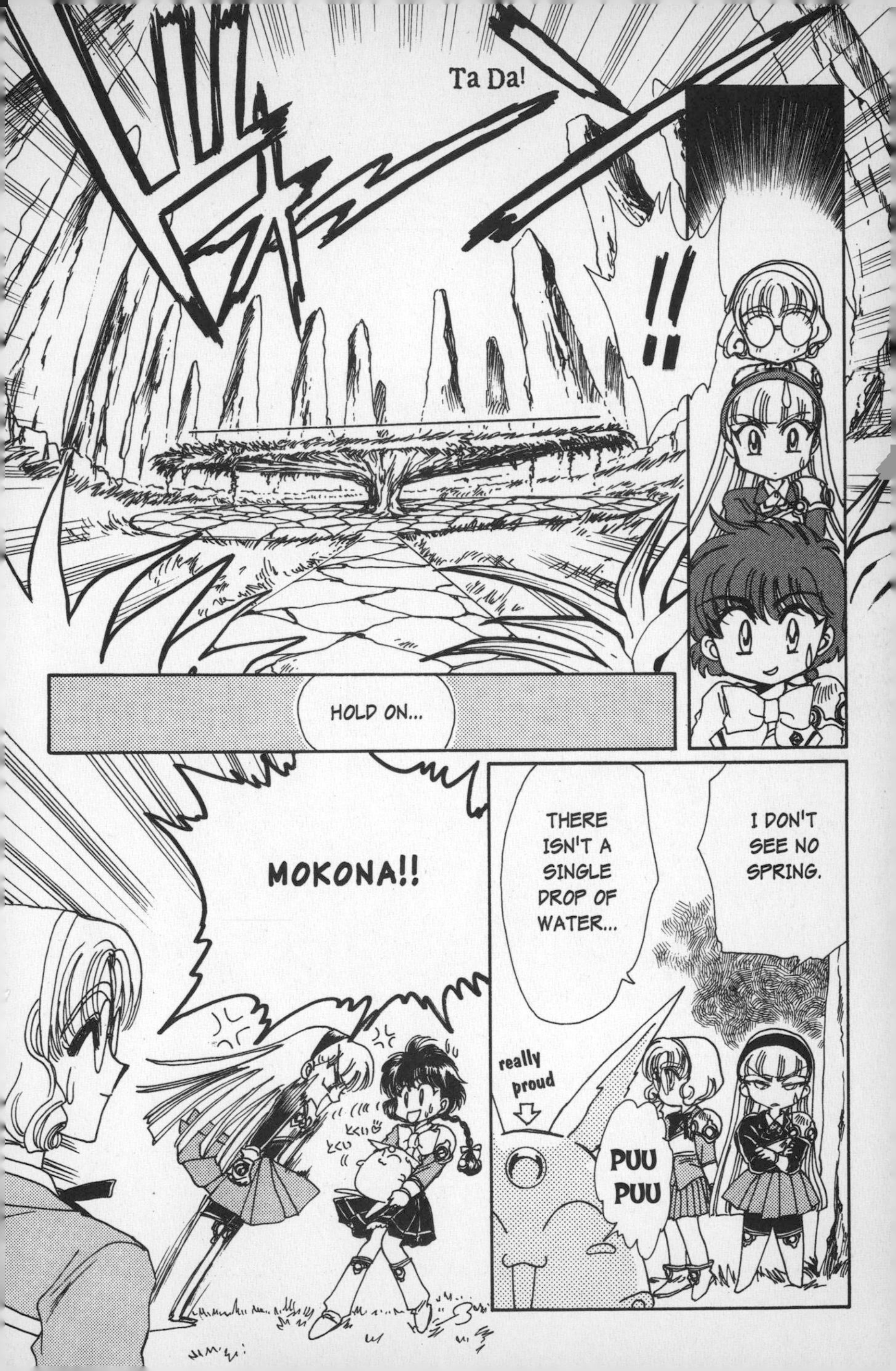

Ta Da!
!!
HOLD ON...
I DON'T SEE NO SPRING.
THERE ISN'T A SINGLE DROP OF WATER...
really proud
PUU PUU
MOKONA!!

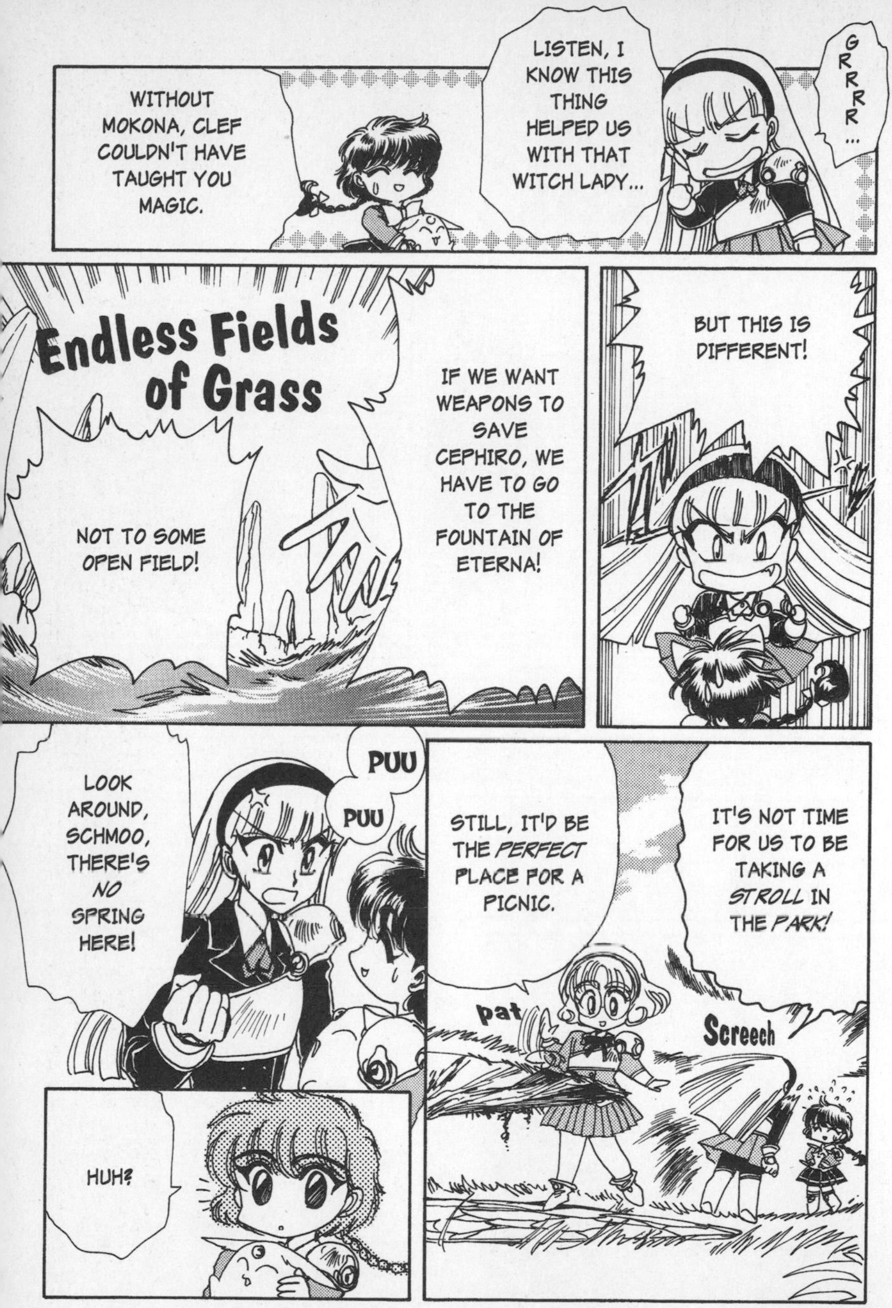
GRRR...
LISTEN, I KNOW THIS THING HELPED US WITH THAT WITCH LADY...
WITHOUT MOKONA, CLEF COULDN'T HAVE TAUGHT YOU MAGIC.
BUT THIS IS DIFFERENT!
IF WE WANT WEAPONS TO SAVE CEPHIRO, WE HAVE TO GO TO THE FOUNTAIN OF ETERNA!
Endless Fields of Grass
NOT TO SOME OPEN FIELD!
IT'S NOT TIME FOR US TO BE TAKING A *STROLL* IN THE *PARK!*
Screech
STILL, IT'D BE THE *PERFECT* PLACE FOR A PICNIC.
pat
PUU
PUU
LOOK AROUND, SCHMOO, THERE'S *NO* SPRING HERE!
HUH?

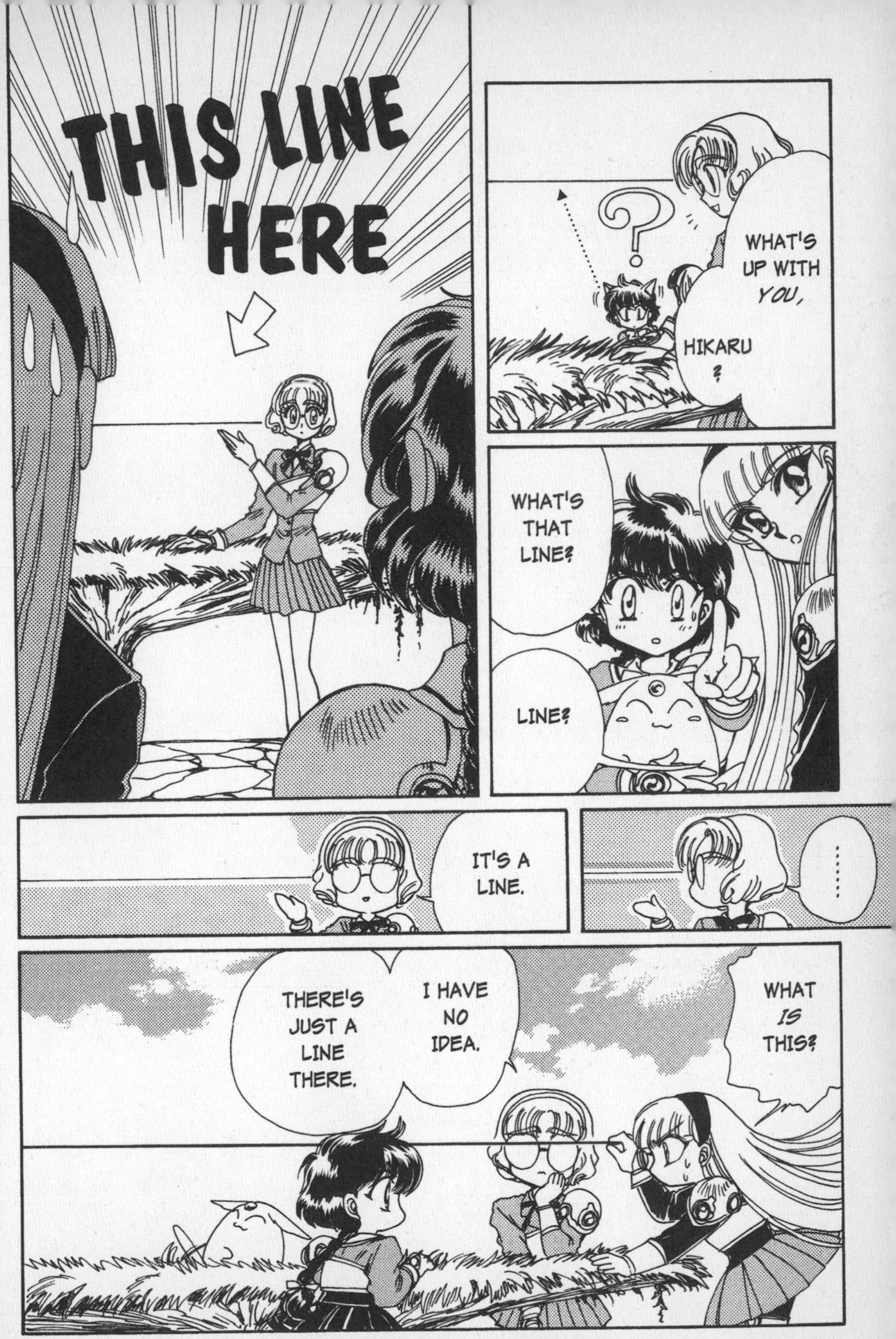
WHAT'S UP WITH *YOU*, HIKARU?
WHAT'S THAT LINE?
LINE?
THIS LINE HERE
......
IT'S A LINE.
WHAT *IS* THIS?
I HAVE NO IDEA.
THERE'S JUST A LINE THERE.

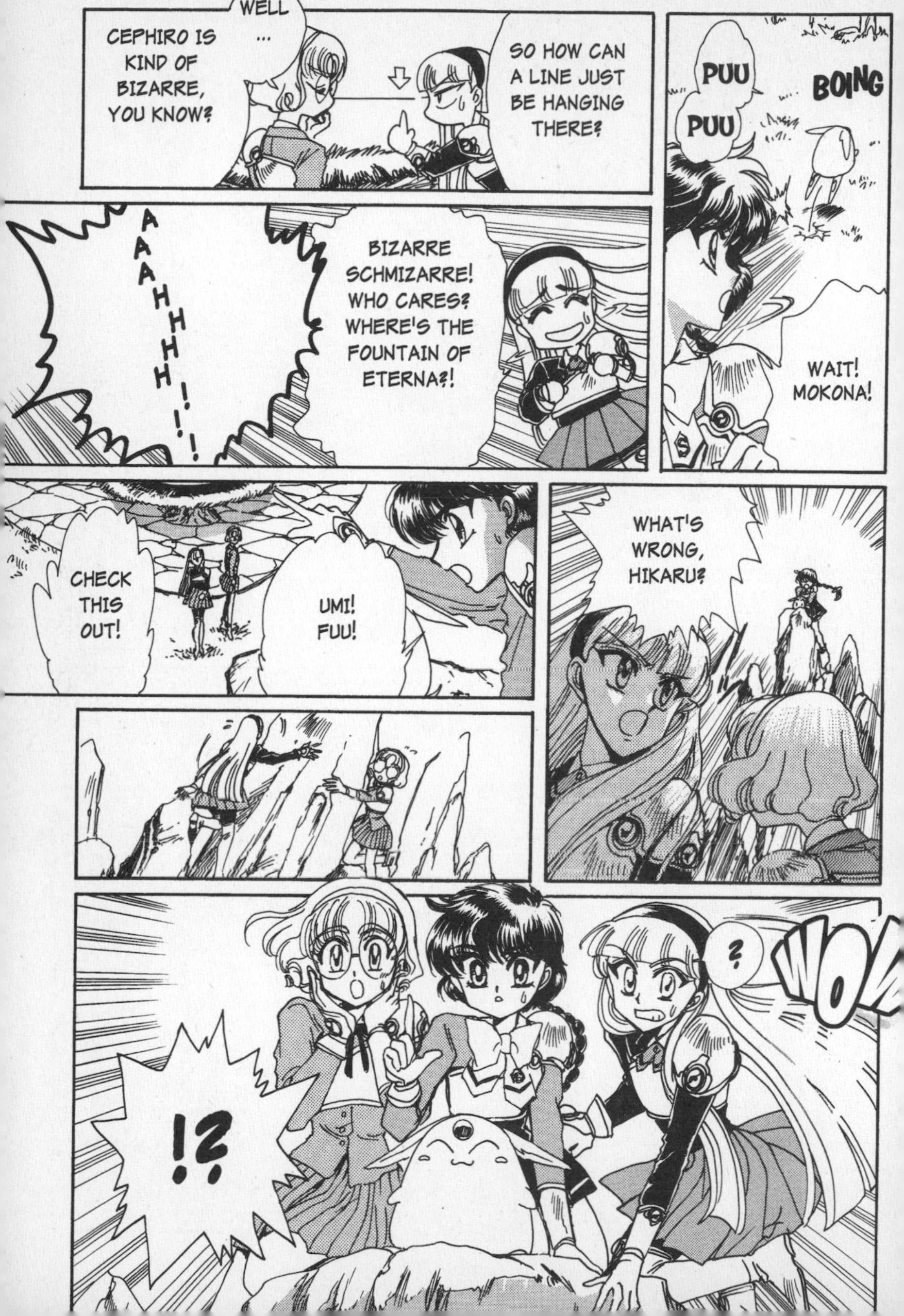
PUU
PUU
BOING
...
WAIT! MOKONA!
SO HOW CAN A LINE JUST BE HANGING THERE?
WELL ...
CEPHIRO IS KIND OF BIZARRE, YOU KNOW?
BIZARRE SCHMIZARRE! WHO CARES? WHERE'S THE FOUNTAIN OF ETERNA?!
AAAHHHH!!!
WHAT'S WRONG, HIKARU?
UMI! FUU!
CHECK THIS OUT!
WOW
?
!?

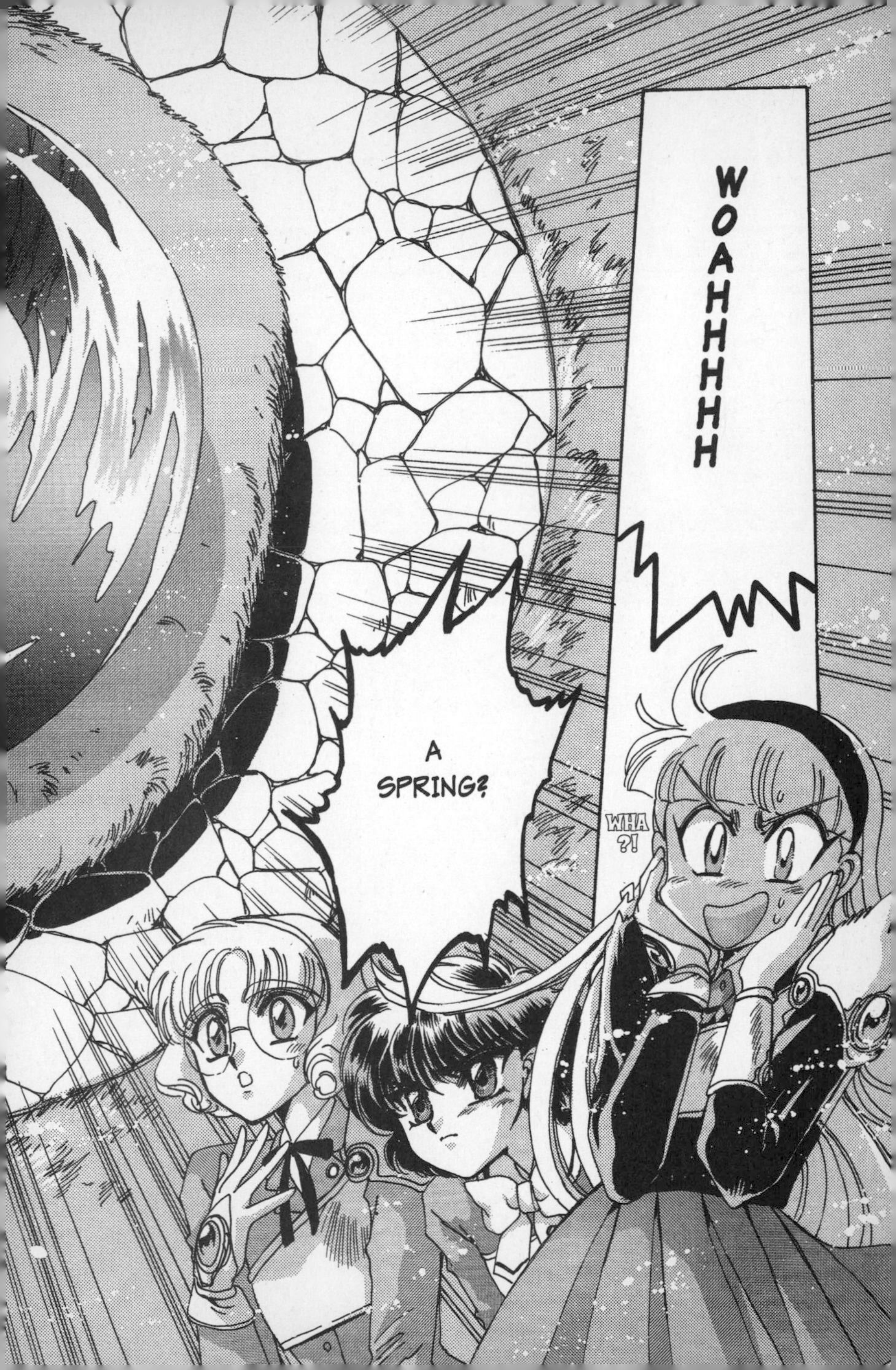
WOAHHHHH
WHA ?!
A SPRING?

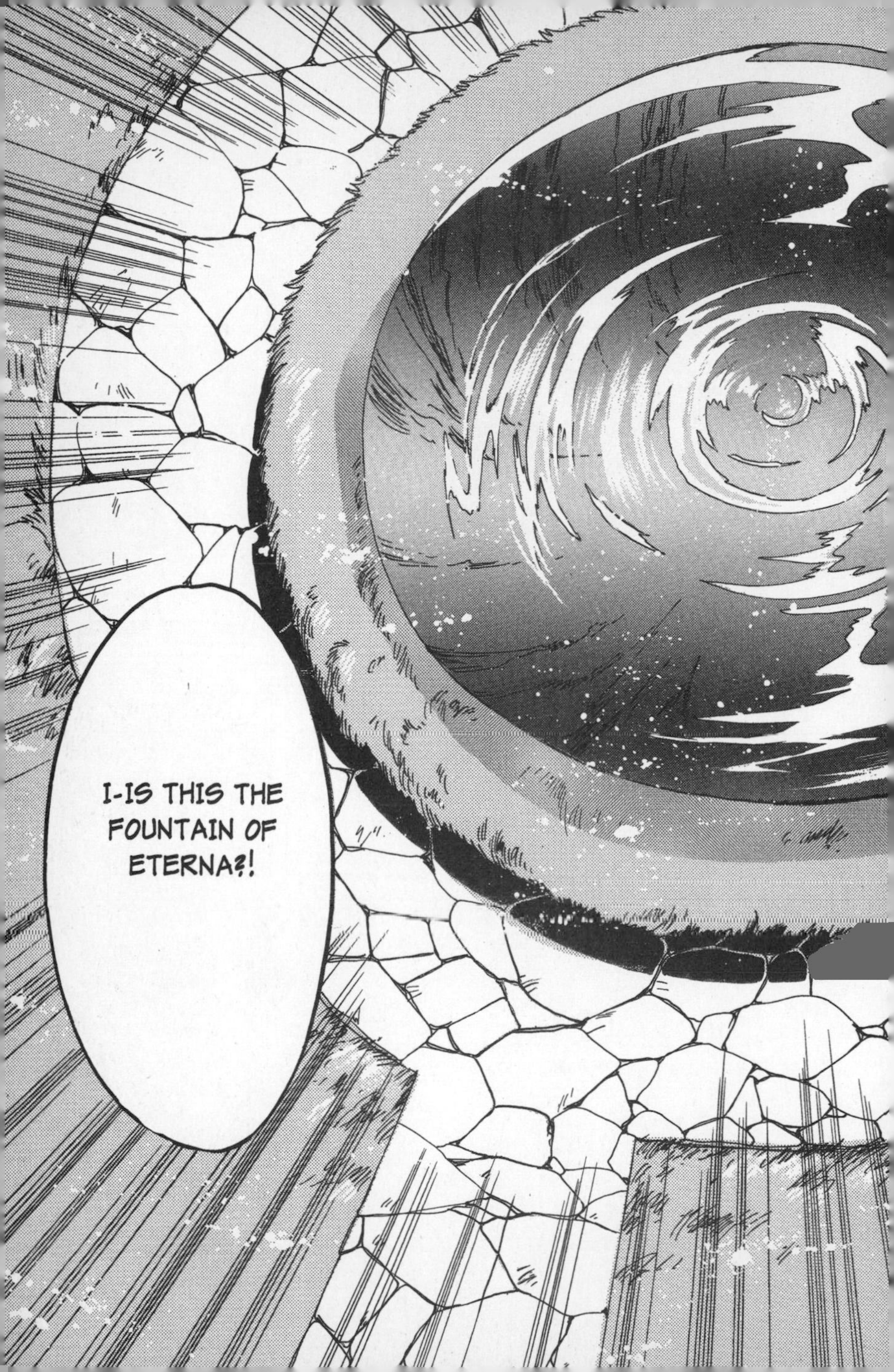
I-IS THIS THE FOUNTAIN OF ETERNA?!

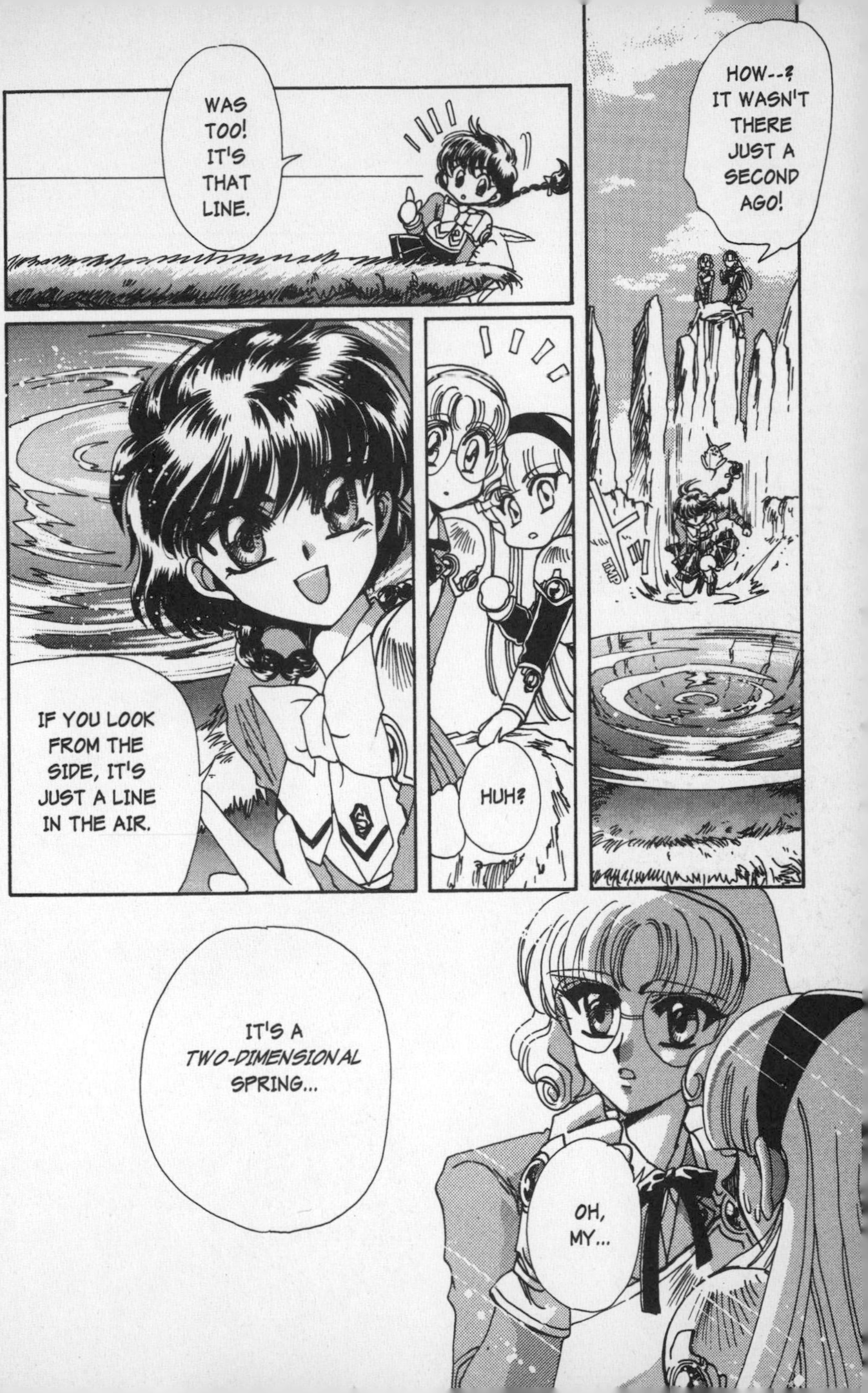
HOW--? IT WASN'T THERE JUST A SECOND AGO!
WAS TOO! IT'S THAT LINE.
HUH?
IF YOU LOOK FROM THE SIDE, IT'S JUST A LINE IN THE AIR.
OH, MY...
IT'S A *TWO-DIMENSIONAL* SPRING...

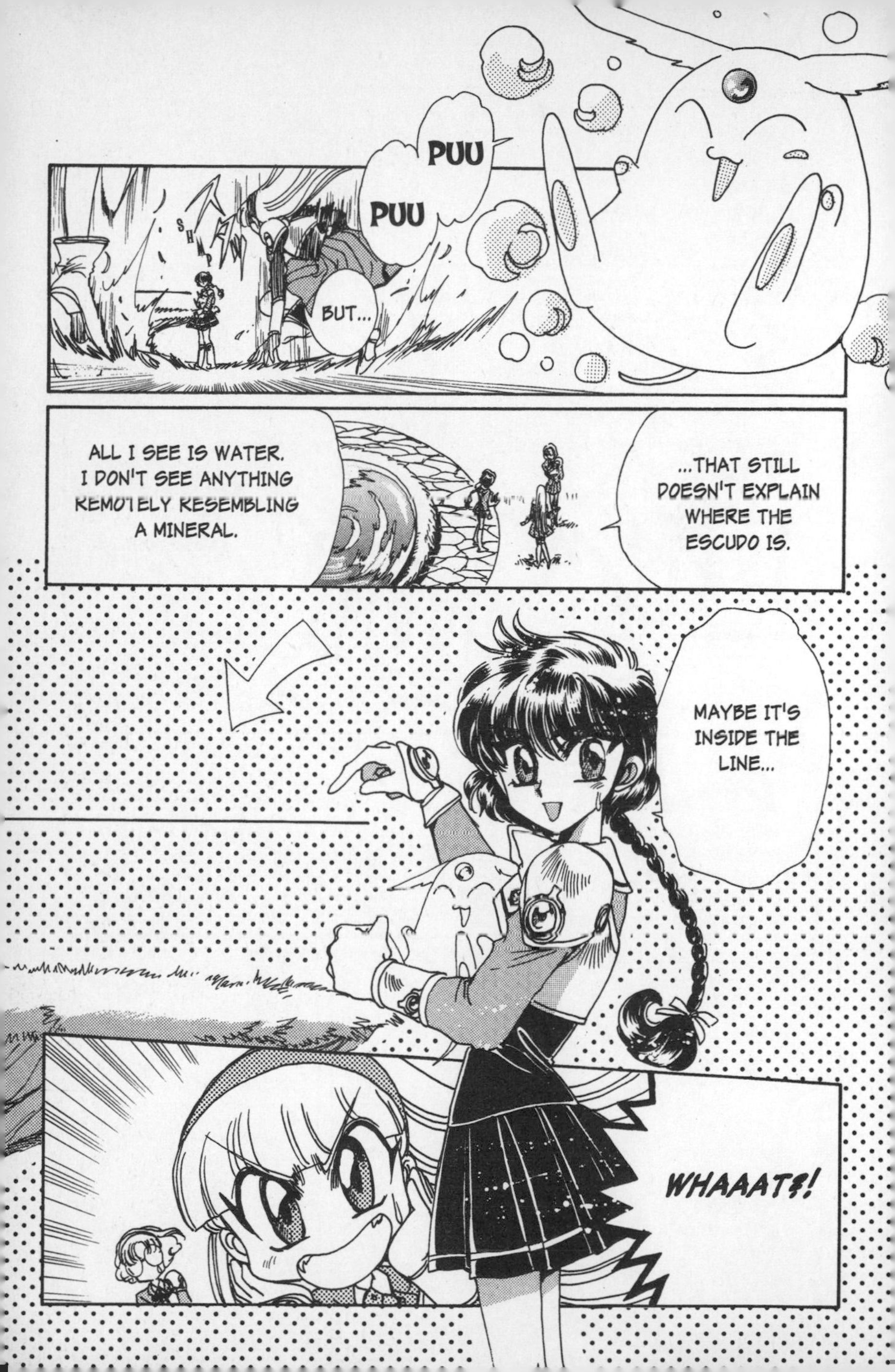
PUU
PUU
BUT...
SHMP
...THAT STILL DOESN'T EXPLAIN WHERE THE ESCUDO IS.
ALL I SEE IS WATER. I DON'T SEE ANYTHING REMOTELY RESEMBLING A MINERAL.
MAYBE IT'S INSIDE THE LINE...
WHAAAT?!

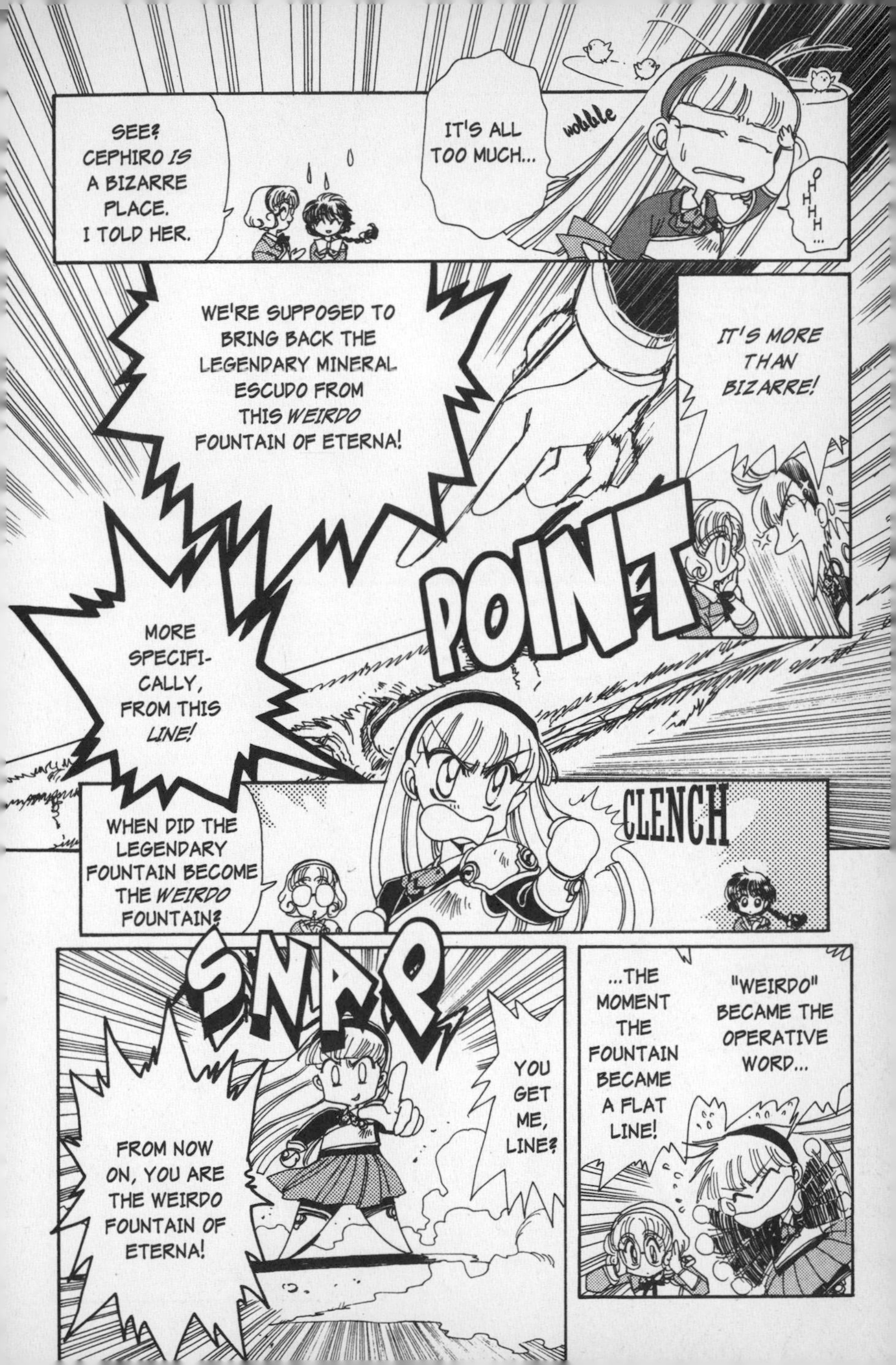
OHHHH...
wobble
IT'S ALL TOO MUCH...
SEE? CEPHIRO *IS* A BIZARRE PLACE. I TOLD HER.
IT'S MORE THAN BIZARRE!
WE'RE SUPPOSED TO BRING BACK THE LEGENDARY MINERAL ESCUDO FROM THIS *WEIRDO* FOUNTAIN OF ETERNA!
POINT
MORE SPECIFI-CALLY, FROM THIS *LINE!*
CLENCH
WHEN DID THE LEGENDARY FOUNTAIN BECOME THE *WEIRDO* FOUNTAIN?
"WEIRDO" BECAME THE OPERATIVE WORD...
...THE MOMENT THE FOUNTAIN BECAME A FLAT LINE!
SNAP
YOU GET ME, LINE?
FROM NOW ON, YOU ARE THE WEIRDO FOUNTAIN OF ETERNA!

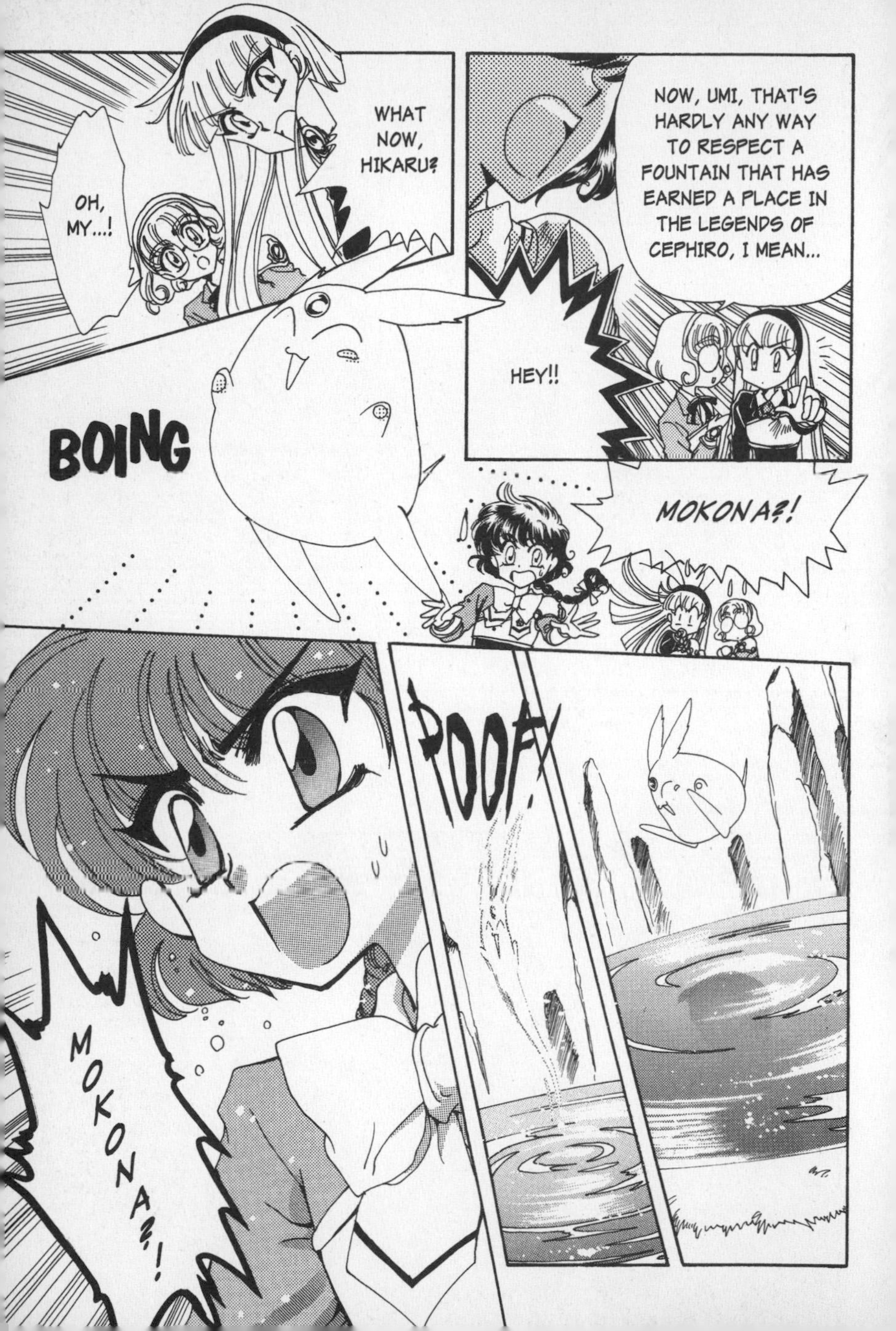
NOW, UMI, THAT'S HARDLY ANY WAY TO RESPECT A FOUNTAIN THAT HAS EARNED A PLACE IN THE LEGENDS OF CEPHIRO, I MEAN...
HEY!!
WHAT NOW, HIKARU?
OH, MY...!
BOING
MOKONA?!
POOF
MOKONA?!

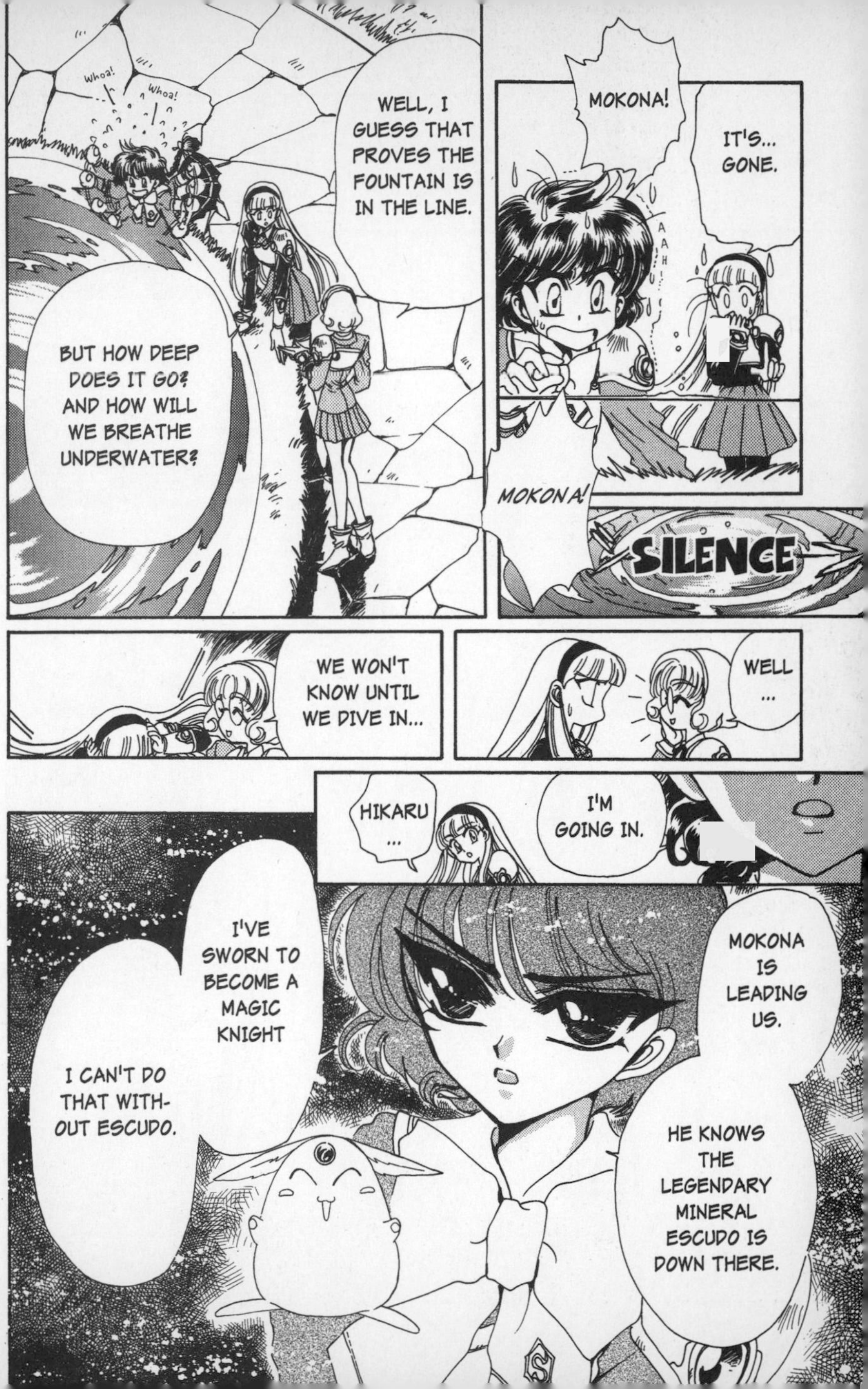
MOKONA!
IT'S... GONE.
AAH!
MOKONA!
SILENCE
Whoa!
Whoa!
WELL, I GUESS THAT PROVES THE FOUNTAIN IS IN THE LINE.
BUT HOW DEEP DOES IT GO? AND HOW WILL WE BREATHE UNDERWATER?
WELL ...
WE WON'T KNOW UNTIL WE DIVE IN...
I'M GOING IN.
HIKARU ...
MOKONA IS LEADING US.
HE KNOWS THE LEGENDARY MINERAL ESCUDO IS DOWN THERE.
I'VE SWORN TO BECOME A MAGIC KNIGHT
I CAN'T DO THAT WITH-OUT ESCUDO.

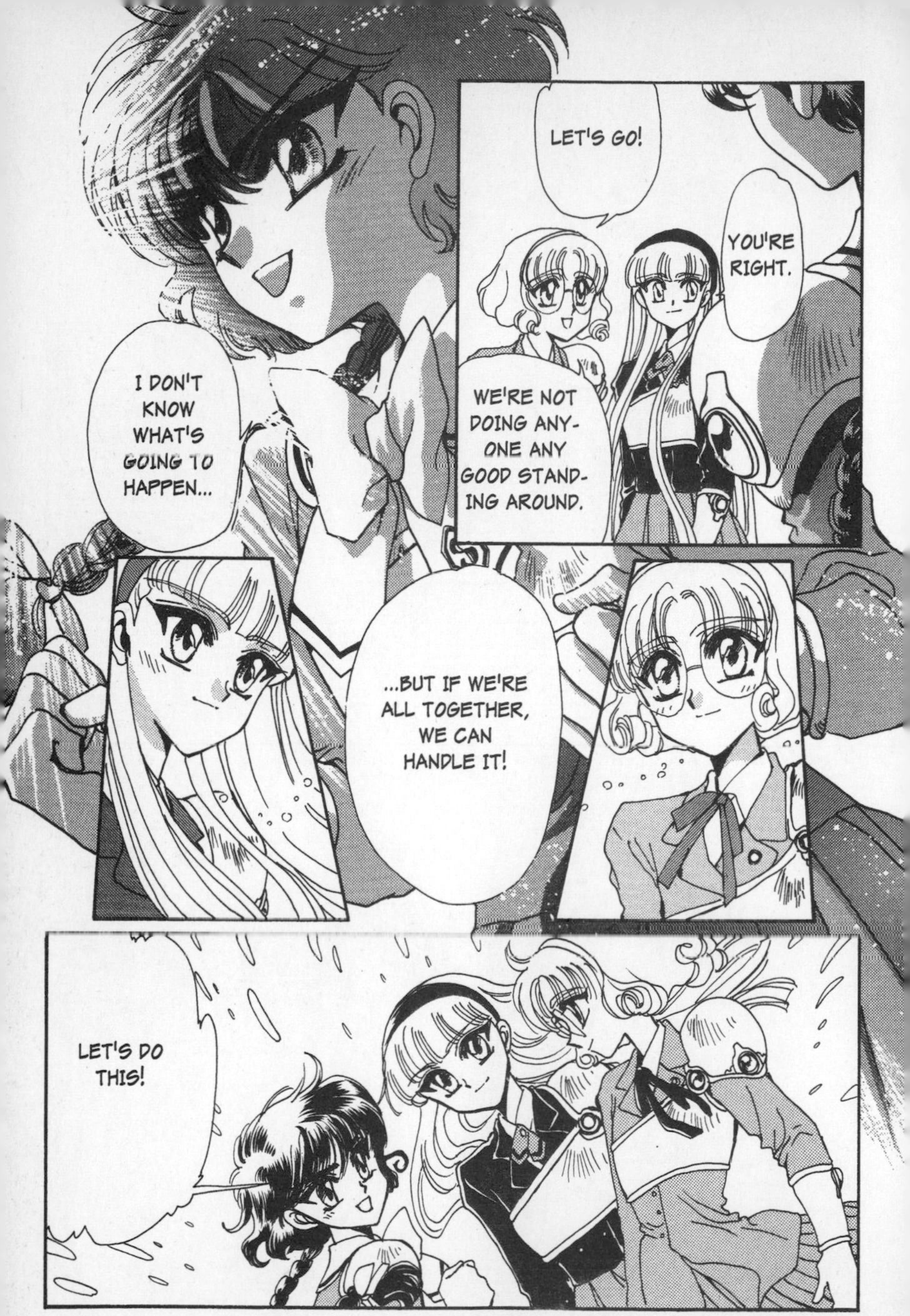
YOU'RE RIGHT.
LET'S GO!
WE'RE NOT DOING ANY-ONE ANY GOOD STAND-ING AROUND.
I DON'T KNOW WHAT'S GOING TO HAPPEN...
...BUT IF WE'RE ALL TOGETHER, WE CAN HANDLE IT!
LET'S DO THIS!

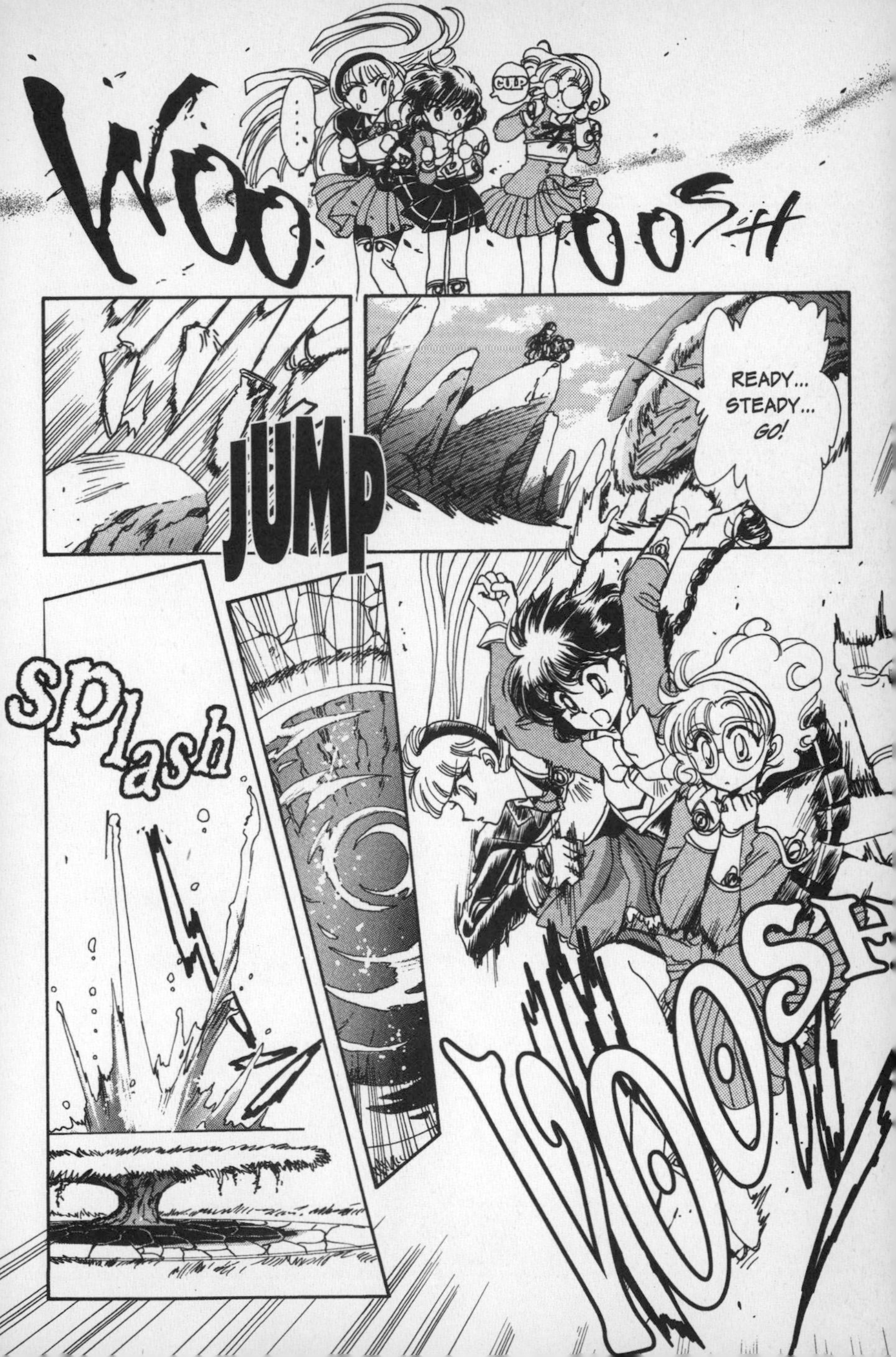
WOOOOSH
GULP
...
READY... STEADY... GO!
JUMP
WOOOSH
splash

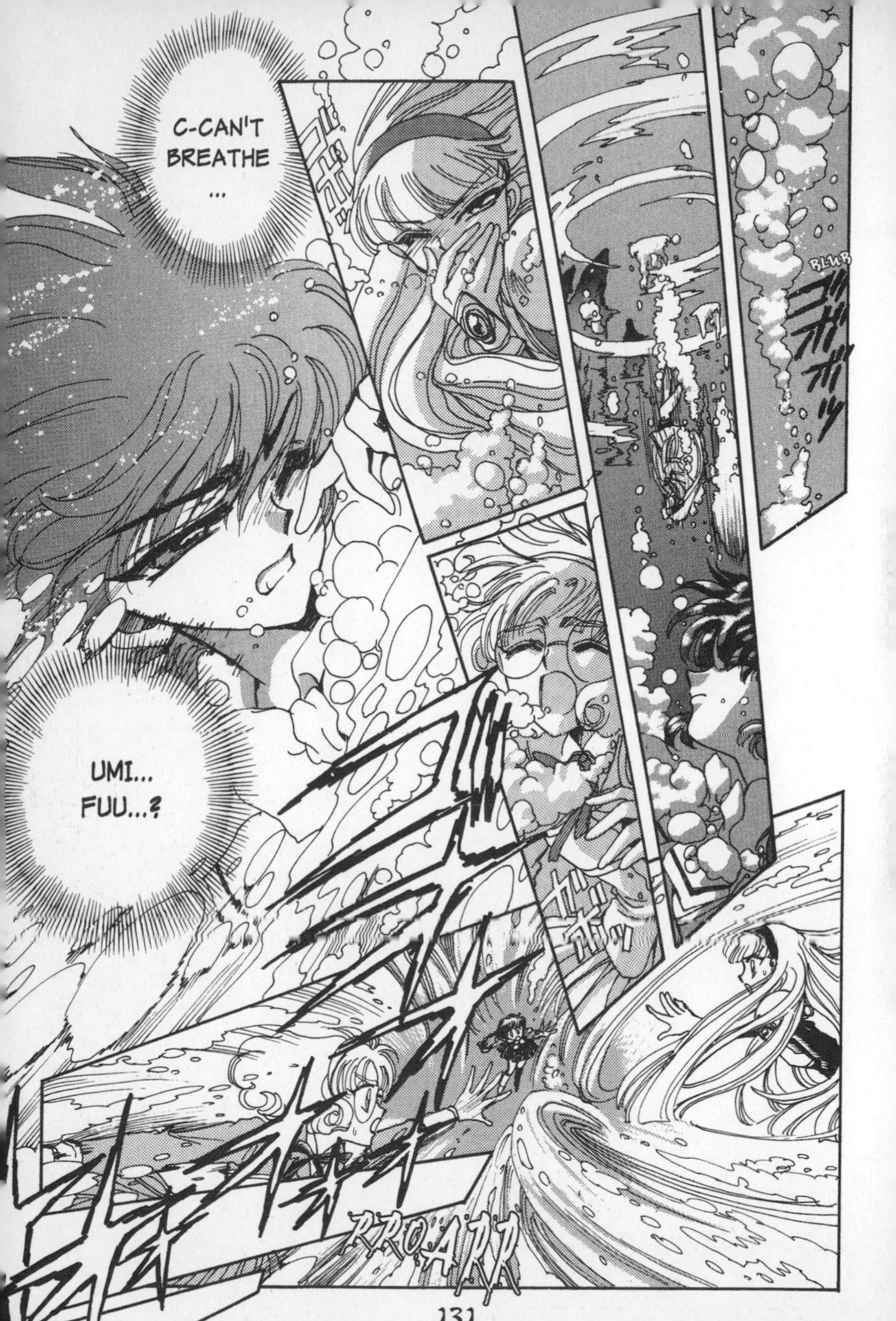
BLUB
C-CAN'T BREATHE ...
UMI... FUU...?
RROARR

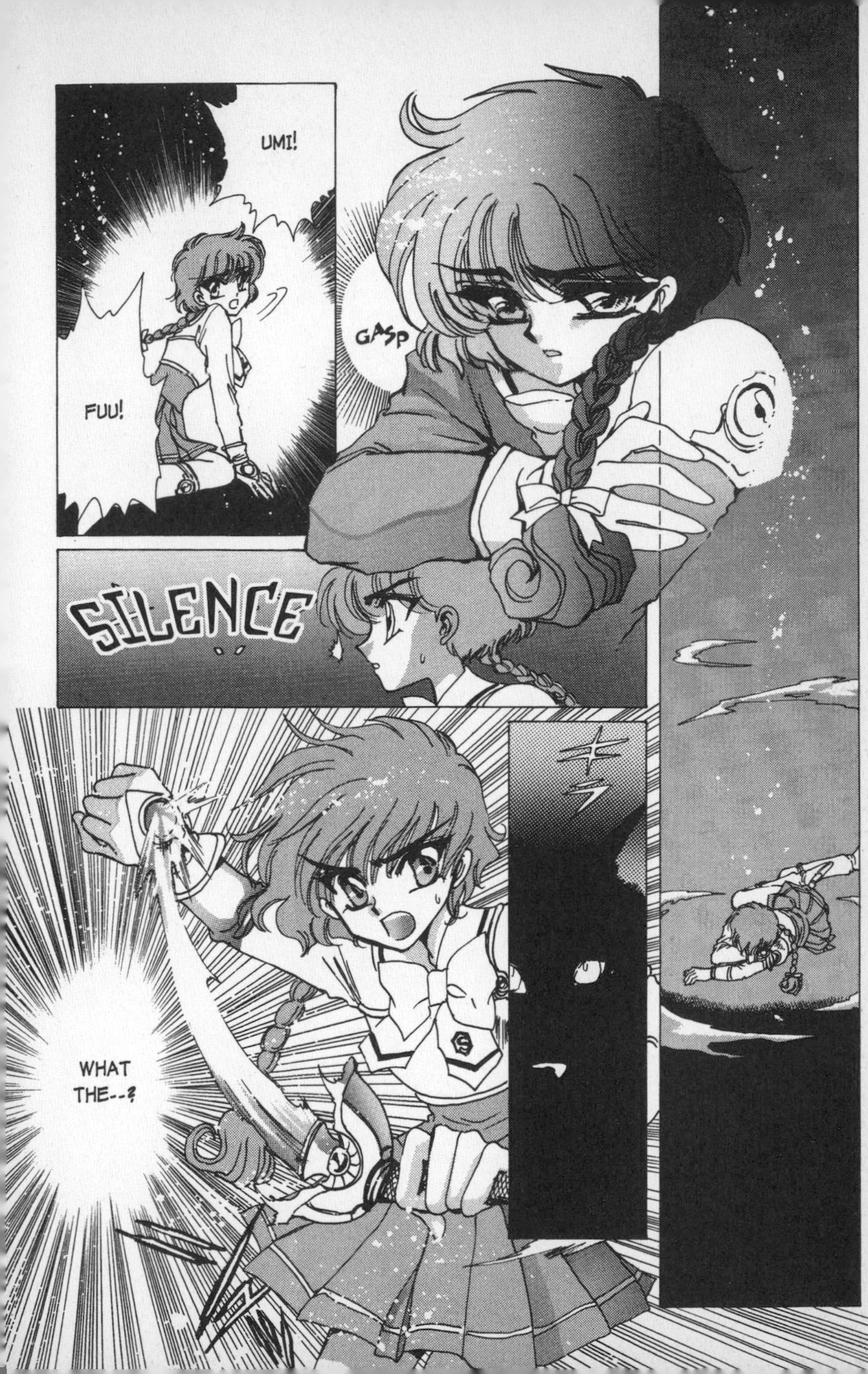
GASP
UMI!
FUU!
SILENCE
WHAT THE--?

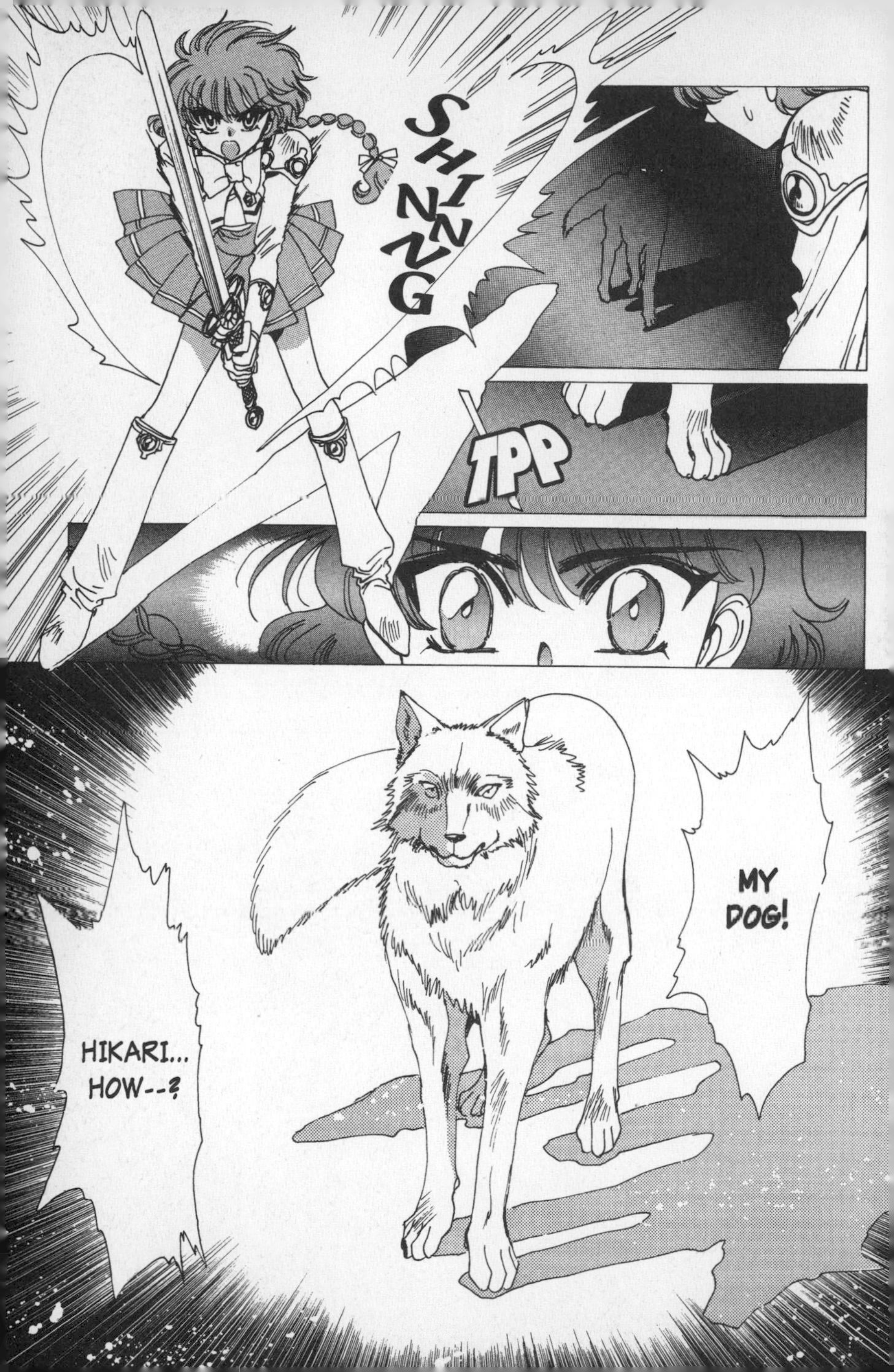
TPP
SHINNNG
MY DOG!
HIKARI... HOW--?

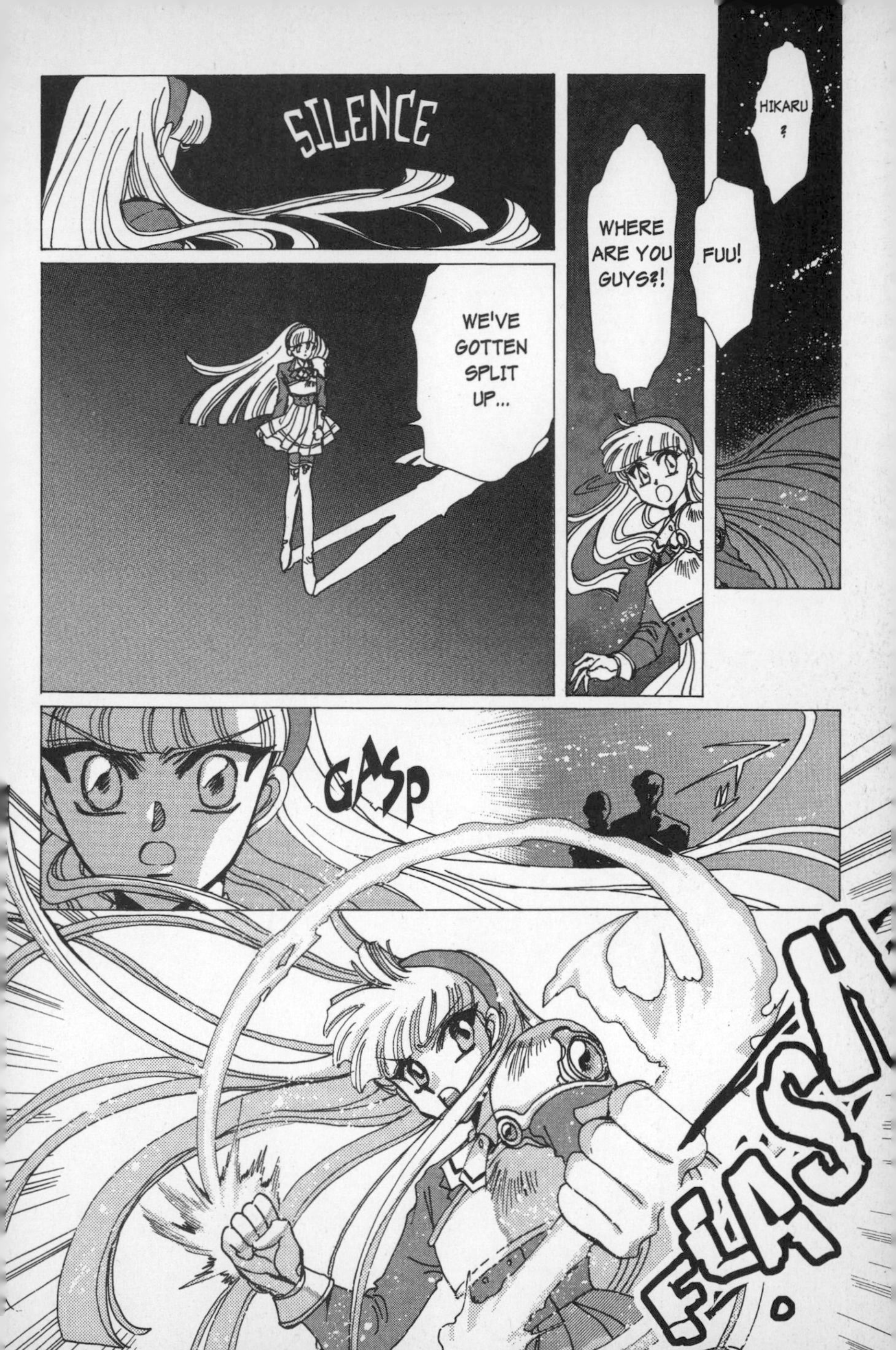
HIKARU ?
FUU!
WHERE ARE YOU GUYS?!
SILENCE
WE'VE GOTTEN SPLIT UP...
GASP
FLASH

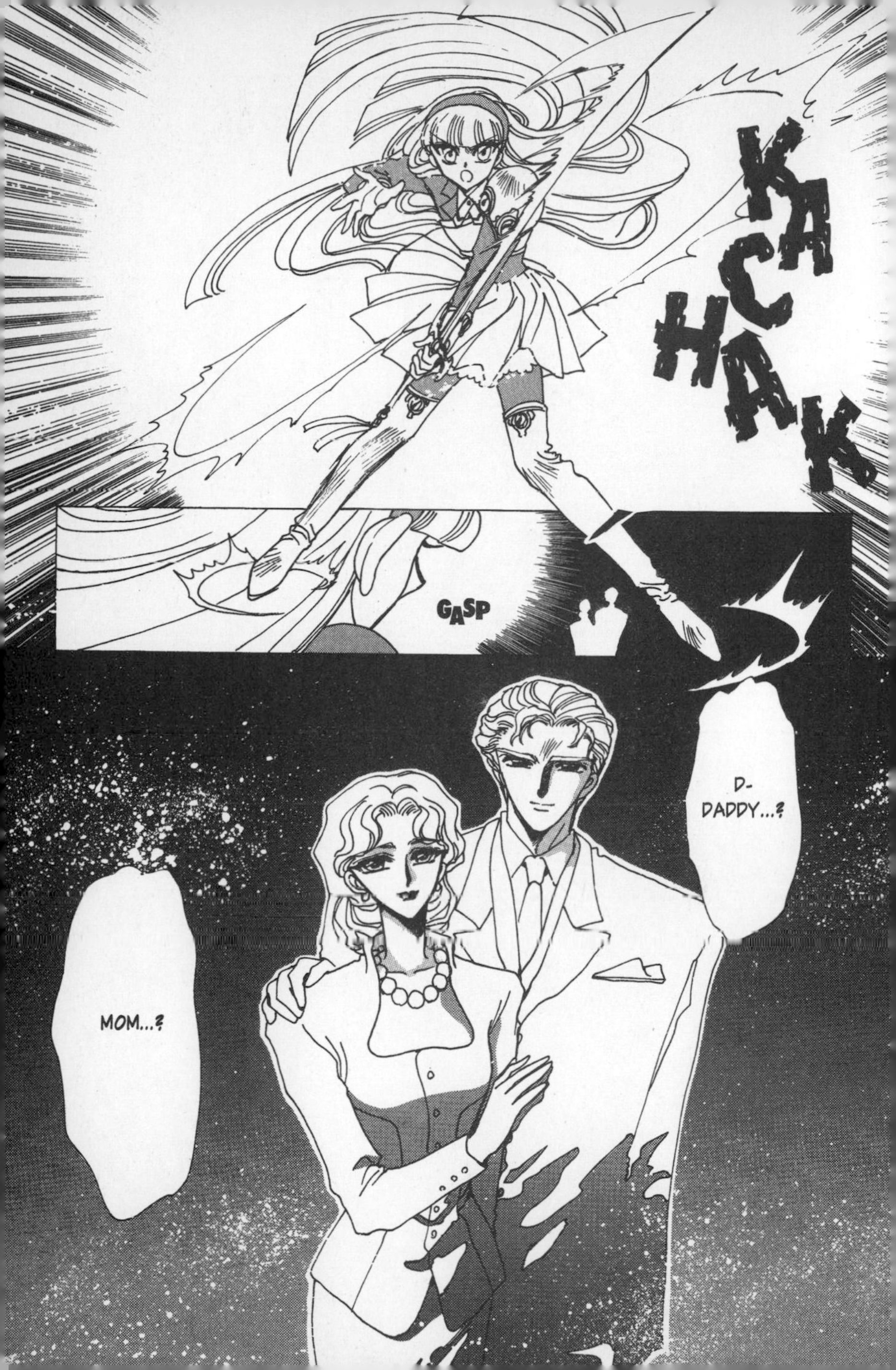
KACHAK
GASP
D-DADDY...?
MOM...?

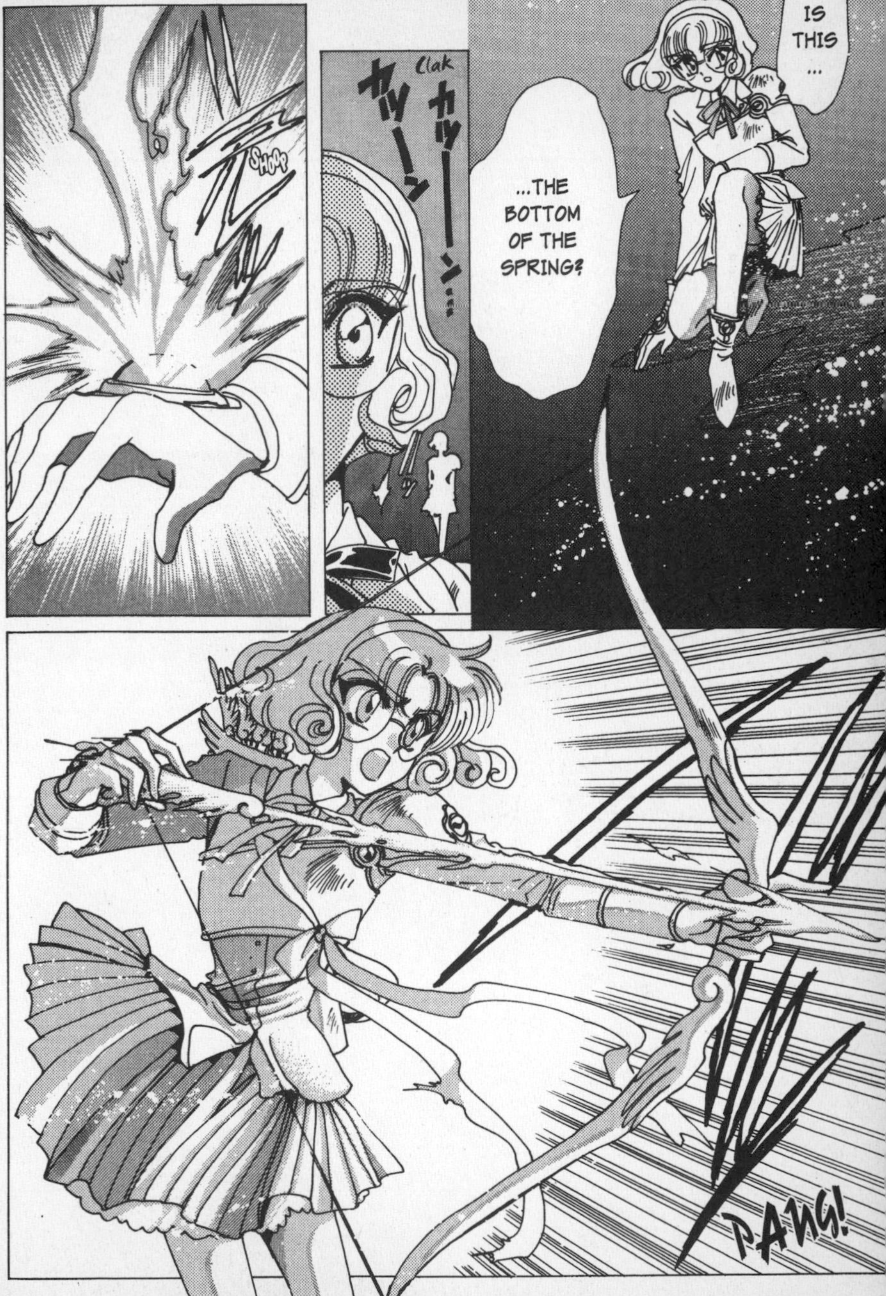
IS THIS ...
...THE BOTTOM OF THE SPRING?
Clak
SHOOP
PANG!

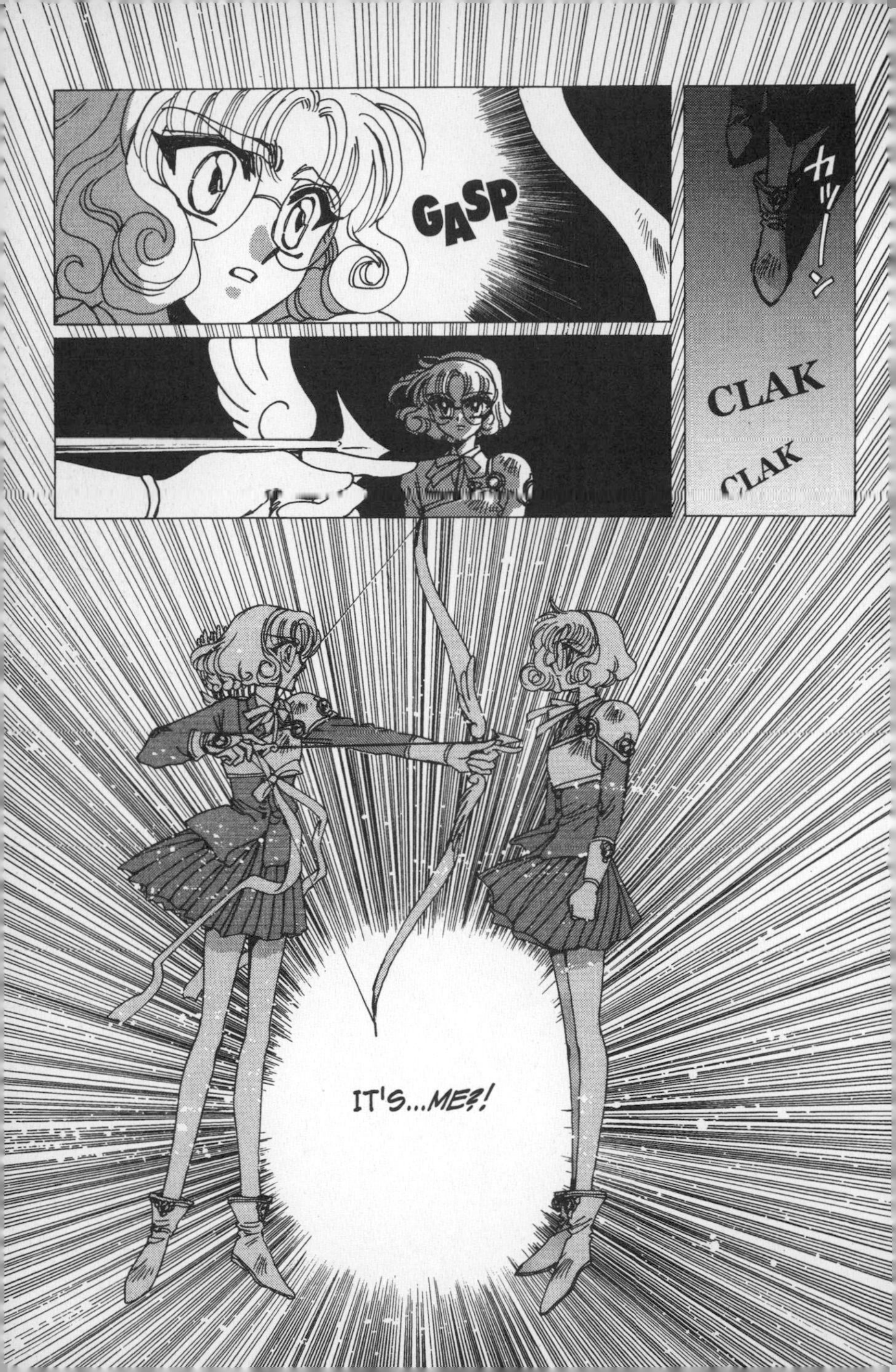

カッーン
CLAK
CLAK
GASP
IT'S...ME?!

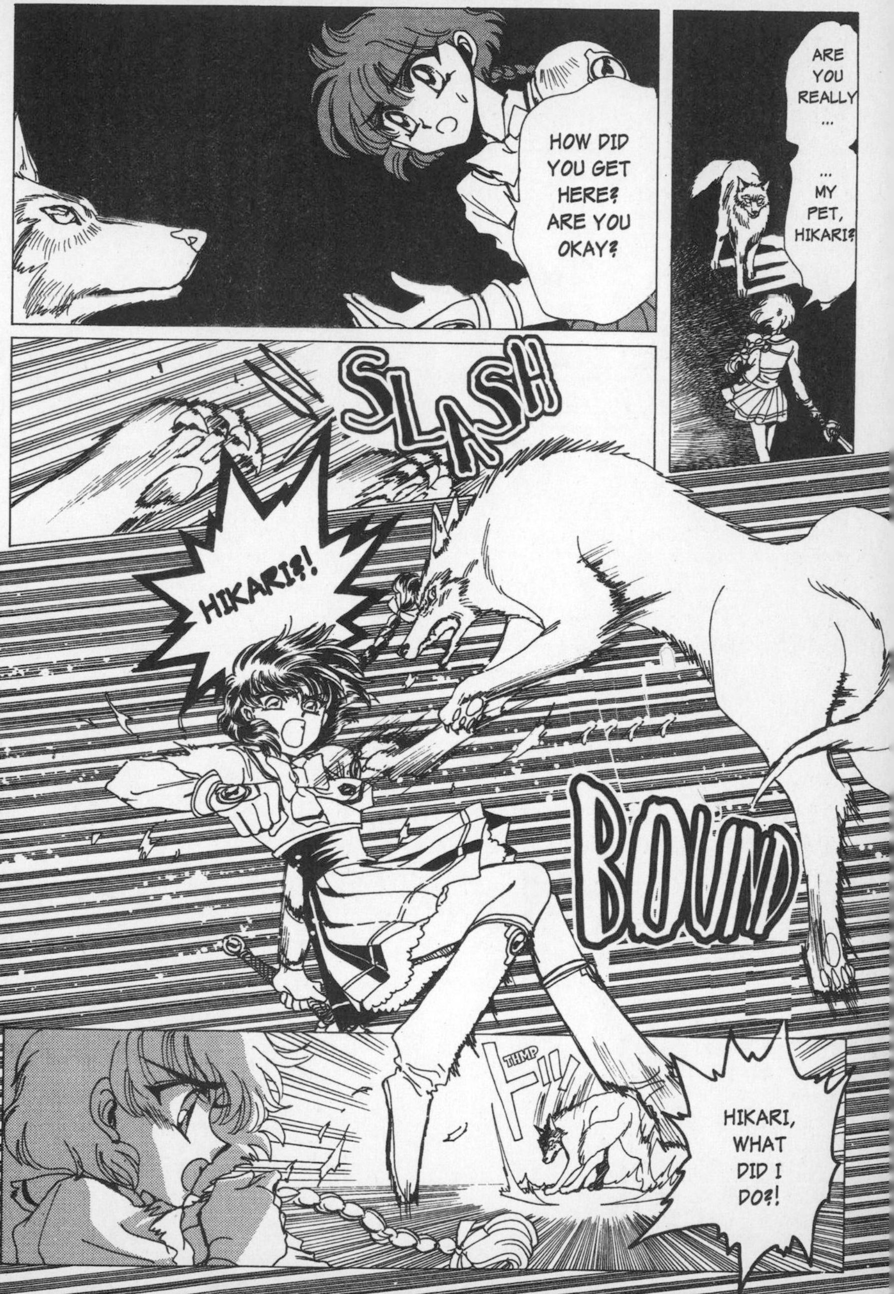
ARE YOU REALLY ...
... MY PET, HIKARI?
HOW DID YOU GET HERE? ARE YOU OKAY?
SLASH
HIKARI?!
BOUND
THMP
HIKARI, WHAT DID I DO?!

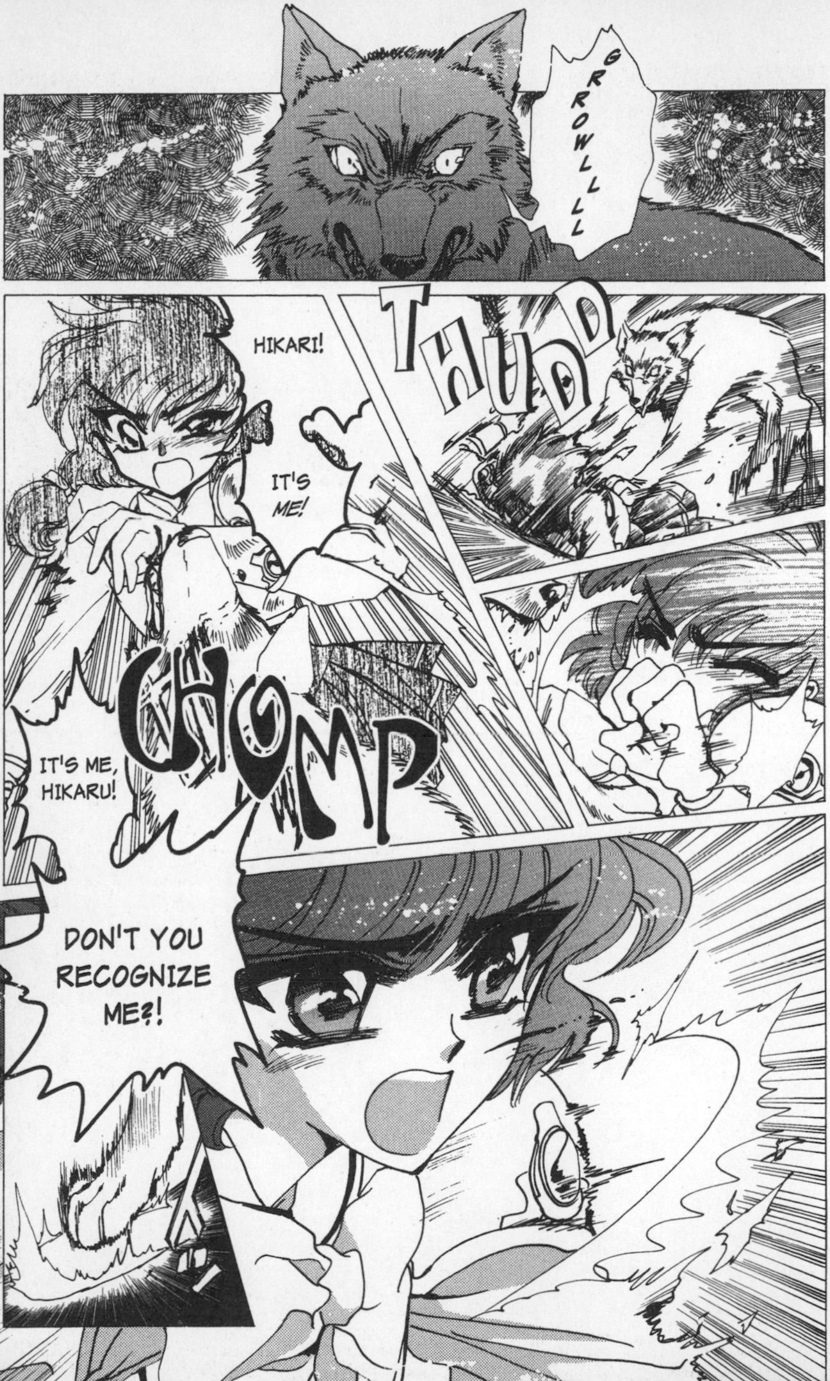
GROWLLLL
THUDD
HIKARI!
IT'S ME!
CHOMP
IT'S ME, HIKARU!
DON'T YOU RECOGNIZE ME?!

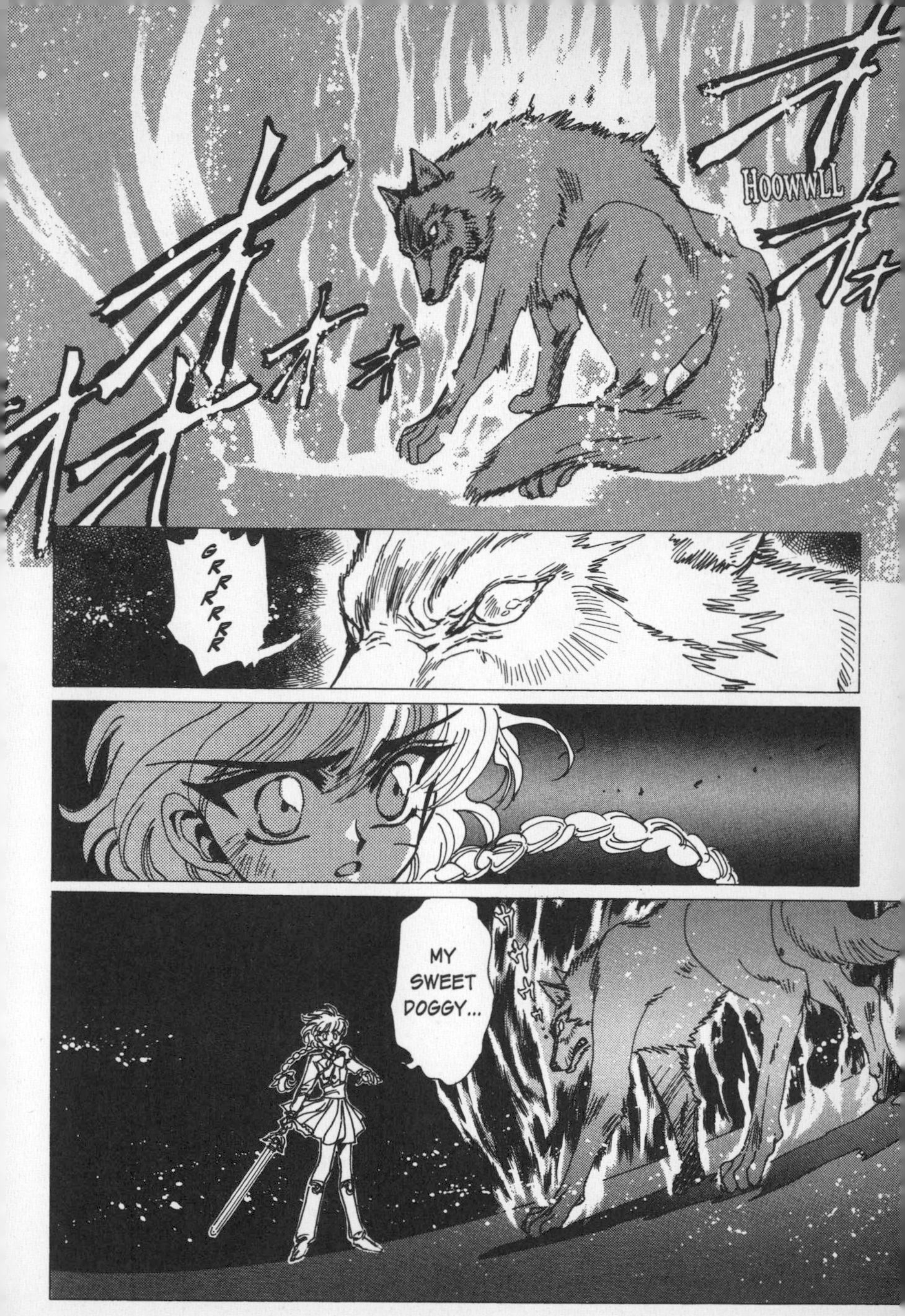
HOOWWLL
GRRRRRR
MY SWEET DOGGY...

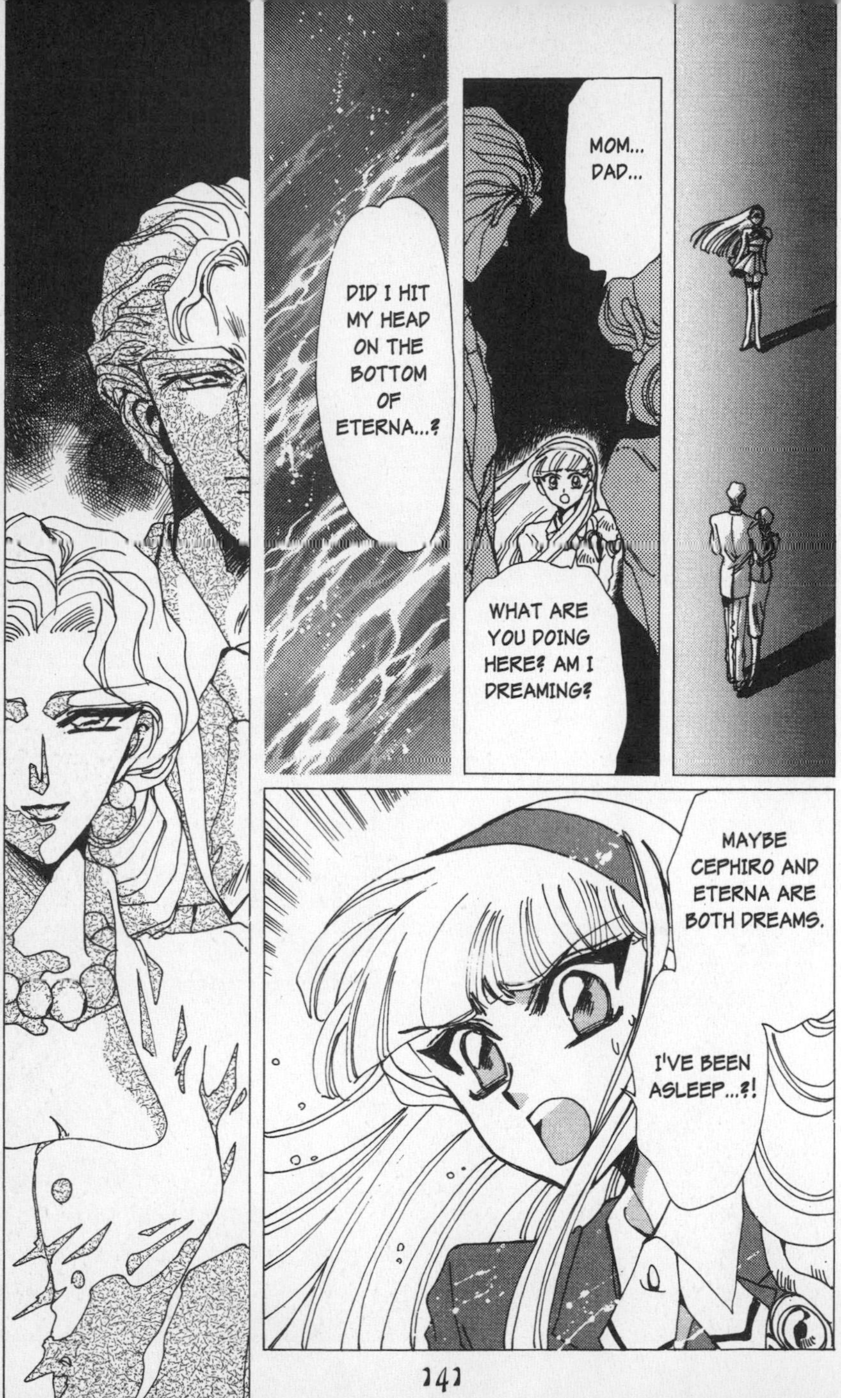
MOM... DAD...
WHAT ARE YOU DOING HERE? AM I DREAMING?
DID I HIT MY HEAD ON THE BOTTOM OF ETERNA...?
MAYBE CEPHIRO AND ETERNA ARE BOTH DREAMS.
I'VE BEEN ASLEEP...?!

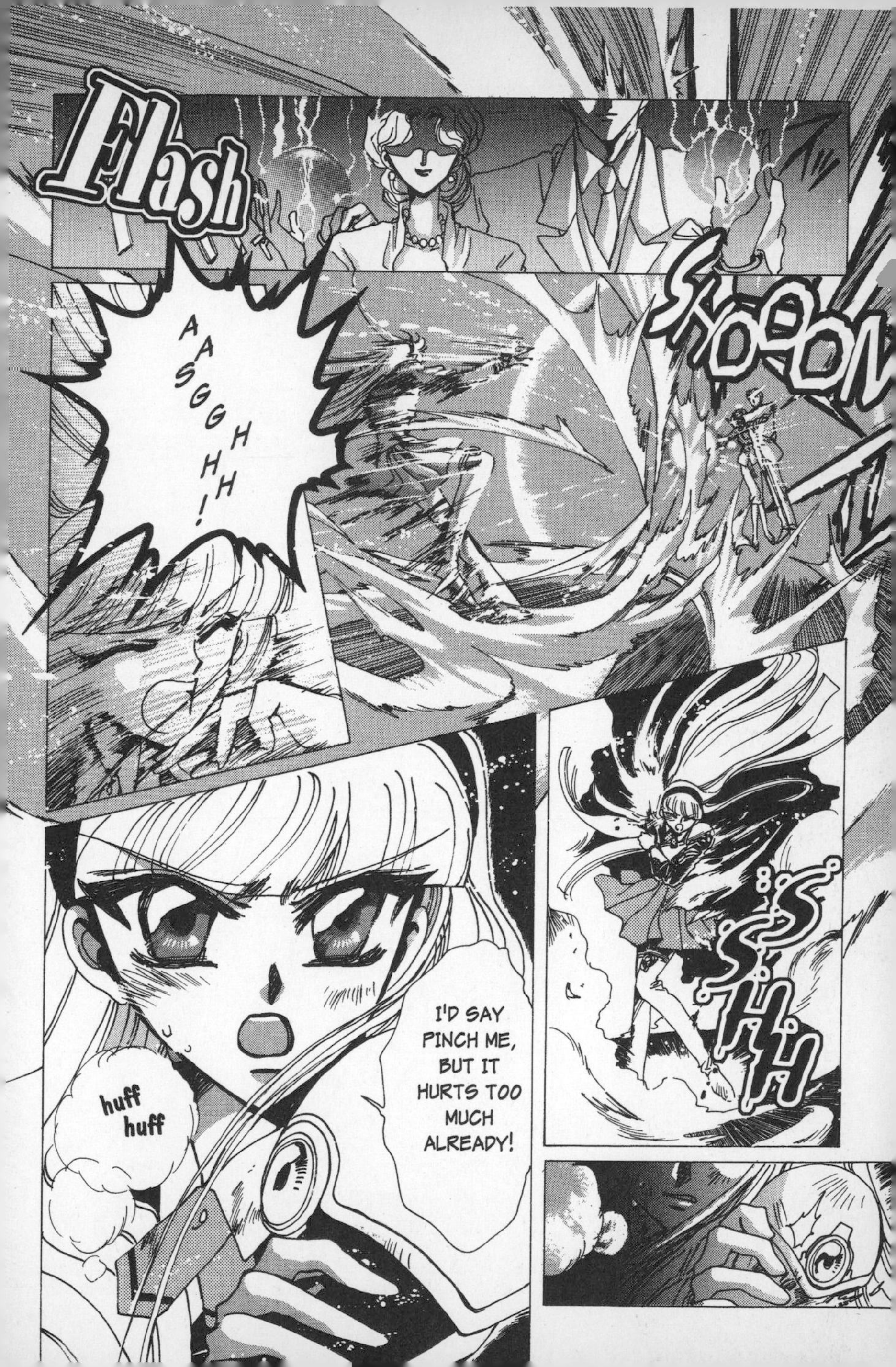
Flash
SHOOOM
AASGGHHH!
SSHHH
I'D SAY PINCH ME, BUT IT HURTS TOO MUCH ALREADY!
huff huff

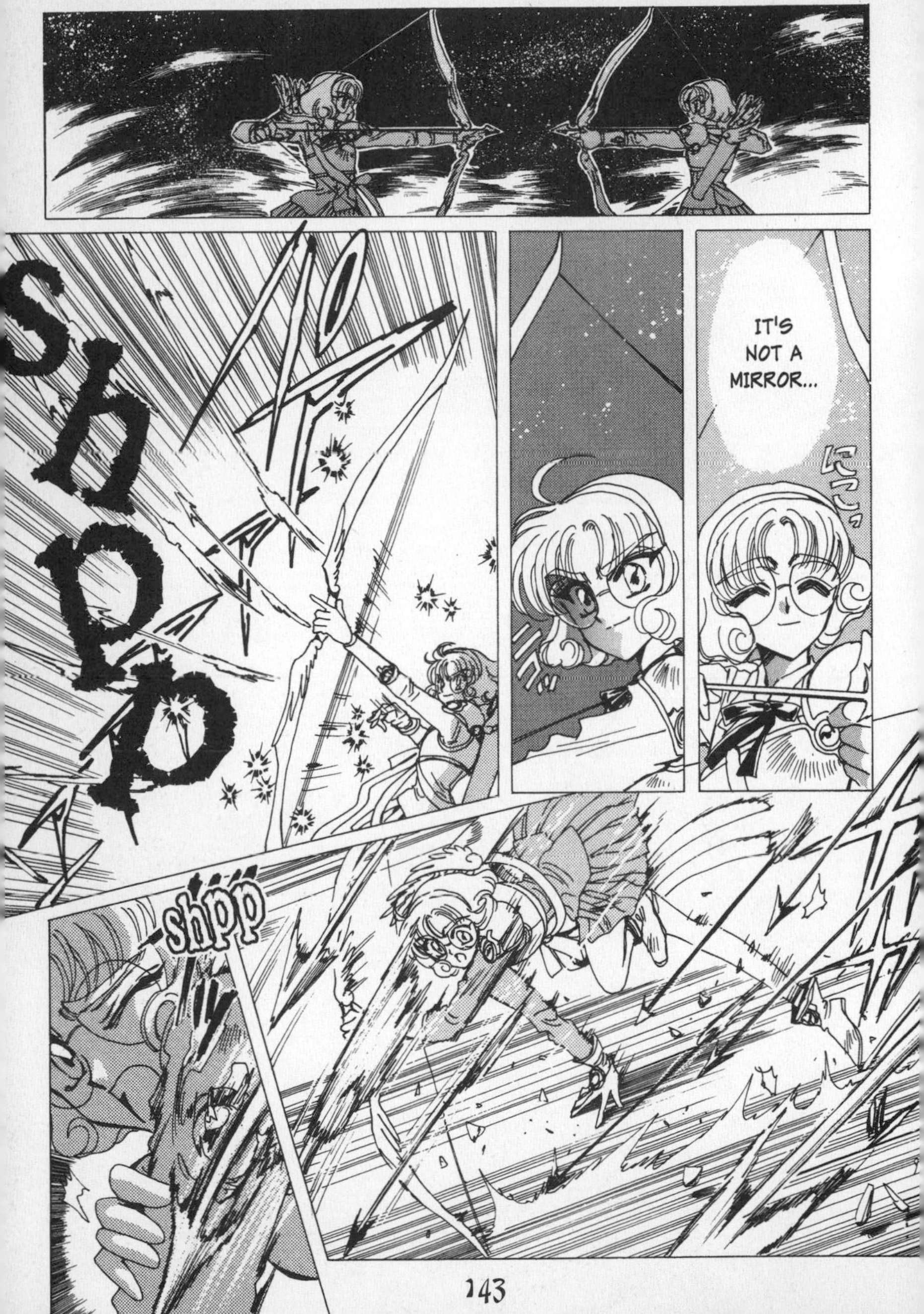
IT'S NOT A MIRROR...
shpp
shpp

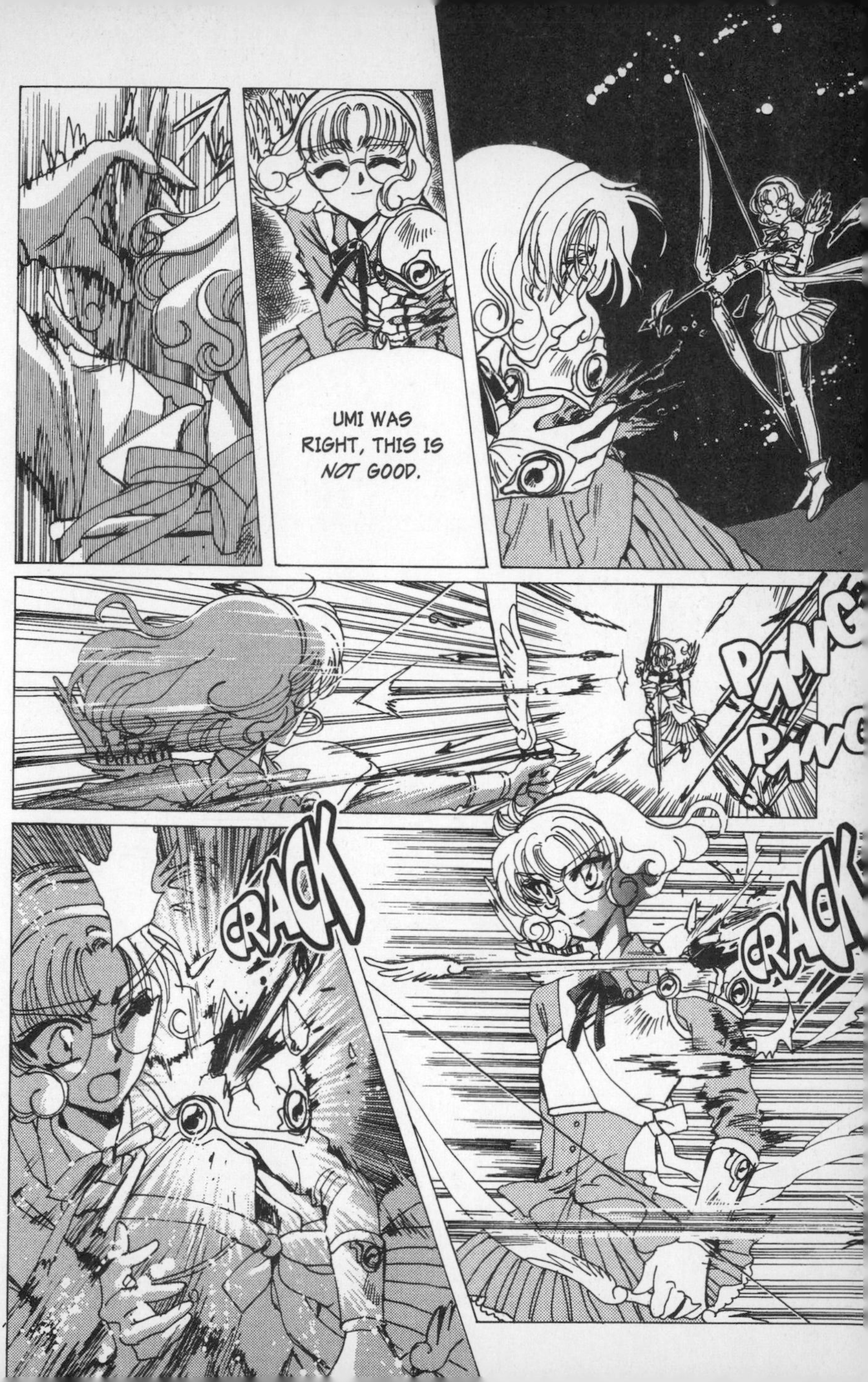
UMI WAS RIGHT, THIS IS *NOT* GOOD.
PANG
PANG
CRACK
CRACK

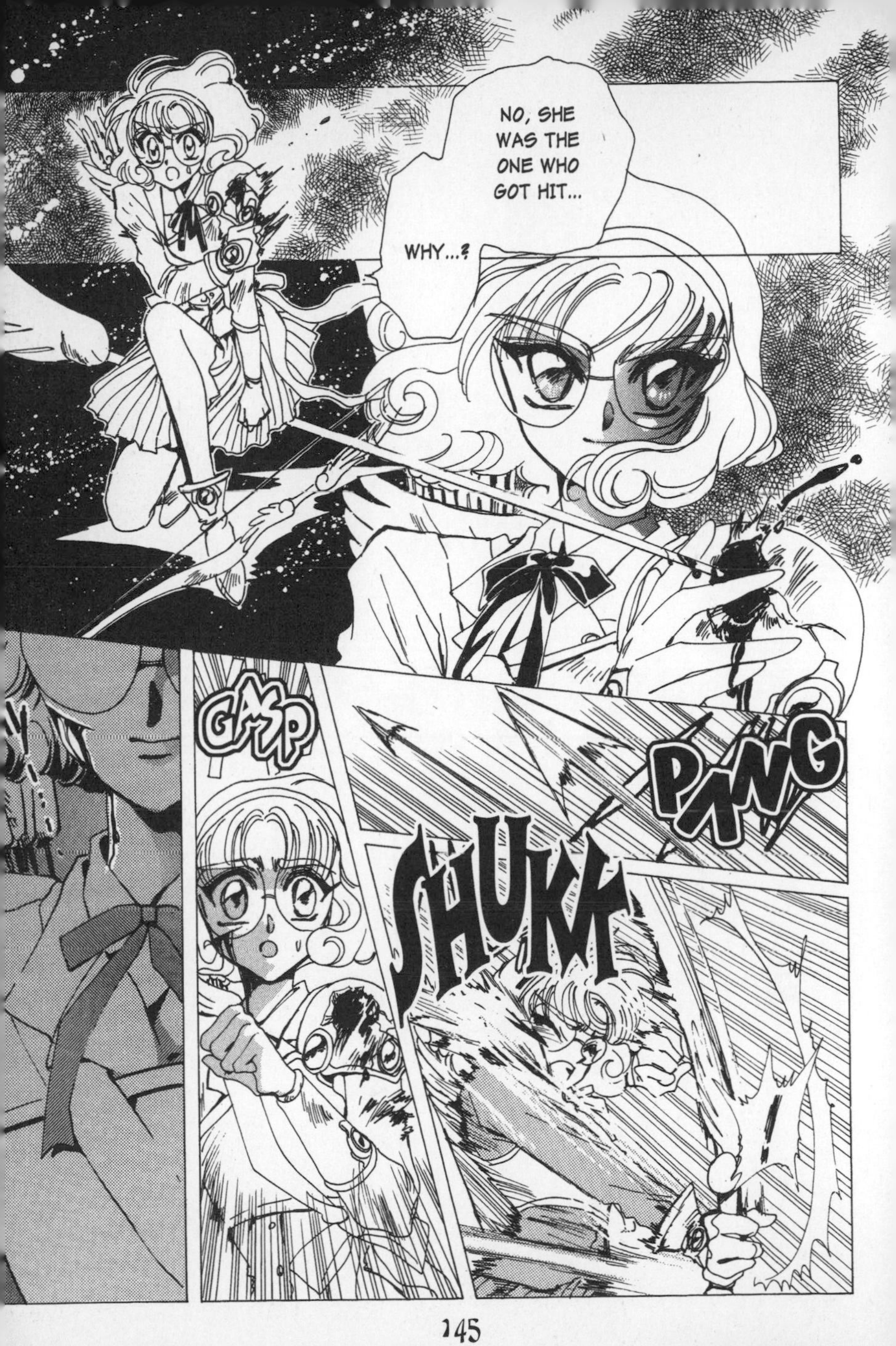
NO, SHE WAS THE ONE WHO GOT HIT...
WHY...?
PANG
SHUKK
GASP

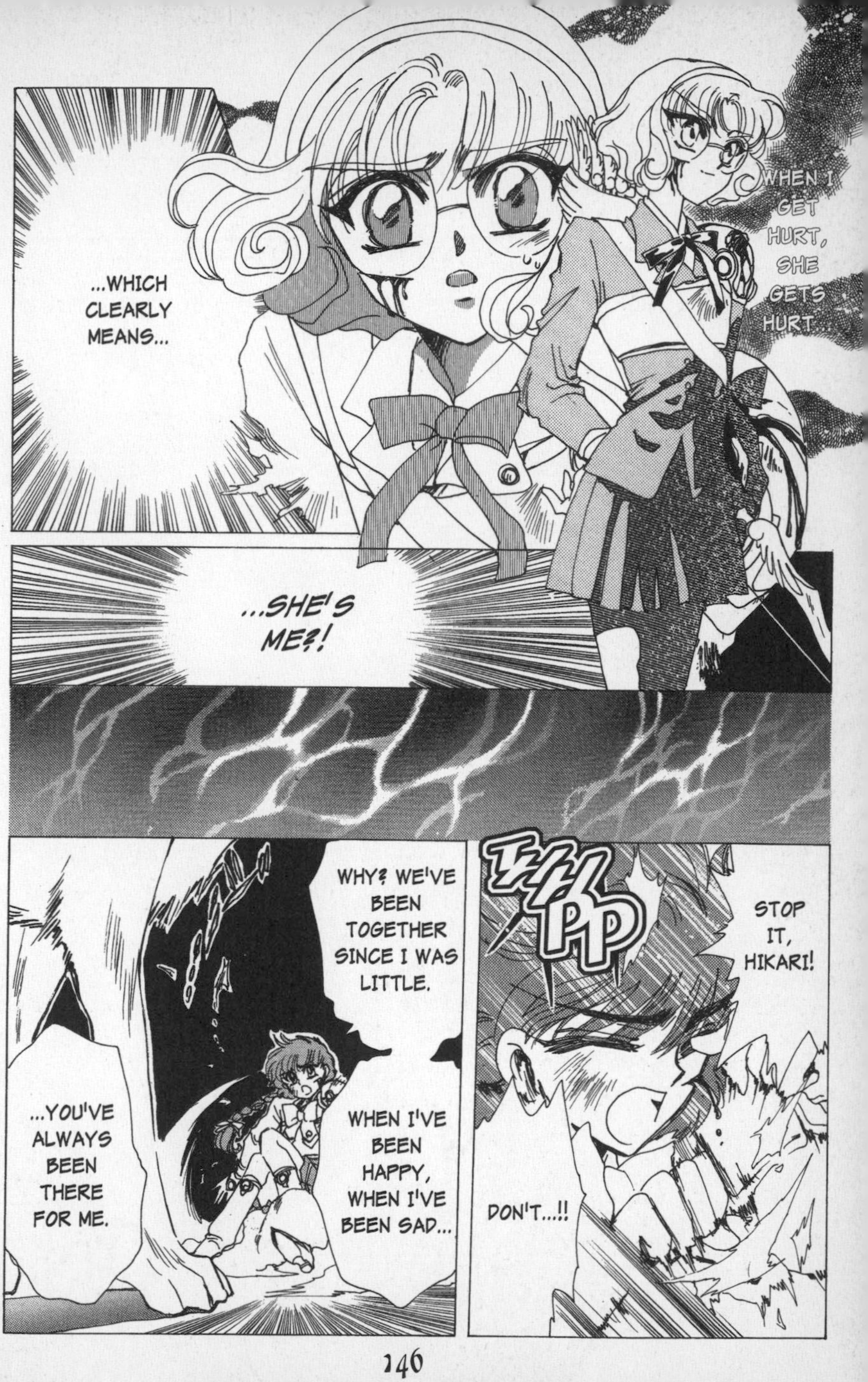
WHEN I GET HURT, SHE GETS HURT...
...WHICH CLEARLY MEANS...
...SHE'S ME?!
STOP IT, HIKARI!
DON'T...!!
WHY? WE'VE BEEN TOGETHER SINCE I WAS LITTLE.
WHEN I'VE BEEN HAPPY, WHEN I'VE BEEN SAD...
...YOU'VE ALWAYS BEEN THERE FOR ME.

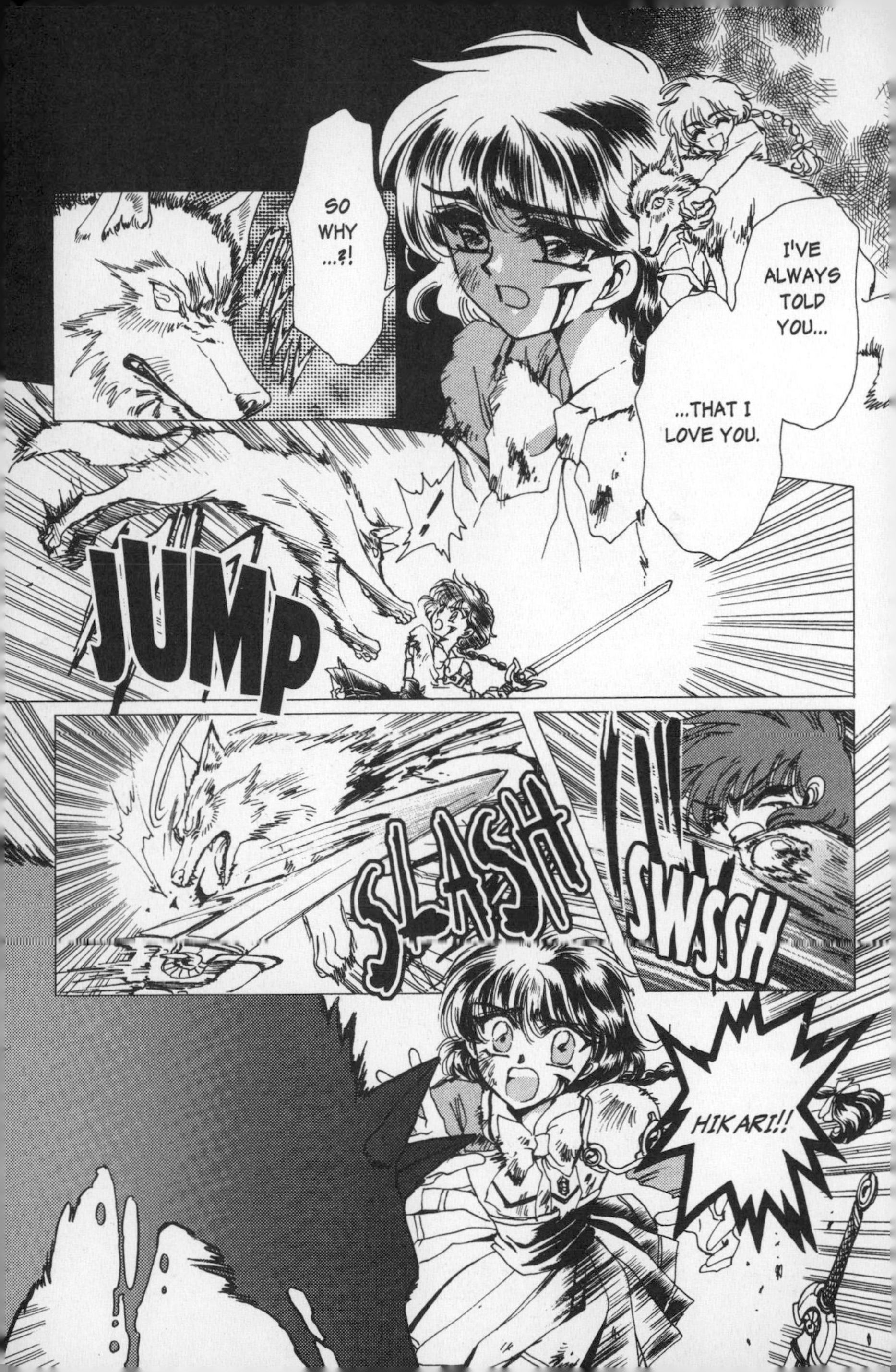

I'VE ALWAYS TOLD YOU...
...THAT I LOVE YOU.
SO WHY ...?!
JUMP
SWSSH
SLASH
HIKARI!!

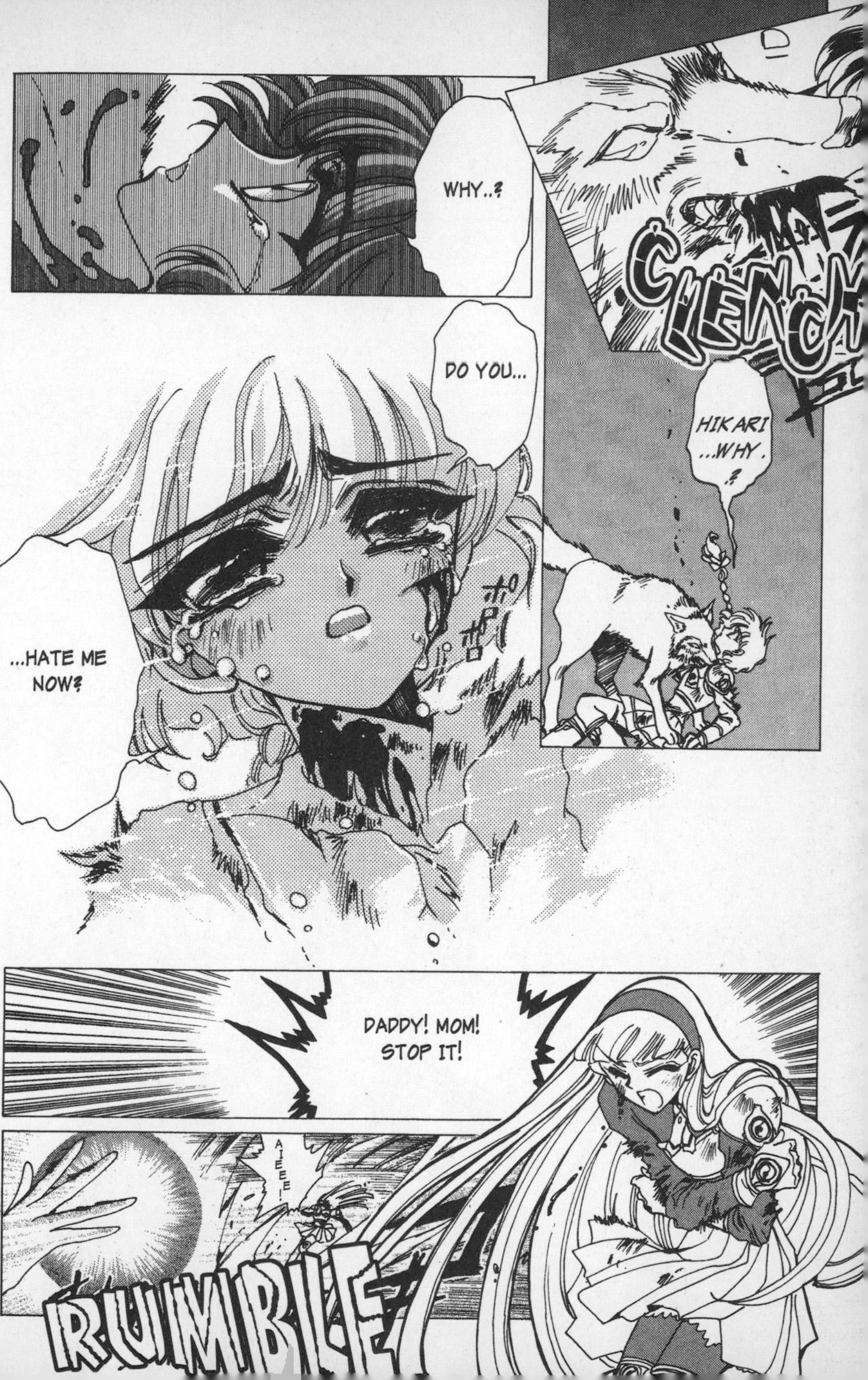
CLENCH
HIKARI ...WHY.?
WHY..?
DO YOU...
...HATE ME NOW?
DADDY! MOM! STOP IT!
AIEEE!
RUMBLE

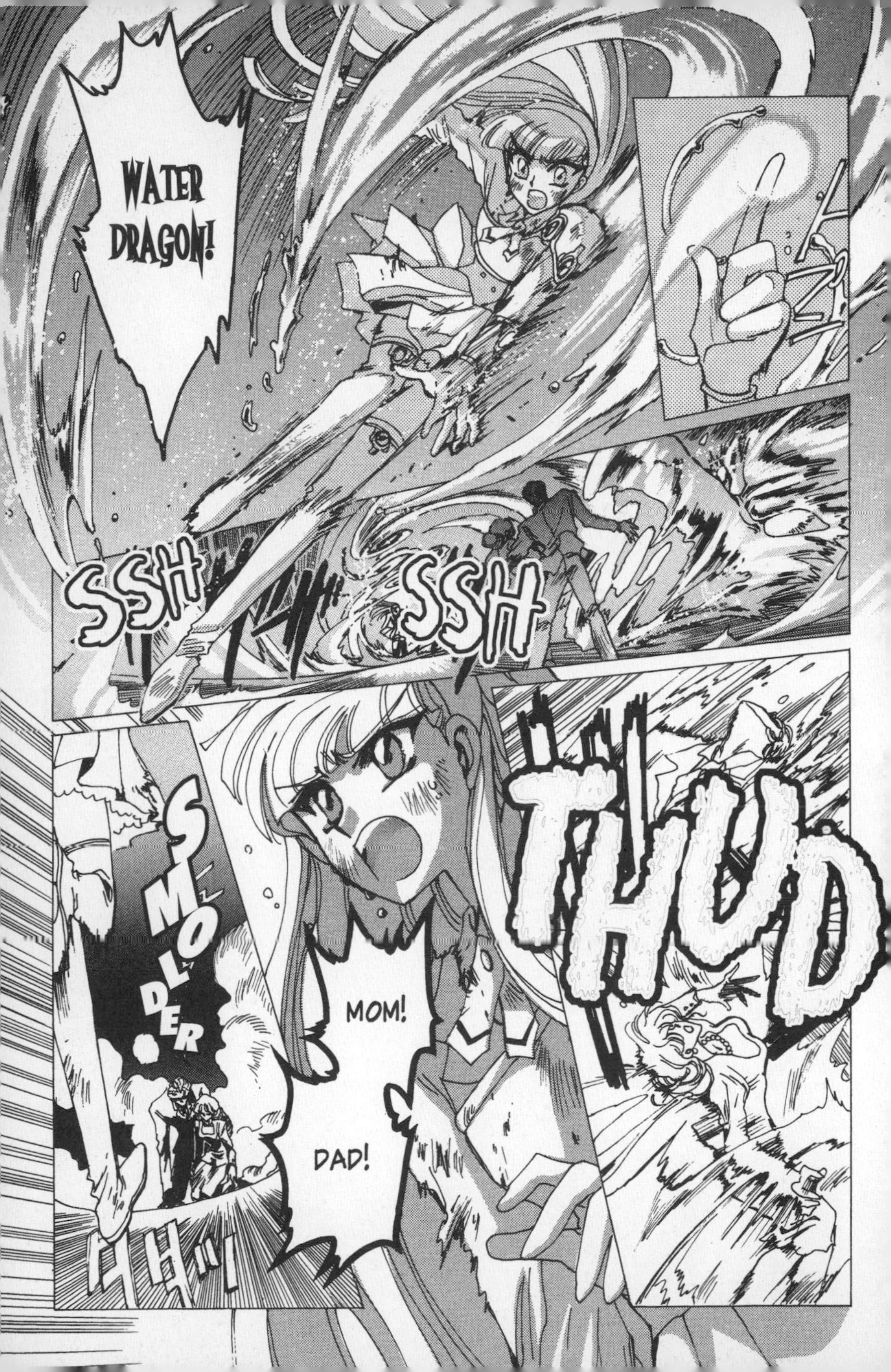
WATER DRAGON!
SSH
SSH
THUD
MOM!
DAD!
SMOLDER

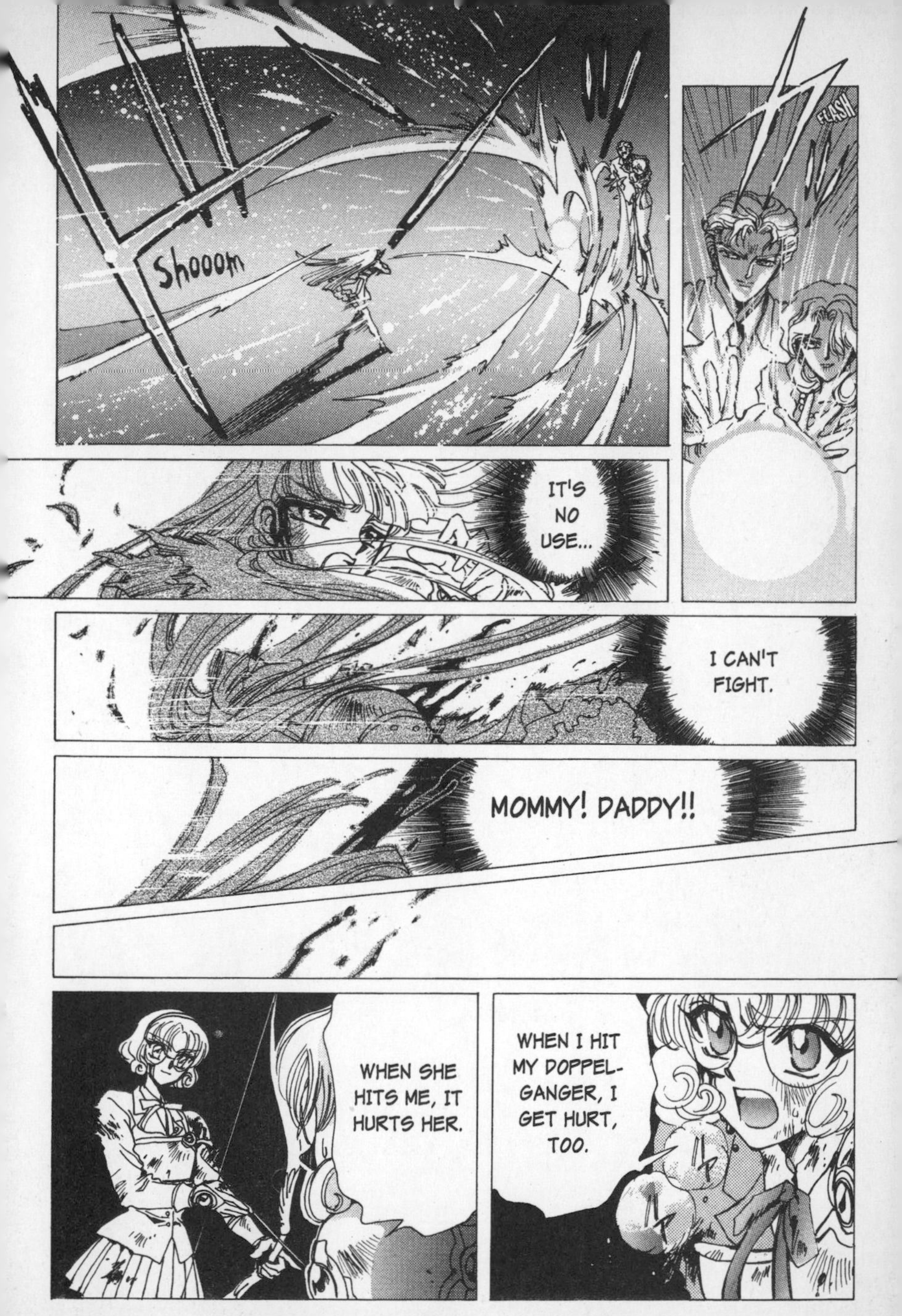

FLASH
Shooom
IT'S NO USE...
I CAN'T FIGHT.
MOMMY! DADDY!!
WHEN I HIT MY DOPPEL-GANGER, I GET HURT, TOO.
WHEN SHE HITS ME, IT HURTS HER.

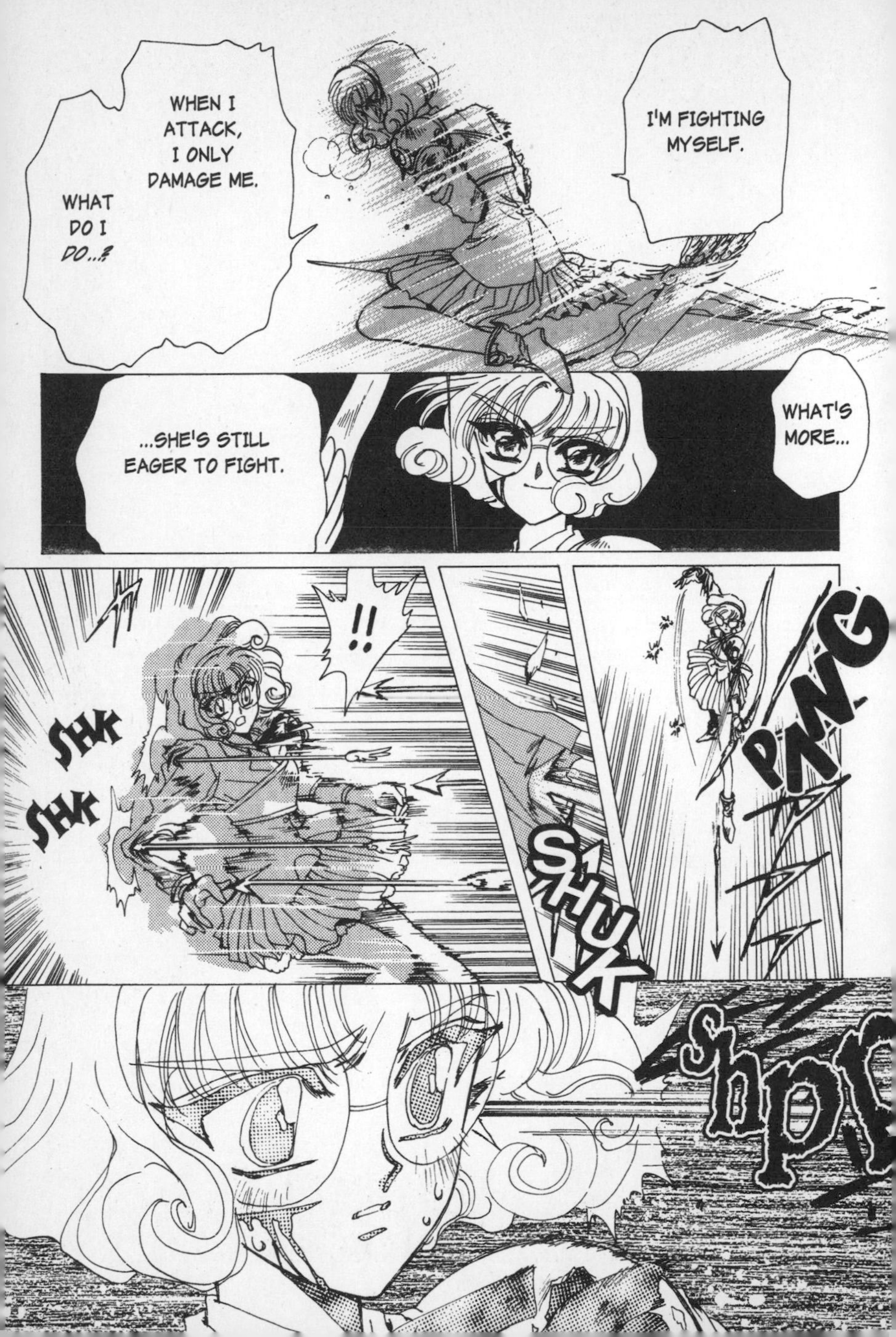
I'M FIGHTING MYSELF.
WHEN I ATTACK, I ONLY DAMAGE ME.
WHAT DO I DO...?!
WHAT'S MORE...
...SHE'S STILL EAGER TO FIGHT.
PANG
SHUK
!!
SHK
SHK

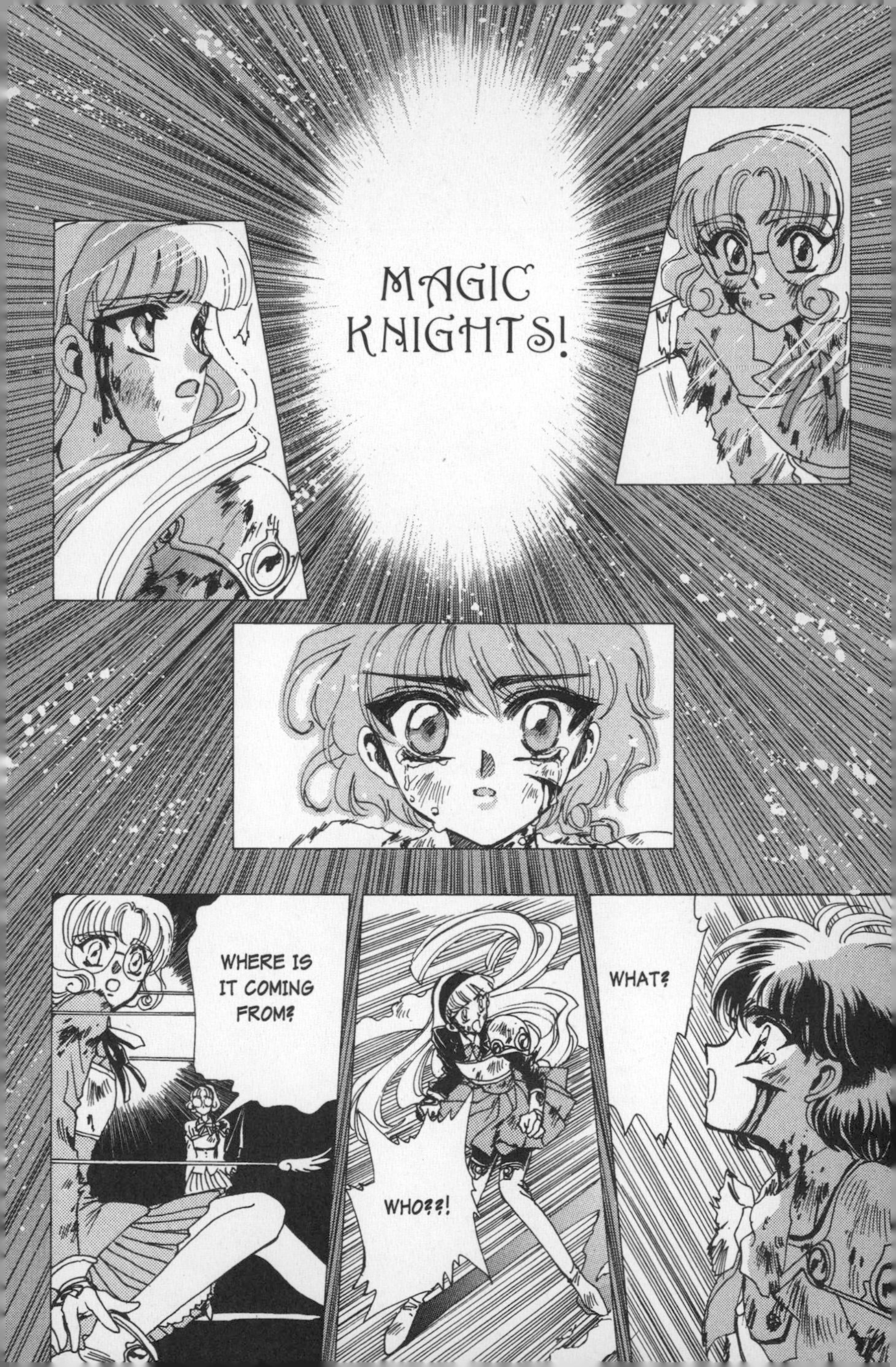
MAGIC KNIGHTS!
WHAT?
WHO??!
WHERE IS IT COMING FROM?

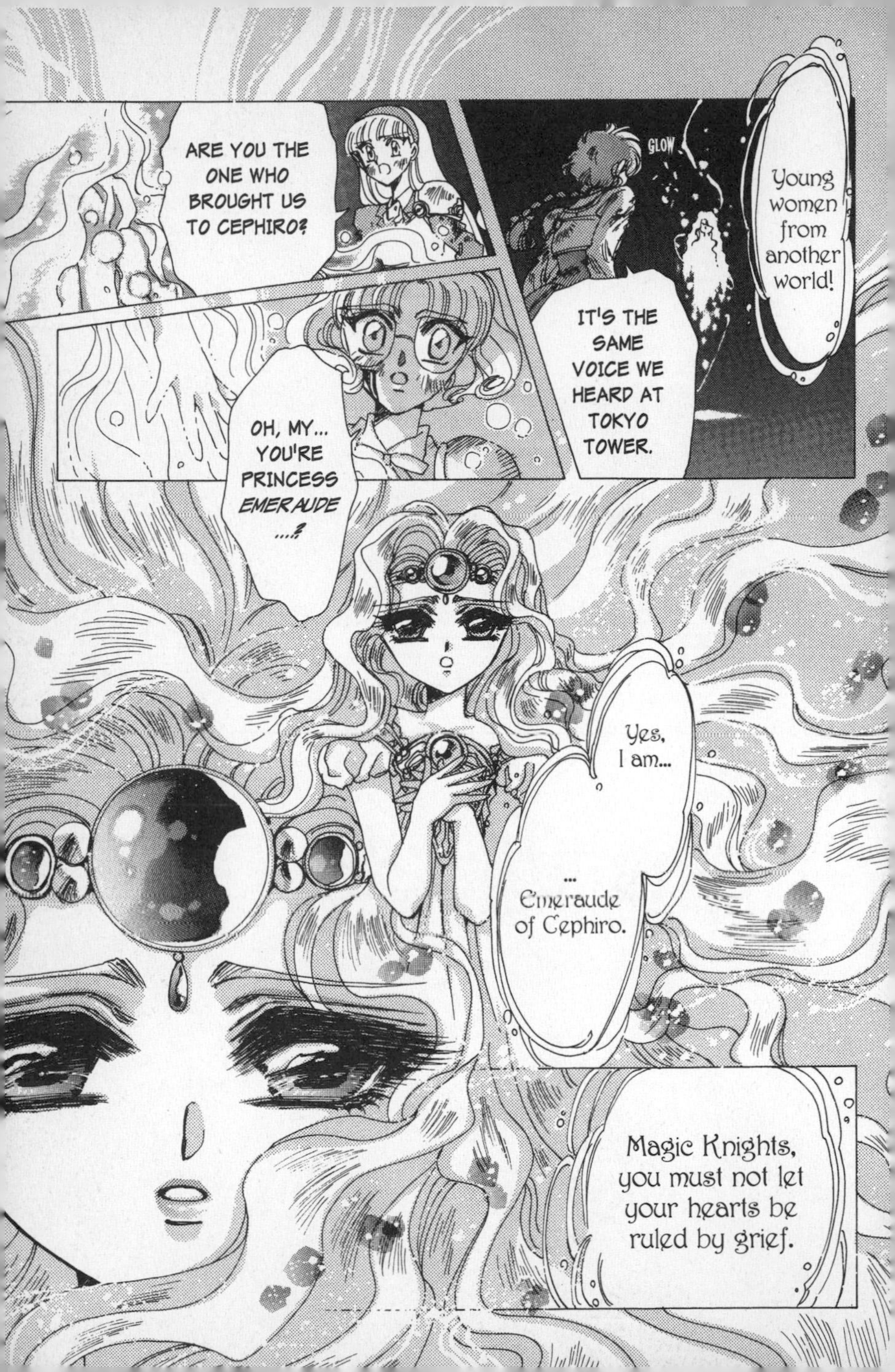
GLOW
Young women from another world!
IT'S THE SAME VOICE WE HEARD AT TOKYO TOWER.
ARE YOU THE ONE WHO BROUGHT US TO CEPHIRO?
OH, MY... YOU'RE PRINCESS *EMERAUDE* ...?
Yes, I am...
... Emeraude of Cephiro.
Magic Knights, you must not let your hearts be ruled by grief.

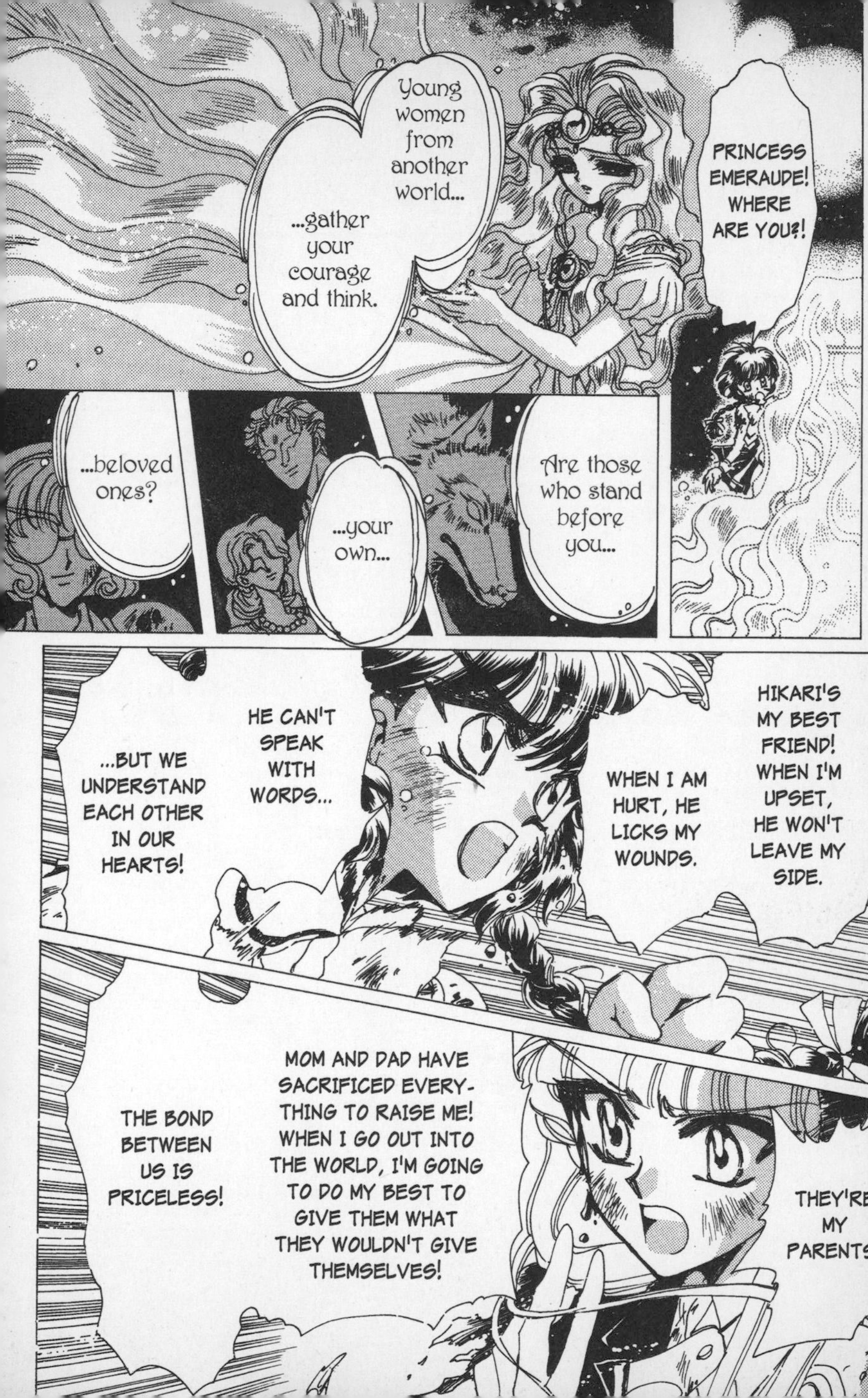

PRINCESS EMERAUDE! WHERE ARE YOU?!
Young women from another world...
...gather your courage and think.
Are those who stand before you...
...your own...
...beloved ones?
HIKARI'S MY BEST FRIEND! WHEN I'M UPSET, HE WON'T LEAVE MY SIDE.
WHEN I AM HURT, HE LICKS MY WOUNDS.
HE CAN'T SPEAK WITH WORDS...
...BUT WE UNDERSTAND EACH OTHER IN OUR HEARTS!
THEY'RE MY PARENTS!
MOM AND DAD HAVE SACRIFICED EVERY-THING TO RAISE ME! WHEN I GO OUT INTO THE WORLD, I'M GOING TO DO MY BEST TO GIVE THEM WHAT THEY WOULDN'T GIVE THEMSELVES!
THE BOND BETWEEN US IS PRICELESS!

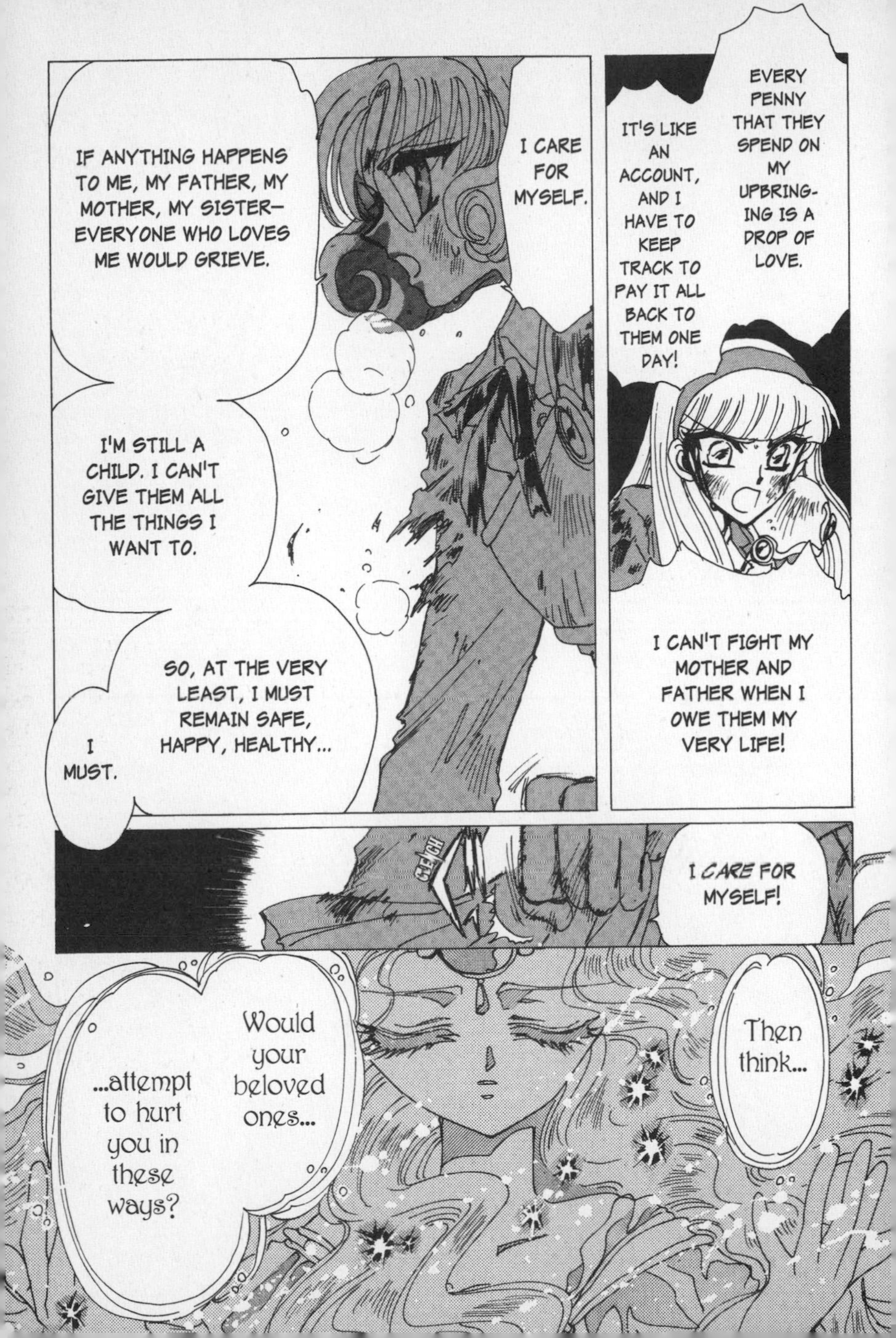
EVERY PENNY THAT THEY SPEND ON MY UPBRING-ING IS A DROP OF LOVE.
IT'S LIKE AN ACCOUNT, AND I HAVE TO KEEP TRACK TO PAY IT ALL BACK TO THEM ONE DAY!
I CAN'T FIGHT MY MOTHER AND FATHER WHEN I OWE THEM MY VERY LIFE!
I CARE FOR MYSELF.
IF ANYTHING HAPPENS TO ME, MY FATHER, MY MOTHER, MY SISTER—EVERYONE WHO LOVES ME WOULD GRIEVE.
I'M STILL A CHILD. I CAN'T GIVE THEM ALL THE THINGS I WANT TO.
SO, AT THE VERY LEAST, I MUST REMAIN SAFE, HAPPY, HEALTHY...
I MUST.
I *CARE* FOR MYSELF!
CLENCH
Then think...
Would your beloved ones...
...attempt to hurt you in these ways?

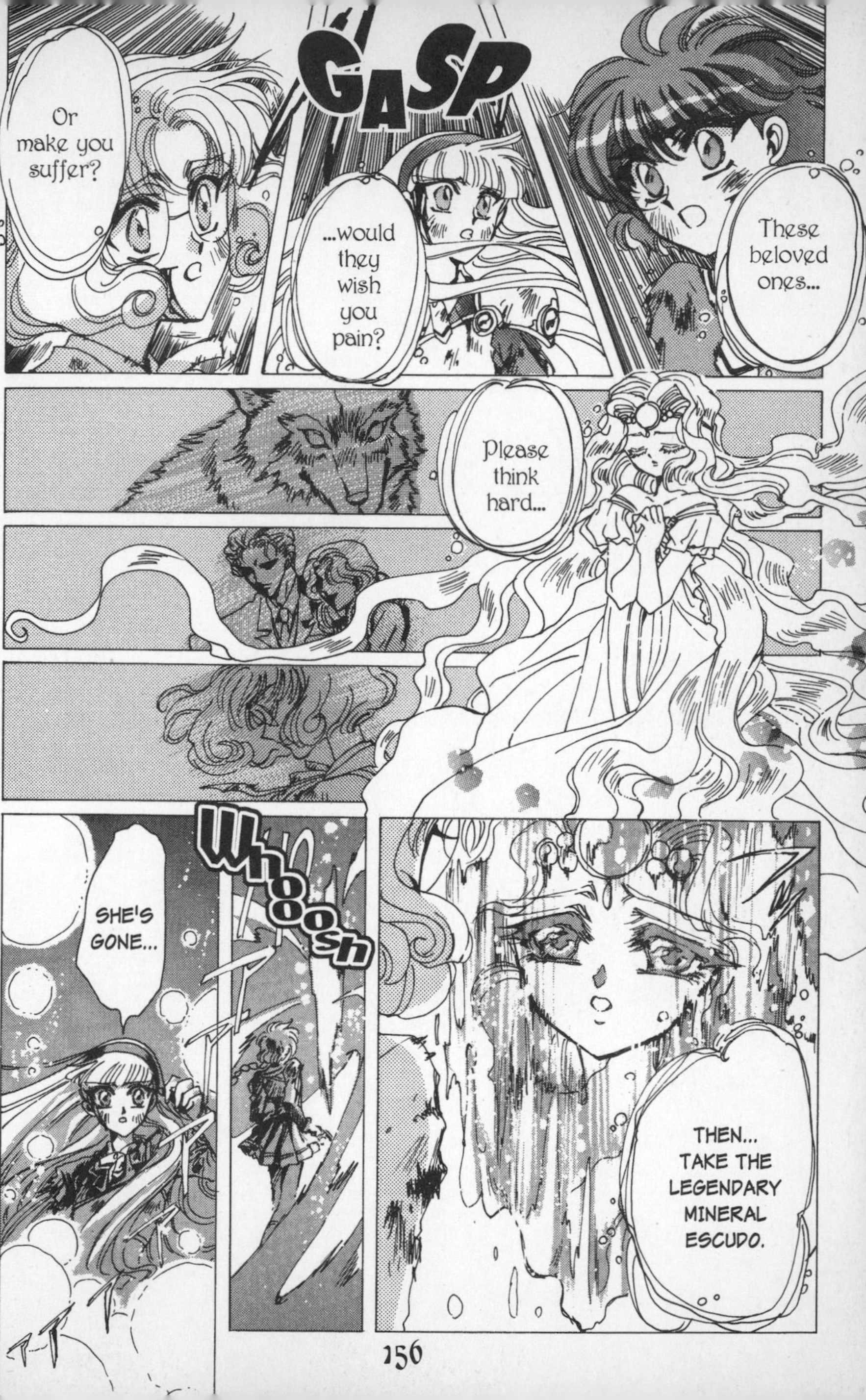
These beloved ones...
GASP
...would they wish you pain?
Or make you suffer?
Please think hard...
THEN... TAKE THE LEGENDARY MINERAL ESCUDO.
Whoooosh
SHE'S GONE...

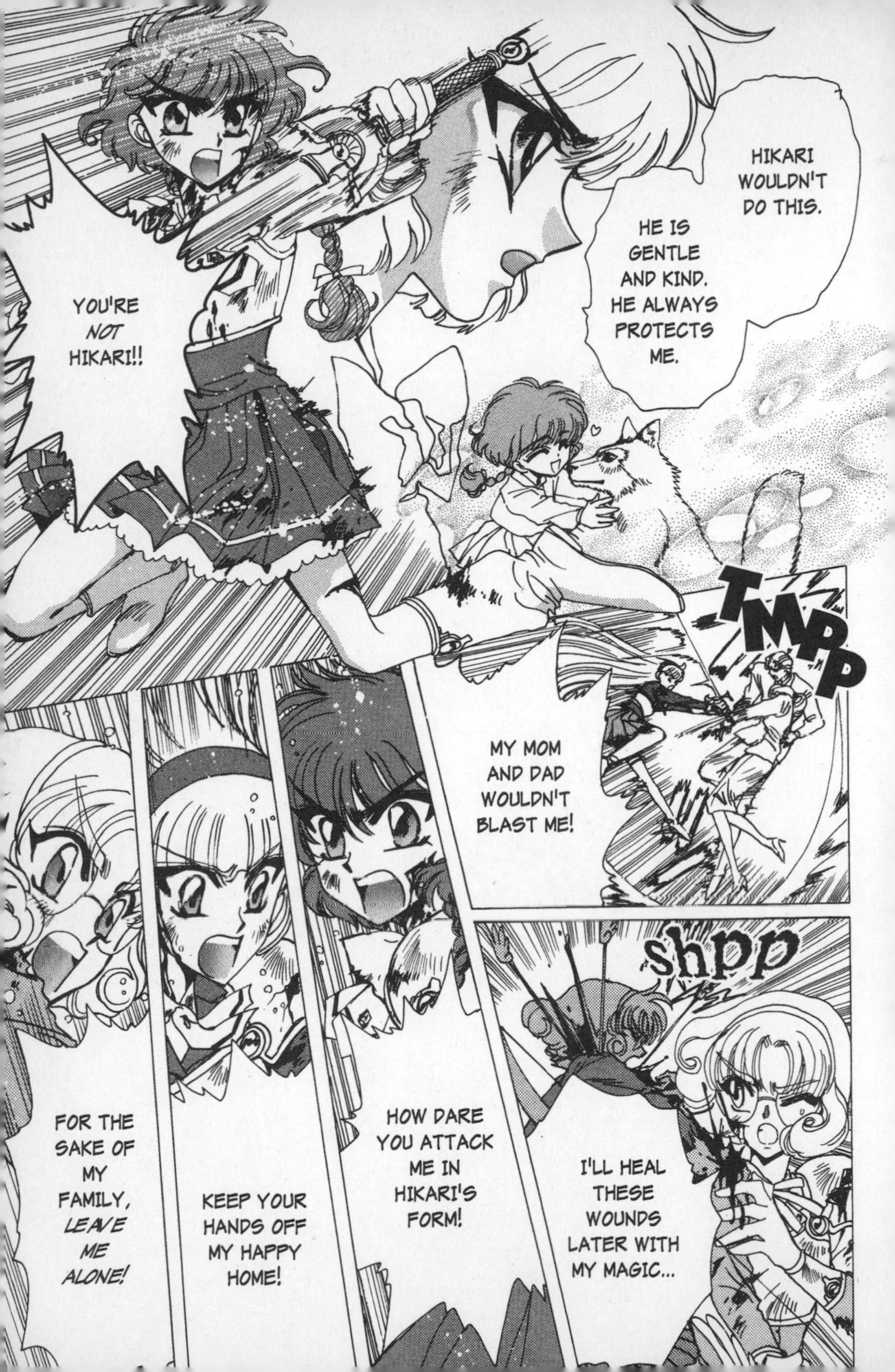
HIKARI WOULDN'T DO THIS.
HE IS GENTLE AND KIND. HE ALWAYS PROTECTS ME.
TMPP
MY MOM AND DAD WOULDN'T BLAST ME!
YOU'RE *NOT* HIKARI!!
shpp
I'LL HEAL THESE WOUNDS LATER WITH MY MAGIC...
HOW DARE YOU ATTACK ME IN HIKARI'S FORM!
KEEP YOUR HANDS OFF MY HAPPY HOME!
FOR THE SAKE OF MY FAMILY, *LEAVE ME ALONE!*

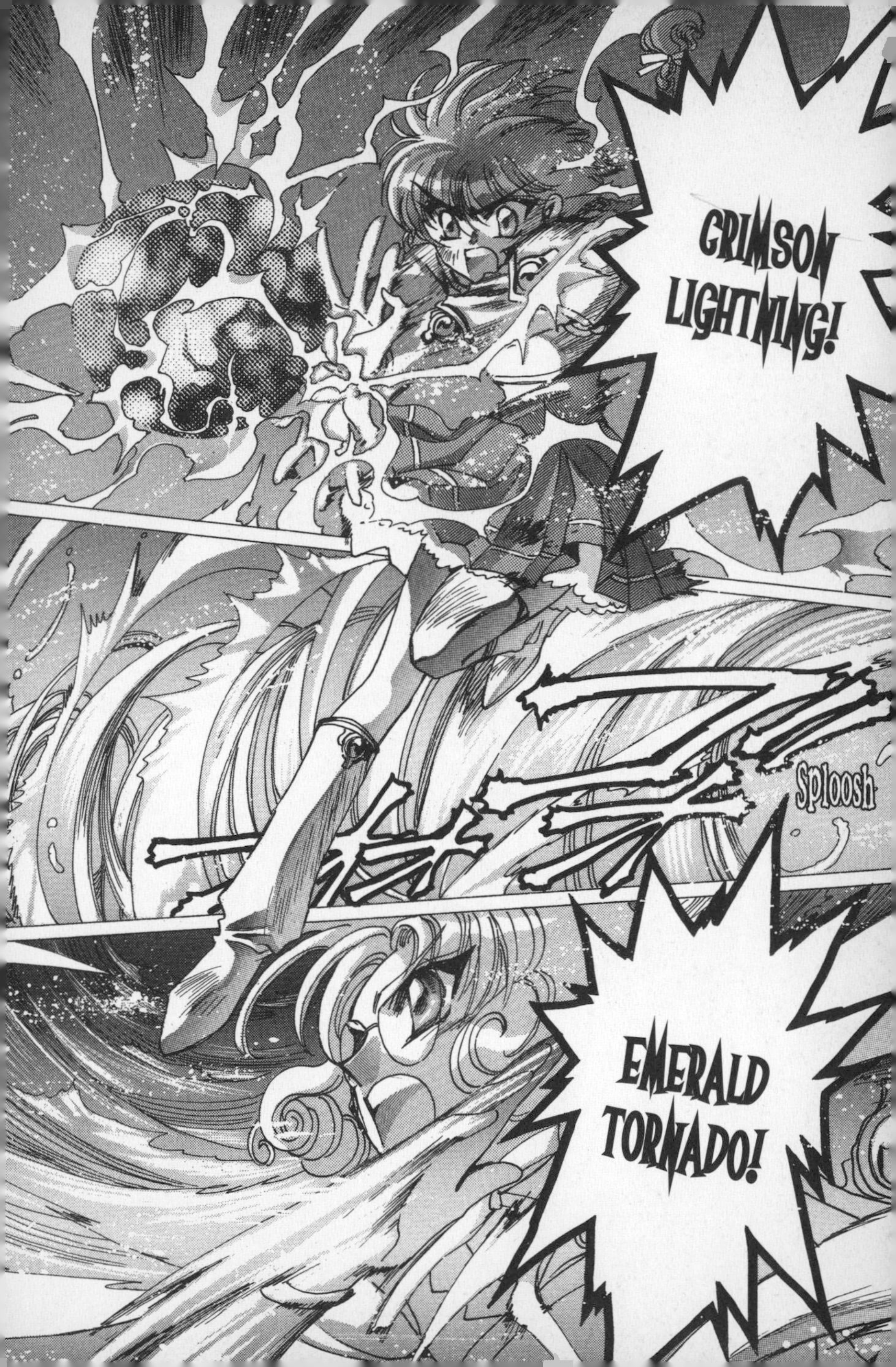
CRIMSON LIGHTNING!
Sploosh
EMERALD TORNADO!

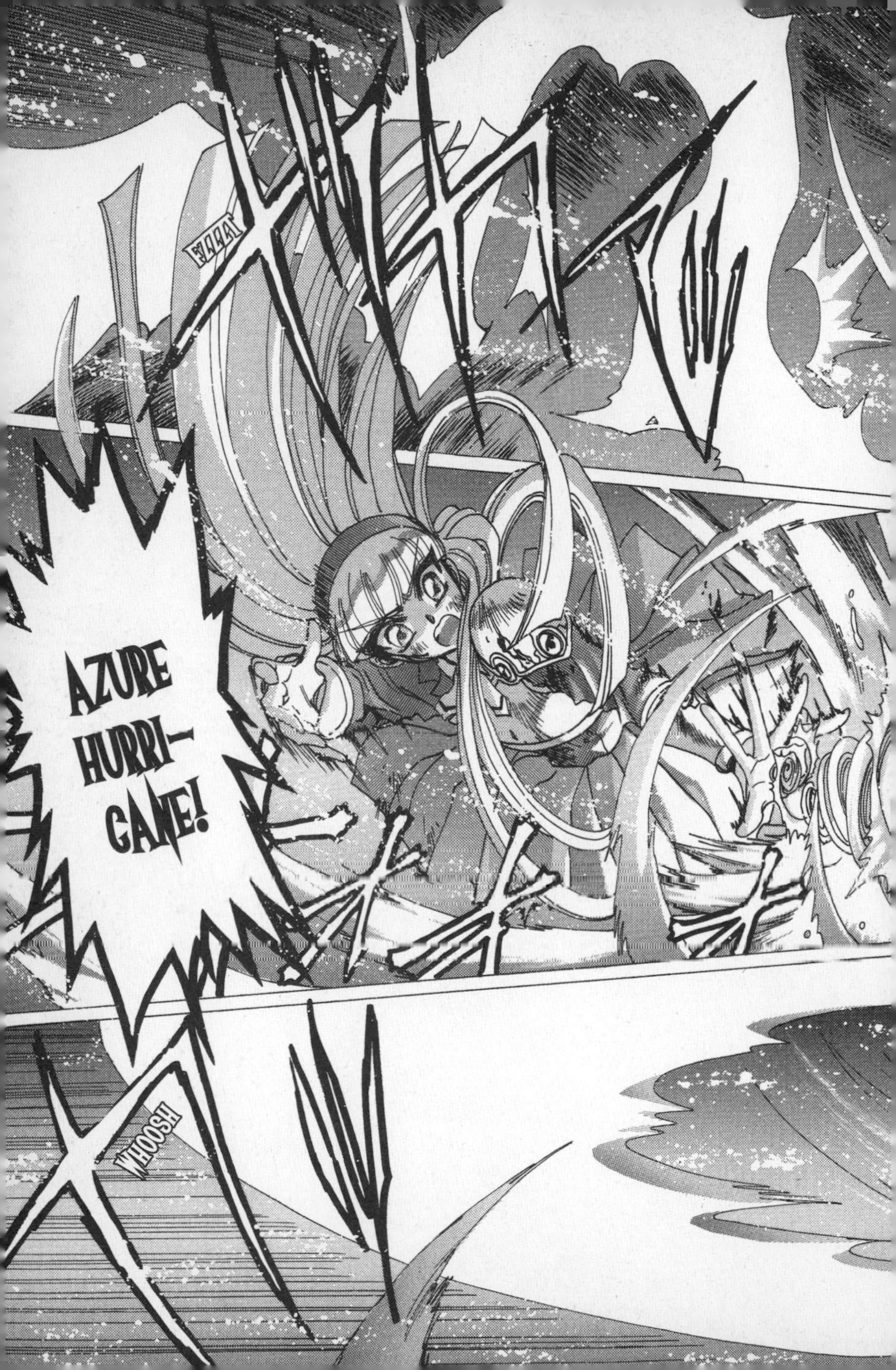
AZURE HURRI-CANE!
WHOOSH

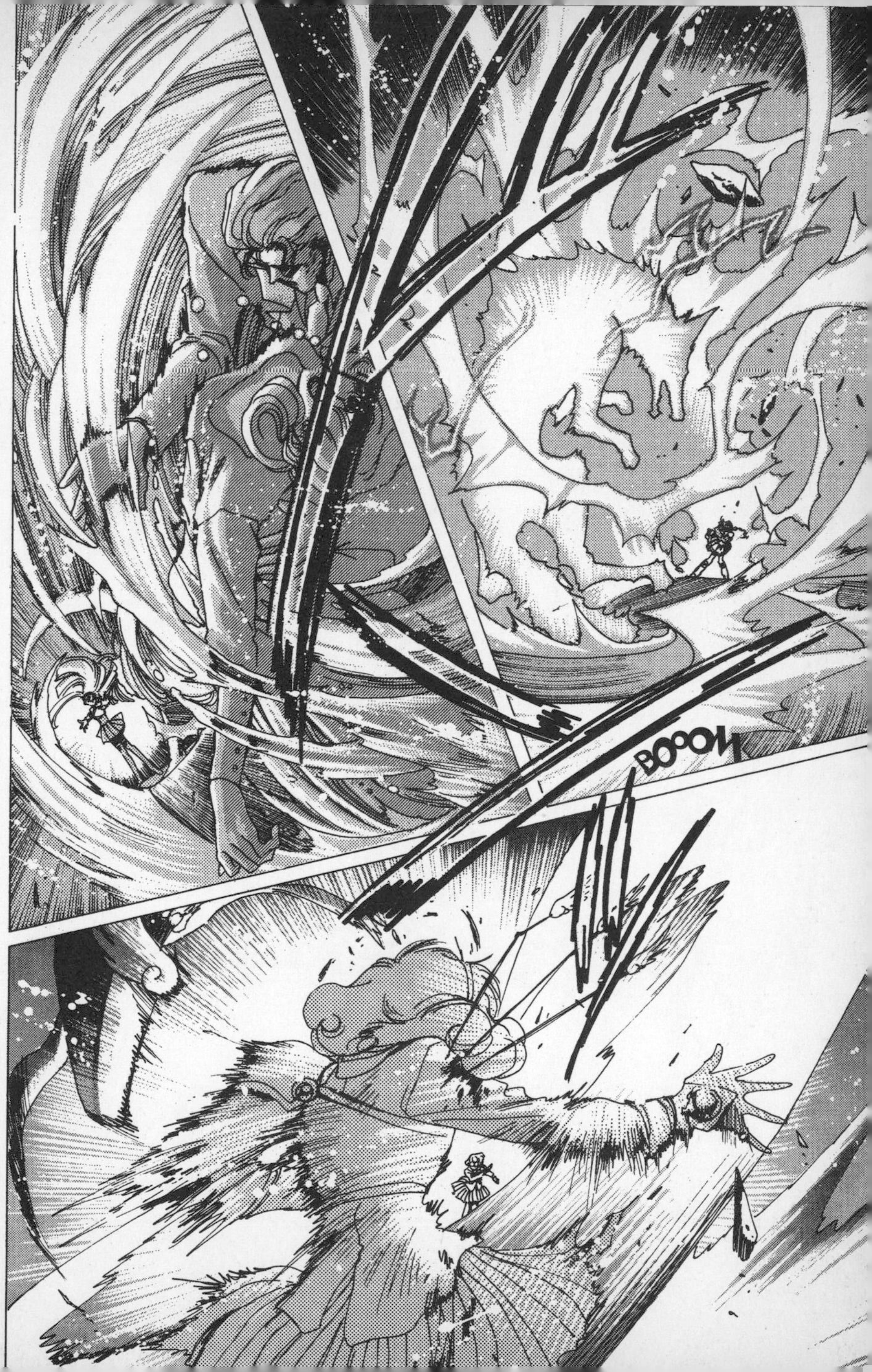
BOOOOM

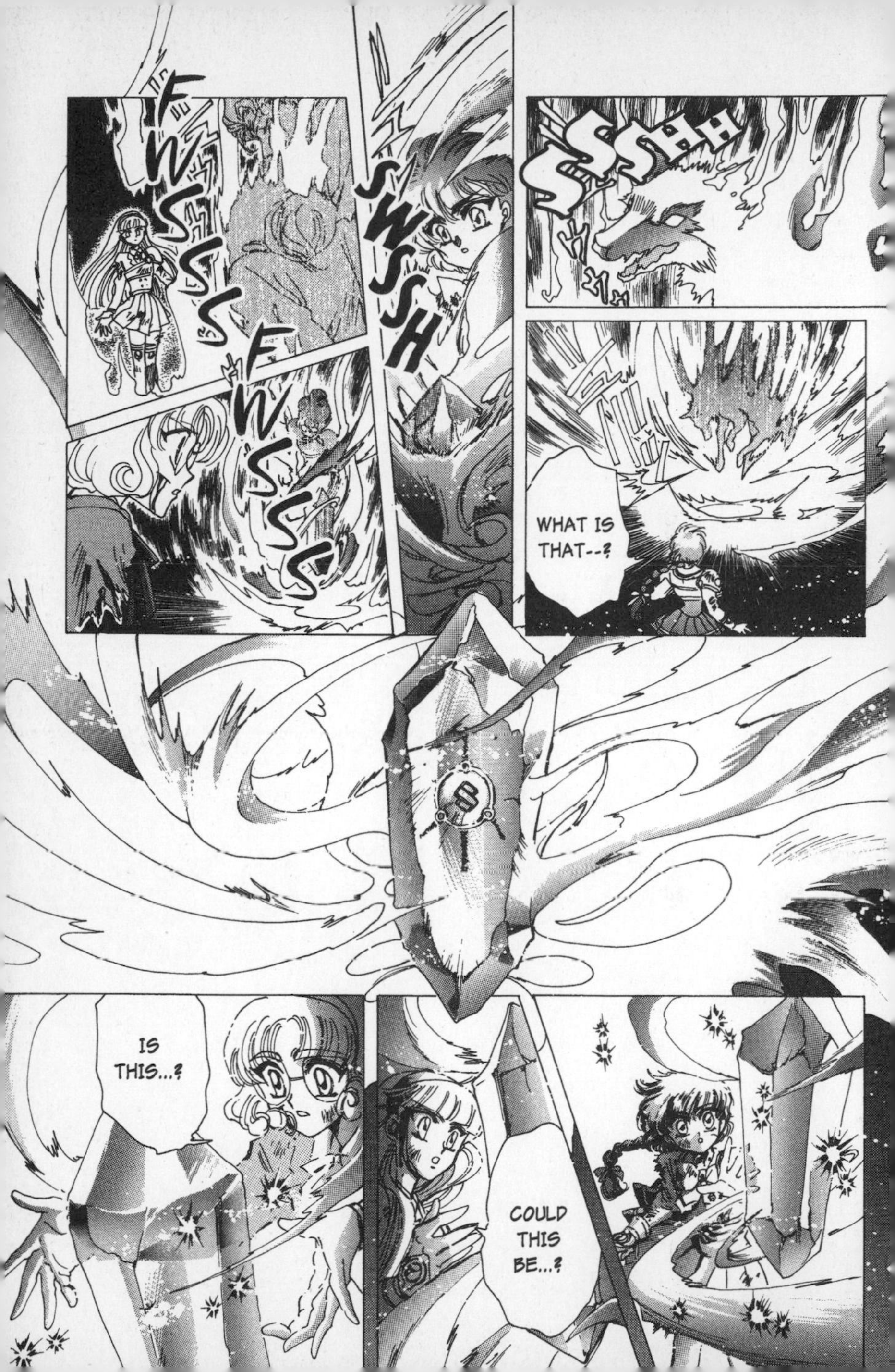
SSHH
WHAT IS THAT--?
SWSSH
FWSSS
FWSSS
COULD THIS BE...?
IS THIS...?

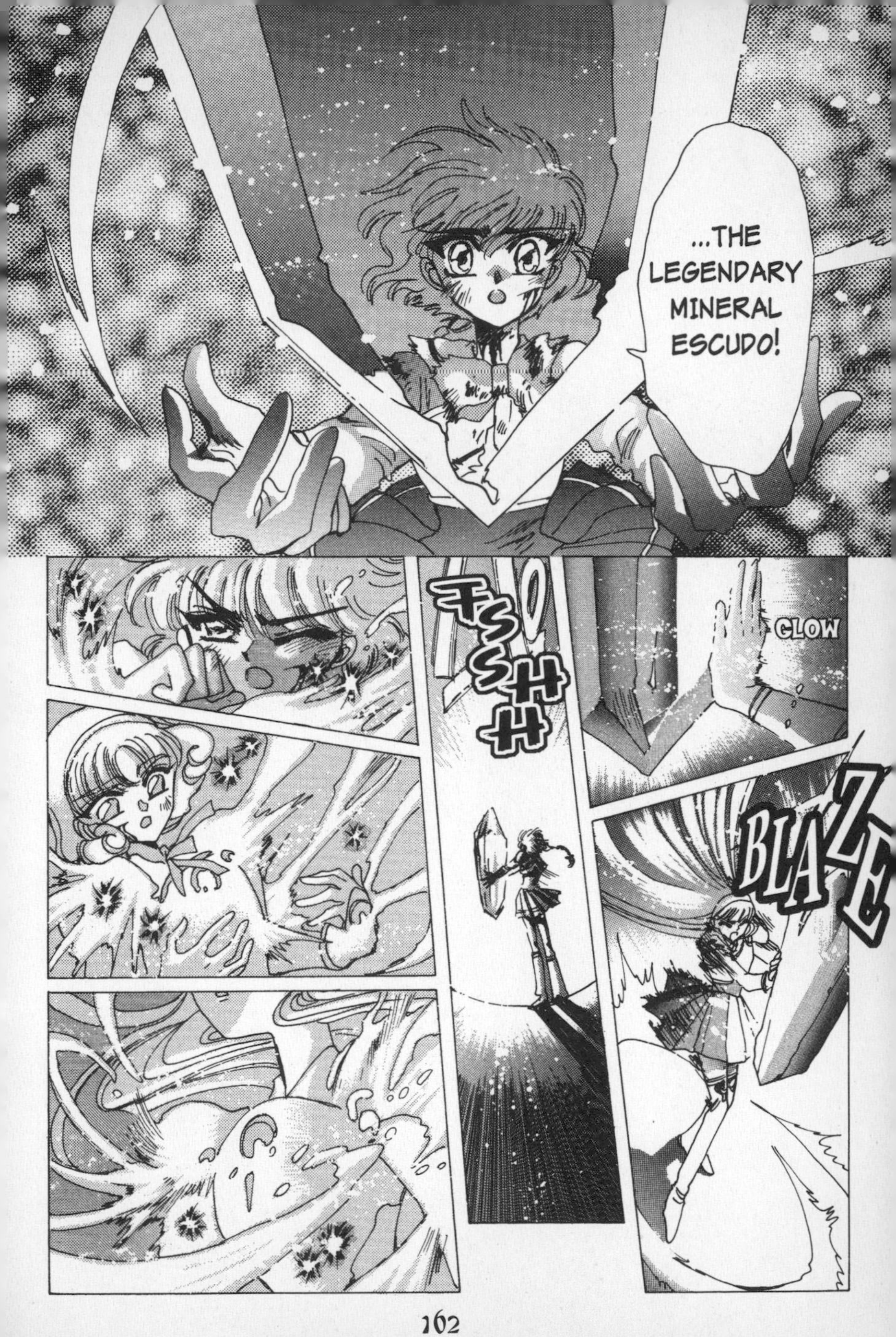
...THE LEGENDARY MINERAL ESCUDO!
GLOW
BLAZE
FSSHH

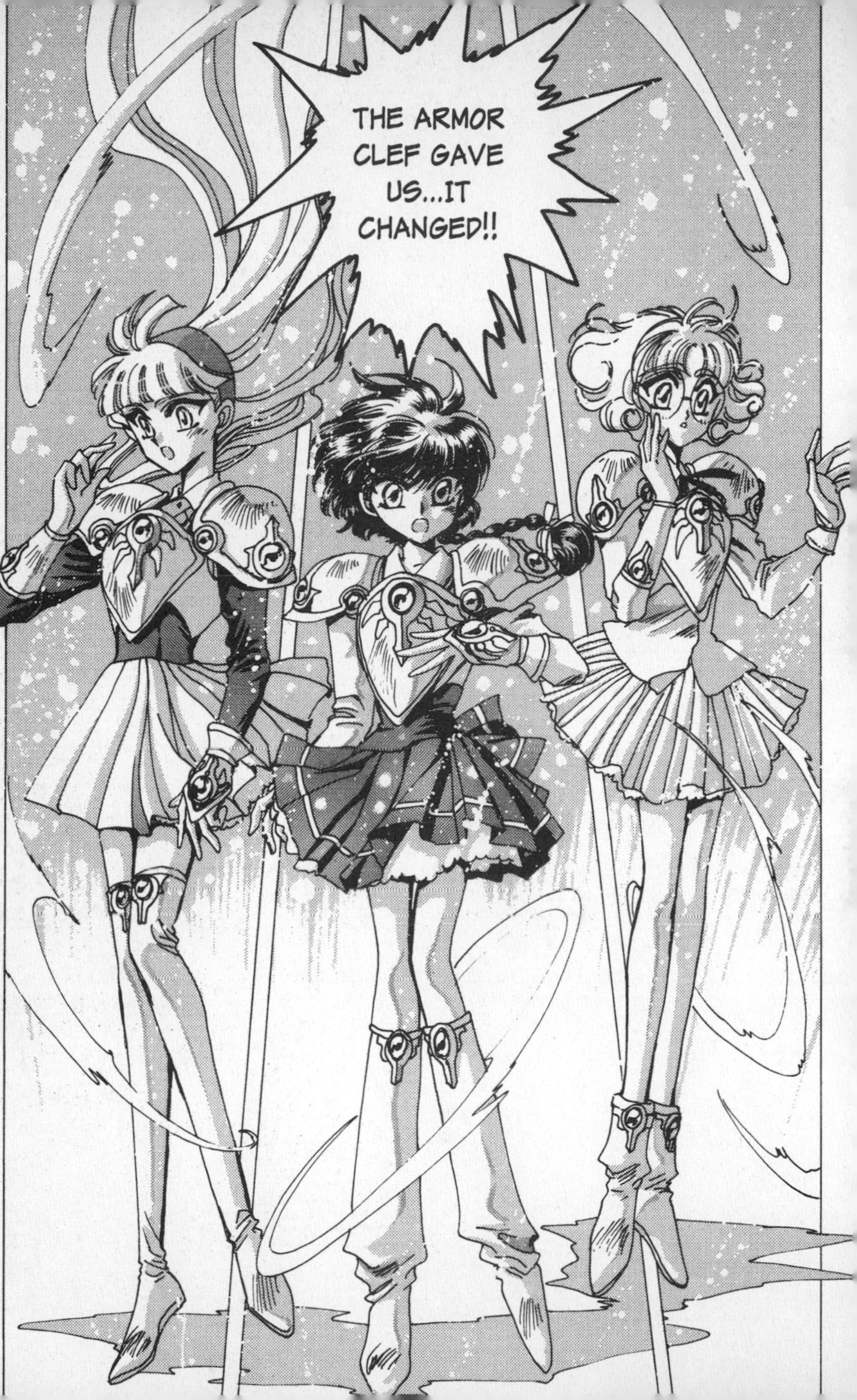
THE ARMOR CLEF GAVE US...IT CHANGED!!

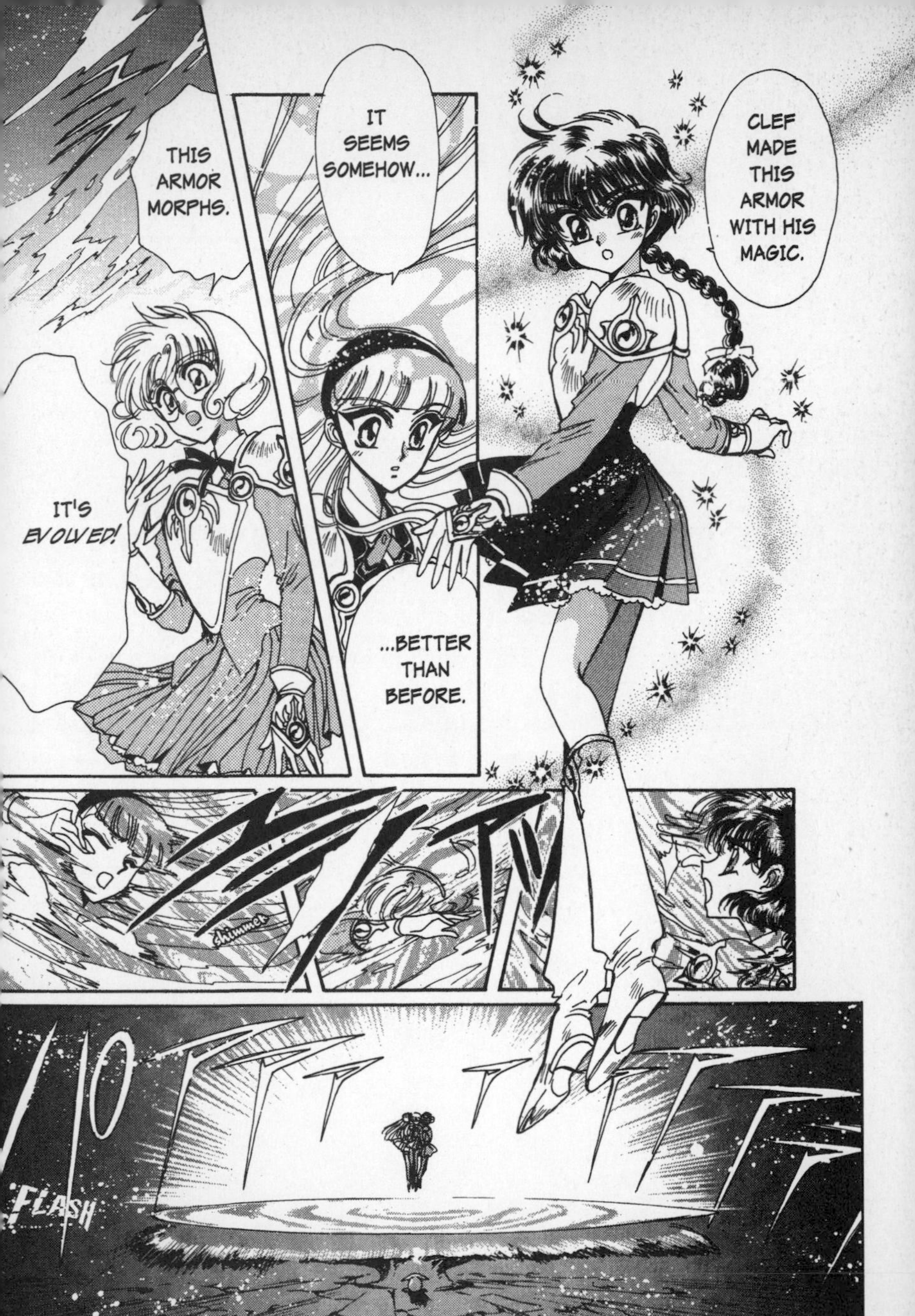
CLEF MADE THIS ARMOR WITH HIS MAGIC.
IT SEEMS SOMEHOW...
...BETTER THAN BEFORE.
THIS ARMOR MORPHS.
IT'S EVOLVED!
shimmer
FLASH

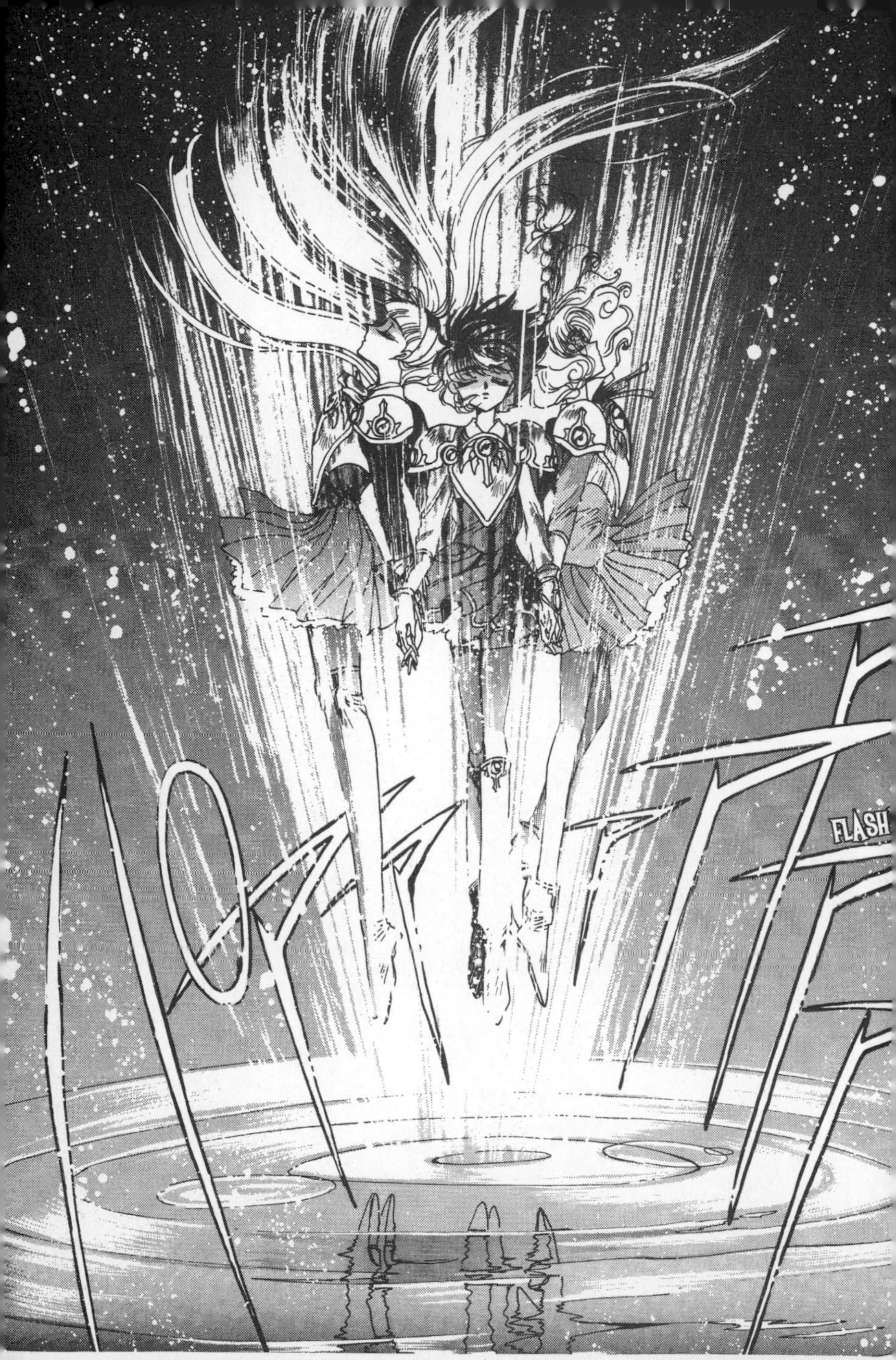
FLASH

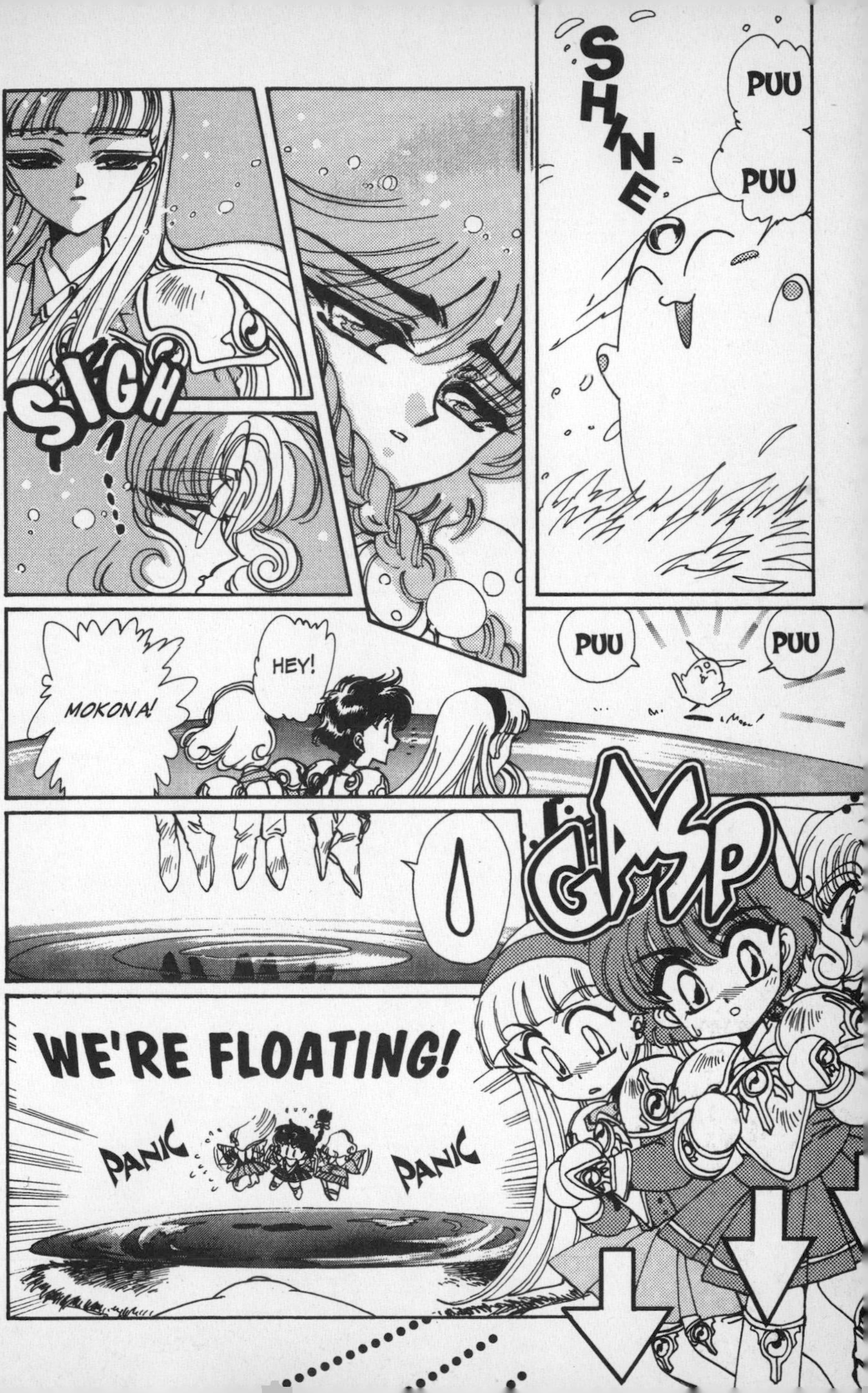
SHINE
PUU
PUU
SIGH
PUU
PUU
HEY!
MOKONA!
GMP
WE'RE FLOATING!
PANIC
PANIC

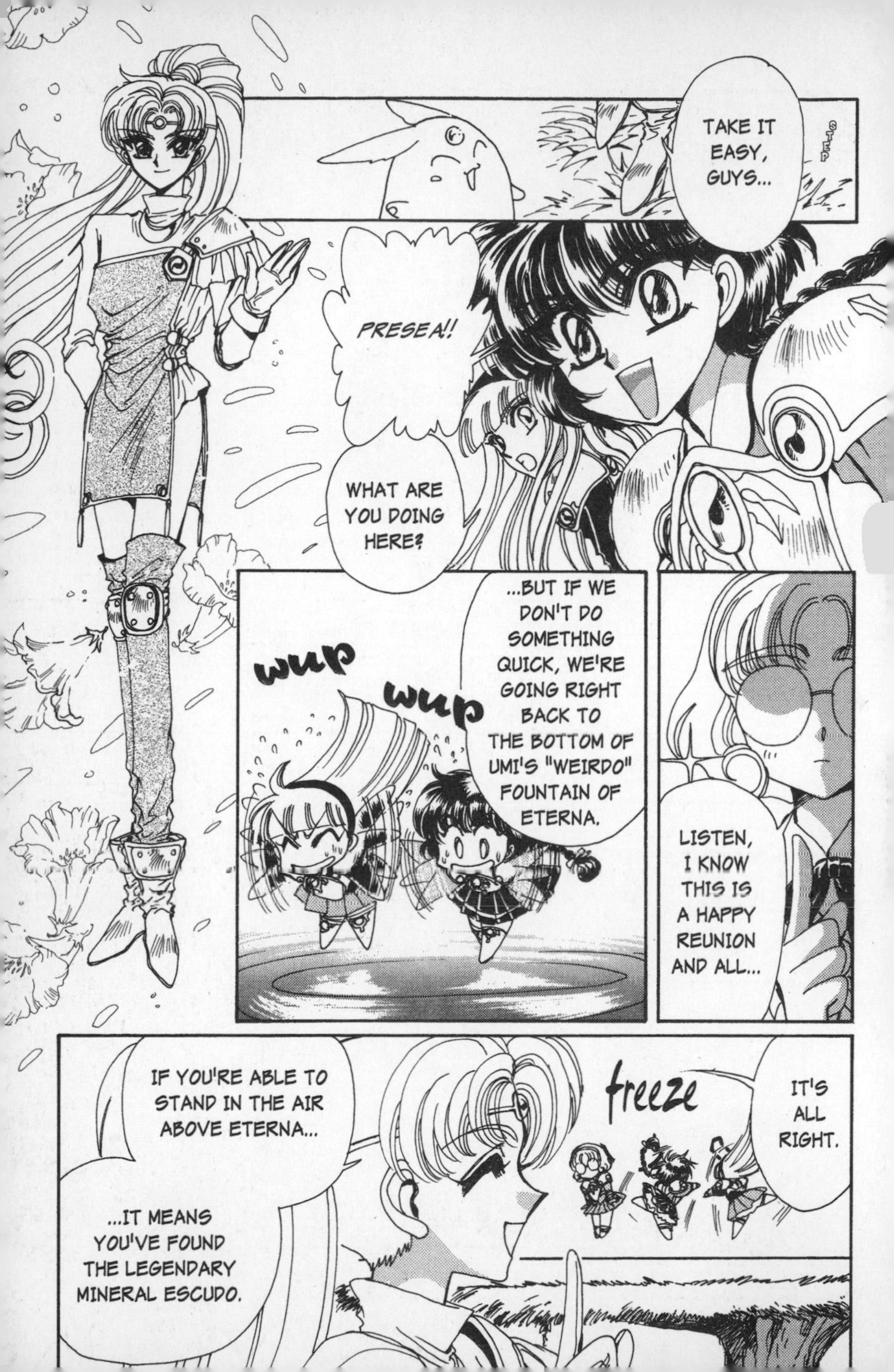
TAKE IT EASY, GUYS...
STEP
PRESEA!!
WHAT ARE YOU DOING HERE?
LISTEN, I KNOW THIS IS A HAPPY REUNION AND ALL...
...BUT IF WE DON'T DO SOMETHING QUICK, WE'RE GOING RIGHT BACK TO THE BOTTOM OF UMI'S "WEIRDO" FOUNTAIN OF ETERNA.
wup
wup
IT'S ALL RIGHT.
freeze
IF YOU'RE ABLE TO STAND IN THE AIR ABOVE ETERNA...
...IT MEANS YOU'VE FOUND THE LEGENDARY MINERAL ESCUDO.

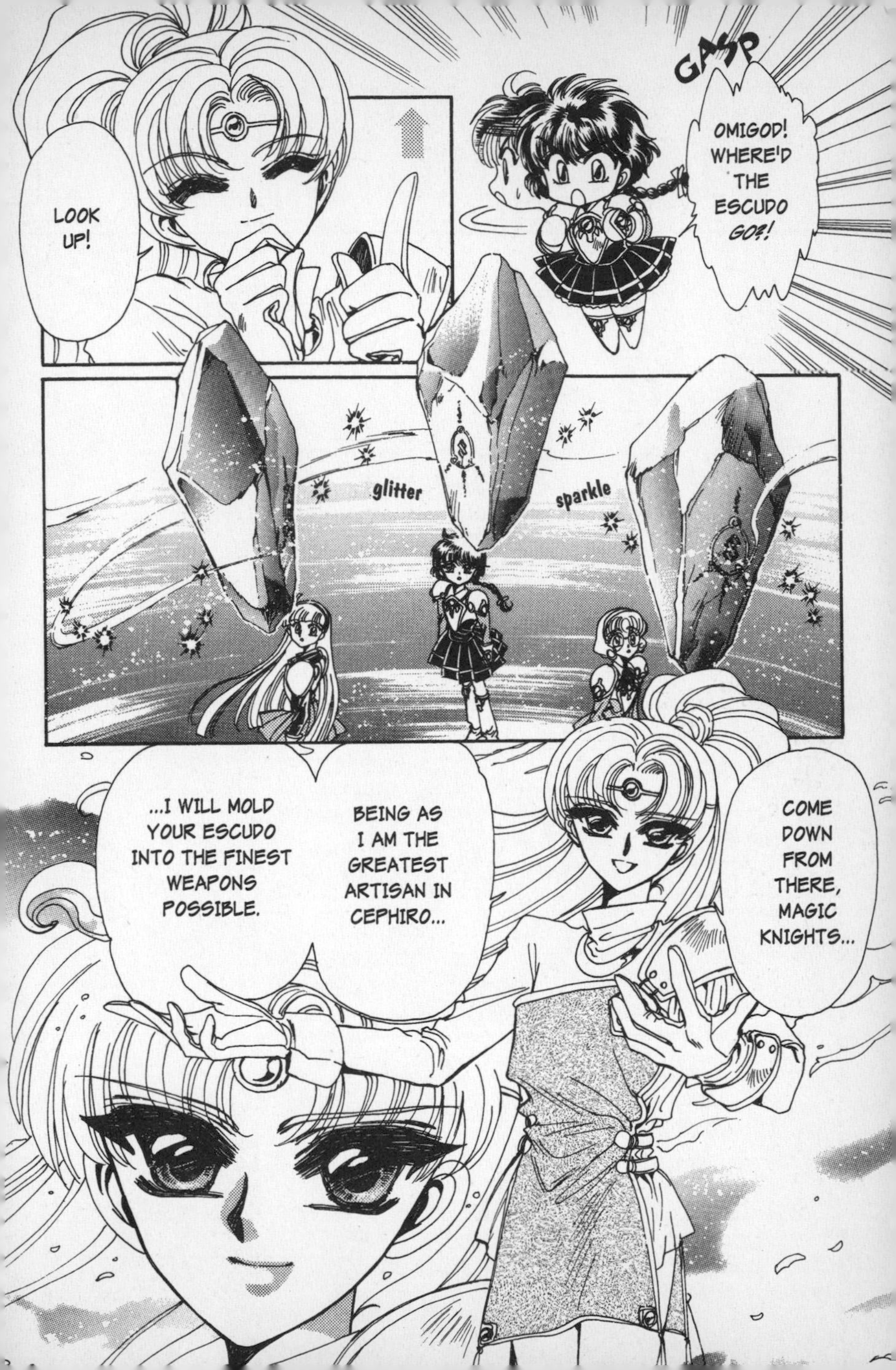
GASP
OMIGOD! WHERE'D THE ESCUDO GO?!
LOOK UP!
sparkle
glitter
COME DOWN FROM THERE, MAGIC KNIGHTS...
BEING AS I AM THE GREATEST ARTISAN IN CEPHIRO...
...I WILL MOLD YOUR ESCUDO INTO THE FINEST WEAPONS POSSIBLE.

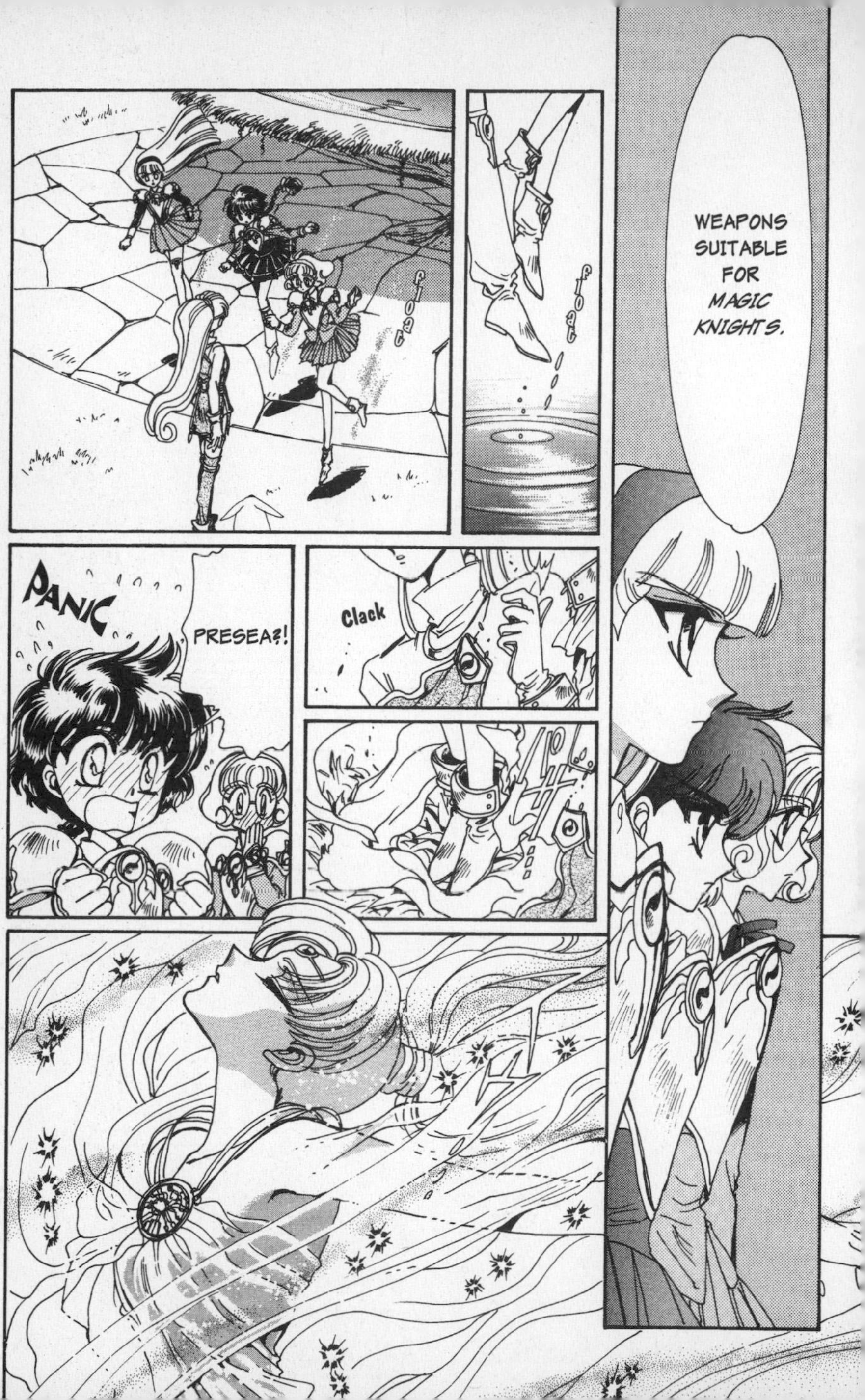
WEAPONS SUITABLE FOR MAGIC KNIGHTS.
float
float
Clack
PANIC
PRESEA?!

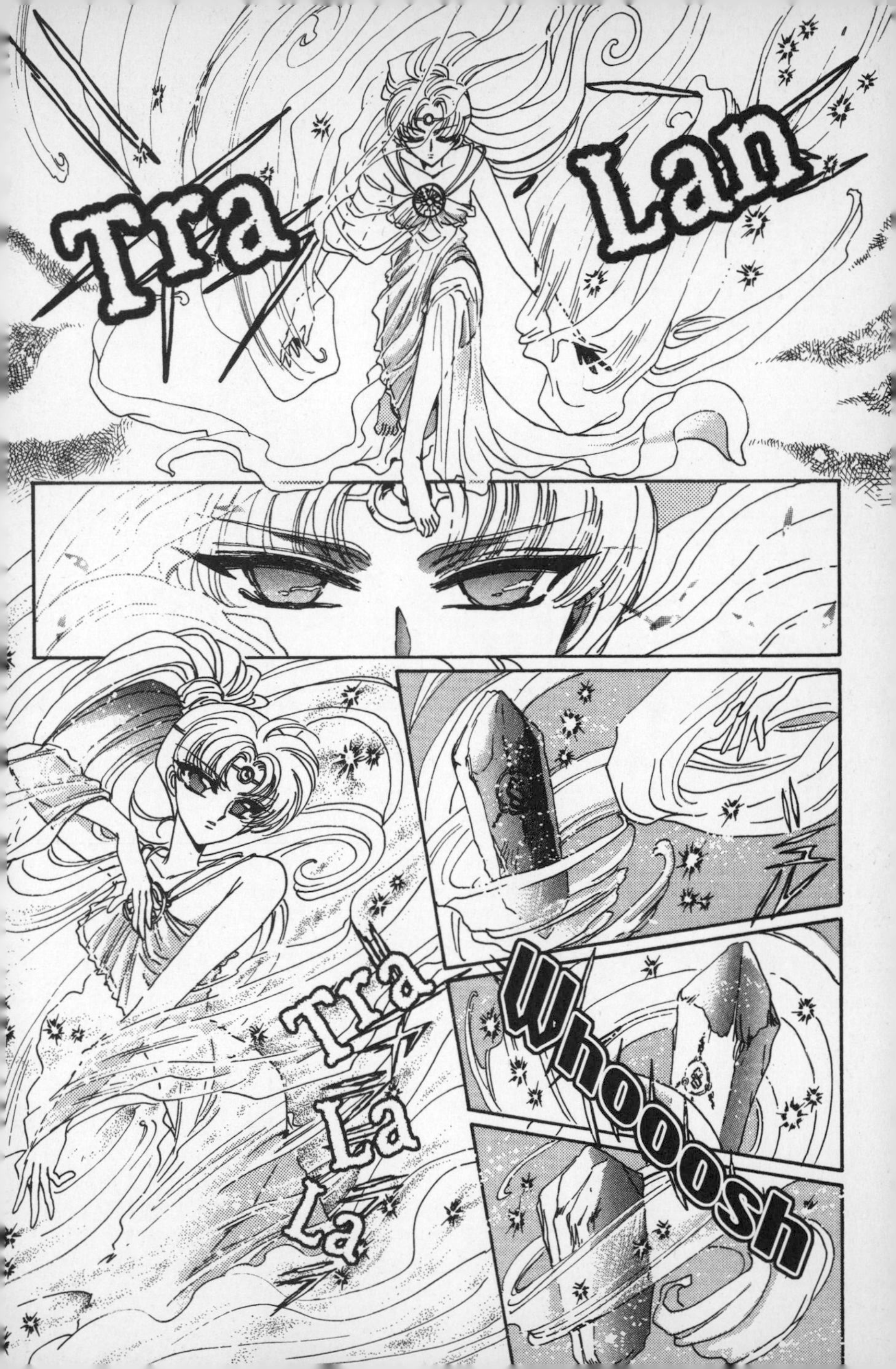
Tra Lan
Whoooosh
Tra La La

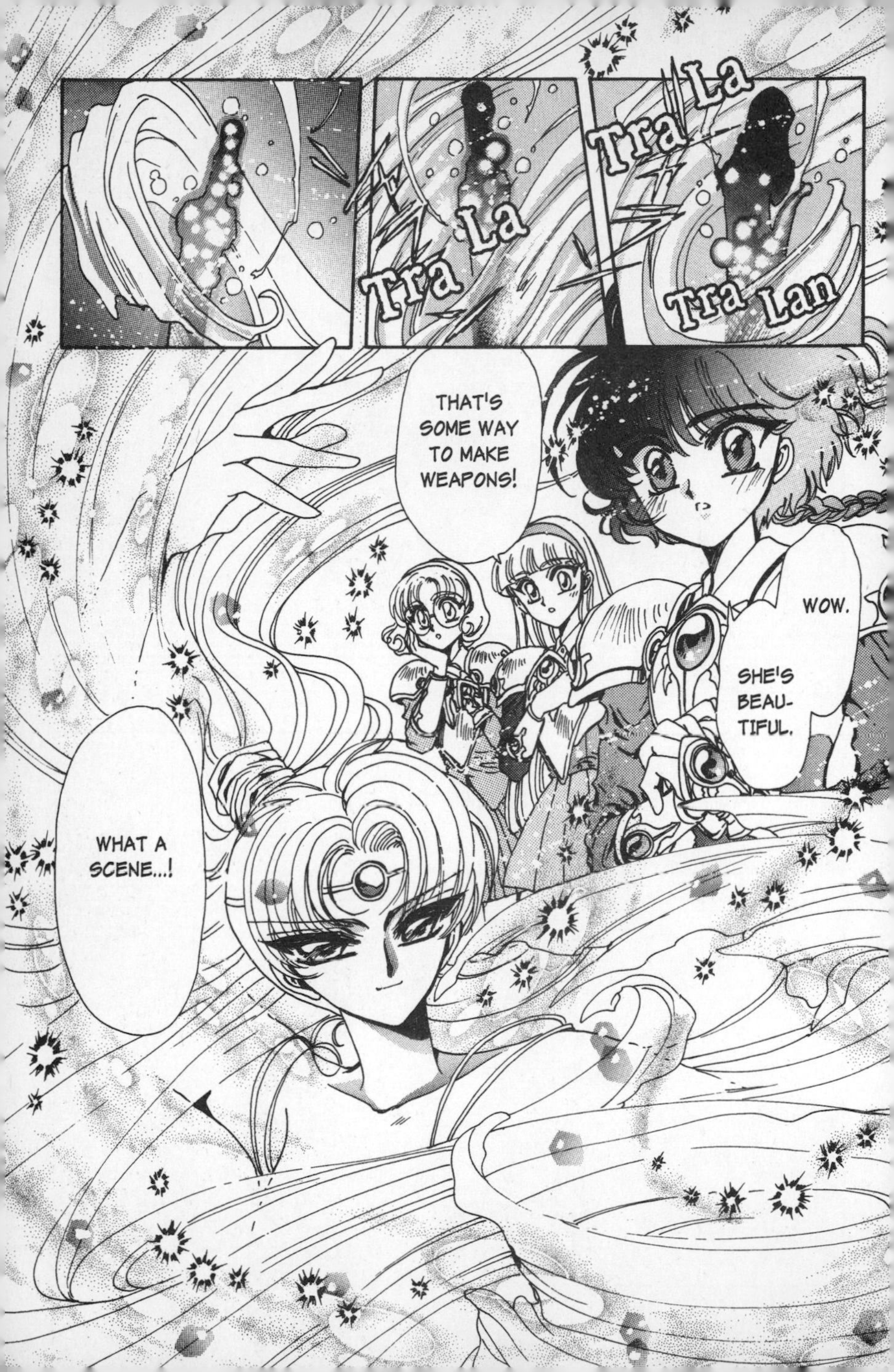
Tra La
Tra Lan
Tra La
WOW.
SHE'S BEAU-TIFUL.
THAT'S SOME WAY TO MAKE WEAPONS!
WHAT A SCENE...!

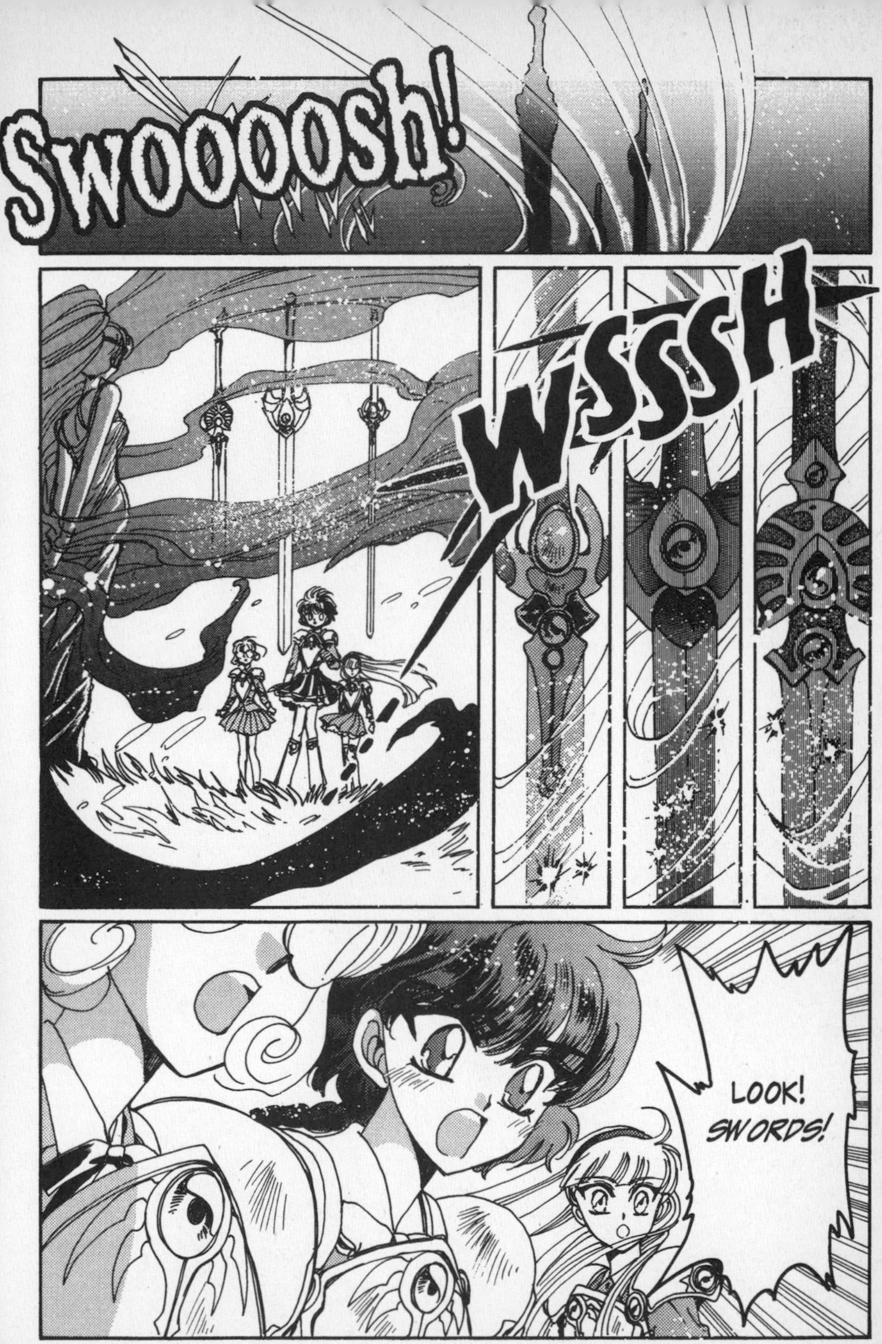
Swoooosh!
WSSSH
LOOK! SWORDS!

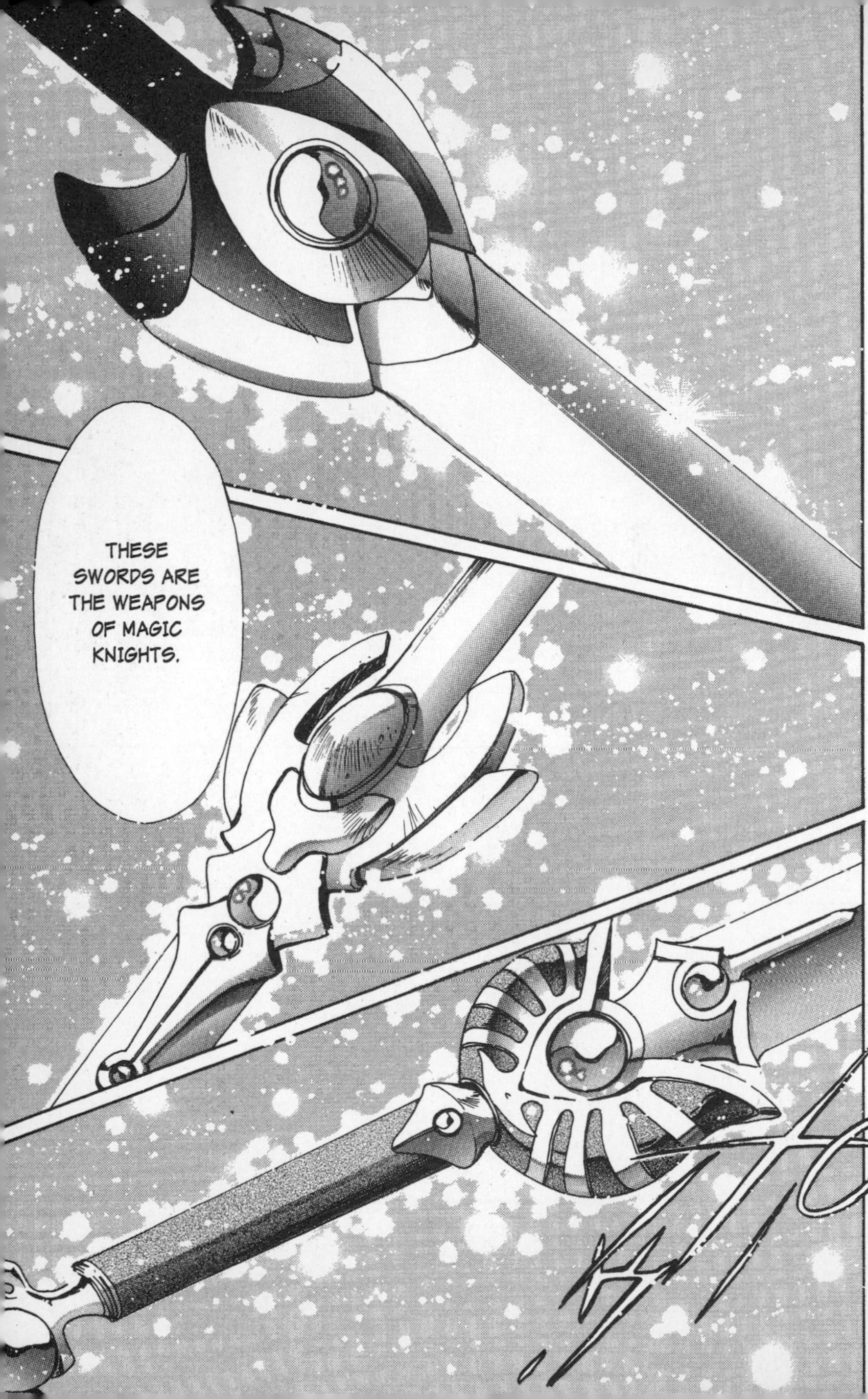
THESE SWORDS ARE THE WEAPONS OF MAGIC KNIGHTS.

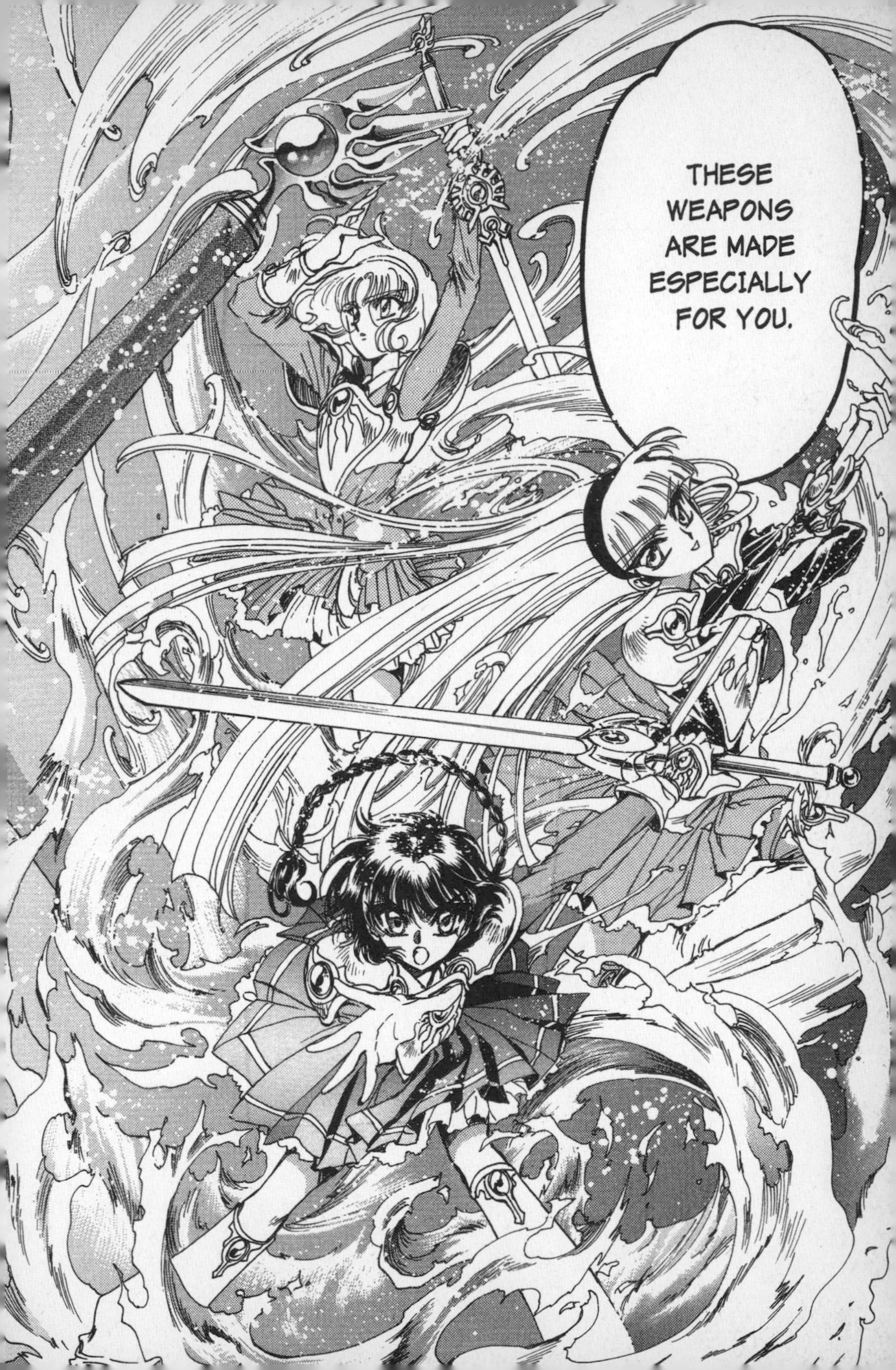
THESE WEAPONS ARE MADE ESPECIALLY FOR YOU.

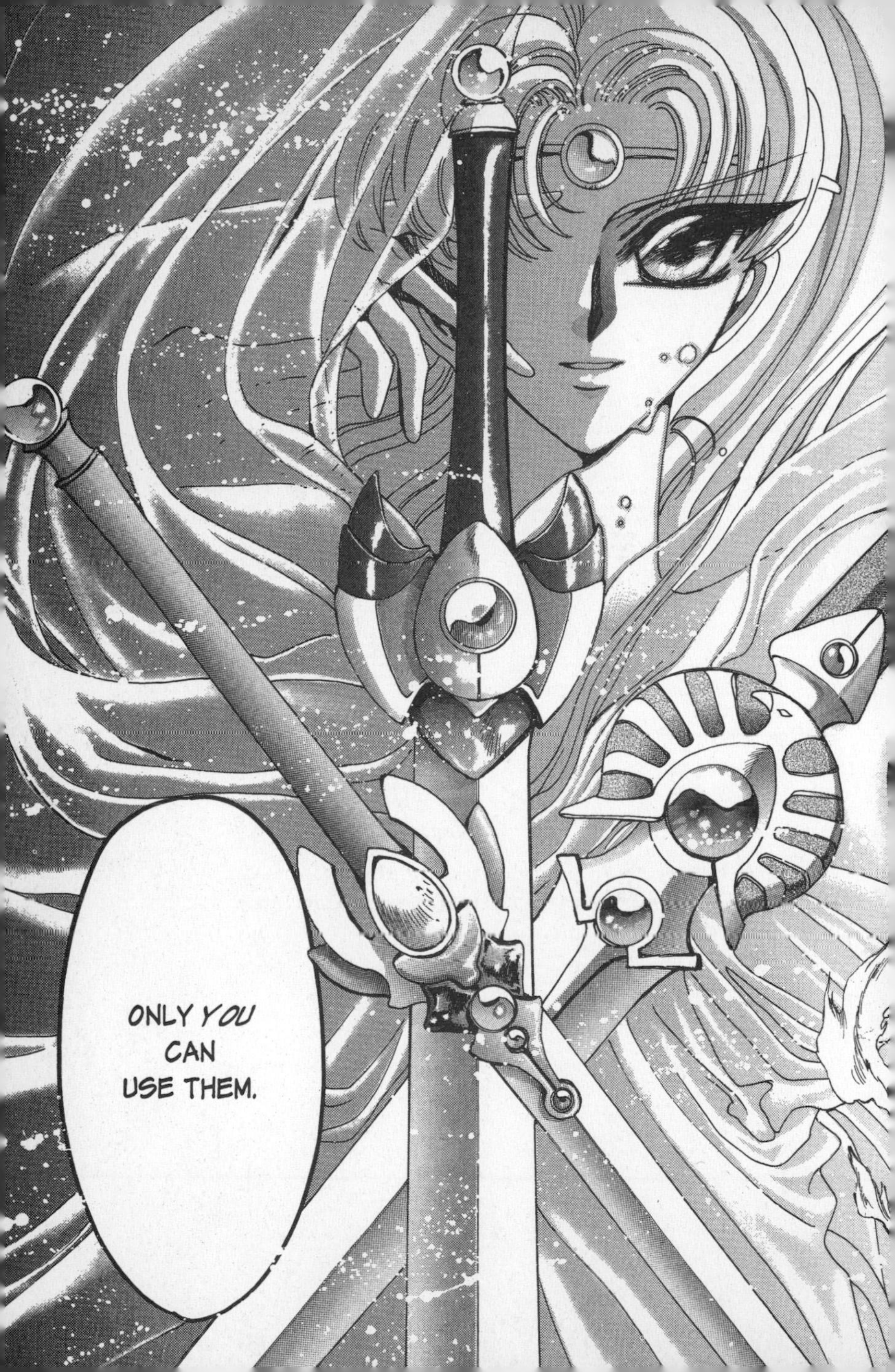
ONLY YOU CAN USE THEM.

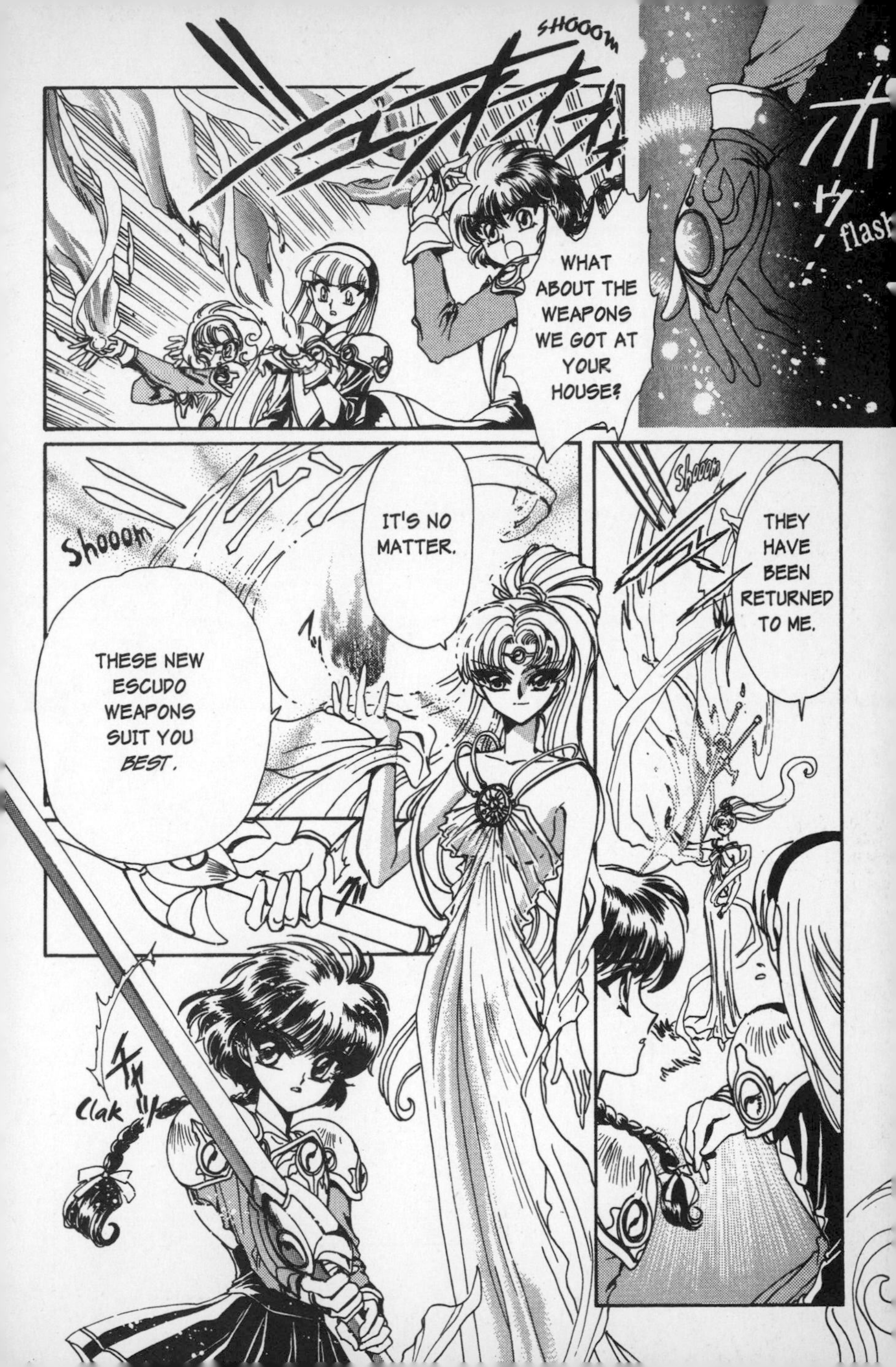
flash
SHOOOM
WHAT ABOUT THE WEAPONS WE GOT AT YOUR HOUSE?
Shooom
THEY HAVE BEEN RETURNED TO ME.
IT'S NO MATTER.
Shooom
THESE NEW ESCUDO WEAPONS SUIT YOU *BEST*.
Clak

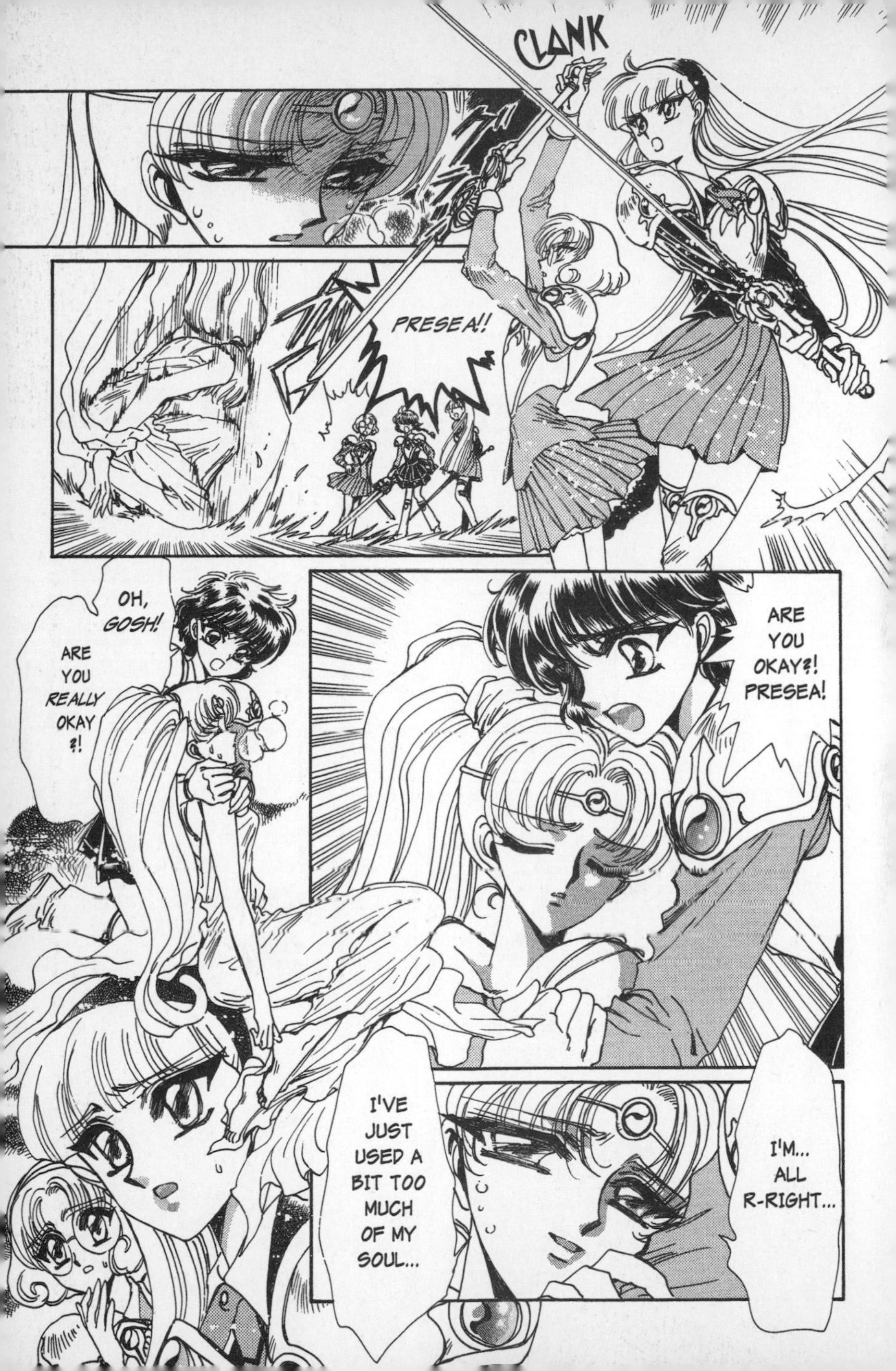
CLANK
PRESEA!!
ARE YOU OKAY?! PRESEA!
OH, GOSH!
ARE YOU REALLY OKAY?!
I'M... ALL R-RIGHT...
I'VE JUST USED A BIT TOO MUCH OF MY SOUL...

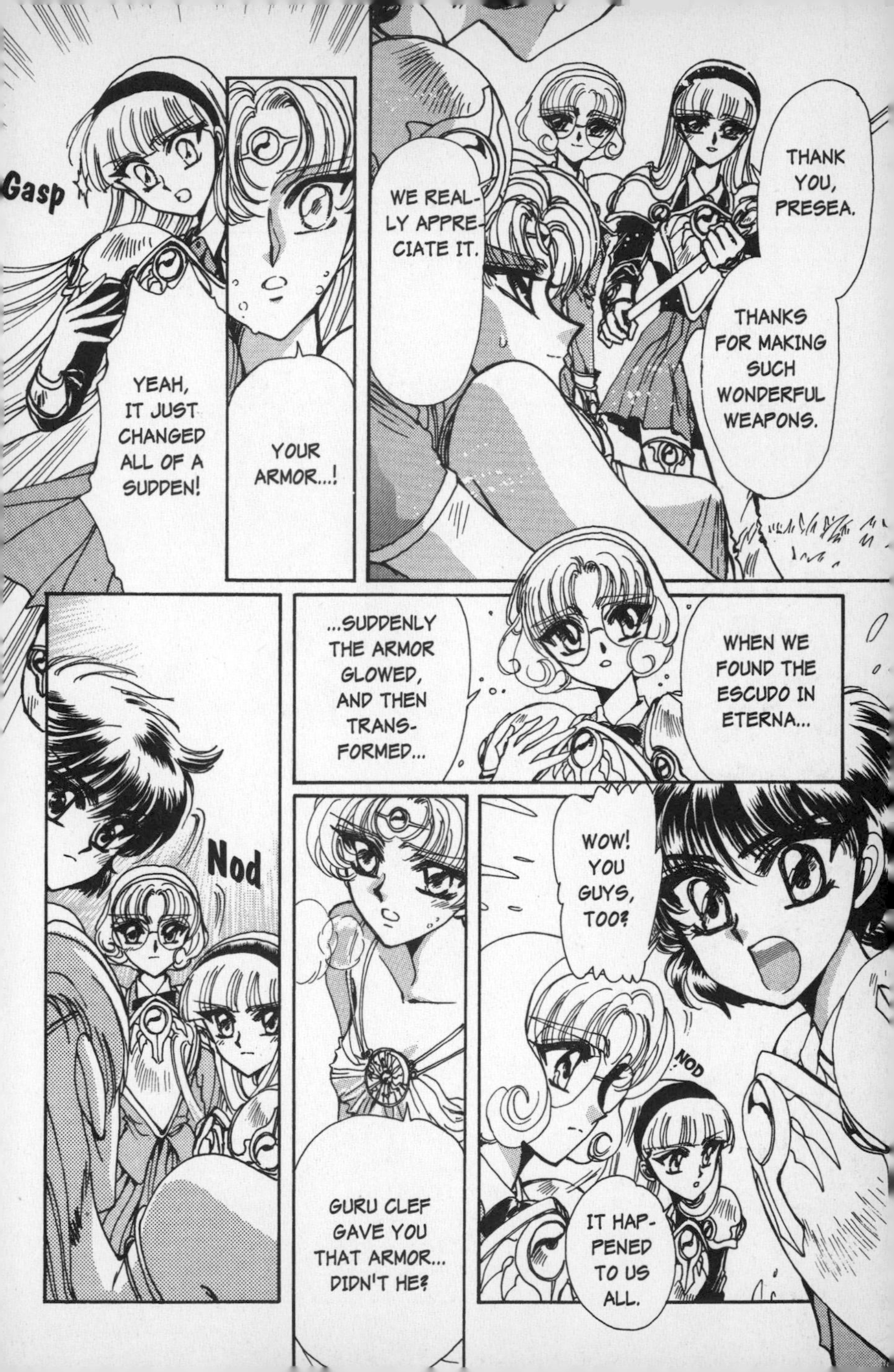
THANK YOU, PRESEA.
THANKS FOR MAKING SUCH WONDERFUL WEAPONS.
WE REAL-LY APPRE-CIATE IT.
YOUR ARMOR...!
Gasp
YEAH, IT JUST CHANGED ALL OF A SUDDEN!
WHEN WE FOUND THE ESCUDO IN ETERNA...
...SUDDENLY THE ARMOR GLOWED, AND THEN TRANS-FORMED...
WOW! YOU GUYS, TOO?
NOD
IT HAP-PENED TO US ALL.
GURU CLEF GAVE YOU THAT ARMOR... DIDN'T HE?
Nod

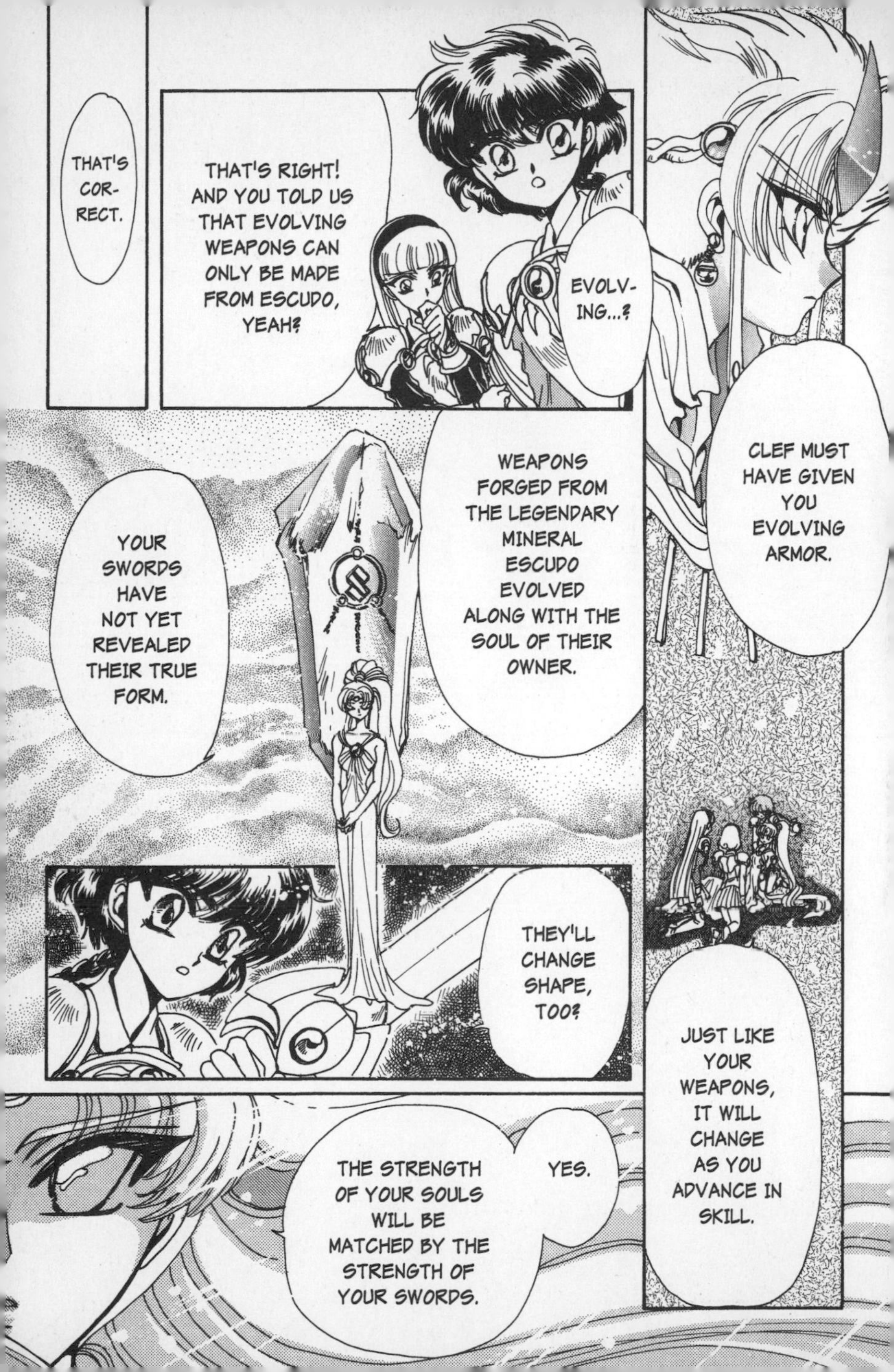
CLEF MUST HAVE GIVEN YOU EVOLVING ARMOR.
JUST LIKE YOUR WEAPONS, IT WILL CHANGE AS YOU ADVANCE IN SKILL.
EVOLV-ING...?
THAT'S RIGHT! AND YOU TOLD US THAT EVOLVING WEAPONS CAN ONLY BE MADE FROM ESCUDO, YEAH?
THAT'S COR-RECT.
WEAPONS FORGED FROM THE LEGENDARY MINERAL ESCUDO EVOLVED ALONG WITH THE SOUL OF THEIR OWNER.
YOUR SWORDS HAVE NOT YET REVEALED THEIR TRUE FORM.
THEY'LL CHANGE SHAPE, TOO?
YES.
THE STRENGTH OF YOUR SOULS WILL BE MATCHED BY THE STRENGTH OF YOUR SWORDS.

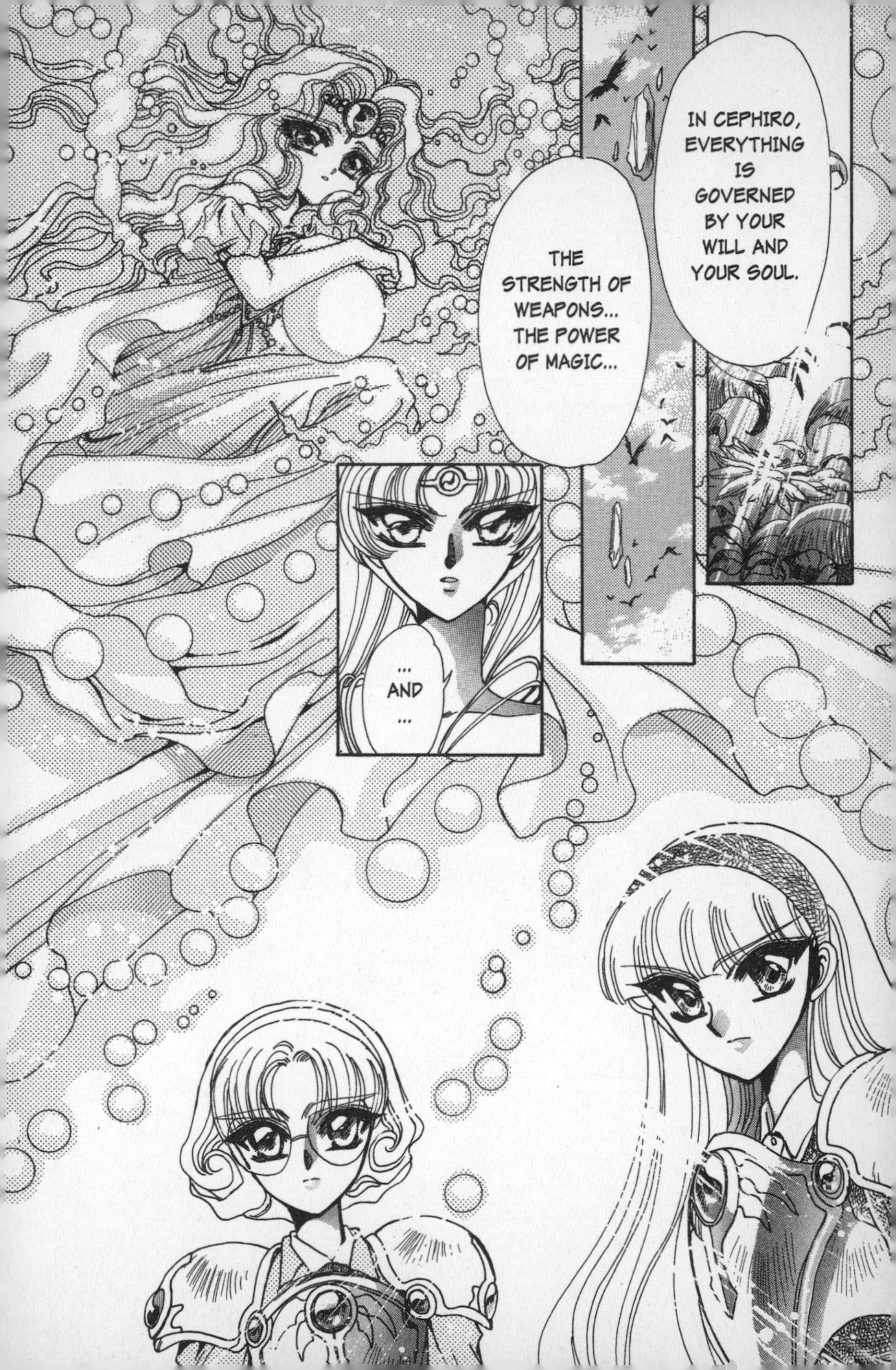
IN CEPHIRO, EVERYTHING IS GOVERNED BY YOUR WILL AND YOUR SOUL.
THE STRENGTH OF WEAPONS... THE POWER OF MAGIC...
... AND ...

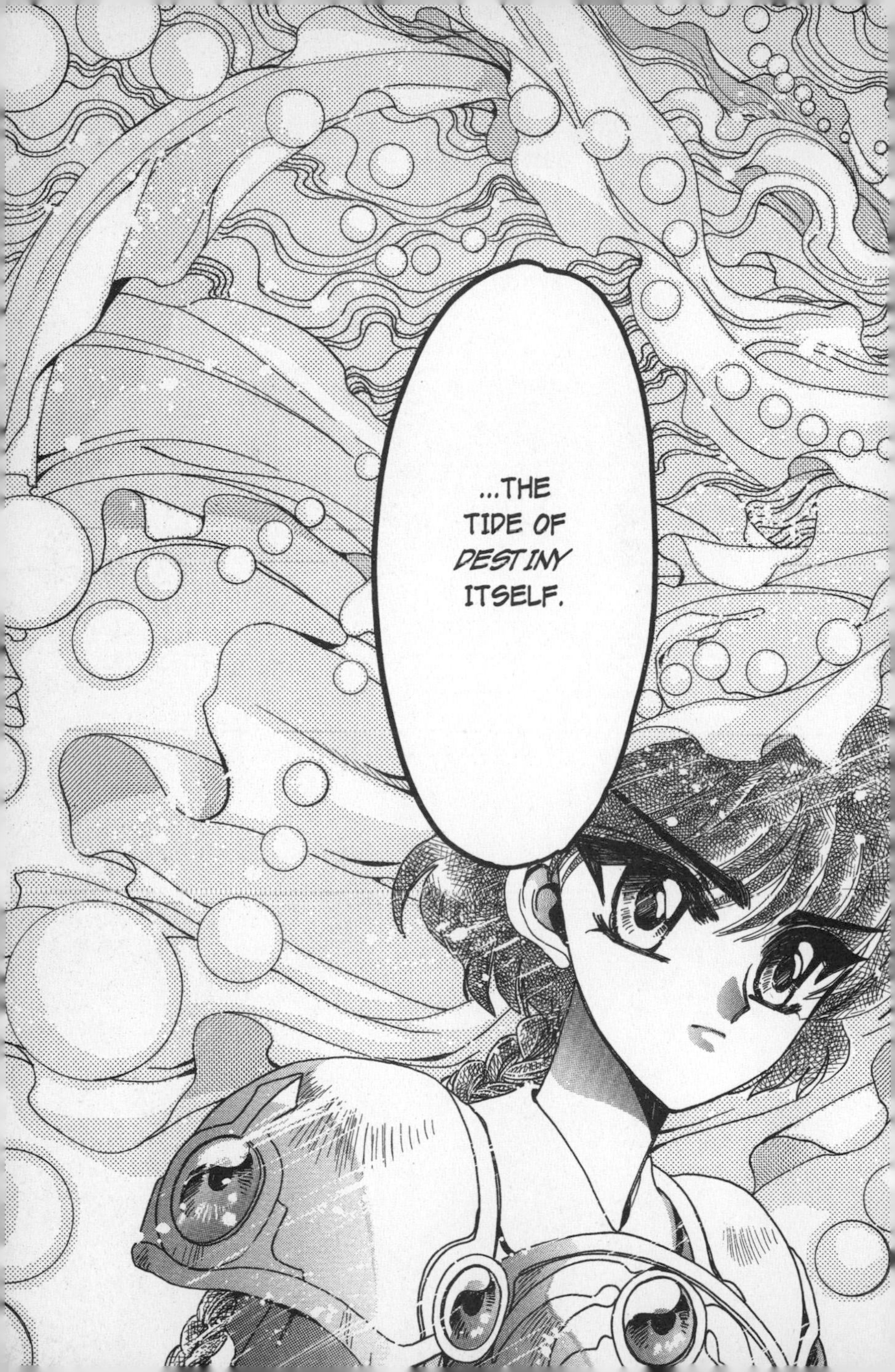
...THE TIDE OF *DESTINY* ITSELF.

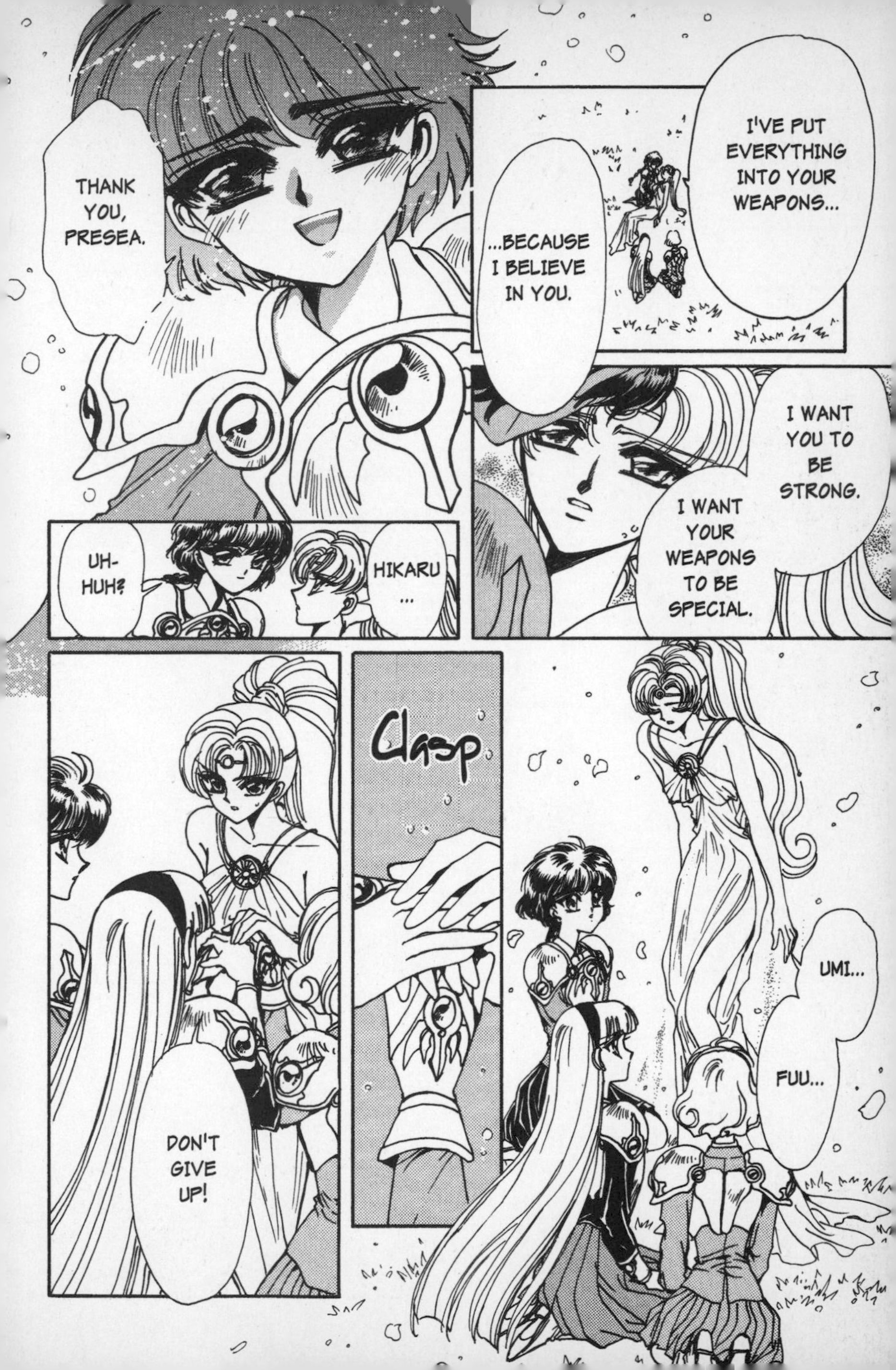

I'VE PUT EVERYTHING INTO YOUR WEAPONS...
...BECAUSE I BELIEVE IN YOU.
I WANT YOU TO BE STRONG.
I WANT YOUR WEAPONS TO BE SPECIAL.
THANK YOU, PRESEA.
HIKARU ...
UH-HUH?
UMI...
FUU...
Clasp
DON'T GIVE UP!

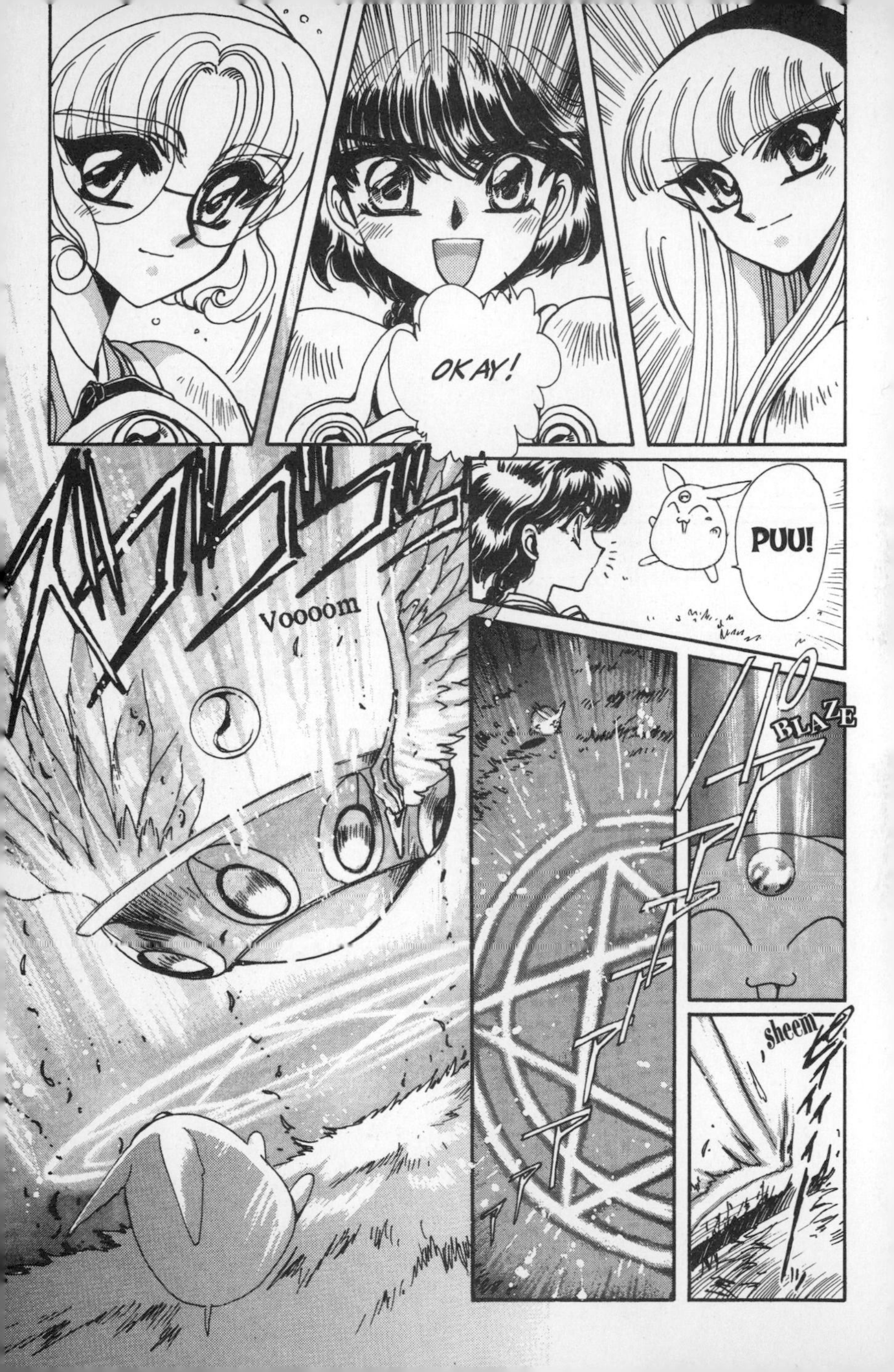
OKAY!
PUU!
Voooom
BLAZE
sheem

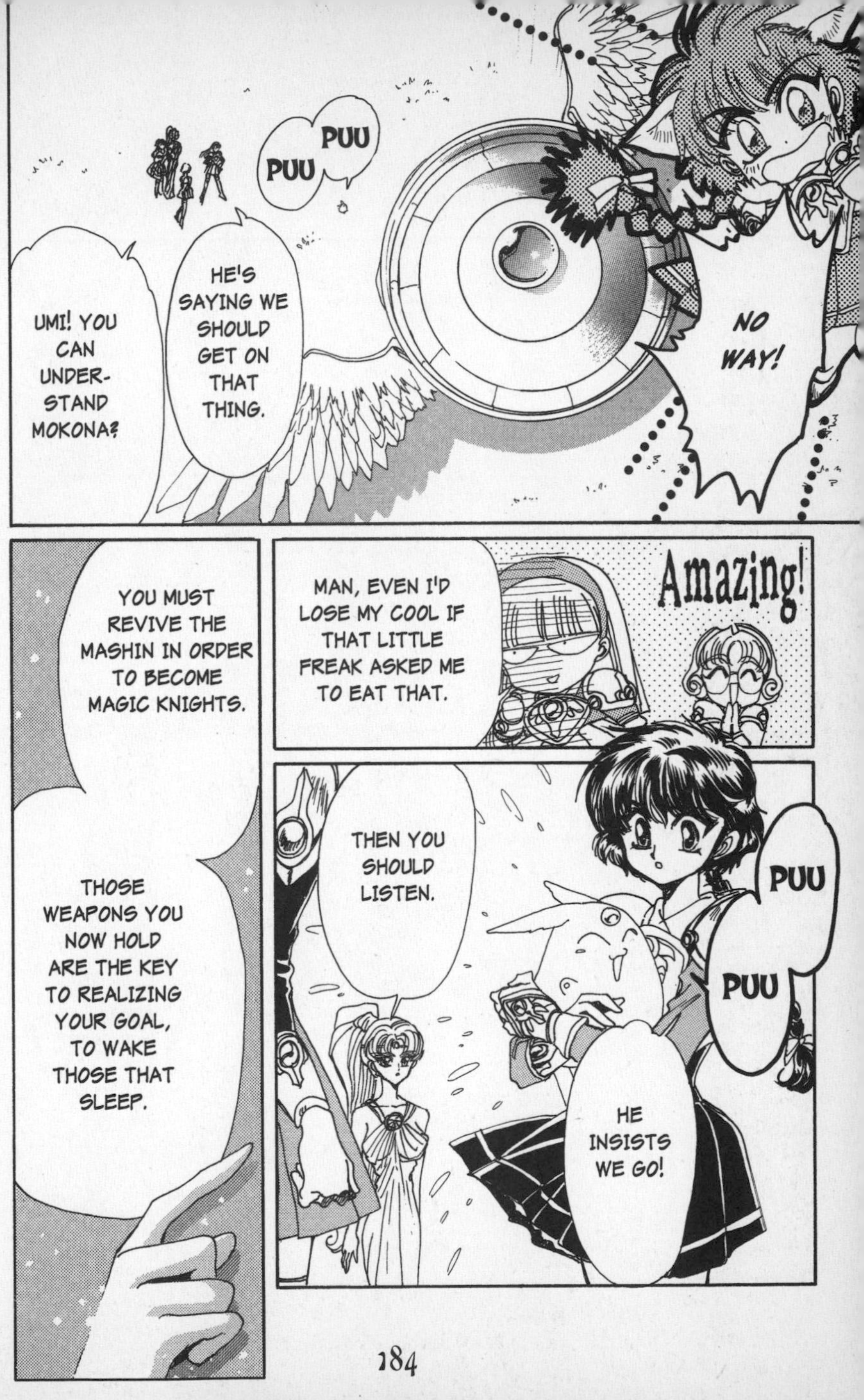
PUU
PUU
HE'S SAYING WE SHOULD GET ON THAT THING.
UMI! YOU CAN UNDER-STAND MOKONA?
NO WAY!
Amazing!
MAN, EVEN I'D LOSE MY COOL IF THAT LITTLE FREAK ASKED ME TO EAT THAT.
PUU
PUU
HE INSISTS WE GO!
THEN YOU SHOULD LISTEN.
YOU MUST REVIVE THE MASHIN IN ORDER TO BECOME MAGIC KNIGHTS.
THOSE WEAPONS YOU NOW HOLD ARE THE KEY TO REALIZING YOUR GOAL, TO WAKE THOSE THAT SLEEP.

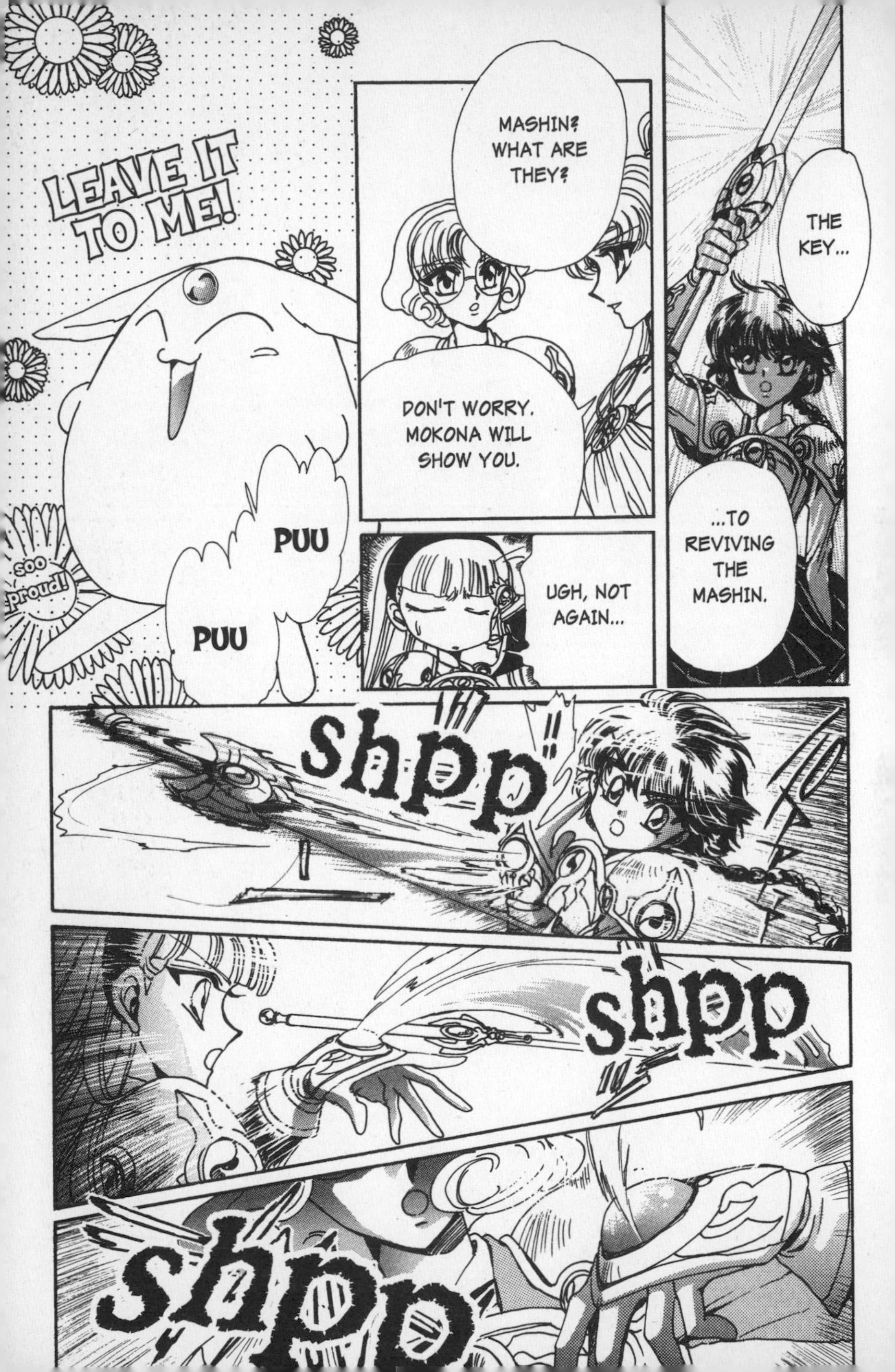
THE KEY...
...TO REVIVING THE MASHIN.
MASHIN? WHAT ARE THEY?
DON'T WORRY. MOKONA WILL SHOW YOU.
UGH, NOT AGAIN...
LEAVE IT TO ME!
PUU
PUU
soo proud!
shpp
shpp
shpp

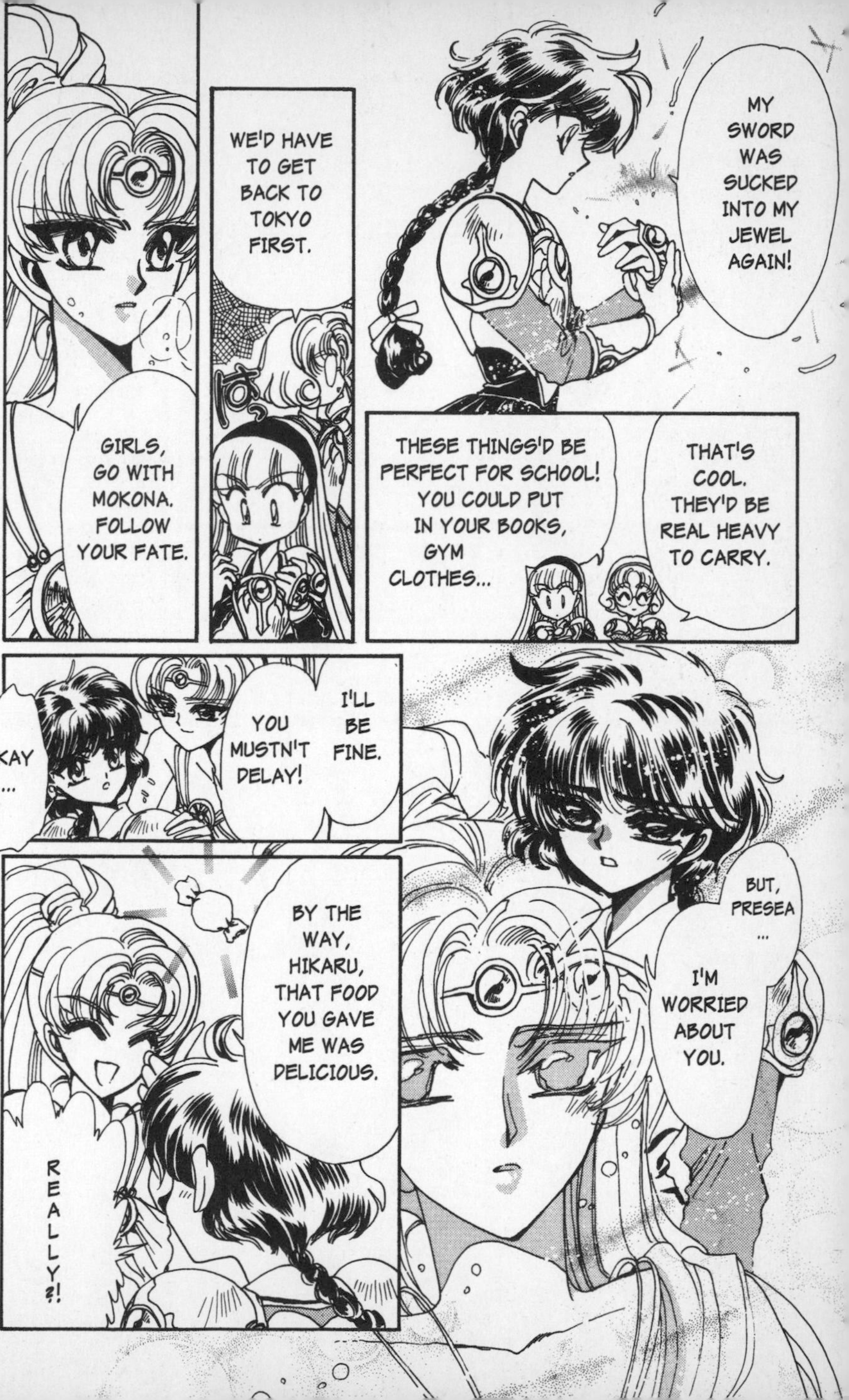
MY SWORD WAS SUCKED INTO MY JEWEL AGAIN!
THAT'S COOL. THEY'D BE REAL HEAVY TO CARRY.
THESE THINGS'D BE PERFECT FOR SCHOOL! YOU COULD PUT IN YOUR BOOKS, GYM CLOTHES...
WE'D HAVE TO GET BACK TO TOKYO FIRST.
はっ
GIRLS, GO WITH MOKONA. FOLLOW YOUR FATE.
BUT, PRESEA ...
I'M WORRIED ABOUT YOU.
I'LL BE FINE.
YOU MUSTN'T DELAY!
OKAY ...
BY THE WAY, HIKARU, THAT FOOD YOU GAVE ME WAS DELICIOUS.
REALLY?!

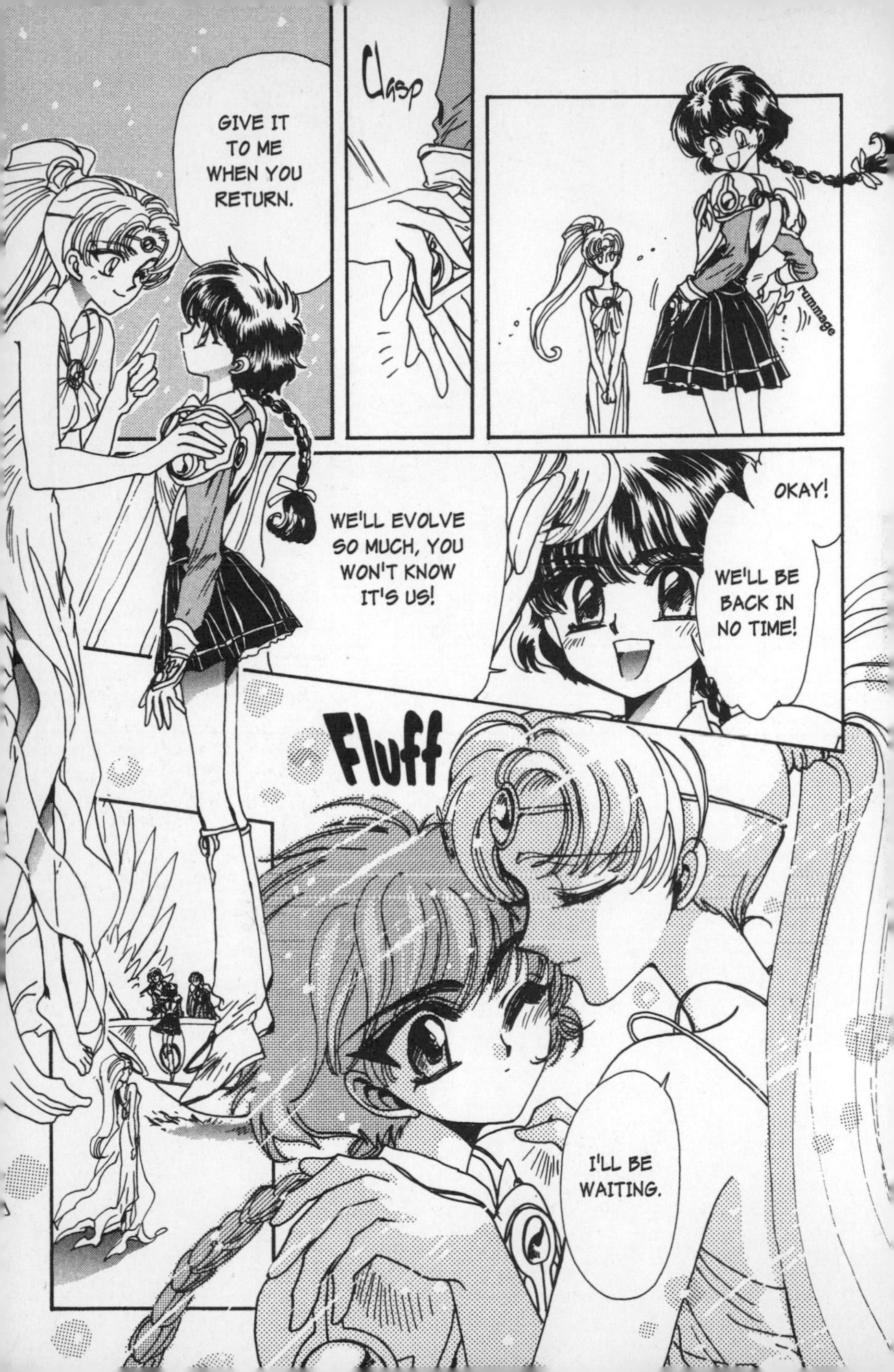
rummage
Clasp
GIVE IT TO ME WHEN YOU RETURN.
OKAY!
WE'LL BE BACK IN NO TIME!
WE'LL EVOLVE SO MUCH, YOU WON'T KNOW IT'S US!
Fluff
I'LL BE WAITING.

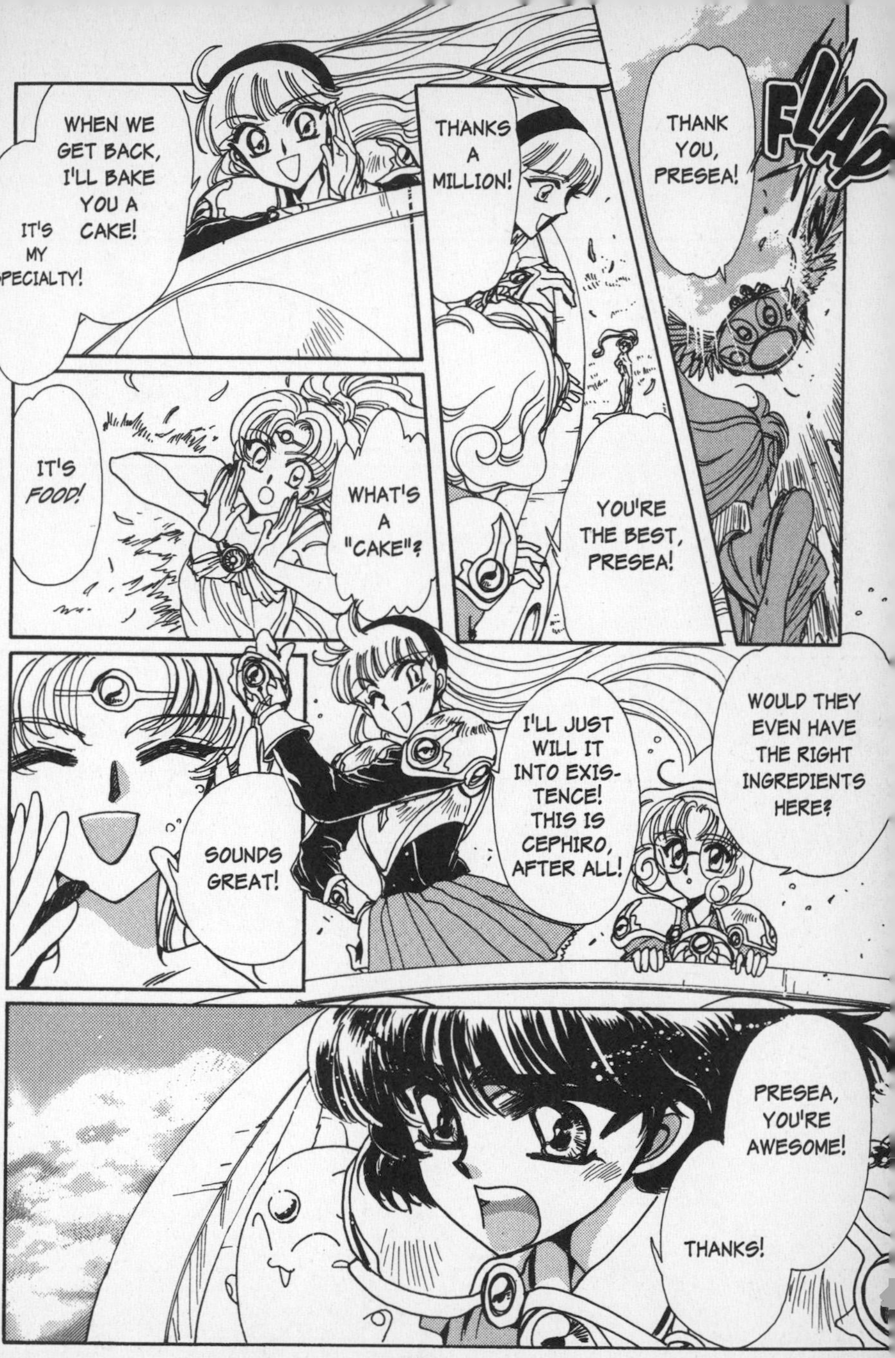
FLAP
THANK YOU, PRESEA!
THANKS A MILLION!
YOU'RE THE BEST, PRESEA!
WHEN WE GET BACK, I'LL BAKE YOU A CAKE!
IT'S MY SPECIALTY!
WHAT'S A "CAKE"?
IT'S *FOOD!*
WOULD THEY EVEN HAVE THE RIGHT INGREDIENTS HERE?
I'LL JUST WILL IT INTO EXISTENCE! THIS IS CEPHIRO, AFTER ALL!
SOUNDS GREAT!
PRESEA, YOU'RE AWESOME!
THANKS!

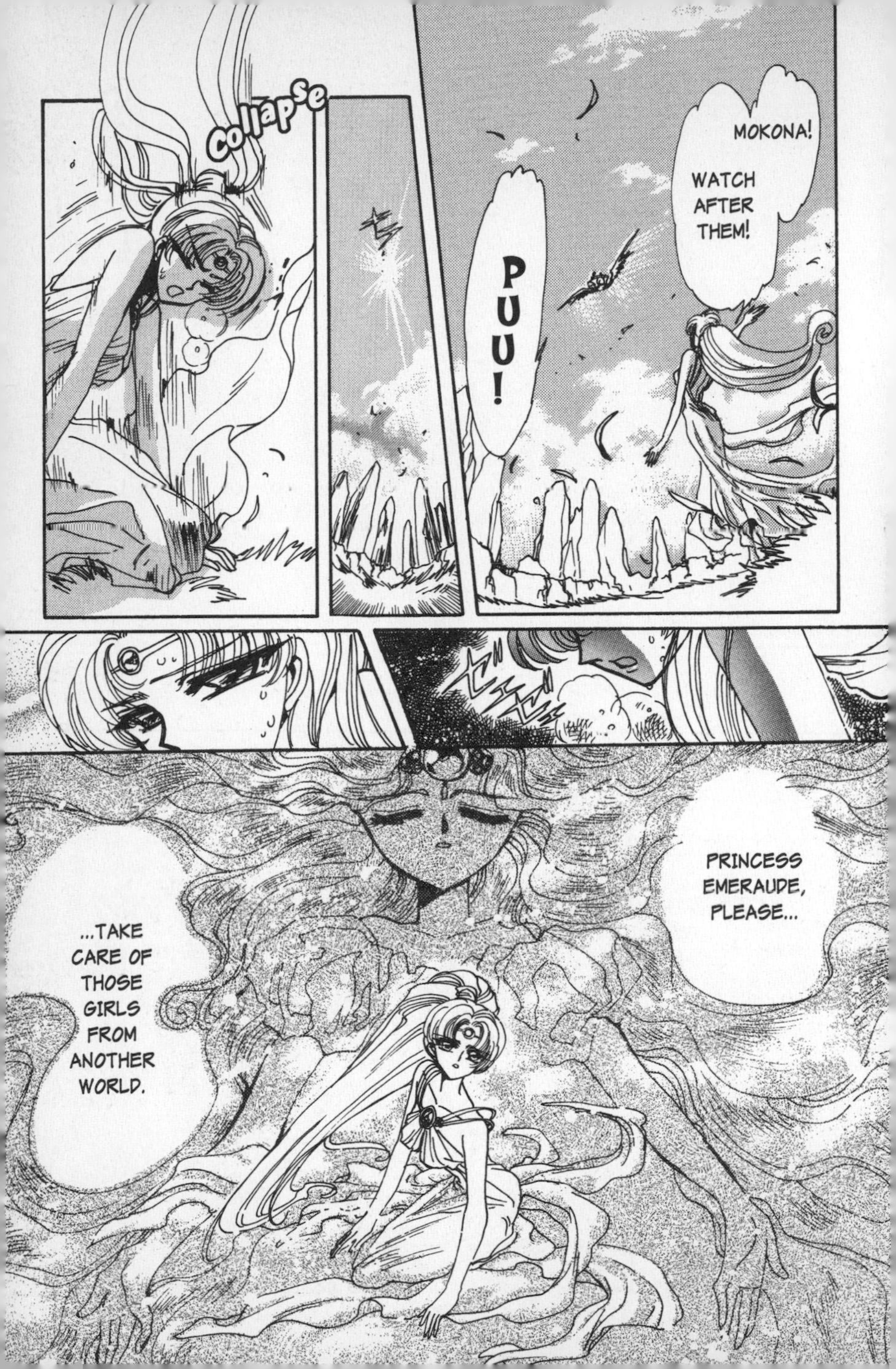
MOKONA!
WATCH AFTER THEM!
PUU!
Collapse
PRINCESS EMERAUDE, PLEASE...
...TAKE CARE OF THOSE GIRLS FROM ANOTHER WORLD.

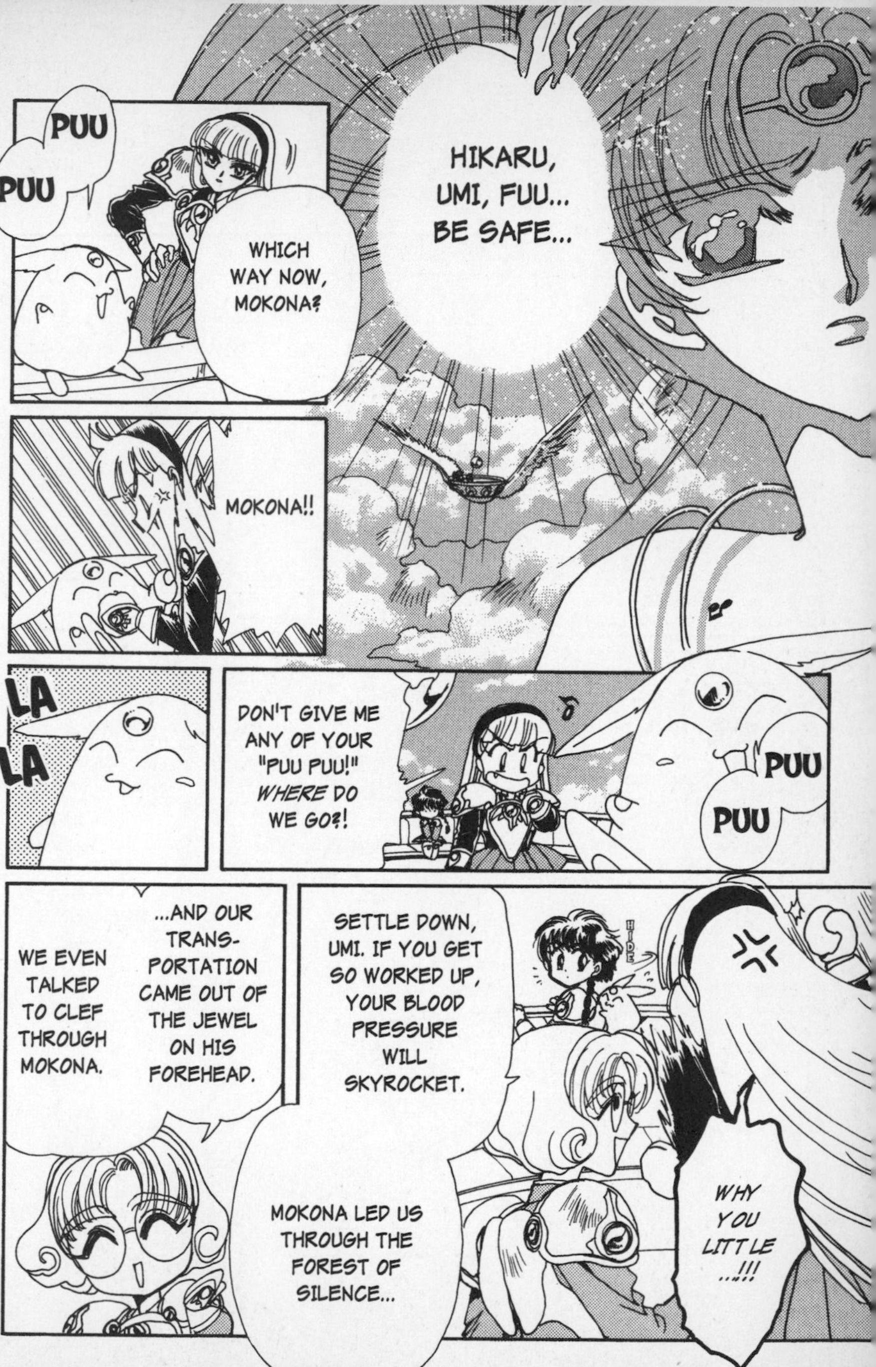
HIKARU, UMI, FUU... BE SAFE...
PUU
PUU
WHICH WAY NOW, MOKONA?
MOKONA!!
PUU
PUU
DON'T GIVE ME ANY OF YOUR "PUU PUU!" *WHERE* DO WE GO?!
LA
LA
WHY YOU LITTLE ...!!!
HIDE
SETTLE DOWN, UMI. IF YOU GET SO WORKED UP, YOUR BLOOD PRESSURE WILL SKYROCKET.
MOKONA LED US THROUGH THE FOREST OF SILENCE...
...AND OUR TRANS-PORTATION CAME OUT OF THE JEWEL ON HIS FOREHEAD.
WE EVEN TALKED TO CLEF THROUGH MOKONA.

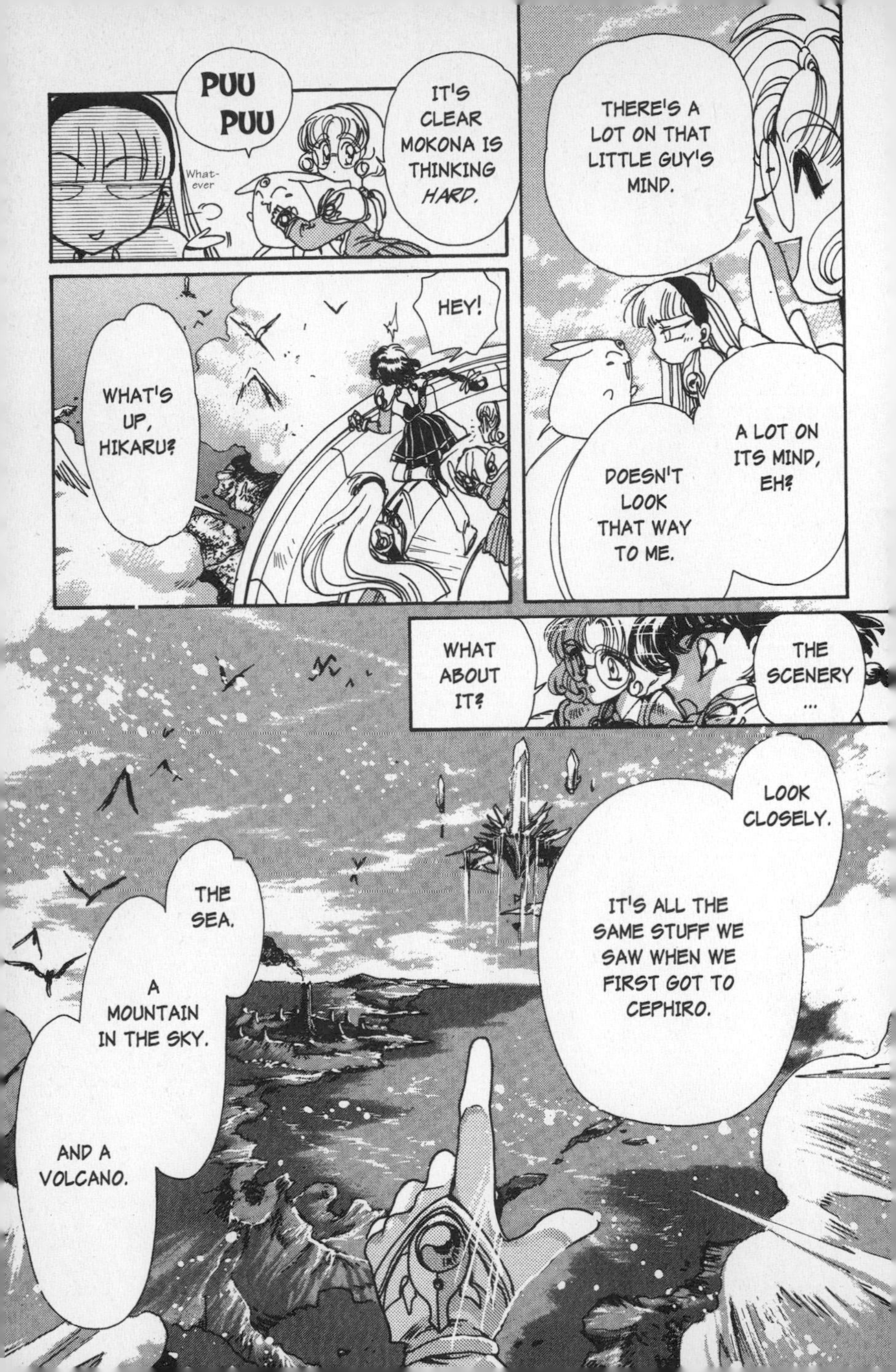
THERE'S A LOT ON THAT LITTLE GUY'S MIND.
A LOT ON ITS MIND, EH?
DOESN'T LOOK THAT WAY TO ME.
IT'S CLEAR MOKONA IS THINKING *HARD*.
PUU PUU
What-ever
HEY!
WHAT'S UP, HIKARU?
THE SCENERY ...
WHAT ABOUT IT?
LOOK CLOSELY.
IT'S ALL THE SAME STUFF WE SAW WHEN WE FIRST GOT TO CEPHIRO.
THE SEA.
A MOUNTAIN IN THE SKY.
AND A VOLCANO.

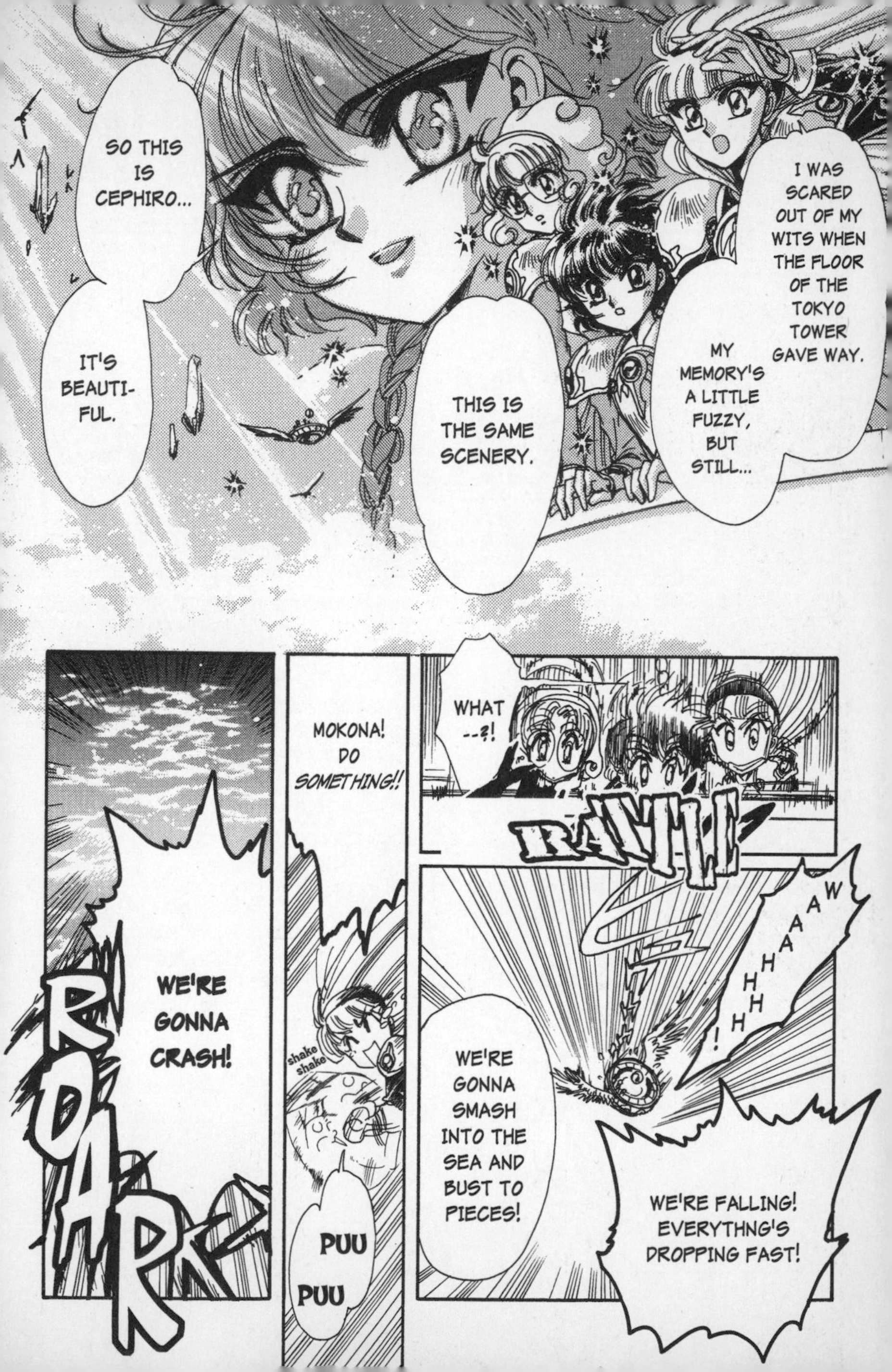
I WAS SCARED OUT OF MY WITS WHEN THE FLOOR OF THE TOKYO TOWER GAVE WAY.
MY MEMORY'S A LITTLE FUZZY, BUT STILL...
THIS IS THE SAME SCENERY.
SO THIS IS CEPHIRO...
IT'S BEAUTI-FUL.
WHAT --?!
RATTLE
WAAAHHHH!
WE'RE GONNA SMASH INTO THE SEA AND BUST TO PIECES!
WE'RE FALLING! EVERYTHNG'S DROPPING FAST!
MOKONA! DO *SOMETHING*!!
shake shake
PUU
PUU
WE'RE GONNA CRASH!
ROAR

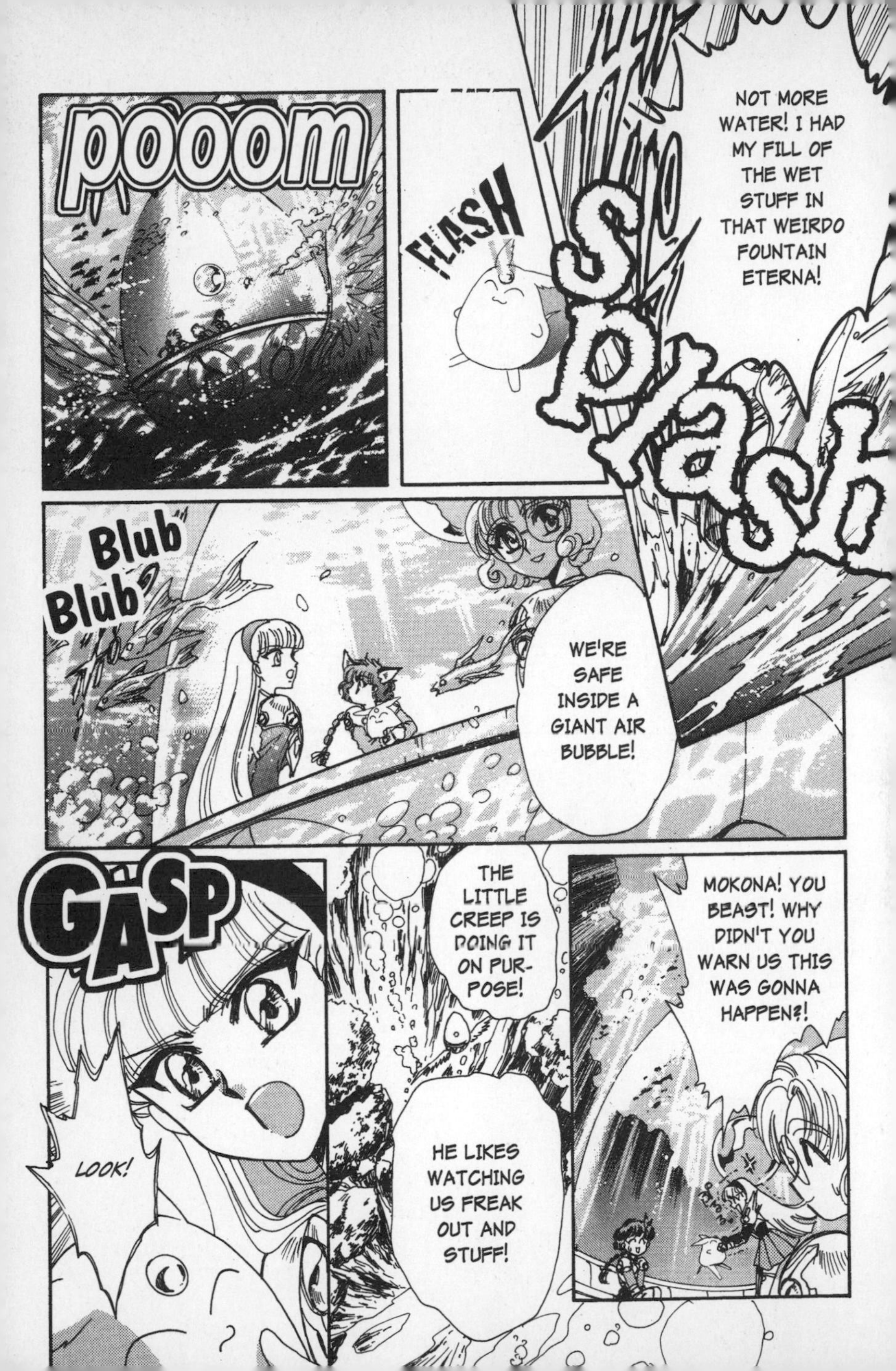

NOT MORE WATER! I HAD MY FILL OF THE WET STUFF IN THAT WEIRDO FOUNTAIN ETERNA!
Splash!
FLASH
pooom
Blub Blub
WE'RE SAFE INSIDE A GIANT AIR BUBBLE!
MOKONA! YOU BEAST! WHY DIDN'T YOU WARN US THIS WAS GONNA HAPPEN?!
THE LITTLE CREEP IS DOING IT ON PUR-POSE!
HE LIKES WATCHING US FREAK OUT AND STUFF!
GASP
LOOK!

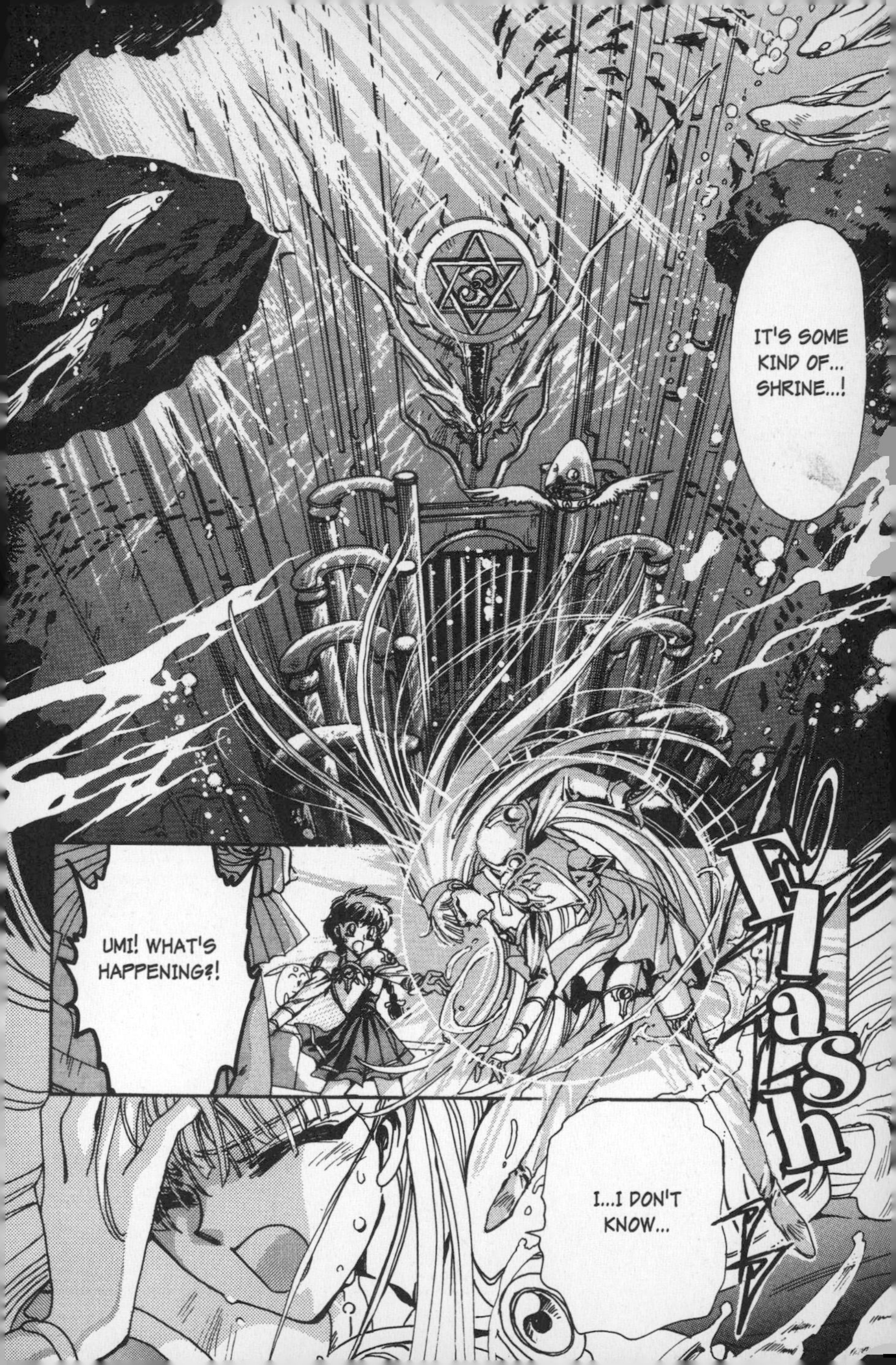
IT'S SOME KIND OF... SHRINE...!
Flash
UMI! WHAT'S HAPPENING?!
I...I DON'T KNOW...

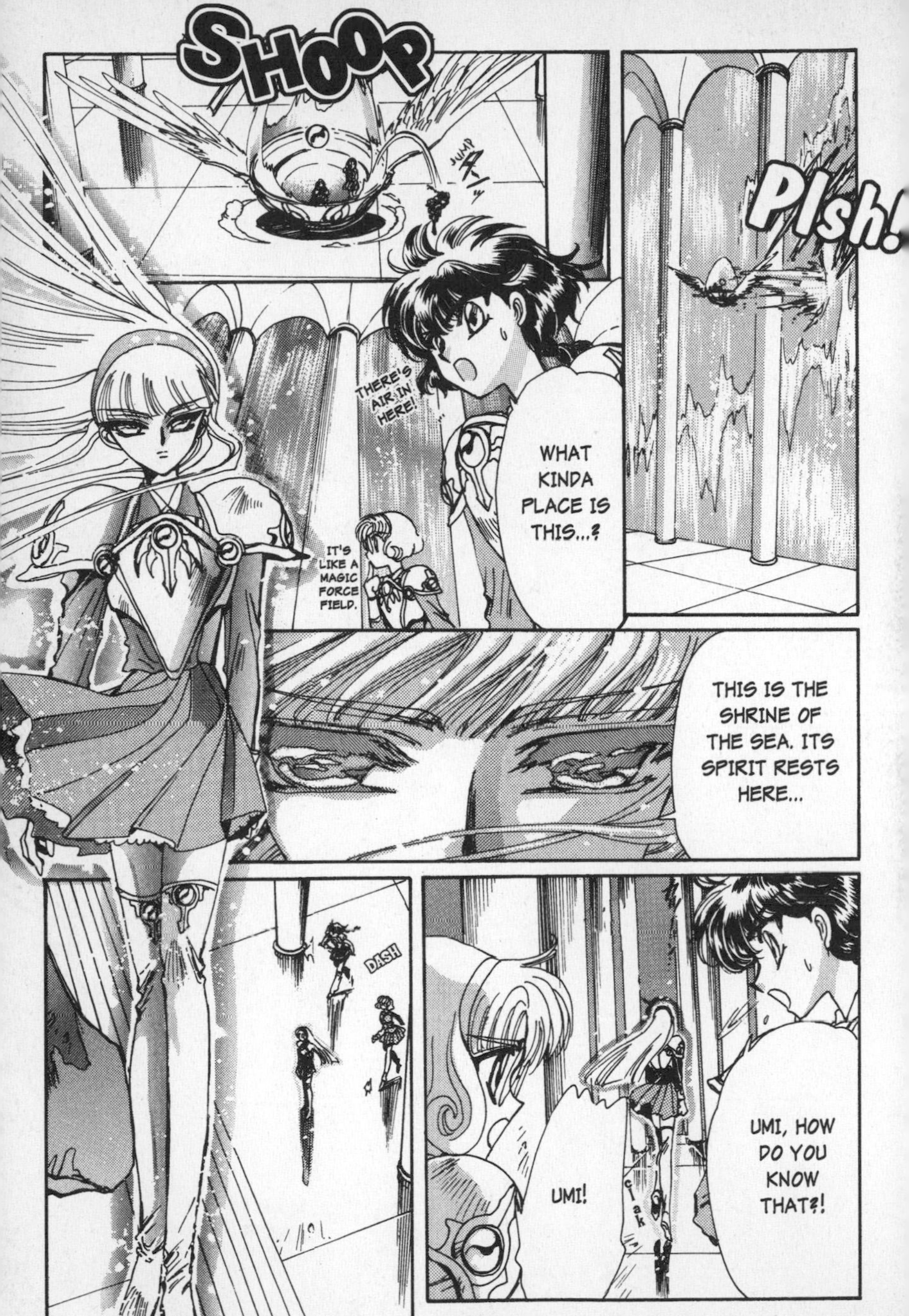
Plsh!
SHOOP
JUMP
THERE'S AIR IN HERE!
WHAT KINDA PLACE IS THIS...?
IT'S LIKE A MAGIC FORCE FIELD.
THIS IS THE SHRINE OF THE SEA. ITS SPIRIT RESTS HERE...
UMI, HOW DO YOU KNOW THAT?!
UMI!
clak
DASH

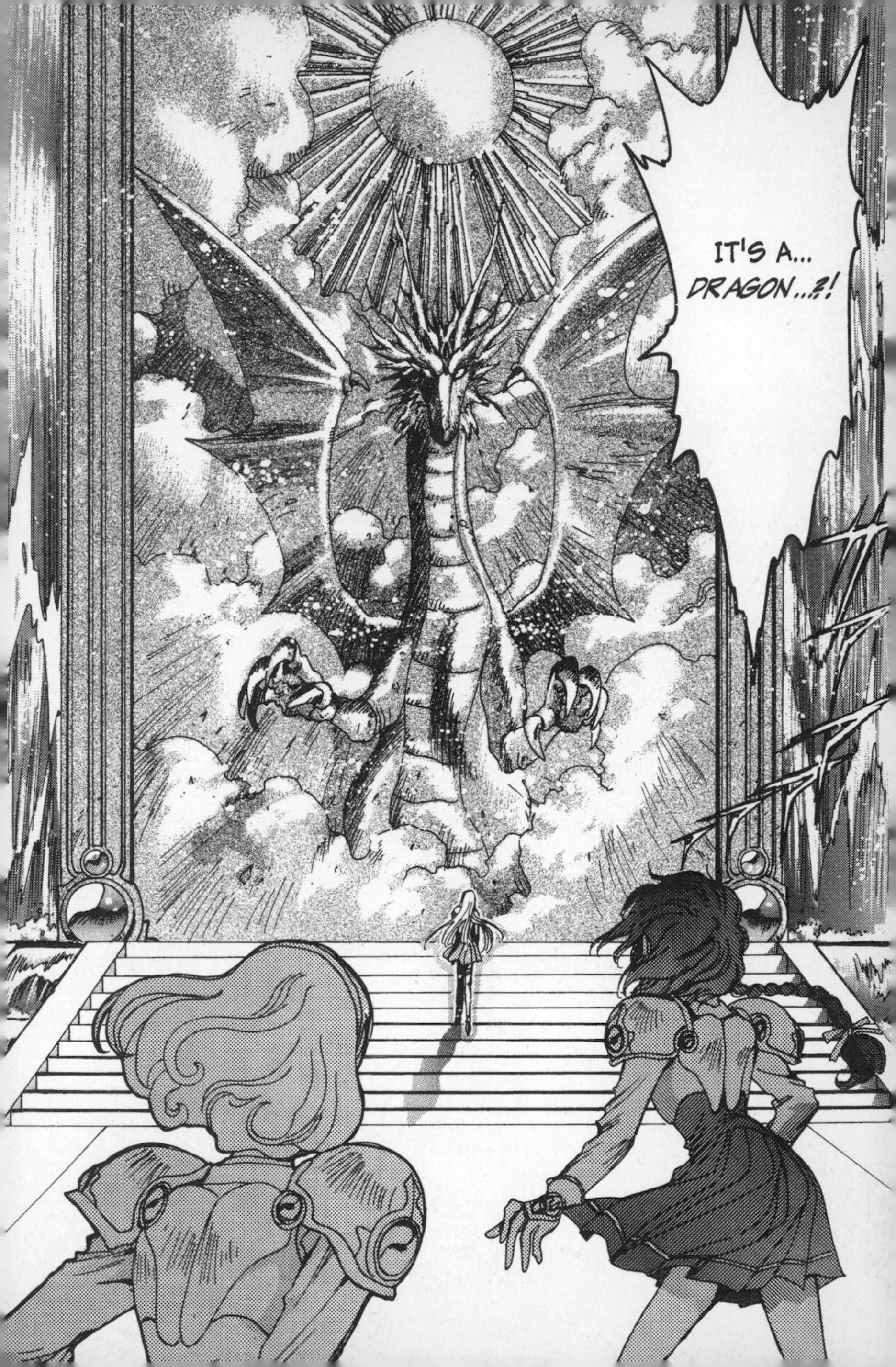
IT'S A...
DRAGON...?!

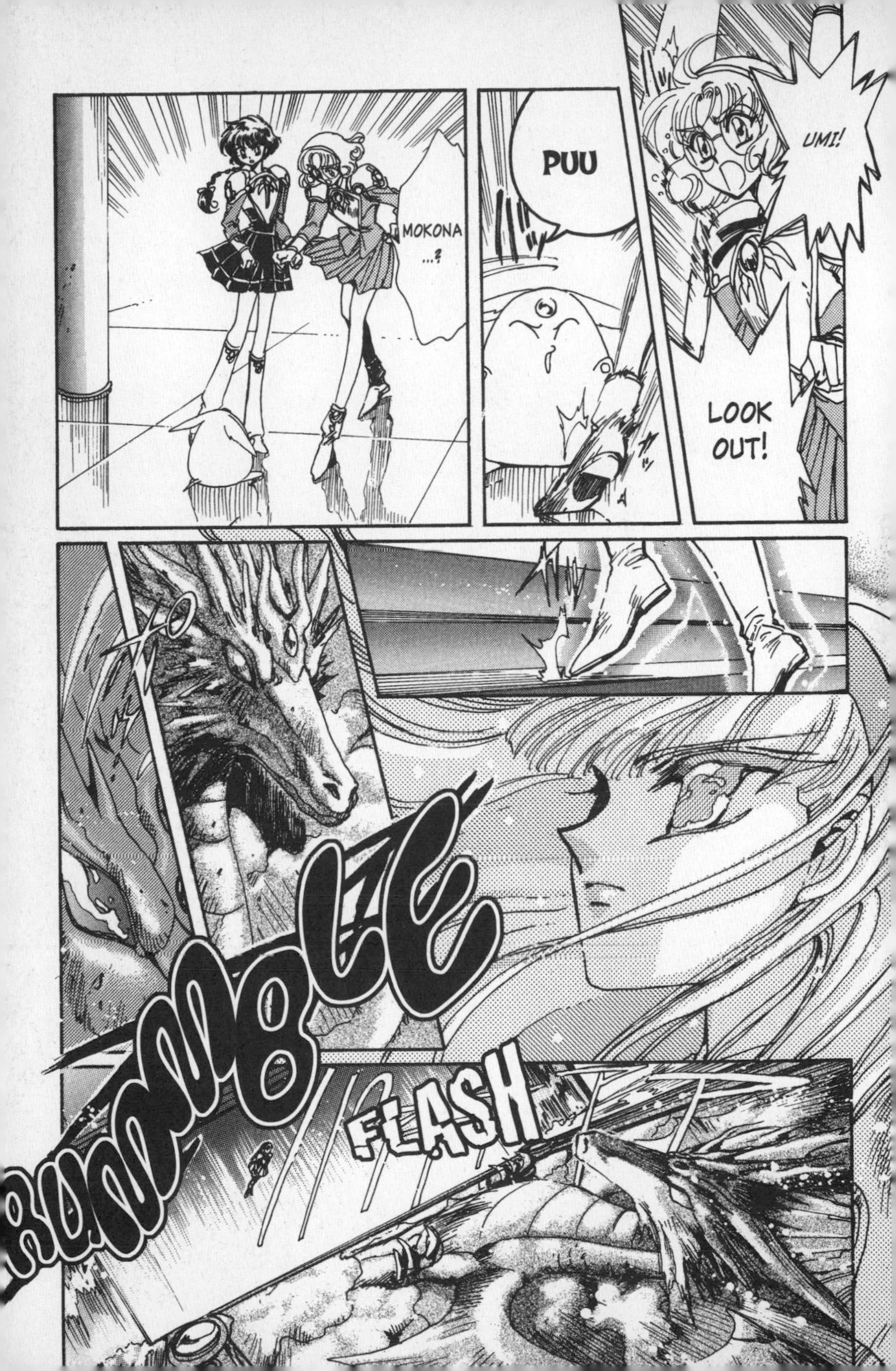
UMI!
LOOK OUT!
PUU
MOKONA ...?
FLASH

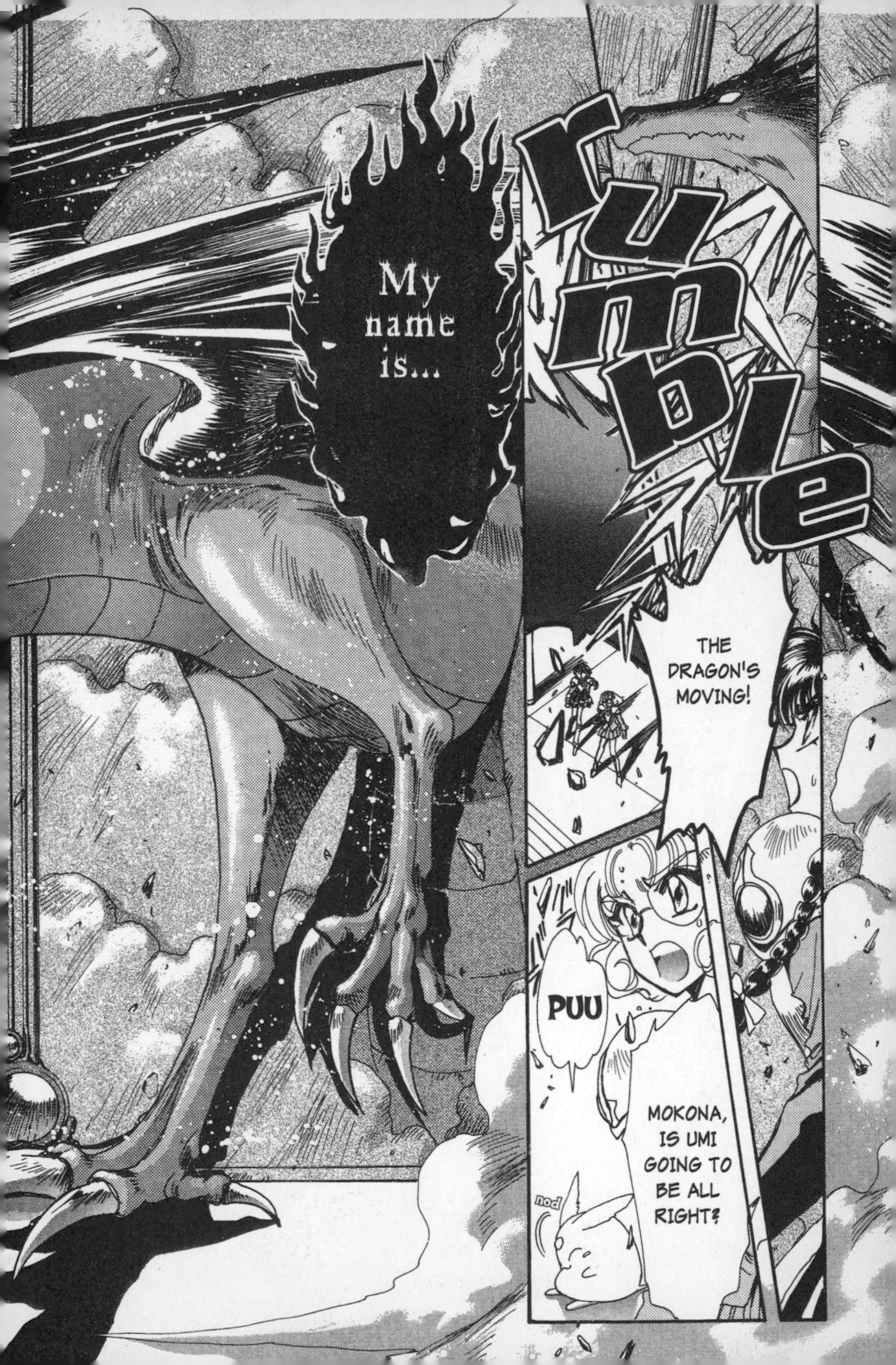
rumble
THE DRAGON'S MOVING!
MOKONA, IS UMI GOING TO BE ALL RIGHT?
PUU
nod
My name is...

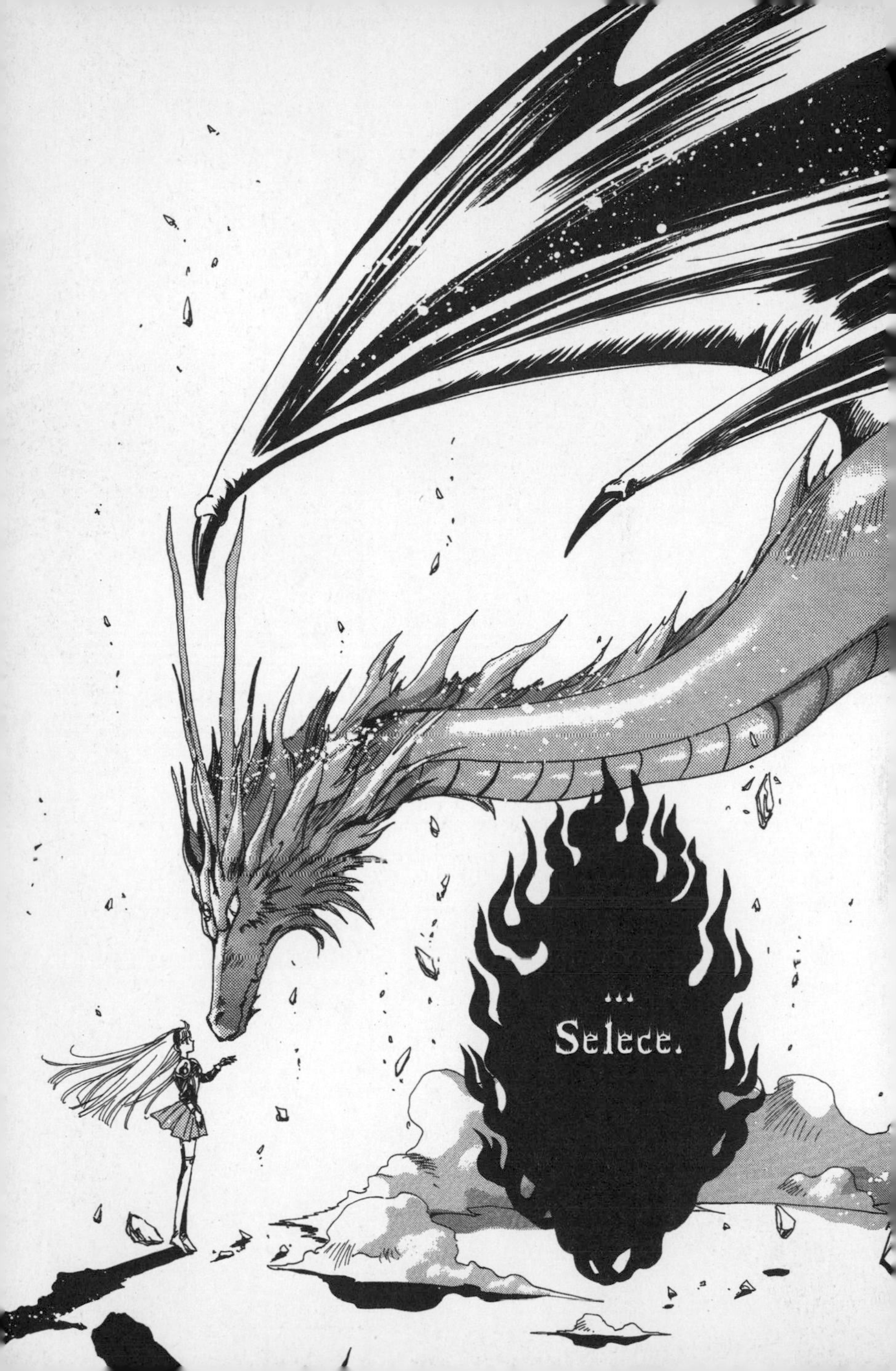
... Select.

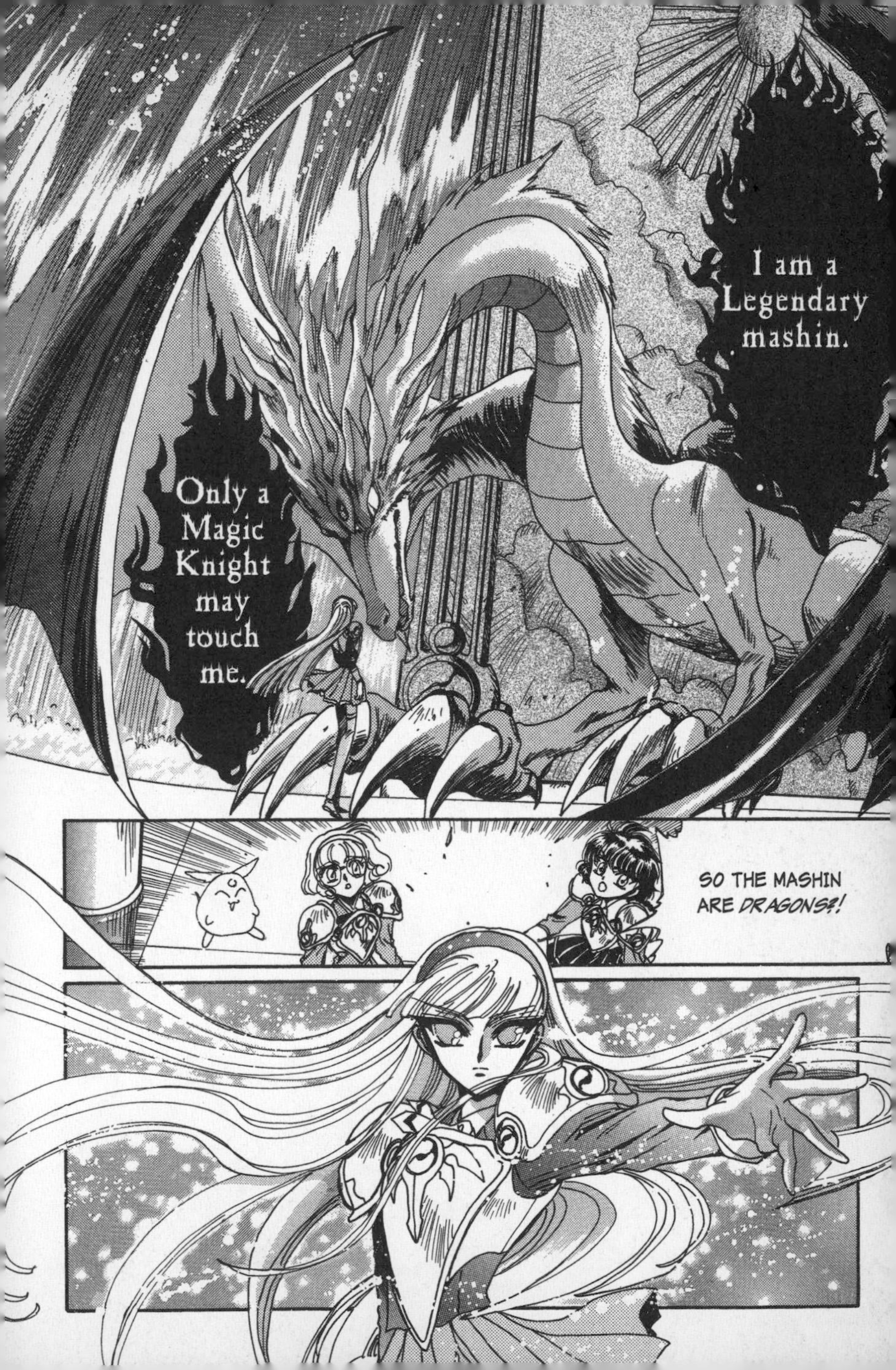
I am a Legendary mashin.
Only a Magic Knight may touch me.
SO THE MASHIN ARE DRAGONS?!

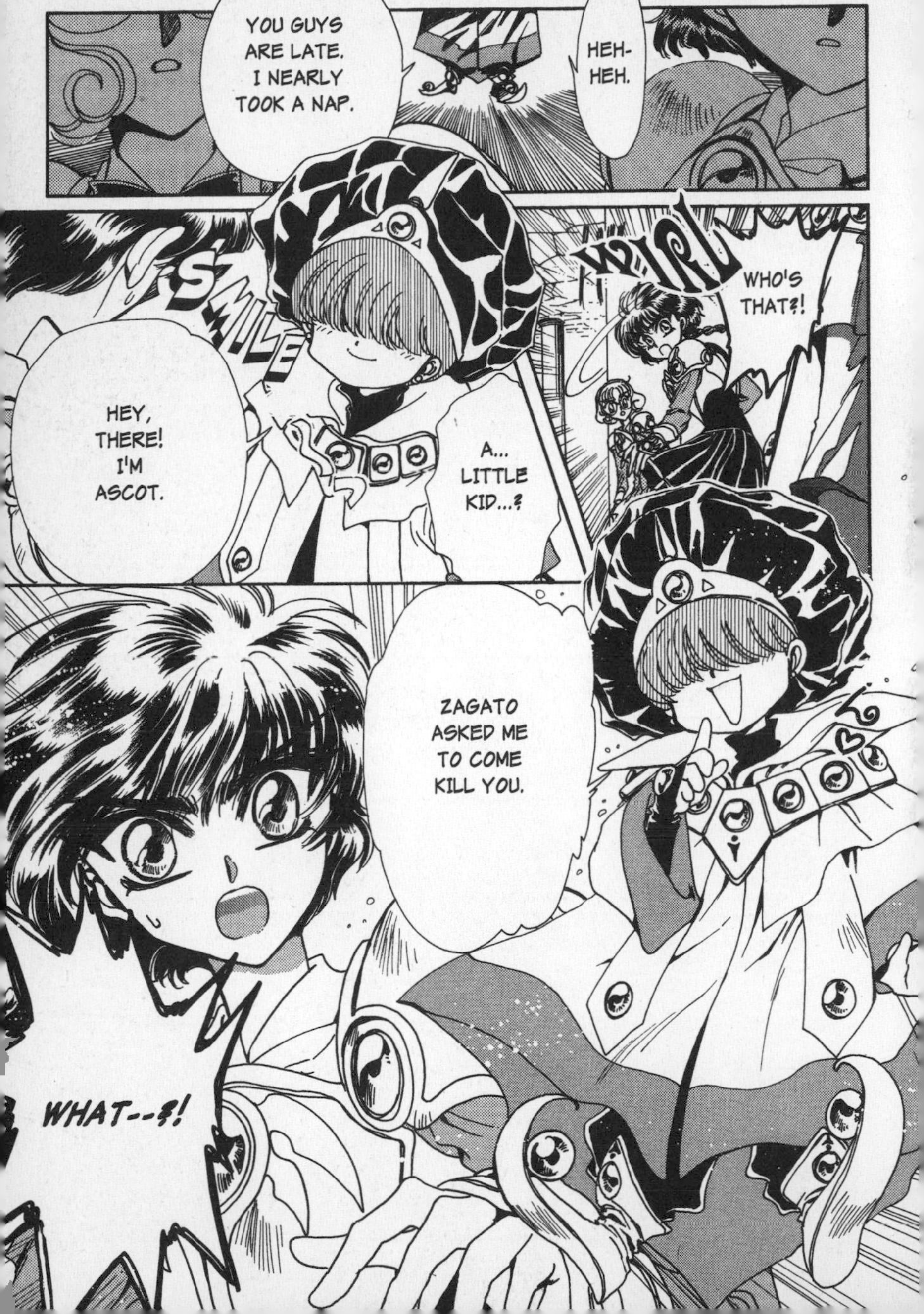
HEH-HEH.
YOU GUYS ARE LATE. I NEARLY TOOK A NAP.
WHO'S THAT?!
A... LITTLE KID...?
SMILE
HEY, THERE! I'M ASCOT.
ZAGATO ASKED ME TO COME KILL YOU.
WHAT--?!

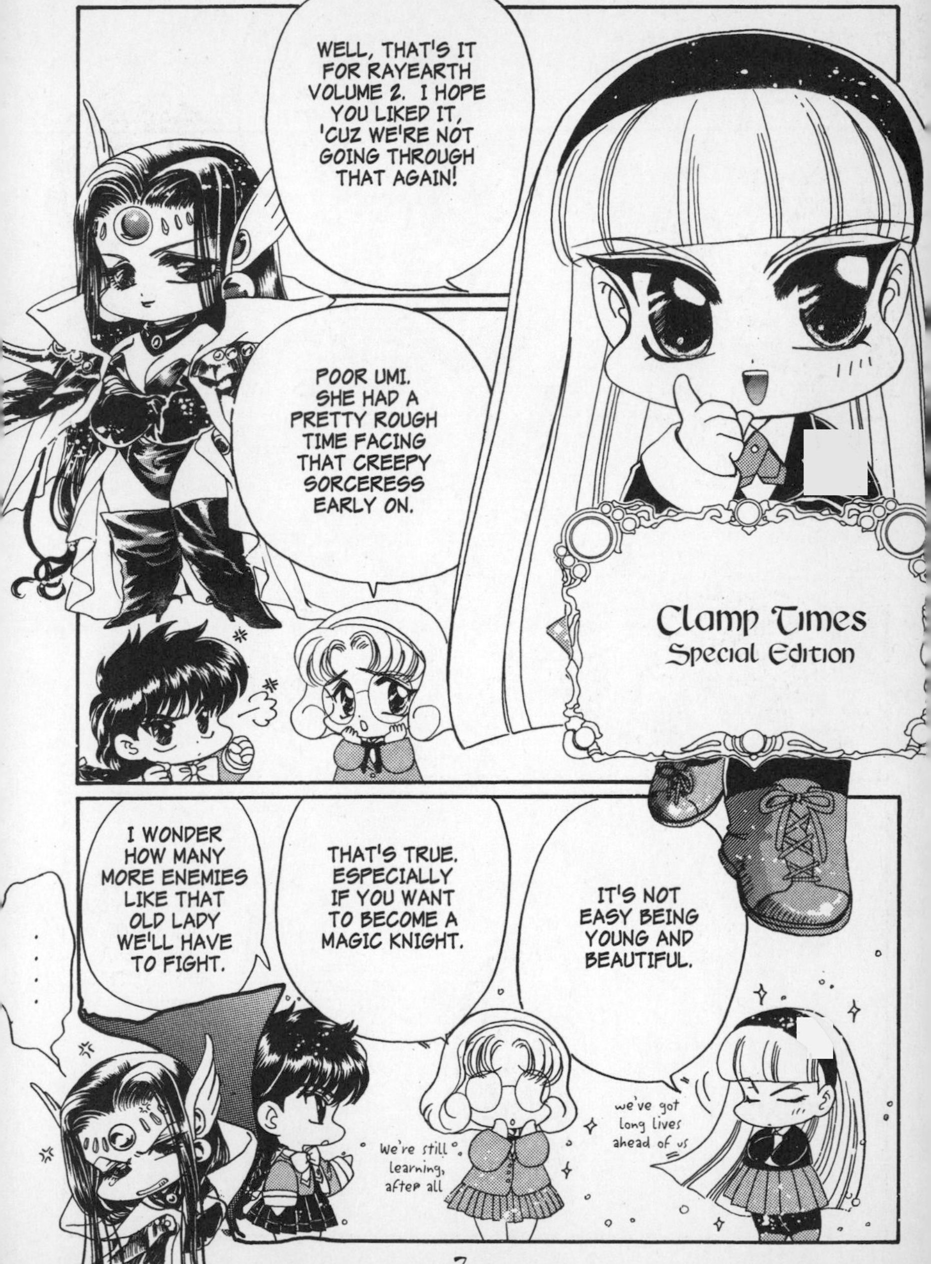
Clamp Times
Special Edition
WELL, THAT'S IT FOR RAYEARTH VOLUME 2. I HOPE YOU LIKED IT, 'CUZ WE'RE NOT GOING THROUGH THAT AGAIN!
POOR UMI. SHE HAD A PRETTY ROUGH TIME FACING THAT CREEPY SORCERESS EARLY ON.
IT'S NOT EASY BEING YOUNG AND BEAUTIFUL.
THAT'S TRUE. ESPECIALLY IF YOU WANT TO BECOME A MAGIC KNIGHT.
I WONDER HOW MANY MORE ENEMIES LIKE THAT OLD LADY WE'LL HAVE TO FIGHT.
we've got long lives ahead of us
We're still learning, after all

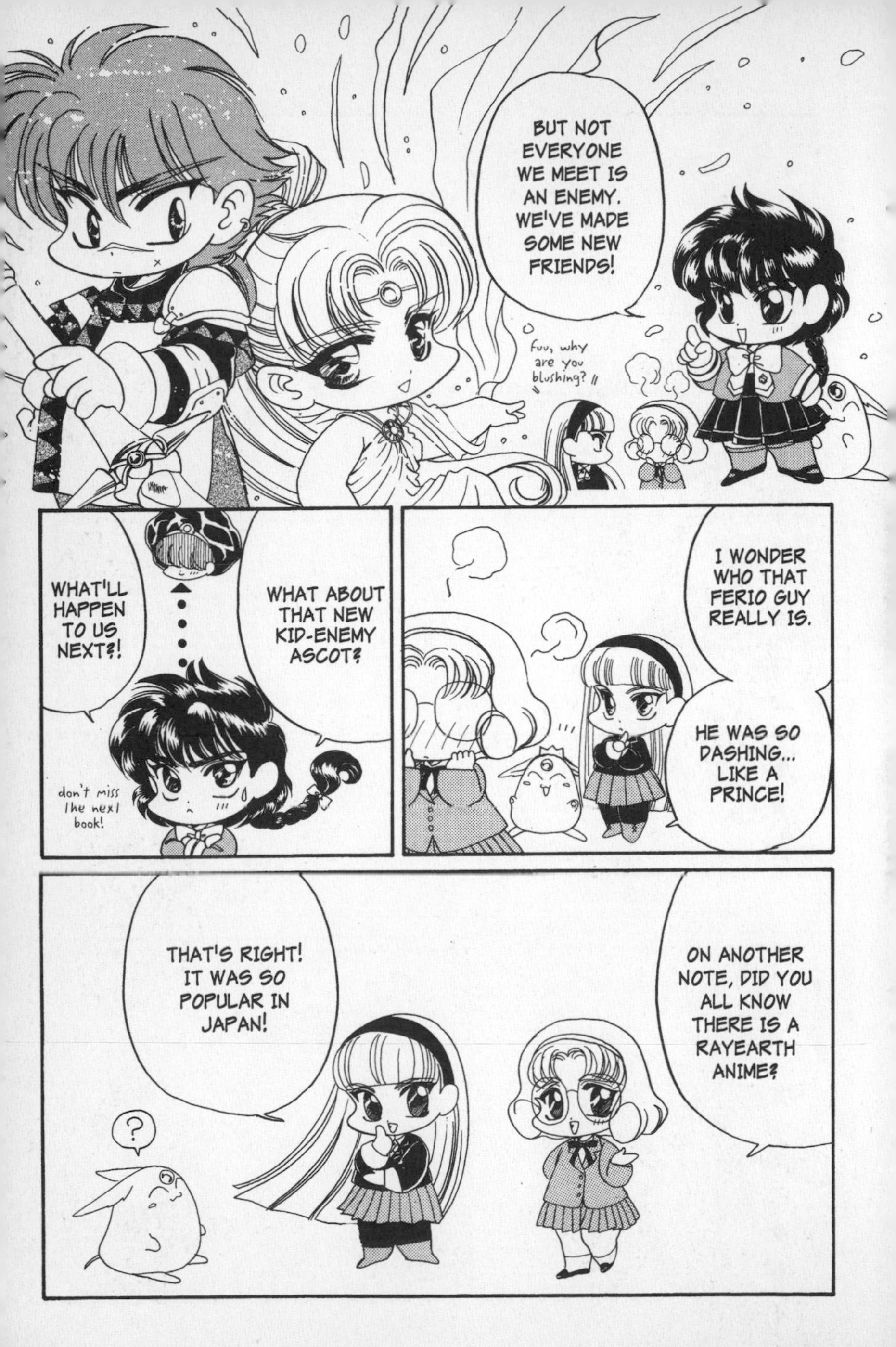
BUT NOT EVERYONE WE MEET IS AN ENEMY. WE'VE MADE SOME NEW FRIENDS!
fuu, why are you blushing?
I WONDER WHO THAT FERIO GUY REALLY IS.
HE WAS SO DASHING... LIKE A PRINCE!
WHAT ABOUT THAT NEW KID-ENEMY ASCOT?
WHAT'LL HAPPEN TO US NEXT?!
don't miss the next book!
ON ANOTHER NOTE, DID YOU ALL KNOW THERE IS A RAYEARTH ANIME?
THAT'S RIGHT! IT WAS SO POPULAR IN JAPAN!
?

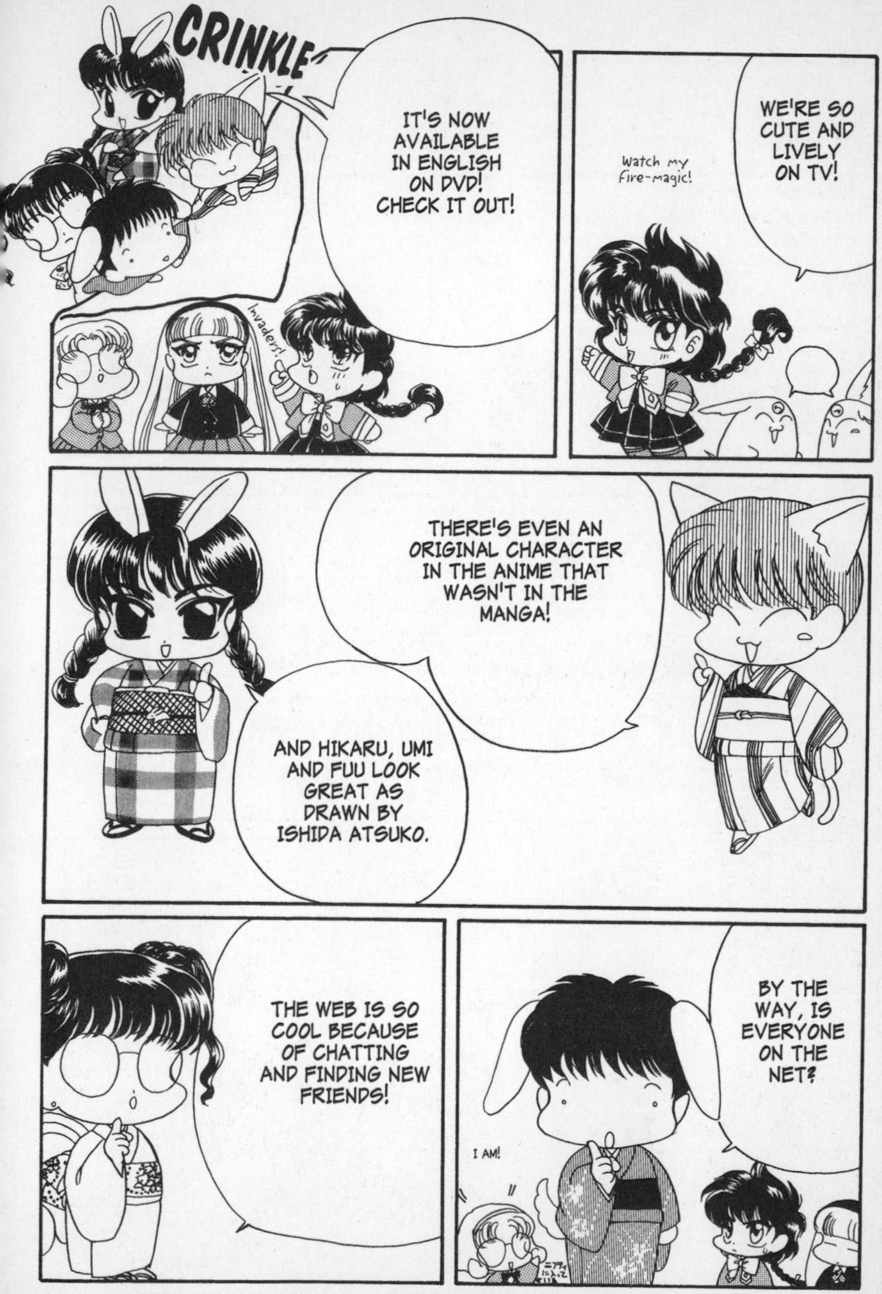
WE'RE SO CUTE AND LIVELY ON TV!
Watch my fire-magic!
CRINKLE
IT'S NOW AVAILABLE IN ENGLISH ON DVD! CHECK IT OUT!
Invaders!
THERE'S EVEN AN ORIGINAL CHARACTER IN THE ANIME THAT WASN'T IN THE MANGA!
AND HIKARU, UMI AND FUU LOOK GREAT AS DRAWN BY ISHIDA ATSUKO.
BY THE WAY, IS EVERYONE ON THE NET?
I AM!
THE WEB IS SO COOL BECAUSE OF CHATTING AND FINDING NEW FRIENDS!

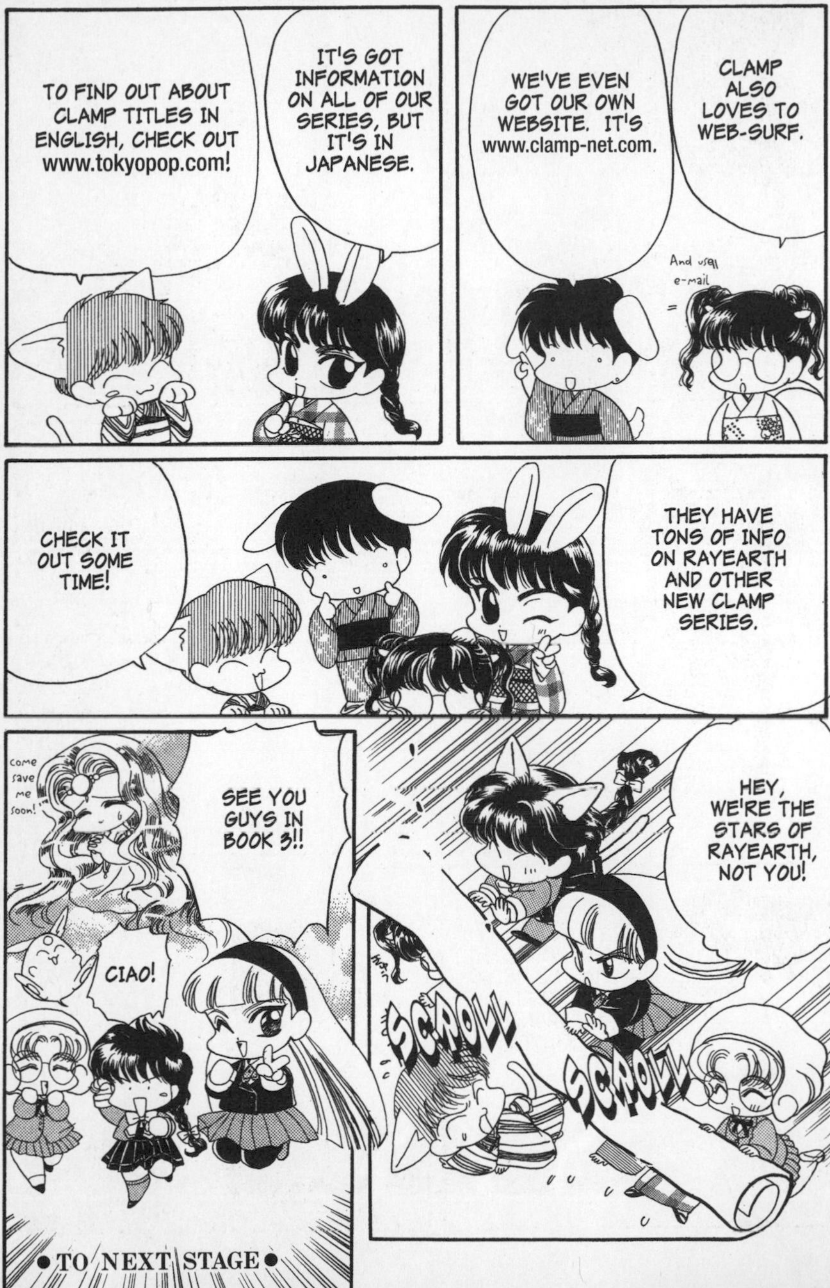

CLAMP ALSO LOVES TO WEB-SURF.
And usual e-mail
WE'VE EVEN GOT OUR OWN WEBSITE. IT'S www.clamp-net.com.
IT'S GOT INFORMATION ON ALL OF OUR SERIES, BUT IT'S IN JAPANESE.
TO FIND OUT ABOUT CLAMP TITLES IN ENGLISH, CHECK OUT www.tokyopop.com!
THEY HAVE TONS OF INFO ON RAYEARTH AND OTHER NEW CLAMP SERIES.
CHECK IT OUT SOME TIME!
HEY, WE'RE THE STARS OF RAYEARTH, NOT YOU!
SCROLL
SCROLL
SEE YOU GUYS IN BOOK 3!!
come save me soon!
CIAO!
•TO NEXT STAGE•

STOP!

This is the back of the book.
You wouldn't want to spoil a great ending!

This book is printed "manga-style," in the authentic Japanese right-to-left format. Since none of the artwork has been flipped or altered, readers get to experience the story just as the creator intended. You've been asking for it, so TOKYOPOP® delivered: authentic, hot-off-the-press, and far more fun!

DIRECTIONS

If this is your first time reading manga-style, here's a quick guide to help you understand how it works.

It's easy... just start in the top right panel and follow the numbers. Have fun, and look for more 100% authentic manga from TOKYOPOP®!